DAUGHTER ZION

Society of Biblical Literature

Ancient Israel and Its Literature

Steven L. McKenzie, General Editor

Editorial Board

Suzanne Boorer
Victor H. Matthews
Thomas C. Römer
Benjamin D. Sommer
Nili Wazana

Number 13

DAUGHTER ZION
Her Portrait, Her Response

DAUGHTER ZION

HER PORTRAIT, HER RESPONSE

Edited by

Mark J. Boda, Carol J. Dempsey, and LeAnn Snow Flesher

Society of Biblical Literature
Atlanta

DAUGHTER ZION
Her Portrait, Her Response

Library of Congress Control Number: 2012952534

Printed on acid-free, recycled paper conforming to
ANSI/NISO Z39.48-1992 (R1997) and ISO 9706:1994
standards for paper permanence.

Contents

Abbreviations

AB	Anchor Bible
ABD	*Anchor Bible Dictionary.* Edited by David Noel Freedman. 6 vols. New York: Doubleday, 1992.
AnBib	Analecta biblica
ANETS	Ancient Near Eastern Texts and Studies
ASV	American Standard Version
ATANT	Abhandlungen zur Theologie des Alten und Neuen Testaments
ATD	Das Alte Testament Deutsch
BBET	Beiträge zur biblischen Exegese und Theologie
BDB	Francis Brown, Samuel Rolles Driver, and Charles A. Briggs, *A Hebrew and English Lexicon of the Old Testament.* Oxford: Clarendon, 1907.
BHS	*Biblia Hebraica Stuttgartensia.* Edited by Karl Elliger and Wilhelm Rudolph. Repr., Stuttgart: Deutsch Bibelstiftung, 1983.
BibInt	*Biblical Interpretation*
BibOr	Biblica et orientalia
BIS	Biblical Interpretation Series
BKAT	Biblischer Kommentar, Altes Testament
BLS	Bible and Literature Series
BR	*Biblical Research*
BS	Biblical Seminar
BZ	*Biblische Zeitschrift*
BZAW	Beihefte zur Zeitschrift für die alttestamentliche Wissenschaft
CBQ	*Catholic Biblical Quarterly*
CC	Continental Commentaries
CTJ	*Calvin Theological Journal*
CTM	*Concordia Theological Monthly*

CurBS	*Currents in Research: Biblical Studies*
DCH	*Dictionary of Classical Hebrew.* Edited by David J. A. Clines. Sheffield: Sheffield Academic Press, 1993–.
DJD	Discoveries in the Judaean Desert
ESV	English Standard Version
EvT	*Evangelische Theologie*
FAT	Forschungen zum Alten Testament
FCB	Feminist Companion to the Bible
FOTL	Forms of the Old Testament Literature
GBS	Guides to Biblical Scholarship
GKC	*Gesenius' Hebrew Grammar.* Edited by Emil Kautzsch. Translated by A. E. Cowley. 2nd ed. Oxford: Clarendon, 1910.
GCT	Gender, Culture, Theory
HALOT	*Hebrew and Aramaic Lexicon of the Old Testament.* Edited by Ludwig Koehler, Walter Baumgartner, and Johann Jakob Stamm. Translated and edited by M. E. J. Richardson. 5 vols. Leiden: Brill, 1994–2000.
HBS	Herders biblische Studien
HBT	*Horizons in Biblical Theology*
HCOT	Historical Commentary on the Old Testament
HTR	*Harvard Theological Review*
IB	*Interpreter's Bible.* Edited by George A. Buttrick. 12 vols. New York: Abingdon, 1951–1957.
IBC	Interpretation: A Bible Commentary for Teaching and Preaching
Int	*Interpretation*
JANESCU	*Journal of the Ancient Near Eastern Society of Columbia University*
JAOS	*Journal of the American Oriental Society*
JBL	*Journal of Biblical Literature*
JFSR	*Journal of Feminist Studies in Religion*
JNSL	*Journal of Northwest Semitic Languages*
Joüon	Paul Joüon, *A Grammar of Biblical Hebrew.* Translated and revised by Takamitsu Muraoka. 2 vols. Subsidia biblica 14/1–2. Rome: Pontifical Biblical Institute, 1991.
JPS	Jewish Publication Society Version
JR	*Journal of Religion*
JSJSup	Journal for the Study of Judaism Supplement Series

JSOT	*Journal for the Study of the Old Testament*
JSOTSup	Journal for the Study of the Old Testament Supplement Series
LHBOTS	Library of Hebrew Bible/Old Testament Studies
NAB	New American Bible
NASB	New American Standard Bible
NCB	New Century Bible
NEchtB	Neue Echter Bibel
NIB	*The New Interpreter's Bible.* Edited by Leander E. Keck. 12 vols. plus index. Nashville: Abingdon, 1994–2004.
NIBC	New International Bible Commentary
NICOT	New International Commentary on the Old Testament
NIDOTTE	*New International Dictionary of Old Testament Theology and Exegesis.* Ed. Willem A. VanGemeren. 5 vols. Grand Rapids: Zondervan, 1997.
NIVAC	NIV Application Commentary Series
NJB	New Jerusalem Bible
NJPS	New Jewish Publication Society
NLT	New Living Translation
NRSV	New Revised Standard Version
OBT	Overtures to Biblical Theology
OTL	Old Testament Library
OTM	Oxford Theological Monographs
OtSt	Oudtestamentische Studiën
POut	De Prediking van het Oude Testament
PSB	*Princeton Seminary Bulletin*
RB	*Revue biblique*
SBB	Stuttgarter biblische Beiträge
SBL	Society of Biblical Literature
SBLABib	SBL Academia Biblica
SBLDS	SBL Dissertation Series
SBLEJL	SBL Early Judaism and Its Literature
SBLSP	SBL Seminar Papers
SBLStBL	SBL Studies in Biblical Literature
SBLSymS	SBL Symposium Series
SBS	Stuttgarter Bibelstudien
SBT	Studies in Biblical Theology
SemeiaSt	Semeia Studies
SHBC	Smyth & Helwys Bible Commentary

SJOT	*Scandinavian Journal of the Old Testament*
SOTSMS	Society for Old Testament Studies Monograph Series
SSN	Studia semitica neerlandica
SubBi	Subsidia biblica
TB	Theologische Bücherei
TDOT	*Theological Dictionary of the Old Testament.* Ed. G. Johannes Botterweck, Helmer Ringgren, and Heinz-Josef Fabry. Translated by J. T. Willis et al. 15 vols. Grand Rapids: Eerdmans, 1974–2006.
TNIV	Today's New International Version
TOTC	Tyndale Old Testament Commentaries
TynBul	*Tyndale Bulletin*
TZ	*Theologische Zeitschrift*
VTSup	Supplements to Vetus Testamentum
WBC	Word Biblical Commentary
WMANT	Wissenschaftliche Monographien zum Alten und Neuen Testament

Preface

The study of the Hebrew Bible has undergone significant changes over the past half century, shifting from a discipline dominated by studies focused on the diachronic development of a text rooted in ancient communities to a discipline with multiple foci, with greater emphasis on the synchronic presentation of the text and the hermeneutical experience of reading communities both ancient and modern. This shift has occurred not merely because of continued refinement of methodologies, but also through the inclusion of a broader set of voices within the biblical guild. Once nonexistent or at best minority voices have been given space within research programs and academic societies, and the impact is seen in the breadth of approaches and topics that now typify the Hebrew Bible guild. One of the most exciting developments in this shifting hermeneutical scene has unquestionably been the virtual explosion of presentations, articles, edited volumes, and monographs focused on the study of the feminine dimension of the Hebrew Bible. This has reached a feverish pitch in the publication of key volumes on the role of female characters, especially as related to the city of Jerusalem and God in the prophetic corpus of the Hebrew Bible.[1]

---

1. A quick sampling of the past decade includes: Gale A. Yee, *Poor Banished Children of Eve: Woman as Evil in the Hebrew Bible* (Minneapolis: Fortress, 2003); Gerlinde Baumann, *Love and Violence: Marriage as Metaphor for the Relationship between YHWH and Israel in the Prophetic Books* (trans. Linda M. Maloney; Collegeville, Minn.: Liturgical Press, 2003); Sarah J. Dille, *Mixing Metaphors: God as Mother and Father in Deutero-Isaiah* (JSOTSup 398; GCT 13; London: T&T Clark, 2004); Mary E. Shields, *Circumscribing the Prostitute: The Rhetorics of Intertexuality, Metaphor, and Gender in Jeremiah 3.1–4.4* (JSOTSup 387; London: T&T Clark, 2004); Carleen Mandolfo, *Daughter Zion Talks Back to the Prophets: A Dialogic Theology of the Book of Lamentations* (SemeiaSt 58; Atlanta: Society of Biblical Literature, 2007); Mignon R. Jacobs, *Gender, Power, and Persuasion: The Genesis Narratives and Contemporary Portraits* (Grand Rapids: Baker Academic, 2007); Christl Maier, *Daughter Zion, Mother*

A key representative of this now firmly established trajectory in biblical studies is Carleen Mandolfo's 2007 monograph, *Daughter Zion Talks Back to the Prophets*. Building on her earlier dialogical approach to the Psalms,[2] she moves the discussion onto the canonical plane, bringing the voice of Daughter Zion expressed in the book of Lamentations into conversation with the voices addressing or depicting Zion throughout the prophetic corpus. The result is provocative and leads to hermeneutical reflection on the role of gender in text and interpretation.

The present volume has been shaped by the dialogic hermeneutic so foundational to Carleen's work. The volume began its life in a lively oral session in the Biblical Hebrew Poetry Section of the 2008 Annual Meeting of the Society of Biblical Literature in Boston, Massachusetts. Four initial papers were commissioned for that session, and these papers were made available to Carleen prior to the session to give her time to prepare a response. The session was electric, not only because of the quality of dialogue between Carleen and the various presenters, but also because of the discussion prompted among members of the session that day. The session would not be the end of this dialogue, however. In the following months papers were invited from other voices across the Hebrew Bible guild, commissioned to take Carleen's monograph as a point of departure for further reflection on feminine images within the Hebrew Bible, especially as related to the relationship between Zion and God. Carleen was gracious enough to accept our invitation to provide one final dialogue, this one on a written level through a response to the entire volume.

The volume begins with an essay by Barbara Green entitled "Cognitive Linguistics and the 'Idolatry-Is-Adultery' Metaphor of Jeremiah 2–3." Green, through the use of Cognitive Metaphor Theory, has attempted to reinterpret the complex relationship created through scholarly interpretation of the use of the marriage metaphor by the Hebrew prophets and in so doing to "recenter biblical texts as valuable for the believing community." Defining metaphor as a "property of concepts, not words," Green has estab-

---

Zion: Gender, Space, and the Sacred in Ancient Israel (Minneapolis: Fortress, 2008); Hanne Løland, *Silent or Salient Gender: The Interpretation of Gendered God-Language in the Hebrew Bible, Exemplified in Isaiah 42, 46, and 49* (FAT 2/32; Tübingen: Mohr Siebeck, 2008); Sharon Moughtin-Mumby, *Sexual and Marital Metaphors in Hosea, Jeremiah, Isaiah, and Ezekiel* (OTM; Oxford: Oxford University Press, 2008).

2. Carleen Mandolfo, *God in the Dock: Dialogic Tension in the Psalms of Lament* (JSOTSup 357; London: Sheffield Academic Press, 2002).

lished a list of correspondences between the prophetic use of the marriage metaphor and the target domain it is intended to represent. Giving continued attention and credence to the "gender problem," as well as feminist and postcolonial interpretations, Green pushes forward to create a balanced interpretation of the extreme and abusive language of the prophets in light of its being used metaphorically. She concludes, "the point is not whoring wives, but the unfaithful elite … still the language is problematic." In an attempt to "maintain the authority of the Bible as Scripture," Green also concludes we must read better, we must read "less literalistically."

In "Speaking of Speaking: The Form of Zion's Suffering in Lamentations," Jill Middlemas strongly emphasizes the meaning that comes through the use of form in the book of Lamentations. Specifically, Middlemas notes how Mandolfo's work fits in the trajectory of scholarship related to form and meaning that began with James Muilenburg's famous address on rhetorical criticism at the Society of Biblical Literature in the late 1960s, was continued by Phyllis Trible as she defined more carefully how to focus on the text, followed up by Walter Brueggemann's heightening of the importance of speech for a theological perspective, and now concludes with Mandolfo's emphasis on a perspective contrary to mainstream theology. Unique to Mandolfo's work is the naming of the third-person objective reporter in Lam 1 and 2 as a dialogic voice (DV). Middlemas suggests in this article that the DV is an eyewitness narrator that has been persuaded to agree with Daughter Zion's inconsolable protest due to the view of human suffering, with the consequence that the voice of God, or that of mainstream theology, has fallen silent.

Focused on a comparison of the dialogue within Isa 40–55 in relationship to that of Lamentations, Lena-Sofia Tiemeyer, in "Isaiah 40–55: A Judahite Reading Drama," argues that the two biblical texts were originally intended for the same audiences, the people of Judah. Building off of a set of five distinct features in Lamentations outlined by Middlemas, Tiemeyer has created criteria for uncovering the theology of the dialogue of Isa 40–55 in comparison to the dialogue found in Lamentations. She notes "there are good reasons for assuming that substantial parts, if not all, of Isa 40–55 originated in Judah." Her comparisons have led her to conclude that the prophetic voice behaves like a true prophet, at times representing the people to God (including DZ) and alternatively representing God to the people; and that God, in Isa 40–55, speaks a form of Judahite speech that plays down the sin and shame of Jacob-Israel *and* Zion-Jerusalem, seeking instead to comfort them in their sorrows. Consequently, Tiemeyer has noted, the actively lamenting Daughter Zion of Lamentations has not been hijacked by the *golah* community and muted beyond recognition in Isa 40–55 as Mandolfo claims.

Heavy on response to Mandolfo's "dialogic ethic," Stephen L. Cook has focused his essay, "The Fecundity of Fair Zion: Beauty and Fruitfulness as Spiritual Fulfillment," on an interpretation of Isa 49:14–21 and Ezek 26:33–38 that provides, in his thinking, a "more respectful and empathetic approach to prophetic theology." With an emphasis on "fairness and fairness," Cook quotes Elaine Scarry's treatise, *On Beauty and Being Just*, as exemplary, noting that Daughter Zion, once self-absorbed (Lam 1 and 2), decenters in Isa 49:14–21 as she experiences the awe of the Holy and the future fecundity that comes from God's restorative plan. Simultaneously, he quotes Paul Woodruff's theories on the otherness of God, noting that the virtue of reverence is based on this profound, awful otherness. Cook uses Woodruff's otherness theology to confront Mandolfo's desire for a God that will set an example for us of morality and fair play, insisting that God may not function well as a role model. Cook concludes with an interpretation of Isa 49:14–21 and Ezek 26:33–38 that surfaces an aesthetically inspired reciprocity in which Zion experiences God's beauty and as a result finds "her true self recovered, welcomed, and ennobled. She finds that her will and God's will naturally accord."

Giving credence to Mandolfo's work as one of several recent ideological readings of Lamentations, Mary L. Conway has purposed in "Daughter Zion: Metaphor and Dialogue in the Book of Lamentations" a new reading of the final canonical form of the book that incorporates three objectives: to validate lament as an articulation of very real pain and suffering, to acknowledge the reality of sin and punishment, and to find a way forward. In order to achieve these objectives Conway has read dialogically solely within the book of Lamentations itself, providing an alternative approach in several areas—the horizontal dialogue, the multivalent nature of metaphor, and the structure of the book as a whole—in an effort to provide an optional perspective on the character of Daughter Zion and her significance within the Hebrew Bible. Her work surfaces the dialogue between the Speaker (Lam 1 and 2), the *Geber* (Lam 3 and 4), Daughter Zion (Lam 1 and 2), and the community (Lam 3 and 5). She has concluded, "the implied author leads the implied readers to empathize with the anguish of the people, to accept responsibility for sin, to personalize the need for confession and redemption, and to participate in the religious life of the wider community as they seek to find a way forward."

In "Yhwh as Jealous Husband: Abusive Authoritarian or Passionate Protector? A Reexamination of a Prophetic Image," Brittany Kim strives to comprehend how the original audience of Lam 1–2 might have understood these texts. She begins with an analysis of the use of קנא in the Hebrew Bible in relationship to divine jealousy. She concludes that Yhwh in covenant relationship with Israel is both jealous of Israel (with regard to her worship of other gods) and jealous for Israel (with regard to her well-being). She goes on to note that this jealous nature of God is always viewed positively in the Hebrew Bible. Next she moves into the pentateuchal legislation concerning adultery and spousal jealousy with a particular focus on punishment and discipline. Here she concludes, "Yhwh does not derive his authority to judge his unfaithful wife from his metaphorical role as her husband. ... but because he is viewed as the supreme ruler and judge over all people." In her last section, Kim muddies the waters considerably through a lengthy discussion on gender associated with metaphor in the Hebrew Bible. She notes that male *and* female genders are at times associated with things positive and at times with things negative. Consequently, the original audience might have argued that it is difficult to blame the female character of Jerusalem for what befalls male Israel.

John F. Hobbins, in "Zion's Plea That God See Her as She Sees Herself: Unanswered Prayer in Lamentations 1–2," takes issue with Mandolfo's "avowed misreading of biblical discourse, and of Lam 1–2 in particular." Hobbins sets an agenda to fight to allow Daughter Zion to speak in her own voice, not that of Mandolfo, or that of Hobbins. To achieve this goal Hobbins compares Mandolfo's reading of the voice of Daughter Zion found in Lam 1–2 with the tradition of lamentation the book has nourished through the ages as evidenced in the writings of Eicha Rabbah, the *Kinot* and *Tefilot* of Tishah b'Ab, and the poetry of Nahman Bialik. Fundamentally, Hobbins calls Mandolfo to task for reading through her contemporary, postcolonial, feminist lens without giving so much as a nod to "tradition." His major concern throughout the paper is his reading of Mandolfo as one that does not allow Daughter Zion to be penitent. He insists that Zion is fully penitent all the while angry and inconsolable, and that God is not an acquiescent ogre but a Deity who takes up humanity's cause.

The majority of Michael H. Floyd's article, "The Daughter of Zion Goes Fishing in Heaven," focuses on the interpretive translation of בת־ציון as "Daughter Zion" (by Mandolfo and others) instead of "Daughter of Zion." Through the use of grammatical, rhetorical-poetical, and sociocultural realism; numerous examples; and in conversation with various scholars, Floyd concludes that the proper translation for the Hebrew expression is a construct chain, "daughter of Zion." He closes his article with a reading of Lam 1, noting the significance of translating בת־ציון as "Daughter of Zion," mainly that בת־ציון personifies the women of Jerusalem, not the city itself.

Using shared cultural memory theory, Mignon R. Jacobs has presented a thorough analysis on one of the key texts in Mandolfo's work, in "Ezekiel 16—Shared Memory of Yhwh's Relationship with Jerusalem: A Story of Fraught Expectations." This study contends that (1) the use of metaphor defines the text and the interpretive process; (2) the depiction betrays the nature of the relationship and thus presents competing perspectives regarding it; (3) all readings privilege a perspective but do not in the privilege obliterate other perspectives; (4) the Deity is both author and character; and (5) the portrayal of the Deity is as much a theological construct as a sociological one. Jacobs begins by describing the characterization of Jerusalem (female) and the Deity (male) as presented in the text. Once the characters are defined, Jacobs moves on to describe the relational dynamics between the two and concludes with a description of the interrelational tensions. The tensions in the relationship dynamics are depicted in terms of dualities: honor-shame, protection-exposure, and commitment-abuse. This approach surfaces the counterclaims within the text, for example, the Deity's claim to shame is that Jerusalem behaved horribly—but the counterclaim is the Deity failed in the relationship.

In "Zion's Body as a Site of God's Motherhood in Isaiah 66:7–14," Christl M. Maier has spent considerable energy "comprehending textual Jerusalem as a social space produced by a specific society at a certain time." She begins her article with a discussion of Lefebvre's tripartite theory of space, which she uses in combination with Cooey's feminist studies on the female body to interpret Isa 66:7–14. In general Maier expresses an appreciation for Mandolfo's work that addresses our modern questions on justice and in turn critiques Second Isaiah's consoling words and promises as inadequate responses to Zion's lament "because God's kindness is still constrained by the demands of patriarchal hegemony." Maier adds to the conversation, through her reading of Isa 66:7–14, a description of Zion's procreative, nurturing, hospitable, motherly role for the newly developing community—noting the hope and comfort the metaphor brings in a time of distress, especially for people at the margins. She finds in Isa 66:5–14 the voice of the marginalized and those who suffer from oppression. She concludes with the goal to keep feminist readings of Zion texts dialogical in two ways: first, in dialogue with other voices within the text; and second, in dialogue with competing contemporary interpretations.

Womanist scholar Cheryl Kirk-Duggan seeks to further problematize Mandolfo's postcolonial feminist reading of the Daughter Zion–prophet–God dialogic while pushing for contemporary applications of her conclusions in "Demonized Children and Traumatized, Battered Wives: Daughter Zion as Biblical Metaphor of Domestic and Sexual Violence." After providing a thorough rendering of her methodology, Kirk-Duggan launches into a data-driven depiction of domestic and sexual violence in the biblical text and contemporary culture. She concludes this section with a critical question about our own complicity in domestic and sexual violence when we do not address the implicit message portrayed by the use of violent metaphors in the biblical text. Using examples of domestic and sexual violence in literature and film as parallels, Kirk-Duggan drives home the reality of the negative subliminal messages communicated to contemporary audiences through uncritical use of the violent marriage metaphor of Hos 2. With the abolition of domestic and sexual abuse and the establishment of healthy values set as her goal(s), Kirk-Duggan closes her article with a sermon outline for Hos 2 that unpacks the implicit message of the violent marriage metaphor and "provides opportunity to talk about faithfulness and obedience and to decry the abhorrent practice of domestic violence."

In "Mission Not Impossible: Justifying Zion's Destruction and Exonerating the Common Survivors," Kim Lan Nguyen has built an argument, based on an anomaly of form in Lam 2:19, that leads her to conclude (contra Mandolfo) that Zion's punishment is deserved and the innocent common people are exonerated. Nguyen begins with an analysis of the vagueness of Zion's sin—asserting that the personification of Zion incorporates historical Zion, not just the current generation, and that the confession of sin(s) found in Lam 1, 2, and 4 exceeds, as a percentage (this conclusion is data driven), the norm for confession of sin found in the lament psalms. Next she discusses the need for theological revision after the destruction of Jerusalem. Here she notes that the Deuteronomic tradition completely fails to explain the problem of innocent suffering. This conclusion leads her to emphasize the anomalous fourth line of Lam 2:19 (three lines are typical), which for her represents the movement toward a new theology that addresses innocent suffering. This new theology allows for the possibility of recognizing the paradox of God's justice, evidenced in the punishment of Jerusalem for her sins, and for affirming the pleas of Zion's innocent victims, who rightly hope for God's future corrective deliverance.

LeAnn Snow Flesher begins "Daughter Zion: Codependent No More" with an interpretive summary of Mandolfo's book that she then uses as background to continue with a dialogic study of Lam 5 in relationship to Isa 62–66. Using the father motif of Lam 5:3 and Isa 63:16 and 64:7 (Eng. 8) as a point of departure, Snow Flesher maps the corresponding grammatical, semantic, idiomatic, and metaphorical similarities between Lam 5 and the community lament of Isa 63:7–64:11 (Eng. 12). These correspondences, aligned with the theological shifts evidenced by the remnant theology of Isa 62–66 and the corresponding language of Isa 65–66, lead Flesher to a concluding question: "Is the voice of the community that laments in Isa 63:7–64:11 (Eng. 12), that is, the community that Daughter Zion represents, the voice of the faithless remnant? Or does she represent a faith-filled community that understood God in new and different ways, with the result that she was ostracized by an elitist, dominant group?"

In "The Daughter's Joy," Mark J. Boda has studied the association of the speech form *Aufruf zur Freude* (summons to joy) with Daughter Zion. His study begins with the three uses of this speech form at the close of the Book of the Twelve as a call for Daughter Zion to rejoice, for her king is returning to Jerusalem and her salvation is imminent. Boda notes the shift in the rhetoric at the close of the Book of the Twelve from a dominating tone of judgment to the dominating tone of salvation in which Daughter Zion emerges as the key figure to announce this new era of salvation. He then goes on to study additional uses of the *Aufruf zur Freude* speech form related to female characters like Daughter Zion to determine trends, if any, within the examples. He finds striking similarities between the two sets of data, mainly that the summons to joy represented a speech form that called the recipients to a response of joy upon receiving the news of military victory. Conversely, the recipients of the news of military defeat would be called to lamentation. Boda notes in his conclusion the evidence in the Hebrew Bible of Daughter Zion expressing her mourning to Yahweh as well as evidence of a call for her to express joy (Zephaniah and Zechariah). Strikingly, what is missing from the Hebrew Bible is an invitation for Daughter Zion to lament or any record of her actually expressing joy. Boda concludes his chapter with a discussion on the irony of the use of the Daughter Zion metaphor by a male hegemonic elite to attain sympathy in their current plight.

In "'Whose God Is This Anyway?': A Response to Carleen Mandolfo," Carol J. Dempsey has heightened the foundational components of Mandolfo's work that are critical for comprehending Mandolfo's methodological approach as well as her understanding of Scripture. In a comparison between Mandolfo and Sandra Schneiders's views of Scripture, Dempsey has emphasized their points of agreement on the "Word of God" as metaphor and the authority of Scripture as dialogical relative authority. Dempsey notes that Mandolfo pushes Schneiders's conclusions on these two points one step further by suggesting the Bible is not the "Word of God" but the words of God, and by dethroning the unilateral absolute authority of Scripture in order to establish it firmly as having dialogical relative authority. Further, Dempsey surfaces Mandolfo's understanding of the anthropocentric portrayal of God in the Bible as metaphorical, resulting in many portraits of God that reflect the human person and the human condition. It is from these foundational premises that Mandolfo addresses the violent language and imagery of Lamentations and the prophets. Dempsey concludes: "because of the metaphorical nature of Scripture, Mandolfo is able to be critically playful with the text in an honest attempt to deepen the faith of believing communities while offering a way on how to read, understand, and make sense of the biblical text and story in a postmodern world.... Mandolfo has opened the door for dialogue about the God of the Bible ... [and] pointed us toward the Truth."

In the final chapter of this volume, "*Daughter Zion* Talks Back to Her Interlocutors," Carleen Mandolfo is provided an opportunity to talk back. She begins her response with comments on her experience of reading about her work in the preceding articles and follows with a significant conversation around method and her particular goals for reading the biblical text. She concludes: "my intertextual/dialogic approach combined with deconstructive feminist and postcolonial emphases gives my form-critical endeavor a decidedly postmodern cast that serves my theological and moral agenda." Mandolfo then sorts the fifteen articles into two major categories: those that are more *author*-oriented and those that are more *reader*-oriented. Articles sorted into the first category are those most critical of *Daughter Zion* and dissatisfied with Mandolfo's lack of respect for the "intention" of the text. These articles exhibit strong methodologies and rigorous analysis. Only two in the reader camp strongly disagreed with Mandolfo's work, and those disagreements seem to hinge on faith commitments. Mandolfo closes her response with a discussion on interpretation; leaning on Ricoeur's reasoning, she concludes, "interpretation is not complete until analysis gives way to understanding (and that understanding remains naïve unless tempered by analysis)."

What you hold in your hand is thus the result of a long process of reflection and conversation on a key aspect of the Hebrew Bible. Approaches range from the poetic, rhetorical, and linguistic to the sociological and ideological. Participants are from a variety of social locations, in terms of gender as well as phase in their academic careers. Our hope was to bring voices new and old to the table for a rich conversation based on recent research, and the present volume has not only fulfilled but exceeded our expectations.

This volume would not have been possible without the help of many people. First of all, we would like to thank Carleen Mandolfo for her willingness to join us on this journey. Her commitment to excellence was evident from the moment she took the stage at that initial session in Boston, as she handed the various participants her soon-to-be-read written review of their work. She humbly accepted our commission to review the volume and fulfilled this difficult task in a timely way. Second, we are grateful to the various participants in the project, initially those responsible for the superb papers that were presented at the initial session in Boston (Jill Middlemas, Barbara Green, Lena-Sofia Tiemeyer, and Stephen Cook), as well as the many others who joined the conversation through their contributions to the full volume. The various contributors were all open to peer review and revision and turned their essays around in a timely fashion, and for that we are especially thankful. Third, we are thankful to Steven McKenzie for his willingness to embrace this project from its early stages for publication in the then new Society of Biblical Literature Ancient Israel and Its Literature series. This early commitment to the present topic and the project in particular made our job as editors much easier. Fourth, we are grateful for the consistent and careful work of Suk Yee (Anna) Lee, who took the various essays in their draft form and painstakingly transformed them into the SBL House Style. Anna is certainly representative of an emerging generation of scholars whose perspectives will broaden the hermeneutical possibilities for the study of the Hebrew Bible. Finally, we are thankful to you as reader for picking up this monograph and joining the conversation. We hope that the volume and conversation will prompt further dialogue, both oral and written, in the years to come that will bear fruit in deeper reflection on the Hebrew Bible and its rich traditions.

Mark J. Boda, Hamilton, Ontario
Carol J. Dempsey, Portland, Oregon
LeAnn Snow Flesher, Berkeley, California

Cognitive Linguistics and the "Idolatry-Is-Adultery" Metaphor of Jeremiah 2–3

Barbara Green

Entry Questions

When I was first assigned to teach in a high school with boarding and day students, I encountered a family in which every member was acting unhealthily. When, eventually, I figured out I needed help in dealing with the individual whose care fell most directly to me, I consulted the school psychiatrist and told her what I had learned from the daughter, who felt she bore the brunt of the family's allocation of blame. The doctor told me that in a dysfunctional family, the pathology may be projected onto one member who is likely not the root of the family's difficulties, though it comes to appear so in the various recitals. When one member gets most of the negative focus, the others avoid at least some scrutiny. In the case I am thinking of, the one child surely had her problems, but she was not the taproot of sickness in that family of seven. How to order the parts well in relation to the whole is the challenge.

The questions I want to raise here have to do with the centrality of the marriage metaphor, found in several prophets—specifically here in Jeremiah—and handled in criticism generally and urgently in recent decades. Carleen Mandolfo asserts, "God does not author responsibly," maintaining that spousal God never "answers" adequately for divine excesses: never owns culpability, will not concede excess, show empathy, grieve, acknowledge the power imbalance in actions regarding "his" people.[1] My first

---

1. Carleen R. Mandolfo, *Daughter Zion Talks Back to the Prophets: A Dialogic Theology of the Book of Lamentations* (SemeiaSt 58; Atlanta: Society of Biblical Literature, 2007), 19, 121–28. The book raises key issues, among them: How does the Bible speak of God? How do gender and violence construct social reality (past and present)? How

question is indebted to her claim: Have we spoken well of God, authored God responsibly, as we have dealt with places in the biblical text/Scripture that are sacrally violent, that is, authorize violence by God and implicitly or inferably sanction us to act in a similar way? Absolutely: to expose the dynamics of texts open to misuse is an important and necessary step in biblical interpretation. Mandolfo's work on Daughter Zion contributes powerfully to that urgent quest. When the construction of the female as the sustained locus for all that is unhealthy is repeated without any resistance, it moves into our imaginations as true.[2] But a second question: Has the metaphor been pulled so relentlessly out of context that we miss something vital by focusing narrowly on one linguistic referent? Can the prophetic image-set work differently when we reangle the gendered language? With the help of cognitive linguistic metaphor theory and Alice Keefe's socioeconomic and literary analysis of the world of Hosea,[3] I will deal with the text in ways both critically minatory and respectfully encouraging so as to offer readings more healthy for believers who continue to draw on such biblical material as Sacred Scripture. I will begin with the "idolatry-is-adultery" metaphor to expose a situation that is indeed fraught with gender trouble but not reducible simply or essentially to it.

Thesis

A fresh look at the disturbing metaphorical language in Jer 2–3 with the help of cognitive linguistic metaphor theory and revised sociology prompts new insight. Gendered language exposes a struggle for fruitful survival—the economic, political, ecological, and cultic crisis confronting Jeremiah's

---

are we to address the harm done in the name of the biblical God to victims of that authority, which is disrespectful and harsh toward its perceived opponents?

2. Representative questions are those posed and explored by Gerlinde Baumann, *Love and Violence: Marriage as Metaphor for the Relationship between YHWH and Israel in the Prophetic Books* (trans. Linda Maloney; Collegeville, Minn.: Liturgical Press, 2003), revisited compactly in part 2, questions that thread her work: Is the marriage metaphor intrinsically violent, and is God's role also inherently scandalous? Is marriage, and perhaps the general realm of women, ever presented as positive? Though useful, those are not the only questions; they may have the defect of their specific scope, in that they focalize the individual female to the exclusion of her intensively communal context.

3. Alice A. Keefe, *Woman's Body and the Social Body in Hosea* (JSOTSup 338; Sheffield: Sheffield Academic Press, 2001).

seventh/sixth-century setting/likely production. Though marriage is part of the operative metaphor structure, *to resituate the gender imagery in this broader field* expands reference. The female-as-deviant and marriage-in-trouble language contributes to a view of Judah's last kings' temptation to rely on international help rather than disclosing illicit cultic behavior. The main culprit is not so much "female" as "foreign."

SCOPE

Building on the work of those who have examined the marriage metaphor in the Hebrew prophets, I will attempt to reinterpret the complex relationship image so that its potential for misuse is reduced and fresh context suggested at least among those who are responsive to hermeneutical arguments. Much of what critical hermeneutics accomplishes finds its way eventually into the churches and into the lives of believers. My concern here is to avoid contributing to a disillusion with the Bible/Scripture's capacity or assignment to disclose God's self to believers. For me, there is no gain if someone who reads my work slams the Bible shut for the last time. Yet the terrain offered by Jeremiah's pugilistic language is challenging, demanding open-eyed critical engagement. My concern is to do the work necessary to recenter biblical texts as valuable for the believing community. Since to read privileging the categories of twentieth- or twenty-first-century Western feminist women is one but *not the only valid way* to proceed, I will try to make the late monarchic context more visible as well as suggesting a fresh contemporary optic for this language. My sense is that any construction of the biblical material must pay careful attention to what can be known of the original context, though readers may make choices for reading as well.

METHOD

Four critical streams contribute to my paper, two primary and two embedded. First is ongoing social-scientific work on the "inception culture," Israel and Judah in the eighth to sixth century, offering helpful data for our consideration.[4] Second, I will work with my "young" cognitive lin-

---

4. In addition to Keefe, helpful for background have been Phyllis Bird, "'To Play the Harlot': An Inquiry into an Old Testament Metaphor," in idem, *Missing Persons and Mistaken Identities: Women and Gender in Ancient Israel* (Minneapolis: Fortress,

guistic understanding of metaphor.[5] Third, scholars with whom I am in dialogue have drawn fruitfully on reception and ideology criticism, specifically feminist and postcolonial theory, making those tools operative in this work.[6] Fourth, with Mandolfo, I work with the thought of Mikhail Bakhtin, specifically his insistence that dialogical language makes deficient and aberrant any literalistic, reductionistic, or single-stranded reading of rich texts.[7]

1997), 219–36; Marvin Chaney, "Bitter Bounty: The Dynamics of Political Economy Critiqued by the Eighth-Century Prophets," in *Reformed Faith and Economics* (ed. Robert L. Stivers; Lanham, Md.: University Press of America, 1989), 15–30; John Andrew Dearman, *Property Rights in the Eighth-Century Prophets: The Conflict and Its Background* (SBLDS 106; Atlanta: Scholars Press, 1988); D. N. Premnath, *Eighth Century Prophets: A Social Analysis* (St. Louis: Chalice, 2003).

5. Though comparatively new, the field is vast and technical. I am standing at the beginner's edge. For an efficient introduction, see Raymond Gibbs and Gerhard Steen, eds., *Metaphor in Cognitive Linguistics* (Amsterdam: Benjamins, 1999); Zacharias Kotzé, "Metaphors and Metonymies for Anger in the Old Testament: A Cognitive Linguistic Approach," *Scriptura* 88 (2005): 118–25; Zoltán Kövecses, *Metaphor: A Practical Introduction* (Oxford: Oxford University Press, 2002); George Lakoff and Mark Johnson, *Metaphors We Live By* (Chicago: University of Chicago Press, 1980); George Lakoff and Mark Turner, *More Than Cool Reason: A Field Guide to Literary Metaphor* (Chicago: University of Chicago Press, 1989); David Lee, *Cognitive Linguistics: An Introduction* (Oxford: Oxford University Press, 2001); Philip J. Nel, "Yahweh Is a Shepherd," *HBT* 27.2 (2005): 79–103; idem, "'I Am a Worm': Metaphor in Psalm 22," *Journal for Semitics* 14.1 (2005): 40–54.

6. See the work of Richtse Abma, *Bonds of Love: Methodic Studies of Prophetic Texts with Marriage Imagery (Isaiah 50:1–3 and 54:1–10, Hosea 1–3, Jeremiah 2–3)* (SSN 40; Assen: Van Gorcum, 1999); Baumann, *Love and Violence*; Angela Bauer, *Gender in the Book of Jeremiah: A Feminist-Literary Reading* (New York: Lang, 1999); Athalya Brenner, "On Prophetic Propaganda and the Politics of 'Love,'" in *Reflections on Theology and Gender* (ed. Fokkelien van Dijk-Hemmes and Brenner; Kampen: Kok Pharos, 1994), 87–105; A. R. Pete Diamond, "Playing God: 'Polytheizing' *YHWH-ALONE* in Jeremiah's Metaphorical Spaces," in *Metaphor in the Hebrew Bible* (ed. Pierre van Hecke; Leuven: Leuven University Press, 2005), 119–32; A. R. Pete Diamond and Kathleen M. O'Connor, "Unfaithful Passions: Coding Women Coding Men in Jeremiah 2–3 (4:2)," *BibInt* 4 (1996): 288–310; Mary E. Shields, *Circumscribing the Prostitute: The Rhetorics of Intertextuality, Metaphor and Gender in Jeremiah 3.1–4.4* (JSOTSup 387; London: T&T Clark, 2004); Renita Weems, *Battered Love: Marriage, Sex, and Violence in the Hebrew Prophets* (Minneapolis: Fortress, 1995). For a discussion of these tools, see Keefe, *Woman's Body*, ch. 5.

7. Consult Barbara Green, *Mikhail Bakhtin and Biblical Scholarship: An Introduction* (SemeiaSt 38; Atlanta: Society of Biblical Literature, 2000); idem, *How Are the*

PLAN

I will organize around the cognitive metaphor, restating Keefe's work in that framing language, and then introduce and ramify seven steps where Jeremiah's metaphors get a workout, drawing implications and offering fresh insights as I go. By the end I will sum up learning that is new, interesting, and provocative not simply for the text's inception but for contemporary reception as well.

DEVELOPMENT OF THE THESIS

BASICS OF COGNITIVE METAPHOR THEORY

Some basic features of cognitive linguistics metaphor usefully distinguish it from other approaches:[8] metaphor is a *property of concepts*, not of words. Metaphors may receive direct linguistic expression or may remain submerged or embedded.[9] Metaphors are not simply ornamental but are *cognitively useful*, helping us to think and see new things. *Similarity is not the base of cognitive metaphor*, though likeness has a job to do. The point is to talk about one domain in terms of another and claim—establish—similarity. Metaphors are *common*, ordinary, easy—not rarefied. Avoiding them is more difficult than employing them. Hence they are crucial to our human

---

Mighty Fallen? A Dialogical Study of King Saul in 1 Samuel (JSOTSup 365; Sheffield: Sheffield Academic Press, 2003); Carleen Mandolfo, *God in the Dock: Dialogic Tension in the Psalms of Lament* (JSOTSup 357; Sheffield: Sheffield Academic Press, 2002). In *Daughter Zion* the material pertinent to Bakhtin is in ch. 1. Using Bakhtin with biblical texts is a growing and heterogeneous project, some of which can be seen at the website for the SBL group Bakhtin and the Biblical Imagination: <http://home.nwciowa.edu/wacome/bakhtinsbl.html>.

8. For an efficient summary of the general history of metaphor, see Wendell V. Harris, "Metaphor," in *Dictionary of Concepts in Literary Criticism and Theory* (New York: Greenwood, 1992), 222–31. Many biblical scholars who work with metaphor provide this same general information in one way or another as they set up for the particular metaphor theory that they will use. For example, Sarah J. Dille, *Mixing Metaphors: God as Mother and Father in Deutero-Isaiah* (JSOTSup 398; GCT 13; New York: T&T Clark, 2004), 2–17; Abma, *Bonds of Love*, 7–10.

9. Jack R. Lundbom (*Jeremiah 1–20: A New Translation with Introduction and Commentary* [AB 21A; New York: Doubleday, 1999], 129) uses the rhetorical term *abusio*, a similar concept in Jeremiah's rhetoric that seems standard in seventh-century Judah.

processes, not optional.[10] Four criteria diagnose cognitive metaphor. An assertion is a candidate for metaphor if: the statement is *not literally true*; is *not simply an adjectival description*; *mapping* works (see below); we have the sense of *hitting a speed bump* when we meet it.[11]

Implications of these basic claims here include the following: we can—must—anticipate a *vast and interlocked network* of metaphorical thought and language with roots tangled in the life and language of Judah in the eighth to sixth century (presumably drawing on older material as well). Though it is possible to lift out some isolated "idolatry-is-adultery"-linked metaphors, it seems best to find the metaphor marbled throughout Jer 2–3, especially as we recognize that the "idolatry" and "adultery" are not basic kernels but shorthand for the negatives of "orthodoxy/loyalty," "fruitful survival of a marriage," and more. Once the "marbling quality" of the language is claimed, the metaphoric networks of chapters 2–3 extend wall-to-wall, its root system extensive and tangled, manifested in a social setting and in language. The challenge is to construct the networks suitably, positioning them to show something unexpected by what their structure asserts.[12]

Terminology of Cognitive Metaphor Theory

A *target domain*—more abstract and less easy to know—names the field we are most interested to investigate; a *source domain*—better known and easier to talk about—helps us in some ways to explore the target. A process of *mapping* the source onto the target (attempting a fit between them) prompts us to infer—construct—conclusions about the target from information available within the source domain. In cognitive linguistics, the equations are: TARGET is SOURCE; and SOURCE maps to [—>] TARGET.[13]

I will begin here to explore the linguistic metaphor "IDOLATRY is ADULTERY," or "ADULTERY maps to IDOLATRY." I will leave the metaphor

---

10. Lakoff and Johnson, *Metaphors We Live By*, 3–5; Lakoff and Turner, *More Than Cool Reason*, 49–56; Kövecses, *Introduction*, ch. 1; Lee, *Cognitive Linguistics*, 6–7.

11. This metaphor was the contribution of Beringia Zen in a seminar on the book of Jonah, cognitive linguistic metaphor, and intertextuality, taught at the Graduate Theological Union, Berkeley, Calif., spring 2008.

12. In Jer 1–20 there are twenty-seven or so discrete "marriage" metaphors (2:2, 20–24, 25, 27, 31, 32, 33, 35; 3:1, 2, 6–10, 12–13, 20; 4:30–31; 5:7–8; 6:12; 9:1 (Eng. 2); 10:20; 12:7–8; 13:21–22, 26–27; 15:7–9; 16:1–2; 18:13; 20:7). Clustering in chs. 2–3 and occasionally thereafter, they become rare after ch. 20.

13. Lakoff and Johnson, *Metaphors We Live By*, 35–40; Kövecses, *Metaphor*, ch. 2.

in quotation marks to remind us that both the target ("idolatry") and the source ("adultery") are far more complex than those words may suggest: I include in "adultery" female sexual deviance and illicit behavior within the patriarchal household, mapping onto "idolatry," by which I understand behavior that violates Yhwh-alone worship. The goal is to explore idolatry/false worship—which, though constantly mentioned by cliché, is little elaborated and hence not precisely understood. The question is: To what extent and how can something better known—"adultery"—assist in elucidating what is less known—"idolatry"? The cognitive linguistic metaphoric process employing "adultery" and "idolatry," though not named biblically in just this way, is clearly used by Jeremiah. Though the terms need ramifying, they are not "wrong."

Refinements from Sociology and Cognitive Theory

Here I must introduce a basic corrective to my hunch when I first began work on this essay. Though I had read and appreciated Keefe's work on eighth-century Israel and Hosea's language, I had somewhat forgotten it while I worked on cognitive metaphor. However, as I coped with the welter of metaphor and revisited Keefe's book, I realized (and I am not claiming this as Keefe's authorial intention but as my reading) that her thesis can be stated as a cognitive linguistic metaphor—TARGET is SOURCE: SOCIAL BODY is WOMAN'S BODY, or SOURCE maps to TARGET. What is asserted of the female body maps to what is happening in the social body:

> This process of reframing will suggest that one may read Hosea's metaphor of Israel's social body as a fornicating female body in light of a growing atmosphere of crisis in eighth-century Israel concerning matters of community identity, socio-economic practice, sacral meaning and corporate survival. This crisis, which was at once social, political and religious, was precipitated by the erosion of indigenous structures of community life under the pressure of a rising market-based economy revolving around interregional trade, land consolidation and cash cropping. At risk in this transition was not only the well-being of individuals, but the sustainability of an order of world that was oriented around the intimate relationship of families to land and structures of communal solidarity based upon the bonds of proximity and kinship.[14]

---

14. Keefe's words (*Woman's Body*, 12) reference the eighth century and the language of Hosea, but the circumstances are not so different a century or so later—likely

What I draw from her work to correct my initial hypothesis is the larger context for the marriage metaphor, my "IDOLATRY is ADULTERY." To home in on one facet of the patriarchal household, specifically the role of the woman-as-wife, is inevitably to distort vision and restrict insight. I think, analogously, a similar thing can happen if we take a complex culture phenomenon (e.g., crisis in U.S. family farms) and focalize it in terms of one participant (e.g., the main female player). Her particular issues may be lifted up for scrutiny but as symptomatic of something more complex rather than as being simply "about her." Her factors are *part of the situation* and may *need particular focus*, but to pull them out of context can be confusing if we do not constantly recall that our move is somewhat distorting and open to misconstrual.[15]

To complexify source and target is to get something that still works for the metaphoric language in Jer 2–3 but even more usefully. First, the *source*: what seemed to be deviance within a marriage now includes such presence in diverse ways within a patriarchal household context: males and females as spouses and parents, contributing to a subsistence economy based on fruitfulness and an ancestral land/heritage system to be maintained over against its being absorbed into larger units.[16] The expanded *target* includes worship but also, intrinsically, the economic, social, and political as part of the distinctive and theretofore traditional national religion; apparently worship included as well an effort to move closer to aniconicity than might have been the preference of other systems or earlier within Yahwism.[17] If the source domain is the whole patriarchal

---

the territory is even smaller and the circumstances more dire. On page 179 Keefe specifies that the basic image (which she ultimately calls a symbol, without developing that language in much depth) includes not only what the woman does but what is done to her.

15. Diamond and O'Connor ("Unfaithful Passions," 289–90), on the contrary, claim that the marriage metaphor is itself a root or base metaphor, holding together the other images used and in fact progressing as a plot. I contend that marriage is not the root and prefer to read the figures kaleidoscopically.

16. Premnath (*Eighth Century Prophets*, 20–24) lists the systemic character of a culture undergoing such stress; his book then explains in fuller detail and works with prophetic texts to show processes operative.

17. Though this is too vast a topic to detail here, Keefe (*Womans' Body*, 96) does suggest and cite discussion about the links between monarchy and monotheism and seems generally agreeable with the scholarship that sees the emergence of monotheism (such as it was) as a slow process likely related to the politics of the monarchy.

household unit functioning in Israelite society, to focus too extensively on one member facet—the spouses qua spouses and woman qua wife—without recontextualizing can be misleading, distorting. The title of this paper should be: "*Yahwism under threat* from imperialistic cultures" is "patriarchal *household under stress.*" The *target* is the economic/social/political/religious health (productive survival) of the people Judah/Israel sponsored by Yhwh, while the *source* is the particular workings of the household unit. Both target and source are in serious and related trouble, with the more graspable household unit's workings illuminating the larger and more elusive unit.[18] Hereafter I will call my metaphor YAHWISM UNDER THREAT is HOUSEHOLD UNDER STRESS.[19] The risk here, well noted by Mandolfo in her oral response to the presentation of this essay, is that of erasing gendered language from consideration, likely from view. For that reason, Keefe's metaphor articulation is more precise as well as more efficient than mine. But my language raises the stakes in a way I intend: Is the "marriage" aspect of the root metaphor so central that if not named in gender language it is occluded? Is gender really absent from "the household" for us if the female is not named explicitly? I think not—or if it is, we need to envision the household more carefully. To frame this urgent matter in terms of the analogy of the family with which I began this paper: Is the daughter's situation worsened or ameliorated if an accusatory focus is taken off her and distributed within a wider unit?

Returning now to the question of how to correlate source and target contributions to insight: cognitive theory, responding to the recognition that even simple metaphors are compound and complex, offers a refinement of mapping, called *blending.*[20] The elaborations of blending provide

---

Citing the same research, Marvin Chaney agrees ("Accusing Whom of What? Hosea's Rhetoric of Promiscuity," in *Distant Voices Drawing Near: Essays in Honor of Antoinette Clark Wire* [ed. Holly E. Hearon; Collegeville, Minn.: Liturgical Press, 2004], 97–115, esp. 108–9).

18. Worth noting is the virtual absence in Jeremiah of any language that expresses the positive side of the metaphor, i.e., where the patriarchal household unit, functioning productively and healthily as an ancestral heritage, maps to approved worship of Yhwh.

19. Making a different sort of point about metaphor and the construction of Yhwh's identity, Diamond says ("Playing God," 119): "Death, cultural death, is the concern of Jeremiah." That is, in cognitive linguistic metaphor language, "death" (or, arguably, nonsurvival) is the target.

20. For a clear and useful description and utilization of how blending works and

a way to suggest and then exploit the rich, thick set of associations and interactive entailments available in a figure like YAHWISM UNDER THREAT is HOUSEHOLD UNDER STRESS. Blending theory uses four mental spaces rather than simply the two of source and target to show what becomes available from the networks of language, culture, experience—all linked neurally as well as more voluntarily. When HOUSEHOLD UNDER STRESS is mapped onto YAHWISM UNDER THREAT, a generic *mental space* suggests the range of inferences possible; and a *blended space* shows more specifically the sorts of associations hearer/readers are likely to utilize, ranging perhaps well beyond the most obvious and making use of apparent incompatibilities. A chart with a few elements filled in shows how this looks for the metaphor in question: note that the marriage is prominent but not isolated from a wider social matrix:

GENERIC SPACE

threat to orderly, fruitful survival

relational inequity among elites/peasants, males/females, Deity/humans

exclusivity claims and violations

reliance on international players: alliance partners, deities

disintegration

TARGET DOMAIN: YAHWISM   SOURCE DOMAIN: HOUSEHOLD
THREATENED   STRESSED

God-human relationship: =   husband-wife relationship:
violated   violated

---

what the payoff is, see Gilles Fauconnier and Mark Turner, *The Way We Think: Conceptual Blending and the Mind's Hidden Complexities* (New York: Basic Books, 2002); Seana Coulsen and Todd Oakley, "Blending Basics," *Cognitive Linguistics* 11 (2000): 218–23; Pierre J.-P. van Hecke, "Conceptual Blending: A Recent Approach to Metaphor, Illustrated with the Pastoral Metaphor in Hos 4,16," in *Metaphor in the Hebrew Bible* (ed. van Hecke; Leuven: Leuven University Press, 2005), 215–31. Van Hecke resolves a crux from Hos 4:16 by careful attention to theory and data. He demonstrates how the blended space may show up culturally specific detail that is not visible in either the target and source spaces, or in the generic space; once seen, it can be read back into the source and target. His example includes information about whether a shepherd follows or leads animals, and what the difference is for the Yhwh-is-shepherd metaphor. A more theoretical treatment occurs in Kövecses, *Metaphor,* ch. 16.

transgressive acts in social body	illicit acts by female in household
religion: betrayed	patriarchy: under attack or threat
Yhwh alone: transgressed	social mores: violated
love claims: pressed but disregarded	husband's role: threatened
past claims: pressed but renounced	family structures: threatened
worship: flawed	inheritance: made questionable
future gifts: owed but rejected	household goods: plundered
reaction/cure: repudiation	reaction/cure: punishment
anger/outrage	anger/outrage
destruction	shaming

BLENDED SPACE: YAHWISM THREATENED IS HOUSEHOLD STRESSED

threat to larger unit is visible in household

confusion of authority destabilizes and threatens productivity

fertility is threatened by various players

contestation or uncertainty of "father's" authority leads to confusion

patriarchal honor is risked as "father" is disregarded

behaviors as aberrant domestically and internationally

reaction of authority to blame deviant for lack of control

conflicting sense that the needs of the players are not being—
cannot be—met

temptation to select alternative partners in order to attain
desired/needed goods

violence threatened as an antidote to the ensuing chaos

What comes into view is the breakdown of *two interlocked and overlapping systems* (source and target) when intensified pressures are placed on them: the more tangible patriarchal or domestic household/heritage with its patrimonial values, and the more mysterious "national" religious system that is seen to underwrite and sustain it. Once Assyria has awakened from a long quiet phase and begun to encroach upon kingdom(s) that had felt autonomous for some time, threat looms. Judah, having barely and painfully survived Assyria, is more comprehensively threatened by Babylon and Egypt, and so the stakes are raised. The pressures placed upon the patriarchal household unit in order to meet the demands of the imperial power(s) make tangible what is threatening the larger unit: loss of a "mixed subsistence" way of life seen as dependent on Yhwh's patronal largesse. That is, as both Jerusalem and the imperial headquarters demand more efficient trade and a more predictable tribute, land becomes mercantile in a way that appears not to have been part of traditional Yahwism. We can feel the intensity of the danger and perhaps understand the violence of the language, as "the wife" is blamed pervasively for initiating and enjoying these external relationships. God and Jeremiah here and others elsewhere, including interpreters and commentators, drive the language dichotomously: the female is wholly deficient and the male utterly righteous. Readers may discern a clean split between the bodily and the mental, fertility and aniconicity, praxis and language. But *metaphor,* with its vast web of relational subtleties, *should not go unresistingly toward either extreme.*

ADDITIONAL SCRUTINY: METAPHORIC NESTING

A fourth step to perform shows how metaphors agglomerate and nest, from some very simple and intuitive ones, through more culturally specific ones, to others more broadly and powerfully pervasive.[21] Cognitive linguistics maintains, usefully, that there are certain basic metaphors, early sensed and thus neurologically wired in, that underwrite or sustain more complex and culturally specific assertions. A sampling of nested metaphor in Jeremiah, naming "target is source," tabbed from the simplest, to the more specific, to the most pervasive, shows:

simplest:
anger is a hot/expanding fluid that can boil over/burst its confines

---

21. See Lakoff and Johnson, *Metaphors We Live By,* 77–86, for something similar; and also Nel's discussion of shepherd for a good illustration of nesting metaphors ("Yahweh Is a Shepherd").

a relationship is an enclosure or container
love is a close bond
straying is disloyalty
> **more culturally specific:**
> God is a volatile element
> the Deity with surrogates is the enforcer of culture systems
> the Deity is the patriarchal spouse and the people is his wife
> destruction, defeat, devastation is divine agency, anger, and punishment
> > **most complex and pervasive:**
> > the social body in monarchic Israel/Judah is the female body

Other nested figures occur, using the equation "source maps to target":

simplest:
a person maps to a group or entity
individual male/female bodies, actions, characteristics, consequences map to group body
following, obeying, conforming map to fidelity and "orthodoxy"
refusals, denials, straying map to infidelity and disloyalty
> **more culturally specific:**
> man and woman map to patriarchal spouses/parents
> "iconic" or "plural" religious practices map to violation
> the patriarchal household maps to Yhwh's domain
> asymmetrical household interdependence maps to the Yhwh-Israel relationship
> economic, social, and political transactions map to religious ones
> > **most complex and pervasive:**
> > breakdown blamed on the woman maps to fractures afflicting the nation

The alternative charts just presented are really another way to present the information from the previous step on mapping, but they allow—even force—us to confront the pervasiveness of the metaphoric language.[22] Least important to me but central in cognitive linguistics is the

---

22. As part of her oral response to an earlier draft of this essay, Mandolfo questioned the necessity for the elaborate theory and discourse of metaphor. What cognitive theory correctly demands is precise articulation of the metaphoric language,

claim that certain roots of this metaphor are virtually instinctive, due to early "wiring." Consequently, prophetic language of divine anger made tangible as blowing out of control and the prophetic assumption that the divine "system enforcer" causes phenomena construed as punishment and reward are powerfully embedded in biblical texts. If we, rationally, refuse some of these equations, we must take note of our reading process, since the assertions perdure at multiple levels. That is, insofar as we want to resist these equations that the language may proffer, we must do so consciously. Interpretation is not a matter of disconnecting a single wire.

Second, since we will focus less on generic images and rather on those more culturally specific, it is a good time to summarize again what can be known about the "source domain":[23] like eighth-century Israel, eighth-to-sixth-century Judah was a subsistence agrarian society, traumatized by a protracted encounter with imperialistic Assyria, Babylon, and Egypt, who over time made various demands to threaten, annex, or conquer territory. Judah's leaders (including minimally the kings and their bureaucracy, powerful nobles, some priests and prophets) were caught on the horns of a dilemma: to meet the demands for tribute, the subsistence and heritage-based society had to be reordered toward a more "efficient" command economy, resulting in greater flow toward "headquarters," that is, the palace (local and foreign). The ancestral heritage system, comprising domestic households, relied upon the cycles of fruitfulness that allowed survival: fertility of womb, ground, livestock, basket, kneading bowl, as Deuteronomy compactly has it (28:4–5). We may accurately call this system the patriarchal household, so long as we recall it is populated by men and women, parents and offspring, animals and plants, Deity and ancestors, all seen as working in a particular way for productive survival. Moving to the more mysterious and lesser-known target: the culture was basically Yahwistic, though the precise nature of that claim is—and was at the time—under dispute and revision, presumably toward aniconicity, distinguishable from its plural roots. A shorthand name for this is "Yhwh alone," with distinct but related foci: the Deity with no peers or dependents,

---

explicit factoring of it. Such work is necessary, in my view, whether always demanded by the theory under which analysis sails or not.

23. For the base of my gleanings, see Keefe, *Woman's Body*, chs. 3, 4, 6, and passim. Premnath makes the situation tangible as well. Note that they are both talking specifically about the eighth century, though Premnath (*Eighth Century Prophets*, 25–50) gives a thumbnail sketch of a wider span of time.

a Deity adequate over against foreign systems. The fundamental struggle here, perhaps appearing futile from our angle, was whether to remain faithful to the heritage system and its way of life *or* to participate more fully in the "global economy." Judah's elites, likely for a mix of motives, preferred the more global option; Jeremiah and the Deity for whom he spoke urge the more traditional and self-sufficient system. The language of the imagery will cross promiscuously among fields we may normally think of as distinct, since preindustrial agricultural societies will not have imagined the fields distinct.[24]

ADDITIONAL SCRUTINY: METAPHORIC ENTAILMENTS

The fifth step to manage here in the consideration of Jeremiah's metaphorical language of chapters 2–3 is to sort the source factors that are *entailed* in the target.[25] That is, part of the target is *highlighted* by a particular source, while other aspects of it remain hidden or obscure; and certain elements of the source are *utilized* when asked to illumine a target, while others lie more *unused*. No single source is adequate to explicate a complex target, nor does a rich source serve just one target.[26] A target (YAHWISM UNDER THREAT) can be built from many sources (including but not restricted to HOUSEHOLD UNDER STRESS). In Jer 2–3 several source images are specified in addition to gendered ones.[27] When I concluded that I had named target ("idolatry") and source ("adultery") at least adequately, it appeared that "vine stock gone bad" did not gain much illumination in the marriage metaphor, and that gender situations such as the rape of an unwilling

---

24. Chaney, "Accusing," 100.

25. Lakoff and Johnson, *Metaphors We Live By,* 10–13, 22–24, 52–55, 87–94; Lakoff and Turner, *More than Cool Reason,* 70; Kövecses, *Metaphor,* chs. 7–8.

26. Kotzé's ("Metaphors") cognitive linguistic work on God's anger as bodily gestures as well as weather serving as a source for anger provides a good example of several sources utilized for a target.

27. In addition to the "patriarchal household disordered" source domain, there are many other domains used for "idolatry." Note even simply in Jer 2: wander off (vv. 5, 17); not avert to patron (v. 6); pollute (v. 7); experts do not do their job (vv. 8, 26); swap or trade gods (vv. 10–11); ignore spring for leaky cistern or far-off rivers (vv. 13, 18); born a nonslave but plundered (v. 14); devastated by animals (v. 15); yoke animal balking and resigning (v. 20); bad vine stock (v. 21); thief caught (v. 26); rebel, be punished (v. 29); lose way (v. 31); bloodied by poor (v. 34); betrayed by erstwhile allies (v. 36).

woman were not exploited as they might have been, since rape is not part of marriage. However, once I decided that I had read the language too narrowly, the kaleidoscopic pieces reconfigured. If the gender-specific language ("adultery") is *part of a larger complex of ideas*, with charges of false worship being simply *one player on a team of images*, the focus expands.

As suggested above, the fuller *source domain* is the patriarchal household, including of course the male and female as spouses but covering more as well; and the *target* is not worship narrowly considered but *a whole relationality* including politics, economics, ecology, and worship (which together constitute Yahwistic religion). Once I moved to HOUSEHOLD UNDER STRESS maps to YAHWISM UNDER THREAT, then certain underutilized and nonhighlighted elements became urgently useful: the folly of wandering to foreign places, the swapping of good local water sources for poor and distant ones, the outrage of a son taken from a household though he was not born a slave—all these suggest that the target is broader than cult, while of course including it. The source domain is not simply a marriage between a man and a woman but correlates a whole household unit, showing how threats to it are visible when such a household—not simply one individual or a dyadic pair—must abandon the local and go for the foreign. The target being highlighted is the aspect of a relationship suffering betrayal, specifically how the patriarch/patron loses when his beneficence and control are evaded or challenged (though leaving obscure what the whole household suffers from such a situation). This target is "complex Yahwism," not simply in the aspect of worship—though of course including that—but also the basic inheritance: the survival of the system of ancestral land heritage with its communitarian economy and ecology underwritten by the Deity's narrated generosity. The threat is "foreign overtures," not simply sexual acts, female behavior, or fertility; the scope is political-economic, rather than narrowly cultic per se. The threat is that imposed by the heavy hand and bruising heel of Assyria, Egypt, Babylon, and by local elites, insofar as they participate. The chart below shows the overlap:[28]

---

28. Though in much past discussion the specifically sexual use of a nonspouse was seen as part of the target (idolatry), we can now see that the claim rose from an overliteralizing sense of the זנה language. That is, the source was made literally intrinsic to the target instead of being metaphorical. No doubt there were other reasons as well for what seems to be an error. See Keefe, *Woman's Body*, chs. 1–2; Bird, "To Play the Harlot." As Keefe says (*Woman's Body*, 131–32): זנה is about much more than sex.

Entailed from the Cultural Associations, Shared by Target and Source

Promiscuity
basic systems challenged by circumstances and choice
survival threatened
productivity threatened
restrictions and controls transgressed
roles violated by access to outsiders
forbidden and illicit behaviors indulged
violence strategies as antidote

Again we can see more of the source and target. The *target*, stated positively, is the relationality of Israel with a Deity who is not characterized by what is "foreign," not bound by kinship ties, not cast into statuary, not partial to other nations; rather, Yahwism required productive survival locally, at least in the ideology of the book of Jeremiah. The threat highlighted is specifically the *foreign*. The *source* utilized includes straying women but also grapes gone bad, leaky cisterns, and far-off rivers preferred to springs, traders exchanging deities, leaders ceasing to do their traditional jobs. To overfocus on *partners* straying is to mistake the target for something more personal when it is in fact more socioeconomic and political: partners *straying*. What emerges more clearly here is that the target is not simply fertility worship such as deviant females might do or embody, but the whole imperial press, including the command economy and the various temptations contemplated in order to survive. Fertility, surely prized in an agricultural society by everyone, is not the deviance. The disorder under protest by Jeremiah is foreignness, in all its aspects. Female and fertile are part of the source, not the target itself. This claim does not excuse the pejorative use made of the female but resituates it.

Consider another analogy: a cartoon in which a clutch of cows obviously being herded somewhere against their wills muse resentfully: "I'm tired of them treating us like airline passengers!" complains one to another. We have to pick up on the fact that once it would have been airline passengers complaining about being treated like cattle; the object of the humor is not the life of cattle but of frequent fliers. If we miss that switch, we have missed the joke. Only context can cue us to the referents. The possibility of animal abuse surely lies within the "metaphor," but critter misuse is not, as culturally contextualized presently, the part to be highlighted. So with the erstwhile marriage metaphor, *to hear the implications of language where gender is slung as insulting is crucial, though without stopping there.* Gender problem: not solved but resituated.

A second example helps as well. Sarah Dille names the apparent lurch we may feel when considering the metaphor "Yhwh as warrior" and "Yhwh as a woman giving birth." How can such disparate sources (war, childbirth) contribute to a single target? The two images characterizing the Deity appear unrelated, inconsistent, and even incoherent. However, the disconnect is resolved when we recall that these roles are joined by the subject's crying out.[29] The metaphor roots in a situation where outcry is necessary, even unavoidable. The inconsistent need not be incoherent. A text and context, well constructed by a reader, bear coherence where it might not previously have been found, such as Dille's sense of the birthing woman and the engaged warrior.

PUTTING JEREMIAH'S METAPHORS INTO PLAY

A next step in the fuller version of this essay was to investigate whether and then to demonstrate how the tissue of metaphoric language in Jer 2:1–4:4, comprising some nineteen nameable figures, voices YAHWISM UNDER THREAT is PATRIARCHAL HOUSEHOLD UNDER STRESS more adequately than it expresses IDOLATRY is ADULTERY.[30] The diversity of source domain language (including gendered figures but others as well) contributes to a deep and rich sense of target domain language that expresses "going out," or going foreign. Space precludes the detailed examination of all these figures, so a small sampling will indicate the point:

---

29. The metaphor whose unexpected coherence Dille discusses (*Mixing Metaphors*, 14–17) is drawn from the work of Katheryn Pfisterer Darr. The discussion can include two metaphors, or entailed aspects of a single metaphor, depending on the level of abstraction at which they are discussed. Often metaphors that appear inconsistent and incoherent are inconsistent but not at all incoherent.

30. Though there appears not to be much consensus on the structure, the variation is actually more at the level of subunits rather than major chunks. I will adopt Lundbom, *Jeremiah 1–20*, 4–12, as most useful, since he attends so well to rhetorical features of the MT. Various commentators provide charts for the material, ordering for the unit in question the person, number, and gender of addressee if pertinent, the rhetorical features (such as questions, quoted discourse), the themes or topics. See Stuart Macwilliam, "Queering Jeremiah," *BibInt* 10 (2002): 402–4, for several of these.

2:10–13: people trade old gods for new ones who are No Profit // leaders search for allies or trade sponsors, fruitlessly[31]
people exchange spring water to dig leaky cisterns // leaders seek new sponsors

2:25b–27ab: woman denies she is going after strangers // refusal to see what is happening

2:31–32: people are seeking their own way in wilderness where their sponsor no longer is // a refusal of an old relationship
bride forgets the time of her betrothals[32] // breakdown in family unit

2:33–37: woman denies her guilt, takes nonjudgment as permission // a sense that the search for allies is permissible since it has not been stopped
the new partner chosen to replace the former will lead her as an exile or prisoner // new allies are unreliable, counterproductive

3:1–5: the wife has been divorced but thinks to return // customary laws flouted, evidence suggests uncertainty about of what to do about alliances[33]
the woman boldly seeks other lovers who participate willingly // search for allies who seem enthusiastic[34]

---

31. William McKane, *Jeremiah I–XXV* (vol. 1 of *A Critical and Exegetical Commentary on Jeremiah*; ICC; Edinburgh: T&T Clark, 1986), 34: Swapping deities was not generally done, surely not to exchange a good deity for a bad one. He reports that Kimchi was of the view that the cisterns dug were political alliances, with Egypt in particular (pp. 37, 59)—so, false reliance.

32. Bauer (*Gender,* 38) characterizes this female figure as refusing a dress code and ultimately as stripped and naked. It seems excessive as a description, though it raises an excellent question about how to read metaphors: as piled up, so that each female bears the burden of what is said of all females (or of another source image), or as more kaleidoscopic, singly tumbling against each other.

33. Walter Brueggemann (*Commentary on Jeremiah: Exile and Homecoming* [Grand Rapids: Eerdmans, 1998], 43–44) says that the three rhetorical questions posed in 3:1 claim that reunion is not possible; and yet later in this trope it is contemplated.

34. McKane (*Jeremiah I–XXV,* 59–60) cites Kimchi, who says the shared of imagery of waiting has to do with prostitutes and with traders, each awaiting customers. Baumann, who reads the images more literally than I do, worries about Yhwh's having multiple wives (which he ought not), and about the logic of females in *znh* behavior with female deities (*Love and Violence,* 109–12). I think Baumann tangles

woman goes back to her former patron as though he
should meet her needs // uncertainty about whom to seek
as all situations change[35]

Some longitudinal observations: First, the main point is that the many
small metaphors are all readily construable with some specific reference to
the crisis faced by leaders of Judah at the end of the seventh and beginning
of the sixth century. The circumstances will have been generally cognate
with what has been well described regarding Israel and Assyria for the
eighth century, with Judah's options for dealing with Babylon and Egypt
having only become more desperate, not changed in kind. "Going out" is
the most consistent valence of the metaphors.

Second, the rhetoric, as many have noted, is harsh. The plan of the
language emerges from the viewpoint and discourse of Deity/prophet,
who accuses the objects of his tirade crudely, shuts down any response
from them—indeed, saying what he "needs" them to say for him to be in
the right. The Deity evidences no self-reflection on his own role—poor
authoring, as Mandolfo says. But the strategies of metaphor call for language powerful enough so that the interlocutors find themselves and their
circumstances compellingly redescribed.[36] In a time of crisis, urgent language was wanted. The addressees, leaders of Judah, are lampooned and
caricatured, insulted in various ways to get their attention, to shame them
into change.

---

here since she is looking pretty exclusively at simply one part of a metaphor chain that
works systemically.

35. Robert P. Carroll (*Jeremiah: A Commentary* [OTL; Philadelphia: Westminster,
1986]) says here (142) and elsewhere that the religious, political, and sexual overlap
and cannot be neatly separated. I agree, though I differ with him on how much of the
sexual behavior described is literally likely. See Diamond and O'Connor for a brief
discussion of the relationship between what would have been possible to contemplate
in late monarchic Judah, though unlikely to have been common behavior ("Unfaithful Passions," 291–92). Carroll also reminds us that to slur another religion by sexual
innuendo is a classic strategy of belittling a group, and that we need not believe every
slur uttered. See William Holladay, *Jeremiah 1: A Commentary on the Book of the
Prophet Jeremiah Chapters 1–25* (Hermeneia; Philadelphia: Fortress, 1986), 112: "Jrm
has made remarkably free use of the Deuteronomy 24 passage." Sarah Mandell pointed
out informally to a group I was in that "our" modern, Western assumption that ancient
Israelite marriages were "monogamous" for women may be untrue! At the very least,
she reminds us, it is an assumption, not a fact.

36. Brueggemann, *Jeremiah*, 39.

Third, the gender distribution within these sixty-five verses is roughly even: at least thirty-seven are addressed to or spoken of males; some thirty are addressed to or said of females (some are gender-uncertain or -irrelevant, e.g., the heavens).[37] Again, my point is not to contest the effect and possibly the intent of misogyny, but to show its distribution amid other imagery. Needing emphasis is also that for any patriarchal male, and for the Deity in particular, the cuckold identity is far from ennobling.[38] The gender language is not respectful of anyone involved, but perhaps Jeremiah would say that respect was not his objective.

PAYOFF

Finally we must push into greater explicitness some of the insights generated here, and at three levels:[39] first, those that may plausibly have resonated with Jeremiah's *intended audience*; second, those *we may see for them* from our wider angle; finally, for *later readers, specifically ourselves*.

First, how shall we hear the refashioned and extended metaphor *preached by a reconstructable seventh-to-sixth-century Jeremiah and received by leaders of Judah*? Without attempting to be too precise about time, a thirty-year window (e.g., 621–591 B.C.E.) would provide a general situation of toggling threat and promise from empires (Babylon or Egypt) that kings and certain factions would have sought to manage. The threat included Judah's being overwhelmed in one way or another (economic or military), and the choice for Jeremiah's opponents appears to have been whether—and how—to resist the worst absorption and loss of position, with the undesired alternative being capitulation to Babylon.[40] From the perspective I construct for these elites, to play the major powers off each

---

37. Males (not worrying about person or number here): 2:3–15, 26–32; 3:12–18, 20–25; 4:1–4; females: 2:1–2, 16–25, 33–37; 3:1–11, 19.

38. Carroll, *Jeremiah*, 142.

39. I do not feel too well accompanied by the cognitive theory at this point, i.e., I do not understand its complexity well enough to be informed about the tangles of the text I am working on. Useful, however, are comments by Lakoff and Johnson about innovation (*Metaphors We Live By*, 151), and by Lakoff and Turner about the mapping of images (*More than Cool Reason*, 89–100). Kövecses (*Metaphor*, ch. 5) talks about metaphor sustained in works of literature.

40. This reduction to two options is, of course, oversimplified, since multiple choices will have been available at any given moment and factions to urge and contest them.

other, to seek allies of Judah's own small size, and to wring from their own people as much as they could manage was a sensible choice. The efforts of leaders to make effective alliances and command tradable products was a matter of exerting control on those producing goods. Judah's political and religious leaders presumably felt constrained to urge a policy that would work effectively *for themselves* under the circumstances to salvage what was salvageable, their own positions not least of all. Keefe suggests that urban elites may themselves have felt little pull toward the values that were more village- or subsistence-based, may have felt justified in practices like latifundialization that eroded the traditional way of life so as to attain greater economic efficiency. For Judah to attempt survival with at least nominal independence—surely with palace and monarchy, temple and priesthood, territory and landholders—would have seemed important and possible to those holding those positions.

The dominant view expressed by prophet and Deity in the book of Jeremiah differed.[41] To sum up a complex viewpoint before moving to his rhetorical strategies: survival at the cost of a way of life—what we would call a religious relationship—was not an option for him. To eke out an unstable position as a "willing vassal" was incompatible with "surviving." To trade the self-sustaining way of life of Yahwism for negotiated dependency upon a foreign potentate was not viable. The prophet's alternative: walk on your own to Babylon. How does Jeremiah present his viewpoint in the circumstances, where it has to have become ever clearer that options were slipping away? He uses metaphor, with its strategies of "shock and awe."[42] Since metaphors work strategically and rhetorically, Jeremiah hurls them at his addressees to persuade change, sets up unusual and controversial scenarios, offering material to be unpacked and explored by those who dare to do such work. Metaphor trades in anthropomorphism, personification, exaggeration, characterizing people in unexpected and insulting roles, subverting the expected or banal: here male elites are made to be

---

41. Keefe (*Woman's Body*, 194) reminds us that such a prophet was not simply one who urged traditional values but was charged with the responsibility to make such a way of life seem worth fighting for in the face of new pressures. In other words, the prophets were both radical and conservative, creative and traditional.

42. Shields (*Circumscribing the Prostitute*, 86–87) reminds us that though hearers may have been familiar from Hosea's use of the marriage trope, the metaphoric language using the female as a source domain (my wording here) would have worked best if it had not become trite and a cliché.

deviant females (of various sorts), and also grape stock somehow gone bad. Royal leaders and their surrogates are shown forgetful and irresponsible, willing to risk the patrimonial legacy as they barter it for the uncertain goods to be had from outsiders. And Jeremiah paints the Deity, aggrieved at such betrayal, jealous and possessive, angry and retaliatory, pushed to the wall and running out of forgiveness and fresh starts. Metaphor piles up and compounds insult and shame, drawing features almost to the breaking point—perhaps past it.

All the source domain language is extreme, exaggerated. The language of female sexual deviance is overwrought and cannot be assumed to reference a clear practice.[43] Women were surely not wildly out of control of the patriarchal household, waylaying strangers on the road, rushing up to hilltops to recline under every leafy tree.[44] Over the past few decades, scholars have backed off from taking "cultic prostitution" as a literal part of "Canaanite religion."[45] And though we can see that there would have been a spectrum of how Yhwh was to be worshipped—with how little or how much "non-aloneness"—in the late monarchy, the choice was not a stark "Yahwism" *or* "a fertility-laden Baalism," though it has taken us a long time to see it.[46] Mandolfo talks about the "dirty little secret" of mono-

---

43. Bird ("To Play the Harlot," 221–25) details how the root זנה is used for both literal and figurative behavior, for male and female behavior (though distinctively), and confusingly (to us) for both prostitution and for promiscuity, and that there are other terms to understand as well, e.g., נאף more specifically for adultery. She argues that "cultic prostitution" is either a misunderstanding or perhaps a slur but in any case ought not be taken as an accurate description. See Baumann, *Love and Violence,* 1–2, 9–22, 43–46, as well.

44. Diamond and O'Connor ("Unfaithful Passions," 308–9) note how dangerous such behavior would have been, and to imagine it was widely indulged is not likely. It was rather language that played upon fear of what would happen in the land-based society where productivity on one's ancestral heritage and reproductivity there were threatened.

45. Keefe (*Woman's Body,* 196, and ch. 6 in general) provides the argument that "Baal" represents not simply a foreign deity but the cultural sponsorship of economic practices. In other words, the collaboration here must be seen in political and economic terms as well as within a religious system. Chaney ("Accusing," 110–21) summarizes what "baal" sponsors and underwrites: a particular way of life of elites, centered on maintaining profitable production and unambiguous reproduction, with issues of legitimate inheritance clear.

46. Keefe, *Woman's Body,* 10–11, 42–65.

theistic, Yhwh-alone worship as distinctively complicit with misogyny.[47] This "secret" is one of her points I have found most intriguing. I do not, however, find the link essential, any more than I hold that the vineyard planted at great cost and then somehow gone bad is inherently connected with monotheism. Again, I am far from denying the misogyny with its attendant problems. In extant ancient Near Eastern literature it does not occur. But the *intrinsic* link with monotheism I cannot discern. And if we resituate the metaphor, widen "IDOLATRY IS ADULTERY" to YAHWISM UNDER THREAT IS PATRIARCHAL HOUSEHOLD UNDER STRESS, any illusion of tight equivalence vanishes. Misogyny is not limited to monotheistic cultures; and as has been pointed out, the presence of deities of both genders does not mean women were not disfavored. The taproot for misogyny is androcentrism and patriarchy, not monotheism. If René Girard and James Alison are correct, androcentrism and patriarchy themselves are more deeply rooted still.[48]

A similar point can be made about the familiar dichotomy between "spiritual" and "sensual," which when polarized cannot be accepted.[49] The images of abandoning well-functioning springs to dig leaky cisterns, turning against rain-dependent agriculture and its way of life for life at the big rivers, are as effective in their way as are the gendered images, though not so emotionally charged. What unites them is Jeremiah's outrage at the foreign: that Yhwh's leaders would so heedlessly swap a traditional way of life with their Deity for something alien and ultimately uncertain. Fertility and the feminine were not the main focus, nor was foreign *cult* per se. The basic evil is to *choose* the *alien* and thereby reject their own heritage, whether or not the elites knew or agreed that one way of proceeding excluded or eliminated the other. Jeremiah's language is thoroughly sexist, shoring up and being shored up by the patriarchal household; but "whoring wives" is not his main point, and we do best to see that, lest we reify the language beyond repair.

---

47. Mandolfo, *Daughter Zion*, 76–77: "Outside of rigid YHWHism, polytheism simply does not equal adultery." She quotes Regina Schwartz's work that suggests the homology between a limited-goods viewpoint and harsh "othering." I see the possibility but not the inevitability. Others agree that the "marriage metaphor" is distinctively Israelite (e.g., Abma, *Bonds of Love*, 23–25).

48. For a short edition of Girard's theory, see James Alison, *Knowing Jesus* (Springfield, Ill.: Templegate, 1993).

49. Keefe, *Woman's Body*, 2.

Second, what can *we see about them that it appears they did not
see about themselves*? The choices of Jeremiah's opponents—those with
responsibility for maintaining the household—were few, and determined
largely by location. No biblical prophet ever says, "It's not our fault, we
had no choice, the imperial crush was inevitable." Yet the point seems
undeniable.[50] Jeremiah's sense that "heritage Yahwism" *must* survive in
a microclimate of its own, *could* exist in a little niche amid a Babylonian
(or Egyptian or Persian) majority, was not realistic, ultimately. And yet
perhaps that is what he did see: the decision to walk to exile was more
survivable for Yhwh's people than the alternatives—to be dragged there
or to make an arrangement with Egypt. At the macrolevel, Jeremiah looks
to have failed to divert the powerful foe from the city walls. Was Jeremiah
right to think that survival in the traditional mode of production and the
resulting way of life was so intimately connected with Yahwism that to
surrender it was to betray one's Deity? Clearly not, given the Jewish people's survival of that crisis and worse since. Yahwism was not so dependent on the patriarchal household.

The last point to offer about what we can see about Jeremiah and the
others that they cannot have seen is the inappropriateness of the sacrally
violent language, with which the book of Jeremiah abounds. Granting that
bad grapevines and foolish choices about water supplies are less problematic than bad women, still the persistent depiction of God as angry, in or
about to be in the process of boiling over, lashing out as an affronted patriarchal male against feminized ingrates, is all basically problematic. All of
the language of outrage and threat, of insult and shaming, evidently failed
to convince the most important of Jeremiah's hearers, the elites who seem
to have resisted the image of the breakdown he paints with them at fault.
All the moralizing prophetic language was largely beside the point, since
threats from the nations were not really divine punishment for Israel's infidelity. No doubt better leaders might have made better decisions about
many things. We may, without exaggeration, say that Jeremiah's language
was not adequate to the task he was given, and this insight is sobering. Perhaps the language was too strong for its intended hearers, as we ourselves
may find it as well.

Finally, what about *ourselves as readers of this material*? Let me pick
up the point I just made "for them," though shifting it as well. If we can

---

50. Carroll, *Jeremiah I–XXV*, 128.

say that Jeremiah's base metaphor did not work for his hearers, we can say that his language is often counterproductive and overstrong for us as well. The starting point for my essay and that of other scholars with whom I have dialogued is that the gendered metaphoric language is abusive for us, its harm outweighing any advantage. Baumann efficiently suggests that it makes women identify with those who are said to deserve violence and leaves women without recourse to the Deity who inflicts it; males are left too free to identify with the Deity punishing the deviant females; and the Deity looks bad from just about every angle.[51] When we are talking about relationships, is language of brute force appropriate, or ridicule and insult ever helpful? The language of punitive sex and violence is at odds with what needs sustaining. The Bible (stem to stern, not simply the OT/Tanak) must answer for its violence, particularly its sacral violence, abounding here. Charges of misogyny, of reinscription of patriarchal interests, of sexism, classism, and racism are impossible to deny or ignore. To use gender language for insults, to denigrate any group in terms of female or feminine characteristics or behavior, is lethal, cannot go unremarked, uncritiqued, undenounced.

But what are the choices? One likely not chosen by any holding this volume is to abandon the Bible as hopeless. Mandolfo's project, a second option, is to loosen the Bible's religious and cultural authority while continuing to demonstrate its literary excellence. Insofar as the biblical text valorizes gender abuse, it must not be allowed to dominate the lives of its readers as it has long done. To deauthorize the Bible so that its language can be read less restrictively is not an easy matter. A third choice, and mine, anticipates the need for any who wish to maintain the authority of the Bible as Scripture. Here, not dissimilar from Mandolfo's project, the challenge is to learn better reading strategies so that we are able to construct its language afresh. Perhaps the project is too ambitious, but it may not be farther out of reach than seeking to demote biblical authority from the places where it is most securely enthroned. How to read better? In a

---

51. Baumann, *Love and Violence*, chs. 12–13. She moves on to ask if this is recuperable by means of other metaphors that can counter the marriage metaphor with which she has worked, and concludes that there is no metaphor the equal of the marriage metaphor (ch. 15). It is my sense that part of its power comes from having raised "it" out of its fuller context. I am a bit leery of saying that readers have to identify in a particular way. Chaney, for example, holds that Judah's elites will have known that they were being addressed as deviant females ("Accusing," 113–14).

word, less literalistically. Literalism strikes me as the most consistent error. How to take the Bible seriously, if that is our choice and heritage to do, and not overliteralize? It is my contention, shared with Keefe, that overliteralizing and reading too narrowly is what led us astray on this metaphor, resulting in our perpetuating what it utilizes, seeing in it nothing more or less than a total denigration of the female. To read the Bible well is necessary for reading it well as Scripture; in this goal, Mandolfo and I strongly agree. But the choice to maintain the traditional assertion that the Bible is a privileged place of God's self-disclosure is not required for good Bible reading. One can read skillfully without affirming the revelatory nature of the text. On that Mandolfo and I seem to part ways.

The third point here, as we consider the basic metaphor's challenge to ourselves as critical readers, is to see if there is anything salvageable once we have seen the toxic nature of some of its facets, once we have been alerted to its sexism, racism, violence, particularly of the sacral varieties. Recall that my point is that the basic metaphor *target*—stated here positively rather than negatively—is a SUSTAINABLE WAY OF LIVING PRODUCTIVELY OUR RELATIONSHIP WITH GOD, which includes what we moderns parcel out as political, economic, ecological, and cultic. The *source domain* is THE WAY OUR HOUSEHOLDS ARE RUN. As twenty-first-century global citizens, we share with Jeremiah's basic world a crisis of productive survival at a level far greater than pertained in his day. Jeremiah's handling of the metaphor suggests that he felt the Yahwistic base could not survive foreign ways, a point on which history has proved him wrong. If we allow the root metaphor to interrogate our present "survival situation," we resist the equivalence of the prophet's solution, which would be to rescue the family farm (with its patriarchal structures) and to reinvigorate a patron-client relationship with a Deity active as an agent in our lives. Jeremiah's language my help us grasp the relationship between our particular "households" and the practices that sustain them and the larger domain of productive survival with appropriate attention to certain traditional values. One of the reasons for my project of decentering the marriage metaphor was to allow Jeremiah's language to have broader reference than simply gender, without excluding gender as a participant. How will we understand the practices of our households and their link to earth's survival? How will our biblical narratives continue usable when our circumstances are so radically changed? Metaphor invites the acceptance or refusal of its descriptions, its instruction, its explanations, its motivations (whether incentives and disincentives). The way forward for us is surely something more healthily ecological with its underwriting cosmology–which we do not yet quite see.

CONCLUSION

I want to return to the analogy with which I began, the dysfunctional family of parents, four sons, and the daughter whose care fell partially to me in my first year of teaching. She bore for some time the accusation and abuse of being the main player responsible for what happened in the household. At a given point, after that unjust and inaccurate situation had been recognized and diagnosed—its harmful effects made visible— change occurred. The remedial attention was redirected more evenly and aptly within the family. A side effect would have been the daughter's sense that she received less attention than before, was less visible. The negative dynamics were no longer simply about her. Did she find that move basically good news, or did she miss the attention she got in her focal position, even if it was heavily negative? That would have been a challenge, of which I was unaware at the time. Was her life different once she ceased to be the primary explanation for the many things that had gone awry in her family? Did the fact that her parents received counseling and presumably learned to view their children and themselves differently save her from a difficult life? I doubt it. But in that family to take the primary onus off of her may have helped a bit, maybe more than a bit. It certainly helped me on numerous later occasions to recall that the obvious party to blame was not thereby the most blameworthy. And I think the refocus helps here.

Speaking of Speaking: The Form of Zion's Suffering in Lamentations

Jill Middlemas

Speaking of Speaking

A cacophony of speaking voices intertwines and intercepts in the biblical book of Lamentations.[1] They represent the horror and shock of a community in the aftermath of disaster. A significant amount of attention in recent years has turned to interpretations of the female voice—the city of Jerusalem personified—and how it functions in the first two chapters. The figuration of a violated and vulnerable woman presents a human face for the very real consequences of disaster and tragedy. In addition, attention to the voice of Lady Jerusalem shifts the focus away from the theme of the redemptive nature of suffering expressed through the character of the strong man of chapter 3 that has so dominated critical interpretations of these poems.[2]

One of the most recent studies of the words of the personified Jerusalem is that of Carleen Mandolfo,[3] who applies the dialogic approach she developed in her first monograph on the interplay of different speaking

---

1. See William F. Lanahan, "The Speaking Voice in the Book of Lamentations," *JBL* 93 (1974): 41–49, for one interpretation of the variety of speaking voices.

2. For a helpful critique of the concentration on the suffering servant in Lamentations, see Tod Linafelt, *Surviving Lamentations: Catastrophe, Lament, and Protest in the Afterlife of a Biblical Book* (Chicago: University of Chicago Press, 2000); idem, "Zion's Cause: The Presentation of Pain in the Book of Lamentations," in *Strange Fire: Reading the Bible after the Holocaust* (ed. Linafelt; BS 71; Sheffield: Sheffield Academic Press, 2000), 267–79.

3. Carleen R. Mandolfo, *Daughter Zion Talks Back to the Prophets: A Dialogic Theology of the Book of Lamentations* (SemeiaSt 58; Atlanta: Society of Biblical Literature, 2007).

voices in the lament literature of the Psalms.[4] In her examination of the lament literature, Mandolfo drew attention to the alternation between the first- and the third-person speaking voices in a way that led to an analysis of how each could function in a dialogue. She showed how the two represent different, even conflicting worldviews. With a similar interest Mandolfo argues that the voice of personified Jerusalem speaks a counterstory that conflicts with the representation of the adulteress wife motif found in the prophetic literature. In the prophetic literature a common way to explain the downfall of the city of Jerusalem (and Samaria) was to figure the city as a wife who failed to remain committed to a single husband. This, of course, was a strategy to use characterization as a means to capture a sense of the disloyalty of the people as a whole. Mandolfo explores the character of the female Jerusalem in the book of Lamentations and how her testimony challenges the prophetic explanation by presenting other reasons for the disaster than only her own sinfulness. By placing the different perspectives in conversation, Mandolfo highlights the disharmony that is inherent in biblical literature. The comparisons and contrasts she makes leads her to the discovery and articulation of a dialogic theology that in her view "provides humanity an avenue for speaking honestly to God about their experiences of him,"[5] as well as to mirror the text and allow dissenting voices into the conversation.[6]

Three points of interest arise from Mandolfo's analysis that have implications for the current study. First, in Lam 1–2 the voice of Daughter Zion is found balanced by that of a narrating reporter. This fact is well known and documented in the literature on these chapters. What is new in Mandolfo's study is that she speaks of the supposedly third-person objective reporter as a dialogic voice (DV), whose own account alternates with that of Daughter Zion as in conversation. He hears her perspective and responds to it. The interaction between the two characters reveals the validity of Zion's speech in that the narrator refrains from discounting or even ignoring her protestations. In distinction to rhetorical techniques employed in the lament psalms or Lam 3, the conversation partner in the first two chapters of Lamentations speaks no generic, theological platitudes to Zion in order to make sense of or to assuage her agonized

---

4. Carleen R. Mandolfo, *God in the Dock: Dialogic Tension in the Psalms of Lament* (JSOTSup 357; Sheffield: Sheffield Academic Press, 2002).

5. Mandolfo, *Daughter Zion*, 19.

6. Ibid., 22.

cries. Moreover, he never responds to Zion with statements about Yhwh's goodness or mercy, steadfast love, or divine role as judge, rock, savior, and redeemer. Through this strategy the dialogic voice in Lamentations seems to accept, even value, the depth of Zion's suffering.[7] In this way, he stands with Daughter Zion against the prophetic tradition.[8]

Second, Lam 1–2 transform the lament genre. The first two poems in the book represent a mixing of two genres—the dirge and the lament form common to the Psalter. Drawing on new approaches in form-critical studies, Mandolfo suggests that what otherwise appears as a deterioration in form is actually a creative adaptation responding to alterations in circumstances.

Finally, Mandolfo's approach explores how the biblical book of Lamentations fails to blame Zion and presents instead her counterstory, or, in Walter Brueggemann's terminology, her countertestimony. An alternative, woman-centered perspective highlights the painful present, the experience of suffering, and with it, the concomitant feelings of shock, betrayal, anger, sadness, and so on.

Mandolfo's application of a dialogic approach has highlighted the important way the female voice presents a counter, even correction, to the dominant image of personified Jerusalem as a sinful and adulteress wife found in the prophetic use of the marriage metaphor. Personified Jerusalem also provides an effective alternative view to that of the narrator of chapter 1.

The state of the discussion as articulated by Mandolfo actually raises to the fore a question of the techniques employed in the presentation: How is the alternative perspective motivated in Lam 1 and 2? One avenue for further discussion has to do with the difference the form makes. Although Mandolfo has pointed to the appearance of a more varied form,[9] several additional points can be made with respect to the rhetorical strategies employed by the poet, the importance of rhetoric in Lamentations, and how interruptions in the context convey meaning. In addition, her study highlights not only a contrary voice, but one whose efficacy stems from the evocation of suffering. Part of what allows the rhetoric of Lady Jeru-

---

7. This point has been made previously by Linafelt, *Surviving Lamentations*, 52; and Kathleen M. O'Connor, *Lamentations and the Tears of the World* (Maryknoll, N.Y.: Orbis, 2002), 17, 31, 34, 35–41.

8. Mandolfo, *Daughter Zion*, 60.

9. Ibid., 65–67.

salem to offer such an effective contrast to that of the prophets is that it is grounded in her very personal pain. What follows provides an analysis of the important role played by form within the book of Lamentations with particular attention to the interchange between Daughter Zion and the Dialogic Voice as well as how suffering functions as a catalyst within the rhetoric.

THE IMPORTANCE OF FORM IN LAMENTATIONS

The careful artistry of the biblical book of Lamentations suggests that the poet(s) has an interest in issues related to form and structure. Four of the poems follow an alphabetic acrostic structure, while the number of lines in the fifth corresponds to the number of consonants in the Hebrew alphabet. In addition, poems 1, 2, and 4 follow a similar pattern in that each begins with the appropriately mournful איכה, "how," contains a fact half and an interpretive half,[10] as well as a myriad of snapshots of the violence that has taken place following the collapse of Jerusalem.[11] The first two chapters are aligned further in that the voice of a third-person eyewitness reporter (1:1–11; 2:1–19) alternates with that of the city personified as a woman in the midst of abject tragedy (1:12–22; 2:20–22). Moreover, the variety of speaking voices in the first four poems seems to be included in the communal lament that closes the collection.[12] The overall effect of the shape of the collection as a whole represents a lengthy example of an extensive funeral dirge[13] or is evocative of a violent, cyclonic storm.[14]

The form categories of the book of Lamentations participate in the artistry that is discernible on a literary level. The dirge interweaves with the lament in chapters 1, 2, and 4, while the communal lament proper characterizes the final poem (ch. 5). The mixture of categories in the third chapter sets it off as distinct in the collection. It begins and ends with an

---

10. Benjamin Johnson, "Form and Message in Lamentations," *ZAW* 97 (1985): 58–73.

11. Michael S. Moore, "Human Suffering in Lamentations," *RB* 83 (1990): 539–43; and Benjamin Morse, "The *Lamentations* Project: Biblical Mourning through Modern Montage," *JSOT* 28 (2003): 113–27.

12. Lanahan, "Speaking Voice."

13. William H. Shea, "The *qinah* Structure of the Book of Lamentations," *Bib* 60 (1979): 103–7.

14. Jill Middlemas, "The Violent Storm in Lamentations," *JSOT* 29 (2004): 81–97.

individual lament (vv. 1–21, 49–66) and contains a didactic interlude in the exact center (vv. 22–39) that leads into a communal confession of sin (vv. 40–48).[15] These details illustrate that the poems of Lamentations have been carefully fashioned and suggest further that their shaping conveys meaning.

Attention to elegiac elements provides a convenient entry point for attention to how the final shape of the book of Lamentations presents an interpretation. Hedwig Jahnow analyzed in detail the form and genre of the funeral dirge with particular attention to the biblical book of Lamentations.[16] A funeral dirge or Hebrew *qinah* is characterized by a backward glance, akin to the use of the elegy to capture the past achievement of a dead loved one. The dirge elements in Lamentations include the appearance of the question איכה (Lam 1:1; 2:1; 4:1), a contrast between the ignoble present and the glorious past, the figuration of Jerusalem as a widow, and the use of the *qinah* meter.[17] However, the extent of the dirge elements remains debatable, with Claus Westermann emphasizing the precedence of the elements of the communal lament.[18] The interplay of the two forms in chapters 1, 2, and 4 has even led to the categorization of a new genre. For example, Adele Berlin thinks of a Zion lament as a contrast to the Zion hymns of the Psalter,[19] while Nancy Lee has argued that the poems in Lamentations represent a new form that she labels the communal dirge.[20] The ascription of an exact genre is difficult to sustain, however, because

---

15. For an interpretation of how the shape of the chapter conveys meaning, see Jill Middlemas, "Did Second Isaiah Write Lamentations 3?" *VT* 56 (2006): 505–25. Cf. Mark J. Boda, "The Priceless Gain of Penitence: From Communal Lament to Penitential Prayer in the 'Exilic' Liturgy of Israel," in *Lamentations in Ancient and Contemporary Cultural Contexts* (ed. Nancy C. Lee and Carleen Mandolfo; SBLSymS 43; Atlanta: Society of Biblical Literature, 2008), 81–101.

16. Hedwig Jahnow, *Das hebräische Leichenlied im Rahmen der Völkerdichtung* (BZAW 36; Giessen: Töpelmann, 1923).

17. A point noted by a variety of commentators including Jahnow, *Hebräische Leichenlied*; D. R. Hillers, *Lamentations* (2nd ed.; AB 7A; New York: Doubleday, 1992); Frederick W. Dobbs-Allsopp, *Lamentations* (IBC; Louisville: Westminster John Knox, 2002), 54; and Nancy C. Lee, *The Singers of Lamentations: Cities under Siege, from Ur to Jerusalem to Sarajevo* (BIS 60; Leiden: Brill, 2002).

18. Claus Westermann, *Lamentations: Issues and Interpretation* (trans. Charles Muenchow; Minneapolis: Fortress, 1994).

19. Adele Berlin, *Lamentations* (OTL; Louisville: Westminster John Knox, 2002).

20. Lee, *Singers of Lamentation*.

the dirge elements of chapters 1, 2, and 4 recede to be completely replaced by a communal lament in chapter 5. Observing the gradual dominance of the communal lament led Tod Linafelt to suggest that, in form, the book of Lamentations turns away from death to embrace life.[21]

The form of the poems of the book of Lamentations, furthermore, conveys meaning in that another genre, in addition to the dirge and the lament, is present. As has been the source of much discussion, the book of Lamentations also resembles the Mesopotamian city lament genre. That the poems are different enough has led to an important debate about whether the biblical book of Lamentations drew from an ancient Near Eastern template to express the community's grief at the loss of Jerusalem and its infrastructure. The debate has been settled to some extent by the thorough analysis of Frederick Dobbs-Allsopp, who argued that the biblical book of Lamentations shares elements with the Mesopotamian city laments, yet remains distinct by including language consistent with the prophetic traditions of biblical Israel as well.[22]

Studies of the Mesopotamian city laments indicate that the language found therein is exaggerated and hyperbolic in order to encourage the deity to take note of disaster and return the divine presence to enable restoration. The poets employ graphic details to spur the deity to action. Furthermore, the Mesopotamian city laments express the efficacy of prayer and the goodwill of the deity by concluding with the god's return in a way that the biblical book of Lamentations does not. As such, the Mesopotamian laments were often employed in festivals of temple dedication and accompanied by feasting and revelry.

Although the biblical book of Lamentations is akin to the Mesopotamian city lament genre, the difference in the application of elements suggests that the former is used differently. Lamentations employs exaggerated language and fails to come to a resolution. William Gwaltney, for example, pronounces the imagery more gruesome in comparison to its ancient Near Eastern counterparts.[23] The poetic description of events in Lamentations suggests that its language is used like and unlike that of the

---

21. Linafelt, *Surviving Lamentations*, 75. See also the discussion by Lee, *Singers of Lamentations*, 37.

22. Frederick W. Dobbs-Allsopp, *Weep, O Daughter of Zion: A Study of the City-Lament Genre in the Hebrew Bible* (BibOr 44; Rome: Pontifical Biblical Institute, 1993).

23. William C. Gwaltney, "The Biblical Book of Lamentations in the Context of Near Eastern Lament Literature," in *More Essays on the Comparative Method* (ed. Wil-

Mesopotamian city laments. Although presenting a litany of distress, it contrasts significantly by remaining in the midst of the tragedy. Rather than containing a conclusion where feasting celebrates the return of the Deity, the biblical book of Lamentations ends instead on a question of whether the Deity will return: "Unless you have utterly rejected us, are wroth with us forever" (Lam 5:22).[24] The concluding statement places the emphasis on concerns about the continuing lack of divine support and aims to spur Yhwh to action in order to achieve the restoration made possible through divine intervention. The choice of the elements of the form of the Mesopotamian city lament indicates yet again how the form of the biblical book of Lamentations conveys meaning. In this case, the biblical book of Lamentations foregrounds the theme of the relation of the present and ongoing tragedy with the continued withdrawal of divine support. While the final two chapters of Lamentations give the impression of a community struggling with its ignoble fate, it is possible to understand the use of the Mesopotamian city lament genre as oriented toward hope for a future beyond disaster. The choice of the genre suggests a hope for a positive resolution that is an element of its form.

In at least two ways, the book of Lamentations employs form categories that orient a painful present toward future possibilities.[25] The collection moves beyond mere survival to a hopeful outlook that is not expressed explicitly in the poems themselves. The only hopeful section occurs in the center of the third chapter as a didactic interlude that intercedes in the surrounding material (3:22–39), only to be eclipsed by the grave and tragic circumstances that reverberate at the book's conclusion like the sound of a death knell. Closer study of the form of Lam 1 and 2 is required exactly because, in addition to words and images, the form conveys meaning.

---

liam W. Hallo, James C. Moyer, and Leo G. Perdue; Scripture in Context 2; Winona Lake, Ind.: Eisenbrauns, 1983), 208.

24. On the translation see Middlemas, "Violent Storm," 97 n. 47, and the references therein.

25. See also Jill Middlemas, *The Troubles of Templeless Judah* (OTM; Oxford: Oxford University Press, 2005), 220–26.

The Importance of Interruptions of
Form in Lamentations 1 and 2

Daughter Zion speaks in the first two chapters of the book of Lamentations, where she presents an alternative figure to the representations of her by the prophets. Her voice intersperses with that of an eyewitness reporter, who presents in factual detail the destruction that accompanied the downfall of Jerusalem, the myriad experiences of the victims that succumbed to or survived it, and the causes of the disaster. The first and second poems differ, however, with respect to how much the female voice speaks as well as with respect to what is said. The differences between the interplay of the voices of the reporter and Daughter Zion actually provide evidence of how form intersects with speech to convey meaning.

Lamentations 1 is an acrostic poem that contains more dirge elements than any other in the collection. The eyewitness reporter begins his narrative with a dirge or funeral song that presents a portrait of how the fortunes of the city of Jerusalem have changed dramatically. He offers an elegy in which he mourns the death of the city as if it were a person. Two statements of direct address to the Deity intercede in the midst of his recitation at verses 9c and 11c. These are statements of complaint akin to the laments of the Psalter that interrupt what is otherwise a properly mournful elegy.[26] In verse 9c the interrupting voice appeals to Yhwh to consider the triumphant attitude of the enemy, while in verse 11c it asks the Deity to take note of the speaker's humiliation and state of worthlessness. The identity of the speaker has been associated with the personified city of Jerusalem whose own appeal to Yhwh concludes the first poem in verses 12–22.[27] A not quite dead Zion interrupts the narrator's untimely report of her demise to add a personal note to an otherwise rote report of the downfall of the city.

In the first chapter of Lamentations, Lady Jerusalem refuses to accept the cold narrative report of her literary death. Instead she interrupts the eyewitness twice to speak directly to Yhwh: "See, Yhwh, my misery" (v. 9c),

---

26. Linafelt, *Surviving Lamentations*, 37–39.

27. For more on the personification of Jerusalem, see Barbara Bakke Kaiser, "Poet as 'Female Impersonator': The Image of Daughter Zion in Biblical Poems of Suffering," *JR* 67 (1987): 164–82; and Knut M. Heim, "The Personification of Jerusalem and the Drama of Her Bereavement in Lamentations," in *Zion, City of Our God* (ed. Richard S. Hess and Gordon J. Wenham; Grand Rapids: Eerdmans, 1999), 296–322.

and "Look and see, Yhwh, how abject I have become" (v. 11c). Employing language found in the communal laments of the Psalter, she insists that Yhwh take note of her distress. Her suffering motivates the disruption of the form of the dirge. These interruptions function on a number of levels. The first is to grasp onto what remains of life—not necessarily in hope, but in what is more akin to survival. The second is to circumvent the narrator in order to raise very personal and tragic concerns directly to the Deity. By interrupting the narrator and speaking past him to the Deity, Lady Jerusalem points to the important role Yhwh can play in the alleviation of her distress and possibly also to Yhwh's complicity in it. Finally, these interjections shift the focus away from what is otherwise a rather factual account of the effects of the collapse of Jerusalem on the city itself (its walls, its roads, for example) and its inhabitants (young girls and noblemen, among others). Disaster has real consequences that these interjections of complaint capture more poignantly than a news report about them.

By the conclusion of the chapter, the voice of Lady Jerusalem drowns out that of the narrator. One of the important themes raised by the personified city has to do with the divine role in her suffering. She draws attention to Yhwh as the causative force behind her ignoble fate (vv. 12–15, 21–22). The narrator corroborates her viewpoint by interjecting in the midst of her speech confirmation of divine causality: "Yhwh has commanded against Jacob, that his neighbors should become his foes" (v. 17). Her passionate words persuade the narrator to accept her perspective that the reason for the disaster lies with the Deity. Furthermore, she succeeds in convincing the narrator that Yhwh has accomplished the destruction of Jerusalem. The narrator continues this line of thought by describing Yhwh's actions against the city and its populace in the second chapter. The narrator describes Yhwh as the Divine Warrior fighting against his own people (2:1–9). In this case, the pain and humiliation of Daughter Zion convinces the eyewitness of Yhwh's responsibility.

Suffering interrupts in the form of lament and dirge in the second chapter, but in this example it evokes compassion, from which encouragement for direct address to the Deity is made. In Lam 2 the voices of what appear to be an independent eyewitness and Daughter Zion interweave again. The primary emphasis is on the description and designation of the enemy with the ultimate foe being understood quite clearly as Yhwh (2:1–9, 17, 20–22). Human enemies appear, but they are depicted as instruments of the Deity's wrath (2:7, 17, 22a). The appearance of human foes also serves to heighten the sense of distress in that they mock the ignoble collapse of the city of Jerusalem (v. 16). As well as being thematically different from the first chapter, in the second chapter the voice of Daughter Zion appears hesitant. The almost total loss of Daughter Zion's speech gives the impression that the extent of suffering has so cowed the female persona that she becomes the Jerusalem of the first chapter whom the narrator mourned in death. The narrator maintains a lengthy description of the enemy's triumph and the fate of the most vulnerable members of the community—only the weak cry of children out of desperation for food (v. 12) breaks the overwhelming silence of the community at large (v. 10). The community's silence here mirrors that of Daughter Zion.

In the midst of narration about the enemy attack and the resulting distress that has come upon members of society, the narrator breaks off his report and speaks of his own personal reaction. His personal tragedy unfolds in response to the pitiful cries of children for food (vv. 11b–12), and he speaks of the tears streaming down his face, gut-wrenching agony, and feeling physically sick (v. 11). It could be as Linafelt has suggested that it is exactly the distress of the children that ultimately moves the narrator from his otherwise impersonal stance.[28] After realizing the extent of his own personal tragedy, the otherwise impersonal eyewitness drops his impartiality yet again to speak directly to Jerusalem (v. 13), but his attempt at comfort only echoes the sorrows she has expressed (vv. 14–17). The narrator shifts tactics at this point and urges Jerusalem to cry out the extent of her suffering—to vocalize pain (vv. 18–19).[29]

> Let your heart cry out to Adonai, O wall of Daughter Zion;
> Let tears stream down like a wadi day and night;
> Do not let yourself rest, do not still the pupil of your eye.
> Arise, cry out in the night as the watch begins;
> Pour out your heart like water before the presence of Adonai;
> Lift up your hands to him for the lives of your children.
>
> (Lam 2:18–19)[30]

Jerusalem responds to the narrator's encouragement, and her speech concludes the chapter with a focus on the totality of the destruction (vv. 20–22).

---

28. Linafelt, "Zion's Cause," 56.

29. See the careful and sensitive analysis of the speech of personified Zion in Linafelt, *Surviving Lamentations*; and idem, "Zion's Cause."

30. On the translation see Middlemas, *Troubles*, 218.

Suffering provides the motivation for interruptions in the form. Two things happen in this chapter that are worthy of note. The first is that the narrator shifts away from his impartial stance. The extent of the human toll of the disaster, especially the fainting of the children who whimper for food, forces the eyewitness to break off his report and disclose his own personal reactions to disaster. He is physically sickened by what he sees. The narrator, too, feels the agony of the present distress. Moreover, the extent of Zion's personal pain has convinced him to adopt her perspective about Yhwh as the active force behind the disaster. The form of the acrostic is broken in the second chapter in that the order of the Hebrew alphabet is reversed in verses 16 and 17 exactly at the point where the narrator implicates Yhwh as the destructive force behind the fall of Jerusalem and the ongoing tragedy: "Yhwh has done what he purposed, he has carried out his threat" (v. 17a). Many explanations have been brought forward to explain the oddity, but Kathleen O'Connor rightly understands that it results from a literary technique that is used to draw attention to the details of these verses.[31] Although O'Connor has argued that verses 16 and 17 are the focal point of the chapter, it becomes clear through attention to the rhetoric of the chapter that what motivates the narrator is not Yhwh's culpability but the suffering of the children. Concern about their dire fate frames the speech of the narrator. He even drops his impartial stance to speak of his personal reaction to the fainting of infants and toddlers in the street (vv. 11–12) and seeks subsequently to motivate Jerusalem to hold onto life by urging her to cry out "for the lives of your children, who faint from hunger at the head of every street" (v. 19).

The second outstanding feature of this chapter is that the eyewitness reporter appears to be aware that in the second chapter Daughter Zion was not able or has not been so keen to speak up about her situation. Noting her withdrawal, like that of the community reeling from shock (see v. 10), he urges her to cry out (vv. 18–19). The eyewitness has valued Lady Jerusalem's contribution, has adopted her viewpoint, and has recognized the power and possibility of protest. The most sensitive study of Lady Jerusalem and her stance of protest is that of Linafelt, who regards her as a woman who rages in the face of disaster. It is true that she could be described as tenacious particularly in chapter 1; however, in chapter 2 she appears far more reticent. Indeed, she refrains from speaking until

---

31. O'Connor, *Lamentations and Tears.*

encouraged to do so by the narrator. Even she became bowed down in her despair. Nevertheless, the experience of suffering motivates her speech, as well as that of the narrator.

THE CONTRIBUTION OF CLOSER ANALYSES OF
FORM TO THE CURRENT DISCUSSION

Closer analysis of the use of formal categories as well as interruptions in form provide the opportunity for greater awareness of the rhetorical strategies employed in the construction of meaning. Moreover, consideration—particularly of interruptions in form—highlights the motivation for different interpretations of the intersection of the divine and the human spheres.

The approach taken here serves as a complement to that offered by Mandolfo, who also used close attention to form as a basis to place alternative speaking voices in conversation. As she has noted, one aspect of the lament form is the alternation of first- and third-person speaking voices. Different voices seem to participate in a dialogue, and it is often the case that one perspective contradicts the other. In the biblical book of Lamentations the voice of Daughter Zion supported by the Dialogic Voice provides a contrary perspective to the reasons for disaster than that found within the prophetic tradition. The eyewitness reporter provides a measure of support for Daughter Zion and the perspective she offers on the disaster. Both are contrary to the presentation of an adulteress Jerusalem as found in the prophetic tradition.

Mandolfo has used the interplay of the words of the two characters, Daughter Zion and the Dialogic Voice, in the first two chapters of Lamentations as a means to advocate further the importance of recognizing a dialogic theology—whereby one articulation of truth is countered, even undermined, by another within the Old Testament tradition. Her study highlights the importance of attention to what is said and how it becomes part of a wider tradition. The approach I take here departs from this interest in an attempt to be clearer about constructions of meaning, with particular attention to the importance of form and interruptions in form. In part, I therefore concentrate more on how something is said rather than the implications of what is said. An additional interest lay with what motivates the construction of meaning. Abject human suffering functions in Lamentations to prompt differences in perspective. As such, personal pain is a key element in understanding how the alternative perspective

offered by the voice of Daughter Zion persuades the eyewitness narrator (and ultimately other perspectives found in the OT) to adopt an alternative viewpoint.[32] The realities of victims foster the reinterpretation of
explanations, rationalizations, and even accusations that accompanied
and followed disaster.

An association of form to how the biblical writers rhetorically evoke
meaning draws on an interest begun already by James Muilenburg and
continued most successfully by one of his students, Phyllis Trible. In his
Society of Biblical Literature address, Muilenburg acknowledged the
importance of the articulation and analysis of form categories in biblical
literature, but sought to move beyond a descriptive task to embrace how
an interest in rhetoric functioned to create meaning.[33] While he pointed
the way forward with and from form criticism, he was keen to stress
the importance of understanding the methods employed by the biblical
writers in fashioning the text. It was important in his view, therefore, to
understand more fully the artistry of the text and how its message was
articulated. Muilenburg's call for biblical analysis along the lines of what
would become known as rhetorical criticism found support in the work
of Trible, who would define more carefully how to focus on the text.[34] It
would be the task of Walter Brueggemann (another of Muilenburg's doctoral students) to articulate the importance of speech for a theological
perspective.[35] Attention to rhetoric led Brueggemann to advocate a theology that recognized the biblical precedent for the interplay of different
perspectives—mainstream testimony and countertestimony (both within
the OT tradition, but also within the approaches made by interpreters of
the tradition). His vision of Old Testament theology embraces a wide definition of different types of analysis, as well as different perspectives on the
Deity presented. Mandolfo participates in this wider interest by focusing
on the theological implications of the dialogue of biblical characters that
offers a contrary perspective to the mainstream biblical tradition. Furthermore, her approach speaks to a biblical theology that values contrary

---

32. One could also draw a comparison to the role of suffering and speech in the
book of Job.

33. James Muilenburg, "Form Criticsm and Beyond," *JBL* 88 (1969): 1–18.

34. See, e.g., Phyllis Trible, *Rhetorical Criticism: Context, Method, and the Book of
Jonah* (GBS; Minneapolis: Fortress, 1994).

35. Most fully articulated in Walter Brueggemann, *Theology of the Old Testament:
Testimony, Dispute, Advocacy* (Minneapolis: Fortress, 1997).

perspectives about the human relationship to the Divine and the Divine to the human person.

A consideration of the book of Lamentations in its entirety supports Mandolfo's promotion of the counterstory offered by Daugher Zion and accepted by the Dialogic Voice (the eyewitness narrator) therein. In a separate study, I argued that the shape of the biblical book of Lamentations is like that of a violent, cyclonic storm with a peaceful eye (the didactic interlude of 3:22–39) surrounded by storm winds (1:22–3:21 and 3:40–5:22).[36] The peaceful center is characterized by being close in thought to mainstream Old Testament tradition with its emphasis on the justice and power of Yhwh and the role of submission by the human partner.[37] The storm winds that surround this interlude of hope are fashioned by images of suffering and tragedy made more poignant by the illustration of the effects of disaster on members of Judahite society. Moreover, a concern with human sin is downplayed in these chapters. Rather than repeating those arguments here, I think it is more productive to point to how the shape of the book also functions to support a dialogic theology or a theology that honors difference. The biblical book of Lamentations holds together conceptualizations of Yhwh that could be described as the dominant testimony about the Deity and human person found in the Old Testament along with other contrary thoughts about the same.

The shape of the biblical book of Lamentations contributes to an understanding of dialogic theology by its holding together different, even contrary, perspectives in tension, if not in conversation. The hurricane image provides a helpful analogy in that the peaceful eye of the storm exists only because of the howling winds and the rains that surround it. The eye of the storm and the storm winds coexist like the different perspectives about the Divine and the human person in Lamentations and indeed within the Old Testament tradition. An important contribution to the study of the Old Testament theology is awareness of difficulties in systematizing conceptions about God. The contrary perspective offered by Daughter Zion and accepted by the Dialogic Voice/eyewitness reporter undermines explanations that failed to account for and value the horror of human suffering. An important additional step in raising awareness of the

---

36. Middlemas, "Violent Storm."

37. See also Middlemas, "Did Second Isaiah Write Lamentations 3?" 514–25.

variety of theological perspectives found in the Old Testament is attention to the rhetorical means by which meaning was constructed.

Conclusions

The biblical book of Lamentations evidences a mixture of formal categories. The variety and arrangement of the formal elements complements the different understandings of God, the human person, and the nature of existence found represented in the book. Careful analysis of the form and genre of the poems results in greater awareness of how the artistry of the text itself constructs meaning that complements what is actually expressed. Moreover, interruptions and interjections in the form of Lam 1 and 2 result in creative expression. In chapter 1 the elements of the communal lament intervene into what is otherwise a classic funeral dirge. Through her complaint Daughter Zion sought to and does persuade. In the second chapter the dirge was interrupted by the narrator's individual lament. The narrator sought to encourage the personified city in his complaint to resume her accusations to the Deity, and he did so.[38] In both places the disruptions in the form stem from the reality of human suffering.

The use of poetic forms has enabled creative adaptation in which suffering transforms the possibilities of discourse. The vocalization of a painful present in the first instance accomplishes persuasion. Lady Jerusalem persuaded the eyewitness narrator to see things from her point of view. Suffering functions a second way in that it provokes compassion in the sense of "feeling with." The eyewitness reacted to Lady Jerusalem's speech by expressing his own pain. The eyewitness reporter's response to Jerusalem is, of course, what she hopes to (but fails to) achieve from Yhwh. Studies of tragedy and disaster regard one common reaction as the loss of hope in a loving God. Even though Yhwh is the one voice not heard in Lamentations and it is the one most sought, perchance the eyewitness reporter's own sorrow provides an indication of a divine reaction. Finally, the depth of expressed tragedy resulted in calls for survival. The reporter dropped his objective stance when confronted with Jerusalem's silence and

---

38. These accusations against the Deity function in a different way than the theodicy normally associated with the intention of literature of this period. I have termed this alternative *theo-diabole* or accusation against the Deity in order to capture a sense of the difference. See Middlemas, *Troubles*, 212.

urged her to cry out, to challenge the status quo with every fiber of her being, and to continue to refuse the option of death.

Particular attention to the form of speech, as well as its mode of expression, highlights how suffering participates in the formal argumentation of the biblical Lamentations on at least two occasions and in conjunction with the characterizations of Daughter Zion and the eyewitness reporter (Mandolfo's Dialogic Voice). Confronted with human suffering on a divine scale, the Dialogic Voice—representative of mainstream tradition and Yhwh—falls silent. Zion persuades her conversation partner to see through her eyes, and the countervoice, the narrator (and presumably Yhwh as well), pauses for thought. The raw expression of tragedy provides the foundation for a persuasive alternative to the focus of the metanarrative on sin and repentance. As such, the rhetoric speaks immediately within its context of the biblical book of Lamentations, but also within the ongoing theological discussions available in the Old Testament tradition. Discourse in the midst of disaster trumps rationalization of the tragedy.

Isaiah 40–55: A Judahite Reading Drama

Lena-Sofia Tiemeyer

The starting point of this study is Carleen Mandolfo's discussion of the dialogic relationship between Daughter Zion and God as depicted in Isa 40–55. Her discussion builds on the recognition that the divine oracles in the later text of Isa 40–55 respond to the complaints of Daughter Zion as phrased in the earlier book of Lamentations. In particular, Mandolfo looks at the portrayal of Daughter Zion in Isa 40–55, and she reflects on the adequacy of God's response to Daughter Zion. On the one hand, Mandolfo implies that God's response in Isa 40–55 sidesteps Daughter Zion's *main* question in Lamentations: Why did God punish the people of Jerusalem so harshly? Instead, the rhetoric of Isa 40–55 focuses on issues that, from God's perspective, neither question his acts nor threaten his omnipotence but instead demonstrate his power. Notably, the oracles devote much space to God's fulfillment of Zion's request that he punish her enemies. On the other hand, Mandolfo claims that Daughter Zion, in her one response in Isa 49:14, comes across as "pathetic." Indeed, taken as a whole, the rhetoric in Isa 40–55 leaves Daughter Zion a bit in the lurch: instead of speaking to the suffering of those who were left in Judah, the probable creators of Lamentations, it benefits the *golah* community. In this manner, Daughter Zion remains largely an outsider in the rhetoric of reconciliation in Isa 40–55.[1]

In the present study I shall argue for a modified interpretation of Daughter Zion's role in Isa 40–55. First, by reading Isa 40–55 as a Judahite text, and second, by highlighting that Daughter Zion is not the only voice in Isa 40–55 that expresses lament, I aim to show that Daughter Zion should not be regarded as a pathetic lonely mother, hijacked by the interests of the

---

1. Carleen R. Mandolfo, *Daughter Zion Talks Back to the Prophets: A Dialogic Theology of the Book of Lamentations* (SemeiaSt 58; Atlanta: Society of Biblical Literature, 2007), 103–19.

golah community. Instead, she, alongside the voice of the prophet as well as that of Jacob-Israel and, in some respects also the Servant, functions as a metonym for the community left in Judah. As such, Daughter Zion, in both Lamentations and Isa 40–55, serves as the outspoken representative of the people of Judah.

ISAIAH 40–55: A READING DRAMA

Isaiah 40–55 is filled with multiple characters—Jacob, Israel, Jerusalem, (Daughter) Zion, the islands, Cyrus, the traders of Egypt and Ethiopia, the Sabeans, and so on—that speak, that are being spoken to, and that are being spoken of. In this study I investigate the character of these voices *within* the text of Isa 40–55, with a focus on the dialogue between God and Daughter Zion, and then explore who these voices represent *outside* the text.

This study belongs primarily in the realm of historical-critical scholarship. There is no *book* called Isa 40–55, and thus Isa 40–55 does not form a canonical unity. The identification of Isa 40–55 as an independent literary unity composed by an author/authors other than Isaiah ben Amos began as a hypothesis of literary criticism. What holds the various chapters in Isa 40–55 together is primarily their shared dating. In my view, the bulk of the material stems from the middle of the sixth century B.C.E., created by an anonymous prophet and his/her disciples, a so-called Deutero-Isaianic school.[2] This dating sets it apart from especially the preceding chapters 34–35 and the following chapters 56–66, sections that, again in my opinion, contain later material from the final quarter of the sixth century B.C.E. as well as from the fifth century B.C.E. If we reject this shared dating, other possible literary units appear, such as Isa 40–48, or 40–55 and 60–62, or 35; 40–55; 60–62, or even 40–66, and so on. As to shared themes and theology, again many themes in Isa 40–55 can also be found in especially Isa 35 and 60–62. Finally, many of the proposed structures of Isa 40–55 go hand in hand with its dating, as most of the suggested structures of

---

2. Of course, one might say when dealing with biblical scholarship that there is no consensus as to this dating. Much research has been done in this area; see especially the overview in Rainer Albertz, *Israel in Exile: The History and Literature of the Sixth Century B.C.E.* (trans. David Green; SBLStBL 3; Atlanta: Society of Biblical Literature, 2003), 376–427. I remain open to the possibility that some material in Isa 40–55 may have been added later.

Isa 40–55 contain the notion of a core text and subsequent editions, each confined by a ring structure (Isa 40:1–5*, 9–11 and 52:7–12; 40:3aα, 6–8* and 55:6–13*).[3]

At the same time, the various materials that are now part of Isa 40–55 together constitute a distinct body of texts that is the conscious product of its authors/editors. For example, distinct patterns in Isa 40–55 suggest that one could regard these sixteen chapters, in their present form, as a rhetorical unity. A specific example thereof is the interchanging pattern of the oracles dealing with the fate of the Servant and the fate of Daughter Zion.[4] On a larger scale, the many voices present in Isa 40–55 suggest seeing this present form as a type of drama:[5] either a liturgical drama,[6] or a theological drama,[7] or even a script of an actually performed play,[8] or a literary drama. Of these four suggestions, the final one is the most compel-

---

3. Again, see the useful overview in Albertz, *Israel in Exile*, 376–427. He uses asterisks to indicate biblical passages with intrusive sections.

4. E.g., Patricia Tull Willey, *Remember the Former Things: The Recollection of Previous Texts in Second Isaiah* (SBLDS 161; Atlanta: Scholars Press, 1997), 105; Ulrich Berges, "Personifications and Prophetic Voices of Zion in Isaiah and Beyond," in *The Elusive Prophet: The Prophet as a Historical Person, Literary Character and Anonymous Artist* (ed. Johannes C. de Moor; OtSt 45; Leiden: Brill, 2001), 54–82, here 60; Jim W. Adams, *The Performative Nature and Function of Isaiah 40–55* (LHBOTS 448; London: T&T Clark, 2006).

5. For summaries in English of some of these theories, see A. S. van der Woude, "What Is New in Isa 41:14–20? On the Drama Theories of Klaus Baltzer and Henk Leene," in *The New Things: Eschatology in Old Testament Prophecy. Festschrift for Henk Leene* (ed. F. Postma, K. Spronk, and E. Talstra; Maastricht: Shaker, 2002), 261–67; and Charles Conroy, "Reflections on Some Recent Studies of Second Isaiah," in *Palabra, Prodigio, Poesía: Im Memoriam P. Luis Alonso Schökel, S.J.* (ed. Vicente Collado Bertomeu; AnBib 151; Rome: Pontifical Biblical Institute, 2003), 145–60.

6. E.g., Jean M. Vincent, *Studien zur literarischen Eigenart und zur geistigen Heimat von Jesaja, Kap. 40–55* (BBET 5; Frankfurt am Main: Lang, 1977), esp. 253; J. H. Eaton, *Festal Drama in Deutero-Isaiah* (London: SPCK, 1979); Michael D. Goulder, *Isaiah as Liturgy* (SOTSMS; Aldershot: Ashgate, 2004).

7. E.g., James Muilenburg, "The Book of Isaiah Chapters 40–66," in *IB* 5:381–773, here 387–88; Eva Hessler, *Das Heilsdrama: Der Weg zur Weltherrschaft Jahwes (Jes 40–66)* (Hildesheim: Olms, 1988), 30–31; Simone Paganini, *Der Weg zur Frau Zion, Ziel unserer Hoffnung: Aufbau, Kontext, Sprache, Kommunikationsstruktur und theologische Motive in Jes 55,1–13* (SBB 49; Stuttgart: Katholisches Bibekwerk, 2002), 157–58.

8. John D. W. Watts, *Isaiah 34–66* (WBC 25; Waco, Tex.: Word, 1987); Klaus Baltzer, *Deutero-Isaiah: A Commentary on Isaiah 40–55* (trans. Margaret Kohl; Hermeneia; Minneapolis: AugsburgFortress, 2001).

ling. Willem Beuken, for example, argues that Isa 40–55 unfolds a drama. He defines the genre "drama" to imply that the text and the reader move forward chronologically throughout the reading. This means that text and reader of, for example, Isa 45 is in a different position and further ahead than the reader of Isa 41.[9] Henk Leene develops Beuken's ideas further and argues that Isa 40–55 bears witness to what he calls "dramatic progression." In other words, Isa 40–55 presents a consecutive story. Isaiah 40–55 is thus a dramatic *text*, a written composition containing performative moments.[10] Likewise, Annemarieke van der Woude argues that Isa 40–55 has all the characteristics of what she calls a "reading drama." It lacks a narrator, and there is a sense of an immediate presence of the story, both key features of a dramatic text. At the same time, as Isa 40–55 does not rely on anything else but words to appeal to the senses, it was probably meant to be *read* rather than to be performed.[11]

PERSONIFICATION AND HISTORICAL REALITY

Who, then, are the different voices *within* this reading drama? Moreover, *outside* the text, what historical communities are being represented by these voices? Finally, who were the originally intended audience of the drama?

To illustrate this issue, let us look more closely at one of the main characters, namely, Daughter Zion/Zion-Jerusalem. In many instances in Isa 40–55, Zion-Jerusalem is personified as a female entity. As such, she is often described using metaphors that are associated with the traditional realm of women. It is widely recognized today that in most cases it is impossible to replace metaphors with literal speech without losing some

---

9. Willem A. M. Beuken, *Jesaja deel II* (POut 2A; Nijkerk: Callenbach, 1979), 10–13. I depend in part on the English overview of Beuken's theory by Richtsje Abma, *Bonds of Love: Methodic Studies of Prophetic Texts with Marriage Imagery (Isaiah 50:1–3 and 54:1–10, Hosea 1–3, Jeremiah 2–3)* (SSN 40; Assen: Van Gorcum, 1999), 58.

10. Henk Leene, *De Vroegere en de Nieuwe Dingen bij Deuterojesaja* (Amsterdam: Free University of Amsterdam Press, 1987), 30–37. Again, I depend in part on the English overview of Leene's theory by Abma, *Bonds of Love*, 59–60.

11. Annemarieke S. van der Woude, "'Hearing Voices While Reading': Isaiah 40–55 as a Drama," in *One Text, a Thousand Methods: Studies in Memory of Sjef van Tilborg* (ed. Patrick Chatelion Counet and Ulrich Berges; BIS 71; Leiden: Brill, 2005), 166–73.

of the impact and meaning of the metaphor.[12] In the present context of Isa 40–55, the female personification of Zion-Jerusalem is an important aspect of the text and it has exegetical consequences. As a result, most recent research on Zion-Jerusalem has explored the particular *choice* of metaphors (mother, daughter, bride, widow, etc.) that Isa 40–55 uses to denote Zion-Jerusalem, and it has highlighted the way in which these metaphors influence our understanding of the persona of Zion-Jerusalem and, by extension, our understanding of Isa 40–55 as a whole.[13]

I fully endorse such a literary approach. In the present context, however, my concerns are more historical than literal. My interest in the persona of Zion-Jerusalem is focused less on her personification and on the metaphors that denote her *within the text*, and more on the identification of the people that she represents *outside the text*. I hold it likely that the persona of Zion-Jerusalem, as well as the other personae within Isa 40–55, is used as a symbol or a metonym for something in the authors' own surroundings. In other words, when referred to, Zion-Jerusalem represents a group of people that is intimately associated with her. This view is based on the assumption that the texts in Isa 40–55 were addressed to the prophets' contemporaries, aimed at confronting them and their ideas as well as comforting them.[14] A symbol or a metonym only works if it alludes to and

---

12. For a recent discussion of metaphors and their roles in Isa 40–55, see Øystein Lund, *Way Metaphors and Way Topics in Isaiah 40–55* (FAT 2/28; Tübingen: Mohr Siebeck, 2007), 31–33.

13. E.g., Katheryn Pfisterer Darr, *Isaiah's Vision and the Family of God* (Literary Currents in Biblical Interpretation; Louisville: Westminster John Knox, 1994), 165–204; Abma, *Bonds of Love*, 53–109; Knut M. Heim, "The Personification of Jerusalem and the Drama of Her Bereavement in Lamentations," in *Zion, City of Our God* (ed. Richard S. Hess and Gordon J. Wenham; Grand Rapids: Eerdmans, 1999), 129–69; Kathleen M. O'Connor, "'Speak Tenderly to Jerusalem': Second Isaiah's Reception and Use of Daughter Zion," *PSB* 20 (1999): 281–94; Gerlinde Baumann, *Love and Violence: Marriage as Metaphor for the Relationship between Yhwh and Israel in the Prophetic Books* (trans. Linda M. Maloney; Collegeville, Minn.: Liturgical Press, 2003), 180–86; Sarah J. Dille, *Mixing Metaphors: God as Mother and Father in Deutero-Isaiah* (JSOTSup 398; GCT 13; New York: T&T Clark, 2004), 128–51, 157–62; Mandolfo, *Daughter Zion*, 103–19; Sharon Moughtin-Mumby, *Sexual and Marital Metaphors in Hosea, Jeremiah, Isaiah, and Ezekiel* (OTM; Oxford: Oxford University Press, 2008), 117–55; Christl M. Maier, *Daughter Zion, Mother Zion: Gender, Space, and the Sacred in Ancient Israel* (Minneapolis: Fortress, 2008), 161–210.

14. See the various discussions of the so-called disputation speeches (*Diskussionsworte*) in Isa 40–55. It goes beyond the confines of the present essay to look at the

reflects sentiments that the target audience can identify with and relate to. Against this background, I set out to identify the voices within Isa 40–55 with existing communities outside the text at the time(s) of its composition. I shall, alongside Mandolfo, focus on what I call the countervoices in Isa 40–55, the voices that dialogue with and in some instances also oppose the divine voice.

GEOGRAPHY AND THEOLOGY:
WHAT THEOLOGY DEFINES JUDAHITE SPEECH?

How, then, does one identify a voice within a text with a historical community of people outside the text? In order to answer this question, we shall look at Jill Middlemas's research on Lamentations. Lamentations was in all likelihood composed in Judah sometime between 586 and 520 B.C.E., in what Middlemas calls the templeless period;[15] and it is also a book that presents the perspectives and the voice of Daughter Zion (with the possible exception of Lam 3). As the result of a detailed analysis of select parts of Lamentations, Middlemas outlines five distinct features pertinent to texts originating in the Judahite community during the templeless period: an emphasis on human suffering, the lack of statements of confidence in future hope, a de-emphasis on the instrumentality of sin, the need to verbalize the raw emotions of grief, and the formulation of painful protest.[16] In a sense, what Middlemas is doing is defining the *theology* of texts stemming from templeless Judah. I find Middlemas's way of identifying Judahite texts intriguing, and I suggest that her five criteria can be used fruitfully as a tool for recognizing Judahite texts out-

---

background and *Gattung* of these speeches. What is important in the present context is to clarity their aim to dialogue with the prophet's audience. Joachim Begrich (*Studien zu Deuterojesaja* [1938; repr., TB 20; Munich: Kaiser, 1963], 48–49) sees the disputation speeches in Isa 40–55 as a literary imitation of the controversies that the prophet experienced. Likewise, H.-J. Hermisson ("Diskussionsworte bei Deuterojesaja: Zur theologischen Argumentation des Propheten," *EvT* 31 [1971]: 665–80, esp. 665–67) argues that the prophet aims at confronting the skepticism of the audience and to convince them of the message of salvation. See also the overview of research presented in Adrian Graffy, *A Prophet Confronts His People: The Disputation Speech in the Prophets* (AnBib 104; Rome: Pontifical Biblical Institute, 1984), 6–14.

15. Jill Middlemas, *The Troubles of Templeless Judah* (OTM; Oxford: Oxford University Press, 2005), 4–5.

16. Ibid., 226–28.

side Lamentations. In the present context, I shall investigate the theology of the countervoices in Isa 40–55—how do they relate to God, to the destruction of Jerusalem, to sin, to the future, and so on—and then see how this theology fits with that of Middlemas's five criteria. If there is agreement, I shall conclude that the countervoices in Isa 40–55 adhere to the particular type of Judahite speech/theology that is typical of much of Lamentations (henceforth L speech, short for Lamentations speech). Taking an additional step, I shall further suggest that this identification constitutes an argument for seeing these voices as representing communities in templeless Judah.

There are two key differences between Isa 40–55 and Lamentations that make a straight comparison difficult. First, unlike Lamentations, the countervoices in Isa 40–55 are not the dominant speakers (God is); and second, unlike Lamentations, the theology of the countervoices is not the dominant theology of Isa 40–55 as a whole. Can we nonetheless argue that the countervoices give clues as to the whereabouts of the target audience? I would answer in the affirmative. As already noted above, these voices represent the kind of sentiments that the authors of Isa 40–55 wanted to confront in their target audience. As such, identifying the theology of the countervoices helps us identify the whereabouts of the target audience.

As to God's voice, the divine oracles in Isa 40–55 are not comparable to any of the laments in Lamentations. This means that Middlemas's criteria for identifying Judahite texts cannot be used for the divine voice in Isa 40–55, and as a result we have to find alternative ways for determining the geographical setting of the divine voice. I suggest comparing the theology regarding human suffering, future hope, and sin found in the oracles of Isa 40–55 with that found in oracles in roughly contemporary texts the geographical origin of which is relatively certain. More specifically, I shall compare briefly the characteristics of the oracles in Isa 40–55 with those in the book of Ezekiel, a book that represents a *golah* perspective. As a result of this comparison, we shall discover in the divine speech an attitude toward sin and divine punishment different from that of Lamentations yet also distinct from that of the exilic book of Ezekiel. I shall further argue that this attitude is also representative of the people of Judah, although to a lesser extent than the one found attested throughout most of Lamentations. In other words, this is also Judahite speech, although it is different from L speech.

The Geographical Setting of Isaiah 40–55

But do we really hear the true *Judahite* voice of Daughter Zion and her companions in Isa 40–55? In contrast to Lamentations, where Daughter Zion represents and speaks for the people of Judah, is not Daughter Zion in Isa 40–55 merely a creature of its exilic authors' imagination?[17] It is widely accepted that Isa 40–55 picks up the Judahite speech of Lamentations.[18] At the same time, it is equally commonly assumed that Isa 40–55 transforms this Judahite speech to serve its own exilic purposes. Daughter Zion is thus mostly seen as a symbol that assures the exiles that their comforted mother is joyously awaiting their return, that is, that the city in the far-off land of Judah is readying her home for the returnees.[19]

This, however, is an unnecessarily roundabout manner of looking at the issue, as there are good reasons for assuming that substantial parts, if not all, of Isa 40–55 originated in Judah.[20] As I have argued elsewhere, the pervading focus on Jerusalem, especially in Isa 49–55, renders it likely that Jerusalem was also the location of the utterances. Moreover, the manner in which Isa 40–55 alludes to and picks up the language of Lamentations makes most sense if both texts were composed within the same

---

17. O'Connor, "Speak Tenderly to Jerusalem," 289 n. 38.

18. E.g., Tod Linafelt, *Surviving Lamentations* (Chicago: University of Chicago Press, 2000), 65–79; Carol Newsom, "Response to Norman K. Gottwald, 'Social Class and Ideology in Isaiah xl–lv,'" *Semeia* 59 (1992): 73–78; Benjamin D. Sommer, *A Prophet Reads Scripture: Allusion in Isaiah 40–66* (Contraversions; Stanford, Calif.: Stanford University Press, 1998); Willey, *Former Things*; Mandolfo, *Daughter Zion*, 103–19.

19. E.g., O'Connor, "Speak Tenderly to Jerusalem," 293.

20. See, e.g., Arvid S. Kapelrud, *Et folk på hjemferd. "Trøstepropfeten"—den annen Jesaja—og hans budskap* (Oslo: Universitetsforlaget, 1964), 26–34; Hans M. Barstad, *The Babylonian Captivity of the Book of Isaiah: "Exilic" Judah and the Provenance of Isaiah 40–55* (Oslo: Novus: Instituttet for Sammenlignende Kulturforskning, 1997). In addition, most contemporary European scholars place the bulk of Isa 49–55 in Judah. See, e.g., Klaus Kiesow, *Exodustexte im Jesajabuch: Literarkritische und motivgeschichtliche Analyses* (OBO 24; Fribourg: Éditions Universitaires, 1979); Odil Hannes Steck, *Gottesknecht und Zion: Gesammelte Aufsatze zu Deuterojesaja* (FAT 4; Tübingen: Mohr Siebeck, 1992); Jürgen van Oorschot, *Von Babel zum Zion: Eine literarkritische und redaktionsgeschichtliche Untersuchung* (BZAW 206; Berlin: de Gruyter, 1993); Reinhard Gregor Kratz, *Kyros im Deuterojesaja-buch* (FAT 1; Tübingen: Mohr Siebeck, 1991); Ulrich Berges, *Das Buch Jesaja: Komposition und Endgestalt* (HBS 16; Freiburg: Herder, 1998).

community.[21] More negatively, the conspicuous lack of explicit mention of Babylon throughout Isa 40–55, with the exception of Isa 47, together with the expectations that exiles will be returning from all the directions of the compass, renders a specifically *Babylonian* setting unlikely. Finally, much of the imagery related to "a way through the wilderness" is best understood as metaphoric descriptions expressing God's care and provision for his people.[22] Therefore, there are no solid reasons that force us to view the speech of Daughter Zion as representing an exilic viewpoint. On the contrary, my hope is that this present article will hammer yet another nail in the (metaphoric) coffin of the theory of a Babylonian-based Deutero-Isaiah. Rather, I hold it plausible that much, if not all, of Isa 40–55 consists of unadulterated Judahite speech.

The Judahite Timbre of the Voices within Isaiah 40–55

Let us now turn to the actual voices in Isa 40–55. Assuming that Middlemas's criteria for identifying Judahite voices are correct, I contend that the voices within Isa 40–55 actually have a strong Judahite timbre.

The Judahite Timbre of the First-Person Prophetic Voice

Beginning with the first-person statements in Isa 40–55 (Isa 40:6aβ–7; 42:24; 45:15–17; 47:4; 49:4, 5b), we encounter a voice that gradually moves from despair to confidence, apparently transformed by God's words. This

---

21. See Lena-Sofia Tiemeyer, *For the Comfort of Zion: The Geographical and Theological Location of Isaiah 40–55* (VTSup 139; Leiden: Brill, 2011); idem, "Two Prophets, Two Laments, and Two Ways of Dealing with Earlier Texts," in *Die Textualisierung der Religion* (ed. Joachim Schaper; FAT 62; Tübingen: Mohr Siebeck, 2009), 185–202. For a similar view, see Christopher R. Seitz, *Word without End: The Old Testament as Abiding Theological Witness* (Grand Rapids: Eerdmans, 1998), 132–49.

22. See, e.g., Horacio Simian-Yofre, "Exodo en Deuteroisaías," *Bib* 61 (1980): 530–53; idem, "La teodicea del Deuteroisaías," *Bib* 62 (1981): 55–72; Ernst Haag, "Der Weg zum Baum des Lebens: Ein Paradiesmotiv im Buch Jesaja," in *Künder des Wortes: Beiträge zur Theologie der Propheten. Josef Schreiner zum 60. Geburtstag* (ed. Lothar Ruppert, Peter Weimar, and Erich Zenger; Würzburg: Echter, 1982), 35–52; Erich Zenger, "Der Gott des Exodus in der Botschaft der Propheten—am Beispiel des Jesajabuches," *Concilium* 23 (1987): 15–22; Hans M. Barstad, *A Way in the Wilderness: The "Second Exodus" in the Message of Second Isaiah* (Journal of Semitic Studies Monograph 12; Manchester: University of Manchester Press, 1989); Lund, *Way Metaphors*.

voice is likely to represent the voice of the prophet within Isa 40–55 and, as such, may represent the voice of the author(s) of Isa 40–55.[23] Some evidence also suggests that the voice of the prophet is identical with or at least overlaps with the voice of the Servant.

First, Isa 40:6aβ–7 probably contains a first-person singular speaker.[24] This voice is characterized by its lack of confidence in future hope, one of the criteria of the type of Judahite speech akin to L speech ("All humanity is grass, and all its loving-kindness is like the flower of the field. Grass withers, blossoming fades, when God's breathe blows upon it. Indeed, the people are grass!").

Second, Isa 42:24b contains a first-person plural voice (זו חטאנו לו).[25] This verse appears in the longer context of 42:18–25, a section that constantly shifts voices and addresses for rhetorical effect.[26] This first-person speech places the responsibility of the suffering on God yet also accepts responsibility for the suffering: God allowed Jacob-Israel to be plundered because Jacob-Israel, including the speaker, had sinned against God. The rest of the verse refers to Jacob-Israel in the third person, accusing him of not having consented to walk in God's ways and having refused to hear God's instruction. As a whole, this verse can be seen as a formulation of painful protest against God's role in their punishment. At the same time, the speaker acknowledges the guilt of the community. This, however, is not in itself an argument against the identification of this voice as L speech, as the voice as Daughter Zion in Lamentations also combines placing the responsibility of the punishment on God yet also acknowledges her sins (e.g., Lam 1:5, 8, 18). It should be remembered that Middlemas's criterion is not the absence of acknowledgment of sin but the de-emphasis on the instrumentality of sin.

Third, Isa 45:15–17 may also contain either the voice of the prophet or that of Daughter Zion. The recipient of the speech in verse 14 is Zion-Jeru-

---

23. We must differentiate between the authors of a prophetic book and the first-person prophetic speaker within the book. Although these two may turn out to be the same, this cannot be taken for granted.

24. Following the reading of the LXX (καὶ εἶπα). Although the MT is pointed as a 3rd masc. sg., the consonantal text can support both a first- and a third-person reading.

25. There is no reason to abandon the MT and follow the third-person reading of the LXX ᾧ ἡμάρτοσαν αὐτῷ, "whom they had sinned against."

26. See the discussion in John Goldingay and David Payne, *Isaiah 40–55* (2 vols.; ICC; London: T&T Clark, 2006), 1:255–56.

salem, as implied by the third feminine singular possessive pronouns. The African merchants will exclaim to (Zion-Jerusalem) that God is with her. In the following verse 15, however, the tone changes and it is the prophet who speaks,[27] exclaiming that God is a god that hides himself.[28] This view of God fits well in with what we heard of the prophet in 40:6aβ–7 and thus conforms to what we call L speech. It also agrees with the statement of the lamenters in 64:6 (Eng. 7), a lament the origin of which is in all likelihood Judahite.[29] The seemingly contradictory claim in verse 15b—that God is God of Israel, the savior—indicates that the speakers waver between despair and hope. The following verses 16–17 continue on the note of verse 15b, declaring that while the idol makers were ashamed and humiliated, Israel was saved by Yhwh. Turning directly to the audience, presumably still Zion-Jerusalem, although addressed in masculine plural, the prophetic voice declares that she/they will never ever be ashamed or humiliated. This again is an example of de-emphasizing the sin: it is mentioned (v. 16) but quickly exchanged for redemption (v. 17).

Fourth, the speaker in 49:4, 5b, traditionally identified with the Servant, wavers between despair and confidence in much the same way as the speaker in 45:15 (above). In verse 4a we meet a person on the brink of despair: ואני אמרתי לריק יגעתי לתהו והבל כחי כליתי ("and I said, 'I have toiled for nothing, and I have spent my strength in chaos and emptiness"), recalling the words of 40:6b–7. In contrast, 49:4b contains a more confident note: אכן משפטי את־יהוה ופעלתי את־אלהי ("but surely my cause is with Yhwh and my reward is with God"), as does verse 5b: ואכבד בעיני יהוה ואלהי היה עזי ("I am honorable in the eyes of Yhwh, and God has become my strength"). Is this a dialogue between what the speaker actually feels versus what she or he ought to feel? Alternatively, does it reflect what she or he used to feel but now, in the light of God's imminent inter-

---

27. See, e.g., Joseph Blenkinsopp, *Isaiah 40–55* (AB 19A; New York: Doubleday, 2000), 256–57; and Berges, *Jesaja 40–48*, 423; contra Jan L. Koole, *Isaiah 40–48* (vol. 1 of *Isaiah, Part 3*; trans. Anthony P. Runia; HCOT; Kampen: Kok Pharos, 1997), 469; and Goldingay and Payne, *Isaiah 40–55*, 2:46, who assume that the foreigners are still speaking but now to God.

28. The reading of the LXX (σὺ γὰρ εἶ θεός καὶ οὐκ ᾔδειμεν ὁ θεός τοῦ Ισραηλ σωτήρ) is probably a conscious change of the MT in order to place the responsibility of God's hiddenness on the people. See further Blenkinsopp, *Isaiah 40–55*, 258.

29. See further my discussion in "Two Prophets, Two Laments," 187–89.

vention, her or his confidence is boosted? In both cases, 49:4, 5 present us with typical L speech, although with a twist.

Finally, the speaker in 50:4–11, again traditionally identified with the Servant, displays the same confidence as 49:4b, 5b and, accordingly, does not conform to Middlemas's criteria. The same is also true for 47:4, which speaks of "our redeemer" (ישׂראל גאלנו יהוה צבאות שׁמו קדושׁ).

In addition, several long sections refer to God in the third person and, as such, may be assigned to the prophet. For example, most of 40:12–31 and much of 42:18–25 (excluding v. 19) may be uttered by the prophet and thus reflect his or her point of view. Nonetheless, I distinguish these longer statements from the specific first-person statements. In the former, despite the references to God in the third person, it is God's viewpoint that is being presented. In contrast, in the latter the prophet is disassociated from God and represents him- or herself.

In conclusion, the voice of the prophet within Isa 40–55 displays a mixture of insecurity and security regarding future hope and God's salvation, and a mixture of assigning the responsibility of the situation to God yet also, but only briefly, acknowledging past sins. Thus this voice can mainly be characterized as L speech, although it at times also displays a viewpoint that is more confident in God's salvation. It is probably fair to say that it wavers between L speech and a divine perspective. This impression is further strengthened by the first-person plural statements in which the prophet emphasizes that she or he sides with the audience. In this manner, the prophetic voice behaves like a true prophet: alternatively representing the people to God and God to the people.

THE JUDAHITE TIMBRE OF THE VOICE OF JACOB-ISRAEL

Turning to Jacob-Israel's voice, he is cited but once, in 40:27. In this passage, Jacob-Israel utters a formulation of painful protest, directed to God and aimed at his behavior toward them, saying: נסתרה דרכי מיהוה ומאלהי משׁפטי יעבור ("my way is hidden from Yhwh and my case is ignored by my God").[30] According to Middlemas's criteria, Jacob-Israel's speech is a showcase of the theology of templeless Judah.

---

30. This opposition between the prophet and his or her audience has been discussed before. See, e.g., John W. Miller, "Prophetic Conflict in Second Isaiah: The Servant Songs in the Light of Their Context," in *Wort—Gebot—Glaube: Beiträge zur Theologie des Alten Testaments. Walther Eichrodt zum 80. Geburtstag* (ed. Hans Joachim

The Judahite Timbre of the Voice of Daughter Zion

As to Daughter Zion, we hear her voice in 49:14 and possibly also in 49:24 and 55:1–3a, and we partake of her thoughts in 49:21.

Zion's speech in 49:14 is the epitome of L speech. Zion is cited as saying: עזבני יהוה ואדני שכחני ("Yhwh has forsaken me, and the Lord has forgotten me"), echoing Jacob-Israel's despondent speech in 40:27. Her speech may continue into 49:15a with the equally despondent words, "Can a woman forget her baby and show no love for the child of her womb?"[31] again stressing her past sorrows.

Isaiah 49:21, part of the divine speech of 49:15b–23, then predicts Zion's thoughts at the future time when her children will be arriving:

מי ילד־לי את־אלה ואני שכולה וגלמודה (אתנחתא)[32]
גלה וסורה ואלה מי גדל
הן אני נשארתי לבדי אלה איפה הם

Who has borne me these? I was bereaved and barren,
an exile and passing away[33] and these, who raised [them]?
Behold, I was left behind alone. These, of what kind are they?

Is Zion happy that she has surviving children, or does her speech betray her own sense of betrayal? In my view, the latter is more likely. This statement, following after her children's rather brusque command in verse 20, sounds much like a hesitant and fearful question.[34] This impression is further strengthened by the use of the expression אמר בלבו. As noted by Michael Carasik, this expression denotes in most cases thoughts or intentions that are a direct challenge to God (e.g., Gen 17:17; 27:41; 1

Stoebe; ATANT 59; Zurich: Zwingli, 1970), 77–85; and Rikki E. Watts, "Consolation or Confrontation? Isaiah 40–55 and the Delay of the New Exodus," *TynBul* 41 (1990): 31–59, here 35, 39, 47.

31. The possibility is stated by Rosario Pius Merendino, "Jes 49:14–26: Jahwes Bekenntnis zu Sion und die neue Heilszeit," *RB* 89 (1982): 321–69, here 329–30.

32. The *ethnachta* (*athnach*), the final and major stress of the first half of the verse, identifies the break between poetic lines.

33. For the translation of וסורה, see the discussion by Goldingay and Payne, *Isaiah 40–55*, 2:191.

34. See further Tiemeyer, "Geography and Textual Allusions," 378–79.

Kgs 12:16–27).[35] God thus anticipates the objection of Daughter Zion to his acts of salvation. This attitude displayed toward God and the displayed lack of future hope defines Zion's speech in Isa 49:21 as L speech.

It should be noted that the literary presentation of Zion's opinion in verse 21 differs from that in verse 14: while verse 14 is a direct quotation of Daughter Zion's speech, verse 21 consists of her thoughts, projected upon her by God. Even so, when we move from inside the text to outside the text, this difference is unimportant. Both Daughter Zion's speech and her thoughts are rhetorical tools for highlighting the opinions of the target audience toward sin and suffering. In this way, both 49:14 and 21 hint at attitudes in the target audience that are akin to those put forward by Daughter Zion in Lamentations. This in turn suggests that the target audience is Judahite.

The biggest obstacle for seeing Isa 49:21 as representing Judahite speech is the verb גלה ("exiled"), often seen as implying a Babylonian location.[36] The situation may not be that clear-cut, however. First, the LXX lacks a corresponding expression for גלה וסורה.[37] Second, it is unwarranted to assume an abrupt change from metaphoric language (v. 21a—motherhood) to literal language (v. 21baα) and back to metaphoric language again (v. 21baβ–21by—motherhood). It is preferable to assume that the metaphor of motherhood persists throughout the verse. Third, if we read the text literally, Zion is both exiled and left behind alone (נשארתי לבדי). How can she be both? The same imagery of exiled Jerusalem is furthermore found in Lam 1:3 and 4:22, texts the provenance of which is clearly Judahite. What we have here is therefore best understood as Isa 40–55 picking up the language of Lamentations directly. I therefore suggest that

---

35. Michael Carasik, *Theologies of the Mind in Biblical Israel* (Studies in Biblical Literature 85; New York: Peter Lang, 2006), 115–18. It should be noted, however, that Carasik himself excludes Isa 49:21, together with Zech 12:5, and argues that אמר בלבו appears to be used positively in texts referring to the eschatological future (n. 110).

36. E.g., Goldingay and Payne, *Isaiah 40–55*, 2:192.

37. Highlighted in ibid. Bernhard Duhm (*Das Buch Jesaia* [HAT III/1; Göttingen: Vandenhoeck & Ruprecht, 1892], 347–48) regards it as a gloss, as does Blenkinsopp (*Isaiah 40–55*, 309). See also Knud Jeppesen, "Mother Zion, Father Servant," in *Of Prophets' Visions and the Wisdom of Sages: Essays in Honour of R. Norman Whybray on His Seventieth Birthday* (ed. Heather A. McKay and David J. A. Clines; JSOTSup 162; Sheffield: JSOT Press, 1993), 114–15, who argues that the LXX preserves the more coherent reading.

גלה וסורה describes the mother Zion metaphorically. She is "exiled" in the sense that she is far away from many of her children.

R. P. Merendino, followed by Ulrich Berges, further suggests that Zion speaks again in verse 24 (היקח מגבור מלקוח ואם־שבי צדיק ימלט, "Can the prey be taken from the mighty, and can the righteous captive be delivered?").[38] This would fit the overall structure of the passage, with verses 14, 21, and 24 introducing an objection or a question by Daughter Zion, and with verses 15–20, 22–23, and 25–26 containing God's response. The theology of verse 24 can again be characterized as akin to that of Lamentations in that it is clearly a statement that lacks confidence in future hope. This identifies 49:24 as yet another example of L speech, placed in the mouth of Daughter Zion.

Mandolfo argues that Zion never really regains her confidence and she never really learns to trust God again. Instead, she remains angry without ever admitting having sinned.[39] It has been suggested, however, that Zion speaks again in 55:1–3a, part of the longer section of 55:1–5, this time with a more confident and joyful tone. Much depends on the division of the passage. On the one hand, if we see all of verses 1–5 as spoken by the same person, then this person must be God, as indicated by verse 3b. On the other hand, if we regard verse 3b as beginning a new section with a new speaker (God), then we are left with an anonymous speaker in the preceding verses 1–3a.

This latter reading depends on two factors. First, it is supported by the fact that Zion-Jerusalem is addressed throughout the preceding 54:11–17. This interpretation of 55:1–3a portrays Zion as finally active and her mistrust gone. She is positive, inviting people to come and drink, even those without money, and she is launching a banquet in Jerusalem and offering out invitations.[40] Second, it depends on the masoretic vocalization of

---

38. Merendino, "Jes 49:14–26," 341–42; Berges, "Personification," 69.

39. Mandolfo, *Daughter Zion*, 103–19, 124.

40. Berges, "Personification," 72. See also Paganini, *Weg zur Frau Zion*, 35–39, 170–72; idem, "Who Speaks in Isaiah 55.1? Notes on the Communicative Structure in Isaiah 55," *JSOT* 30 (2005): 83–92. Alternatively, Hendrik Carel Spykerboer ("Isaiah 55:1–5: The Climax of Deutero-Isaiah. An Invitation to Come to the New Jerusalem," in *The Book of Isaiah* [ed. Jacques Vermeylen; BETL 81; Leuven: Leuven University Press, 1989], 357–59) sees the prophet as the speaker who invites the needy to come to the new Jerusalem. Most commentators, however, identify the speaker with God. See, e.g., Goldingay and Payne, *Isaiah 40–55*, 2:367–69.

the second-person possessive suffix of the last word פָּאֲרָךְ in verse 5. The masoretic vocalization of the second-person possessive suffix of the other words in this verse indicates that the audience is male. The suffix on the word פָּאֲרָךְ, however, can either be understood as either a pausal masculine singular form[41] or, more naturally, a feminine singular form (cf. 60:9).[42]

A closer look at the speakers in verses 3b–5 reveals a complicated pattern. The first-person singular speaker in verse 3b is surely God, who will make a covenant with the audience (addressed as second masculine plural). God then continues to speak in verse 4, referring to a singular masculine person, possibly the Servant,[43] or, more likely, a Davidic figure, as David is the last person mentioned in the preceding verse 3.[44] In verse 5a God is presumably still the speaker, now addressing a male person in the second masculine singular (הן גוי לא־תדע תקרא וגוי לא־ידעוך אליך) to whom nations that do not know him will run. The best, although not ideal, identification of this male person is as a collective address of the same target audience that was addressed in verses 1–3.[45] Finally, the speaker in verse 5b is most likely not God, as he is referred to in the third person (למען יהוה אלהיך ולקדוש ישראל כי פארך), while the target audience is addressed in the second singular, either masculine or feminine (see above). The continuation of 55:6–13 continues along the same lines of alternating speakers. In verses 6–7 someone other than God speaks to a plural audience, while God addresses a plural audience in verses 8–13a. Finally, an anonymous person other than God speaks in verse 13b.[46]

In my view, much favors reading Isa 55 as reflecting multiple speakers. Even so, it seems overly complicated to divide verses 1–5a into more than one speaker. As there is no clear indication that Daughter Zion speaks in verse 1 and as the transition from verse 3a to verse 3b is smooth, I prefer reading all of verses 1–5a as spoken by God. At the same time, verse 5 appears to be merging and thus identifying Daughter Zion with the target audience by mixing the masculine and the feminine possessive suffixes. I thus agree with Mandolfo that Daughter Zion remains questioning

41. See Joüon §61i; and GKC §58g.

42. Paganini, "Who Speaks in Isaiah 55.1," 86–88.

43. Berges, "Personification," 72. Berges suggests that the Servant and Daughter Zion have finally merged. Cf. Isa 54:17.

44. Goldingay and Payne, *Isaiah 40–55*, 2:373.

45. Ibid., 374.

46. Cf. Paganini, "Who Speaks in Isaiah 55.1," 92; and idem, *Weg zur Frau Zion*, 44.

throughout Isa 40–55. One should not see 55:1–3a as her having mellowed down and finally accepting God's point of view. In other words, her speech remains that of L speech to the very end.

God's Voice

God is the dominant speaker in Isa 40–55. In this case, we can no longer use Middlemas's criteria for identifying Judahite speech, as there is no comparison between laments and divine oracles in terms of theology. As Mandolfo phrases it, the Bible is always theodic: God would never be heard saying that his punishment of Israel was out of proportion with its sins.[47] We therefore have to look for other criteria for determining the geographical flavor of the divine speech in Isa 40–55. This brings us back to Middlemas, who claims that the texts of templeless Judah, with their focus on pain and with their reluctance to attribute the fall of Jerusalem to sin, stand in contrast to the joyful message of exilic Isa 40–55 and the hope for restoration of Ezekiel.[48] As we shall soon discover, however, this claim cannot be substantiated. I shall use the book of Ezekiel as a model for exilic theology. The book itself claims to have been composed in exile, and most scholars maintain that most of the material in the book was composed by and reflects the concerns of the *golah* community, either in Babylon or after returning to Judah.[49] As such, it can fruitfully be used as a model for exilic theology. We shall therefore compare, although very briefly, the theology toward sin and punishment in Isa 40–55 with that in Ezekiel.

Beginning with evaluating the attitudes in Isa 40–55 to sin, punishment, and restoration, we immediately notice the marginality in God's

---

47. Mandolfo, *Daughter Zion*, 117.

48. Middlemas, *Templeless Judah*, 226–27.

49. See, e.g., Andrew Mein, *Ezekiel and the Ethics of Exile* (OTM; Oxford: Oxford University Press, 2001), 59–66, who provides a good overview of what is known to us about the exiles' situation in Babylon and how it fits with the situation described in Ezekiel. This, however, has not deterred several scholars from postulating a Judahite setting of all or parts of Ezekiel. See, e.g., Robert Carroll, "Deportation and Diasporic Discourse in the Prophetic Literature," in *Exile: Old Testament, Jewish, and Christian Conceptions* (ed. James M. Scott; JSJSup 56; Leiden: Brill, 1997), 63–85, esp. 80–82; idem, "Exile! What Exile?" in *Leading Captivity Captive: "The Exile" as History and Ideology* (ed. Lester L. Grabbe; JSOTSup 278; Sheffield: Sheffield Academic Press, 1998), 62–79, who argues that the notions of exile in the book of Ezekiel are literary notions, metaphors of the fears of the people in Judah.

speech of sin and punishment and the weak correlation between the two. Here, as in other prophetic books, the exile is viewed as God's punishment for the sins of Judah. Even so, neither the guilt of the people nor the punishment of Zion-Jerusalem is described in detail.[50] In fact, some passages do away with the guilt altogether. Notably, most scholars now understand the "writ of divorce" in Isa 50:1 as rhetorical: the mother was *not* sent away,[51] as she was *not* guilty. Instead God's voice focuses on wooing his people back to him. In the case of Daughter Zion, God never accuses her of sin. In the case of Jacob-Israel, although he (42:24; 43:22–28; 46:8–13; 48:1–11), together with the unidentified audience in 50:1–3, is accused of sin, such accusations are relatively rare and not particularly harsh. For example, 42:24 is a backward-looking passage that despite putting the blame on Jacob-Israel also acknowledges God's own responsibility in the matter. Other passages state that God has removed Jacob-Israel's transgression (44:21–22) or that God pardons abundantly (55:6–7). As shown by Blaženka Scheuer, Isa 40–55 portrays God as offering his salvation freely with no preconditions attached to it. A case in point is 44:22: "Return to me *because* I have redeemed you" (שובה אלי כי גאלתיך). In other words, the return of the people is the hoped-for result of God's salvation. Thus Isa 40–55 envisions a sequence of sin-punishment-deliverance-repentance.[52]

God also renders himself as vulnerable and as open to blame as the theodic perspective of the Hebrew Bible allows for. In 43:25–26, for example, God confronts Jacob-Israel directly, inviting him to present his case. In doing so, God actually lays himself bare by declaring his willingness to submit the matter to a formal judicial procedure and thus giving Jacob-Israel the opportunity to justify himself.[53] In the end, Jacob-Israel will be proven righteous. At the same time, there is an ironic tone to this offer, hinting at God's surety of his side of the case and, in a sense, demonstrating his self-justification.[54] Verse 25 provides the clue to this seemingly contradictory picture: God will tamper with the evidence in that he will erase all evidence of Jacob-Israel's sins. God, and God alone, is responsible

50. Baumann, *Love and Violence*, 186.

51. E.g., Moughtin-Mumby, *Marital Metaphors*, 140–41, with cited bibliography.

52. Blaženka Scheuer, *The Return of YHWH: The Tension between Deliverance and Repentance in Isaiah 40–55* (BZAW 377; Berlin: de Gruyter, 2008).

53. Koole, *Isaiah 40–48*, 349.

54. See further Goldingay and Payne, *Isaiah*, 1:314; Koole, *Isaiah 40–48*, 350; Berges, *Jesaja*, 312.

for Jacob-Israel's salvation. This illustrates well the ambiguous portrayal of God in Isa 40–55: while he is willing to listen to his human counterpart, he remains certain of his own righteousness. He openly acknowledges his responsibility in the destruction, and he offers renewed love, but he never says that he is sorry.

This theological perspective is markedly distinct from that of exilic Ezekiel.[55] Yes, there is restoration, but anything akin to hope is hard to find. There is too much suffering in Ezekiel for a voice of hope to penetrate,[56] and there is very little in terms of consolation, salvation, and grace for Israel.[57] In particular, there is no restoration at all for Daughter Zion, as she is not resurrected in Ezek 40–48.[58] The complaining Zion and the comforting God, both present in Isa 40–55, are also utterly alien to Ezekiel. Along the same lines, the book of Ezekiel is notorious for wallowing in guilt, and it places the blame for the destruction of Jerusalem squarely upon Jerusalem herself (e.g., Ezek 16; 23). Moreover, in contrast to Isa 40–55, where the people's repentance *follows* God's offer of salvation, repentance is presented in Ezekiel as the *precondition* of salvation (e.g., Ezek 14:6; 18:30, 32; 33:10–11). For Ezekiel, repentance is the demonstration of the people of Israel's acceptance of their own responsibility for the destruction of Jerusalem and the ensuing exile. Reversely, the idea of a new heart, found in Ezekiel (Ezek 11:17–21; 36:24–32), is unattested in Isa 40–55.[59]

Summing up, it is possible to argue that God in Isa 40–55 speaks a form of Judahite speech in that he plays down the sin and shame of Jacob-Israel and Zion-Jerusalem and instead seeks to comfort them in their sorrows. In contrast to especially the divine oracles in exilic Ezekiel,

---

55. Contra Dieter Baltzer, *Ezechiel und Deuterojesaja* (BZAW 121; Berlin: de Gruyter, 1971); and Walther Zimmerli, "Jahwes Wort bei Deuterojesaja," *VT* 32 (1982): 104–24, here 113.

56. E.g., Daniel L. Smith-Christopher, *A Biblical Theology of Exile* (OBT; Minneapolis: Fortress, 2002), 75–104.

57. E.g., Baruch J. Schwartz, "Repentance and Determinism in Ezekiel," in *Proceedings of the Eleventh World Congress of Jewish Studies, Division A: The Bible in Its World* (ed. David Assaf; Jerusalem: World Union of Jewish Studies, 1994), 123–30; idem, "Ezekiel's Dim View of Israel's Restoration," in *The Book of Ezekiel: Theological and Anthropological Perspectives* (ed. Margaret S. Odell and John T. Strong; SBLSymS 9; Atlanta: Society of Biblical Literature, 2000), 43–67.

58. Julie Galambush, *Jerusalem in the Book of Ezekiel: The City as Yahweh's Wife* (SBLDS 130; Atlanta: Scholars Press, 1992), 147–48; Baumann, *Love and Violence*, 166.

59. Scheuer, *Return of YHWH*, 122.

God in Isa 40–55 focuses far more on grace for Daughter Zion and her fellows than on their culpability.

CONCLUSION

Within the drama of Isa 40–55, the two key antagonists—Jacob-Israel and Zion-Jerusalem—display attitudes toward sin and divine punishment that are in line with those found in Lamentations.[60] The first-person voice, representing the prophet/the Servant, is less easy to define. His or her first words in the drama of Isa 40–55 are filled with doubts. As the drama unfolds, this voice begins to vacillate between doubt and hope, in order to gradually change into a more confident tone that is also more trusting in God. It further identifies with both God and the people, as it sometimes expresses God's view, and sometimes, using first-person plural, sides with the target audience. Finally, throughout this drama, God is persistently working at getting the other voices to accept his offer of salvation and at getting Daughter Zion in particular to look beyond her current troubles and to rejoice at the bright future that he is arranging for her.

Moving outside the drama of the text, I suggest a scenario where (a group of) prophets seek to convince their target audience of God's salvation. The countervoices in Isa 40–55, that is, those of Jacob-Israel and Zion-Jerusalem, serve as a rhetorical tool, in that they express sentiments that their target audience can identify with. They further emphasize that God listens to the target audience and that he responds to them. The first-person voice reflects these authors' own thoughts on the matter as they alternate between siding with the target audience and siding with God, and as they gradually become convinced of God's imminent salvation.

Going yet one step further, we have seen that the sentiments expressed by the countervoices conform to the five distinct features pertinent to texts

---

60. One reason why Sean McEvenue ("Who Was Second Isaiah?" in *Studies in the Book of Isaiah: Festschrift Willem A. M. Beuken* [ed. Jacques van Ruiten and Marc Vervenne; BETL 132; Leuven: Leuven University Press, 1997], 216–18) does not equate the speaker in Isa 40:6b–7 with Daughter Zion in 49:14 is because he finds it difficult to envision Zion in 40:6 as speaking in such bitter and personal tones. I agree that they should not be equated. Nonetheless, I maintain that both profess to the same negative outlook on life, an outlook that stems from their shared Judahite background in that the prophet in 40:6aβ–7 is from Judah and is called to speak to Judah about God's renewed grace.

originating in the Judahite community. This, in turn, suggests that the intended original audience of Isa 40–55, just like that of Lamentations, was the people of Judah. The lamenting Daughter Zion of Lamentations is thus not hijacked by the *golah* community and muted beyond recognition, as Mandolfo claims. Rather, she remains in Isa 40–55 the outspoken spokeswoman for the people of Judah.

The Fecundity of Fair Zion: Beauty and Fruitfulness as Spiritual Fulfillment

Stephen L. Cook

The persona of Daughter Zion in the Scriptures (the female metaphorical figure representing the people of Israel as God's wife) is now receiving some overdue empathetic attention.[1] Thanks to scholars such as Carleen R. Mandolfo, Zion's personal perspective and subjectivity are coming alive in all their uniqueness. Indeed, Mandolfo's monograph *Daughter Zion Talks Back to the Prophets* allows us to hear Zion's viewpoint in her own words despite the way that many biblical texts seem to squelch her voice.[2]

The seeming highhandedness and violence of God in biblical texts about Daughter Zion has certainly exercised many scholars in recent decades. In particular, a growing body of scholarship has focused a pointed critique on metaphors of God as an outraged, patriarchal husband, who appears to perpetrate a "battered love."[3] Students of biblical literature

---

1. On the captivating personification of Israel, and particularly the city-temple complex of Jerusalem, as the woman Zion, see Frederick W. Dobbs-Allsopp, "Daughter Zion," in *Thus Says the Lord: Essays on the Former and Latter Prophets in Honor of Robert R. Wilson* (ed. John J. Ahn and Stephen L. Cook; LHBOTS 502; New York: T&T Clark, 2009), 125–34.

2. Carleen R. Mandolfo, *Daughter Zion Talks Back to the Prophets: A Dialogic Theology of the Book of Lamentations* (SemeiaSt 58; Atlanta: Society of Biblical Literature, 2007). Mandolfo's line of approach is anticipated in Frederick W. Dobbs-Allsopp, "Rethinking Historical Criticism," *BibInt* 7 (1999): 235–71, here 255–57 n. 68.

3. Representative scholarship highlighting dimensions of "pornography," violence, and abuse in biblical construals of Daughter Zion include: Peggy L. Day, "Adulterous Jerusalem's Imagined Demise: Death of a Metaphor in Ezekiel XVI," *VT* 50 (2000): 285–309; Harold C. Washington, "Violence and the Construction of Gender in the Hebrew Bible: A New Historicist Approach," *BibInt* 5 (1997): 324–63; Diane Jacobson, "Hosea 2: A Case Study on Biblical Authority," *CTM* 23 (1996): 165–72;

are increasingly familiar with the perspective of this divine "batterer" as the prophets present it, but we have been less conscious of his estranged wife's point of view. Mandolfo argues that the cause is God's nearly complete "cognitive authority" in the prophetic texts, God's "epistemological hegemony" over Daughter Zion.[4] She addresses the scandal of Daughter Zion's silencing in her monograph, which lifts up Lam 1–2 as a neglected resource for hearing Daughter Zion's side of things.

What a great service Mandolfo has done by helping us hear Daughter Zion's voice in the wake of God's judgment upon her! Zion's authentic words, uttered on her own terms in Lam 1–2, provide a theologically legitimate countervoice within the canon. We ignore her viewpoint to our own impoverishment and detriment. To use Mandolfo's persistent rhetoric of personification, the least that we can do for Daughter Zion is to pay attention to her often ignored perspective.[5]

Jumping off from one concern of Daughter Zion presented in Mandolfo's work, I focus this essay on Zion's agonizing struggle with loss of children and lack of fertility. In the wake of the tragic devastations leveled against her by the Babylonians in the sixth century B.C.E., Zion emphasizes this particular loss as central to her pain. "I was bereaved and barren … left all alone," Zion confesses (Isa 49:21). In post-exile prophecy, God responds to this tragedy of barrenness and sterility by granting Zion beauty and new life, which issue in an awesome, supernatural fecundity. This divine grant holds tremendous theological significance and redounds with spiritual ramifications.

The miraculous fecundity of Zion, reversing her barrenness, particularly stands out as an eschatological theme in the prophetic poetry of Second Isaiah.[6] These poems portray a renewed Zion of God becoming

---

Renita J. Weems, *Battered Love: Marriage, Sex, and Violence in the Hebrew Prophets* (Minneapolis: Fortress, 1995); Pamela Gordon and Harold C. Washington, "Rape as Military Metaphor in the Hebrew Bible," in *A Feminist Companion to the Latter Prophets* (ed. Athalya Brenner; FCB 8; Sheffield: Sheffield Academic Press, 1995), 308–25; Julie Galambush, *Jerusalem in the Book of Ezekiel: The City as Yahweh's Wife* (SBLDS 130; Atlanta: Scholars Press, 1992). For a general critique of the Bible's association of God with violence, see the stringent arguments and bibliographic references in John J. Collins, "The Zeal of Phinehas: The Bible and the Legitimation of Violence," *JBL* 122 (2003): 3–21.

4. Mandolfo, *Daughter Zion*, 96.

5. Ibid., 123.

6. For the purposes of this essay, I use the term "Second Isaiah" to refer to the

a beautiful paradise, "her wilderness like Eden, her desert like the garden of the LORD" (Isa 51:3). Though once depopulated, barren, and arid, God now comforts Zion by infusing her with verdant new vivification. Across the passages of Second Isaiah, the ideal future Zion is well watered and fructified, her waste places springing with growth, teeming with life (44:26; 49:19; 52:9; 58:12; 61:4). In 49:19–21, for example, her desolate landscapes explode with new inhabitants. Suddenly, Daughter Zion finds herself so blessed with progeny that she is too cramped for comfort. "The place is too crowded for me," her children cry (49:20). What spirituality lies behind this emphasis on luxuriant growth, primordial fecundity? The question plunges us to the heart of the prophetic witness about life lived as God intends. It cries out for explication.

While Mandolfo honors Lamentation's presentation of Daughter Zion's voice and certainly enriches us through its recovery, she leaves us with a strikingly dismal and sour view of the biblical prophetic texts. Mandolfo finds very little to honor, or even to respect, in the prophetic presentation of God intent on squelching Zion. Even God's attempts to reconcile with Zion in Second Isaiah, which glow with promise and which many biblical scholars celebrate, she deems to fall woefully short. The Isaian texts' persuasive power, Mandolfo maintains, is inadequate to meet Zion where she is.[7] Given God's past misdeeds and abuse, Daughter Zion will have trouble ever "trusting again." Why should she, when the God of Second Isaiah "cannot quite admit … that he acted out of all proportion" in the events surrounding the destruction of Jerusalem by the Babylonians?[8] For Mandolfo, Second Isaiah's prophecies of comfort and promise simply do not make up for the fact that God remains an unrepentant abuser in this corpus—a failed, unworthy marriage partner.[9]

One immediately wonders whether Mandolfo's approach of suspicion does justice to Second Isaiah, and, indeed, to such other prophetic books as Jeremiah, Habakkuk, and Zechariah. In Second Isaiah, God *does* in fact acknowledge Zion's incomparable suffering (Isa 51:19–20) and *does* voice sincere regret (54:7–8). God is quite up front about how nations such as Babylonia far exceeded their mandate in dispensing judgment (40:2; 47:6;

---

corpus of prophetic poetry in Isa 40–66. I am aware, of course, that it is possible to subdivide this corpus into Deutero-Isaiah and Trito-Isaiah sections.

7. Mandolfo, *Daughter Zion*, 106–9, 113, 117–19.

8. Ibid., 110–11; cf. p. 123.

9. See ibid., 122–27.

51:22–23). Across the prophets one observes the same grim realism, fully aware of the unjust, excessive injury unavoidably attendant to the exercise of divine judgment within the constraints of history. The prophets are overtly cognizant of the horrible "overreaching" of God's instruments of judgment, which Mandolfo holds that God either ignores or uses as a means of sidestepping divine culpability in Zion's excessive torment (for good examples of prophetic grappling with this issue, see Isa 10:12–19; Hab 1:13; Jer 12:12–14).[10] God openly recognizes the unfortunate problem of overreaching at Zech 1:15, directing extreme anger at the attacking nations of 586 B.C.E., who "overdid the punishment" (NJPS), who went "far beyond my intentions" (NLT).[11]

Despite Mandolfo's grave reservations about any notion of divine retribution, the idea of a divine exercise of judgment upon Israel, personified as Daughter Zion, hardly amounts to an "abusive-god theology."[12] The God of the Hebrew prophets desired all along to encounter his marriage partner in true subjective authenticity, but was frustrated at every turn prior to the judgments leading to the Babylonian exile of 586 B.C.E. Because Mandolfo appears to lack a concept of divine judgment as grace, she is unable to appreciate the people's experience of defeat and exile as a necessary portal to becoming emotionally available, personal, and vulnerable before God, the requisite condition for realizing the truly mutual divine-human dialogue that she treasures. Canonical shaping of the prophetic books insists on an understanding alternative to that of Mandolfo, to wit, that divine judgment is in fact gracious, aimed at opening up space for genuine dialogue, reconciliation, and human transformation.

---

10. For Mandolfo's indictments of God along these lines, see *Daughter Zion*, 106–7, 109, 124. In studying her frustration with Second Isaiah, one receives the impression that she believes God could make divine interventions in human life free from historical contingency, impervious to the unpredictable self-direction of human agents. The Hebrew prophets exercised a more extreme realism about God's limits in working within history.

11. For a most helpful exposition of the biblical understanding of the workings of God's violent judgment, see Terence E. Fretheim, "'I Was Only a Little Angry': Divine Violence in the Prophets," *Int* 58 (2004): 365–75. Other helpful treatments include: idem, "Theological Reflections on the Wrath of God in the Old Testament," *HBT* 24 (2002): 1–26; Erich Zenger, *A God of Vengeance? Understanding the Psalms of Divine Wrath* (trans. Linda M. Maloney; Louisville: Westminster John Knox, 1996); and Abraham J. Heschel, *The Prophets* (New York: Harper & Row, 1962), 177–78, 279–306.

12. Mandolfo, *Daughter Zion*, 126.

To be fair, a major part of the problem here is Mandolfo's insistence on isolating a literary trope—that of Yhwh as husband—as a subject of ethical evaluation. Leaving the God to whom we pray aside, her focus of condemnation is actually a figuration deployed by a text, a "god" with a small *g*. Mandolfo states, "In the prophetic texts focused on the marriage metaphor, God speaks as husband … rather than as a divine being. God assumes an axiological position vis-à-vis Zion that is as particular as any other subject's [and thus as open to our moral outrage]."[13] The Scriptures are all too vulnerable to this line of criticism. They offer their literary trope solely as a means of conveying partial truths about a divine referent outside the text. Slippage between vehicle and tenor is rampant, and the divine "husband" of the text necessarily takes actions that no human spouse, no "particular subject," ever should. Our outrage at this *divine* husband is misplaced.

The particular literary vehicle of Yhwh as the husband of Daughter Zion will never be able to hold its own ethically if cordoned off from its unique (i.e., decidedly nonanthropic, ontologically unindebted) tenor. "Husbands should not be their wives' judges, they should be their partners!" Mandolfo rightly insists.[14] What Mandolfo fails to appreciate, though, is the absolute requirement of our tenor that this distinctively divine husband be both lover and judge. Only the presence of the extratextual tenor explains and justifies the eyebrow-raising (shocking, even appalling!) vehicle that the prophets are daring to utilize. Contrary to Mandolfo, vehicle and tenor must be taken as a package.

Beyond this point, a larger question is at stake that leads directly to this essay's theme of beauty, fecundity, and spirituality. Should we really insist that giving Daughter Zion back her voice, though laudable from the perspective of Mandolfo's "dialogic ethic," must remain God's people's last, best hope?[15] Must allowing the perspective of Zion both power and

---

13. Ibid., 96. In response to my critique at a session on "Daughter Zion: Her Portrait, Her Response," at a meeting of our professional society in 2008, Mandolfo argued as follows: "The big question I must pose to Prof. Cook is, what God are you talking about? The God you pray to or the God of the text? … I'm reading the God of the text. The manner in which God is figured in these texts begs fervent engagement, not quiet reverence" (Mandolfo, "Response" [presented at the annual meeting of the SBL, Boston, Mass., 24 November 2008]).

14. Mandolfo, *Daughter Zion*, 126.

15. Mandolfo writes, "In a post-Holocaust (and post-9/11) world we may feel abandoned by God, but the Bible continues to be a powerful testimony to the human will to survive and make meaning out of the raw material of existence. Every voice in

influence be the one nonnegotiable starting point for any healing of the divine-human relationship? Mandolfo appears to answer in the affirmative. Second Isaiah's offer of salvation to Daughter Zion falls short, she writes, because "as in the earlier prophetic texts, there seems to be no room for her speech.... Monologism reigns."[16] Based on a particular reading of the philosophies of Mikhail Bakhtin and Martin Buber, she has built her case against the prophets on a premise identifying justice with a *voiced* "reclamation of agency." If we are to have any healing and justice, Daughter Zion must speak her mind, God must hear her out, and God must own up to the divine mistakes.[17]

I would counter that prophets such as Isaiah and Ezekiel have alternative algorithms of salvation to offer, ones that recover much more for Zion than an authentic voice with which to express her free, human agency. Might what these prophets are striving after amount to her radical metamorphosis and ennoblement, the eschatological flowering of her authentic personhood and innate, final destiny? I propose to test a more respectful and empathetic approach to prophetic theology than that defended by proponents of a "dialogic ethic" through the investigation of two texts: Isa 49:14–21 and Ezek 36:33–38.

In executing this probe, I reach very different conclusions from Mandolfo about Daughter Zion's treatment at the hands of the biblical prophets. Unlike her, I find myself able to give the prophetic texts about Zion an empathetic reading. Despite our different approaches, my understanding has been markedly sharpened in dialogue with her book. Indeed, I

---

the book has a role to play in that task. Dialogue does not mean everything is 'fixed,' but dialogue is our best hope" (*Daughter Zion*, 124).

16. Ibid., 113. Quoting the work of Patricia Tull Willey, Mandolfo laments that Second Isaiah lacks the competing dialogue of nonauthoritative voices that Mikhail Bakhtin appears to appreciate in the novels of Dostoevsky. See Patricia K. Tull Willey, *Remember the Former Things: The Recollection of Previous Texts in Second Isaiah* (SBLDS 161; Atlanta: Scholars Press, 1997), 75–76.

17. Mandolfo, *Daughter Zion*, 113. For Mandolfo, liberation and ethics must begin with a relatively symmetrical relationship between subjects in which the parties share a truly reciprocal recognition of each other. Real relationship is based on reciprocity, she repeatedly stresses, not on self-interest, power, and hierarchy. Dignity, self-worth, and even personal identity are all dependent on our relationships granting us enough respect and space as free, human agents to voice our subjectivity. An ongoing willingness to hear each other out and admit mistakes is essential. See *Daughter Zion*, 16, 20–21, 47, 51, 53, 83 n. 7, 84, 117, and 121.

can state one of my central observations as a counterthesis to her main proposal. Whereas Mandolfo makes verbal "dialogic" reciprocity an ethical priority, I defend the notion that Second Isaiah prioritizes an alternative nonverbal "dialogue," a reciprocal mode of interaction between God and Zion based on beauty and the appreciation of beauty. This alternative, *beauty-based* interaction with God ennobles Zion as God's human partner, who encounters God in true subjectivity. I intend to sketch my understanding of how this aesthetically inspired "dialogue" functions in Isaiah and how it "bears fruit" for the contemporary reader.

Central to Mandolfo's project is a deeply held commitment that God is answerable to us mortals, subject to the rules of fair play. Utmost among her values are dialogue and reciprocity. Assuming these as normative, she asks readers to judge if God's behavior is responsible and ethical, specifically in God's telling of Daughter Zion's story. "Does God author [the story of Zion] responsibly?" she queries.[18]

Indeed, she argues, "God does not author responsibly." God and God's prophets disregard Zion's viewpoint, brutalize her voice. Theirs is a "crushing monologism."[19] God's callousness is serious, because our understandings of how God acts toward humans will resonate in human expectations for one another. An image of a God who abuses might well sanction human oppression.[20]

Mandolfo's assumptions correlate well with some biblical traditions. Thus God honors Abraham's pleas on behalf of Sodom in Gen 18:16–33. Likewise, the tradition of biblical lament assumes that it is only right for God to attend to the pain and distrust of a supplicant. An axiom of the Psalter is that an ethical God is surely affected by our human perspective and open to our outrage.[21] Other biblical traditions where God towers

---

18. Ibid., 15–17.

19. Ibid., 16, 53, 84, 113, 123.

20. Ibid., 15, 127. Mandolfo (126) expresses wholehearted agreement with Kathleen M. O'Connor's argument that "If God abuses and cruelly and violently controls us, then it is surely fine for humans to be abusive and violently controlling as well. The ways we imagine God encourage, support, and affirm our own behavior. An abusive God leaves abuse and violence unchallenged in families, churches, and nations" (*Lamentations and the Tears of the World* [Maryknoll, N.Y.: Orbis, 2002], 110).

21. In a classic article on the importance to faith of the lament psalms, Walter Brueggemann laid out how in this form of prayer "the speech of the petitioner is heard, valued, and transmitted as serious speech." "The petitionary party is taken seriously and the God who is addressed is newly engaged in the crisis in a way that puts God

above attentiveness and anthropic reciprocity, however, should not be condemned out of hand. Even streams of tradition where God appears *amoral* from our human standpoint may well have a constructive spirituality to offer! Second Isaiah represents one such theological stream.

In *Reverence: Renewing a Forgotten Virtue*, Paul Woodruff advocates our renewed appreciation of *reverence*, recognizing all the while that this virtue entails a perception of profound ethical and relational asymmetries between heaven and earth. Woodruff argues that we should not be dismayed at God's qualitative difference from us, a difference that may even include amorality in God. With sound logic, ancient and modern religions have not balked to understand darkness and evil as an aspect of the Divine. After all, if everything extant emanates from God, where could evil come from except somehow from God? Woodruff's own conclusion is that "we would be wrong to withhold reverence from what we feel to be divine simply because we do not find that it measures up to our human standards."[22]

In my view, the texts of Second Isaiah align well with Woodruff's train of thought. They represent the epitome of *reverence*. Here God openly declares, "I form the light and I create the darkness, I make well-being, and I create disaster [רע, "harm," "evil"], I, Yahweh, do all these things" (Isa 45:7 NJB). This God does not answer to human systems of justice and appears to defy our categories of right and wrong (see 40:14–15). I submit that in this type of biblical theology, we must allow God a moral and ethical license inappropriate to mortals.[23]

---

at risk" ("The Costly Loss of Lament," *JSOT* 36 [1986]: 57–71, here 59). The assumption that God is open to being persuaded by our language of pain and fury is clear at places such as Pss 22:1–2; 42:9–10; 44:17–19, 22; 89:38–39; Jer 15:18; 20:7; Lam 1:9b, 11, 20; 2:18, 19, 20. I would only caution that the forceful accusations against God in this tradition of lament are typically a language of confidence that God is faithful to respond, not instantiations of Mandolfo's observation that supplicants may experience alienation from God beyond healing. Thus note the dialectical shift from outrage to confidence between v. 1 and v. 5 of Ps 13; between vv. 1–2 and vv. 3–5 of Ps 22; between vv. 6–8 and vv. 9–10 of Ps 22; and between v. 7 and v. 11 of Jer 20. By the same token, it is surely telling that the lament form typically concludes with a vow to praise God (e.g., Pss 13:6; 22:22–26; Jer 20:13).

22. Paul Woodruff, *Reverence: Renewing a Forgotten Virtue* (New York: Oxford University Press, 2001), 69; cf. Stephen L. Cook, *Conversations with Scripture: 2 Isaiah* (Anglican Association of Biblical Scholars Study Series; Harrisburg: Morehouse, 2008), 19–37.

23. In her response to my critique at the 2008 SBL meeting in Boston, Mandolfo

Woodruff would surely question Mandolfo's expectation that God should set a moral example for us. God may not function well as a role model, divorced as God may be from practical morality and fair play. Given the possible otherness of God, we should not demand a God we can emulate. Indeed, ethics does not require one! Woodruff insists that "reverence toward evil gods does not put people into danger of becoming evil."[24] The virtue of reverence is based on the profound, awful otherness of the Divine, which humans would be crazy to mimic.

Rather than emulation, divine otherness actually provokes יראת אלהים ("fear of God," "social ethics").[25] For excellent scriptural examples, see Exod 20:20; Deut 4:10; 5:25–29; and, within Second Isaiah, see Isa 57:11; 59:19. The only danger in encountering the uncanny is the danger of becoming moral! The experience of a God of true, spine-tingling otherness—even a Deity understood as capable of evil—leads immediately to consciousness of impurity and guilt within the human being (cf. Isa 6:5). Then, in short order, the experience evokes a profound sense of moral responsibility.[26]

The mystery is hard to fathom, but stands as a phenomenological truth. *Awe* issues in *ought*. *Awe* before the eerily transcendent commonly provokes a deep sense of morality and obligation to God. The *numinous*—that which dwarfs and unnerves us—gives rise to ethical awareness, to moral transformation. Pulled in by the embrace of the Holy, submerged in God's preternatural vastness, the ego releases all selfishness and violence. Dwarfed and humbled before pure tremendousness, one grasps for rela-

---

objected to my characterization of the God of Second Isaiah as an amoral being of incomparable otherness. She insisted that the God of the text is "linguistically fashioned to be taken up axiologically" (Mandolfo, "Response"). I would counter that, in contrast to the ways that some Scriptures render God, Second Isaiah is strikingly "reverent" in emphasizing the alien transcendence of divinity. For a thorough discussion, see Cook, *2 Isaiah*, 2–4, 6–8, 11–14, 20–23, 25–37.

24. See Woodruff, *Reverence*, 68–69.

25. For this sense of the Hebrew, see Gen 20:11; Neh 5:15; Isa 63:17.

26. In my monograph on Second Isaiah, I put it this way: "Discovering God as God truly is, we feel increasing awe before the towering, nonrational dimensions of the Divine. More and more, we recognize our profanity and alienation from ultimate reality. The experience provokes powerful feelings of culpability and awakens a ravenous hunger for purity and virtue. We find ourselves impelled to become freer, nobler, and more selfless" (Cook, *2 Isaiah*, 22–23).

tionship with other mortals, one opens up to the need and plight of one's fellow human beings.

Woodruff's notions of reverence and its relationship to human morality fit Second Isaiah especially well, making the corpus particularly resistant to Mandolfo's grid of expectations. The God of Second Isaiah is the "high and lofty one who inhabits eternity, whose name is Holy" (Isa 57:15). Isaiah's God is the amoral, inscrutable being who declares, "My thoughts are not your thoughts, nor are your ways my ways, says the LORD. For as the heavens are higher than the earth, so are my ways higher than your ways and my thoughts than your thoughts" (55:8–9). Liberal culture may fire away with charges of God's failures at empathy and spousal mutuality,[27] but such charges have a hard time sticking to a nonanthropomorphic Deity of incomparable otherness (e.g., 40:12–18, 22; 44:7–8; 46:5, 9; 48:11–13; 51:12; 55:9). Again, modern psychotherapy has every right to outrage at how God's spouse will have trouble ever "trusting again,"[28] but the sober world of analysis does not reckon with an imminent divine epiphany of alien fairness (e.g., 43:5–7; 44:23; 46:13; 47:18; 49:3; 52:1; 55:5; 60:1–3, 7, 19; 61:3, 10; 62:1–3).

Beyond its stimulation of morality and other-centeredness, an epiphany of alien transcendence may also issue in an emotional and spiritual healing of human life. The Holy One of Second Isaiah longs to grace Israel with an inarticulate appreciation of the value and majesty of God's workings. God uses God's uncanny, beauteous *holiness* as a healing balm to bring about a new spiritual centeredness within the people.

God's healing begins as God's radical, *sublime* otherness reorients the human self. In the presence of that which rises sheer above comprehension, the ego-self instinctively relinquishes its assumed position at the center of existence. The mind clears up to perceive a larger, more encompassing fairness and majesty in reality than had previously been apprehended. The world around tears at the seams and a new universe reveals itself, in which the human subject is standing in a new position with balance and fairness restored to life.[29] Far from feeling demoted or bullied,

27. Mandolfo, *Daughter Zion*, 124.

28. Ibid., 110.

29. See Cook, *2 Isaiah*, 23. Mandolfo has objected to the logic of this argument, sensing some "slippage" in my claims. She states, "You were claiming that we shouldn't expect God to be an ethical role model for us. I think I could have been more with you … if you had stuck to your guns on God's incomprehensibility and recognized

the subject finds herself enlightened and empowered, the soul wondrously stilled, not grievously stifled.

If one grapples seriously with the theology of Second Isaiah, one should simply not expect Daughter Zion's healing to manifest itself in the form of articulate verbal acknowledgments of God's overtures toward her. Mandolfo's hope for such signs is misplaced. Relevant signs are instead to be expected in the form of expressions of awe at God's hidden wonder, issuing in an *inarticulate* appreciation of God's mysterious ways. If the person in pain is being graced with an experience of God's "wholly uncomprehended Mystery, revealed yet unrevealed," that person's objections will appear quieted and gently displaced as her soul senses the way of God's working.[30]

Mandolfo acknowledges the possibility that healing could come in this nonverbal, awe- or reverence-based manner, but finds my argument overconfident, "skewed toward Christian soteriological notions," and, overall, lacking resonance with the biblical text.[31] My rejoinder is straightforward:

---

that the aesthetic considerations you are positing exist entirely outside the realm of fairness or justice. God just is, and Daughter Zion's sense of injustice is beside the point" (Mandolfo, "Response"). But my claim is precisely that an epiphany of inscrutable divine beauty can actually gift us with a palpable new perception of justice. In Second Isaiah the human encounter with sublime beauty issues in a rising experience of "fairness" in the double sense of the word, aesthetic fairness and ethical fairness. I develop my case for this below, drawing heavily on Elaine Scarry, *On Beauty and Being Just* (Princeton: Princeton University Press, 1999). To quote Scarry, "A single word, 'fairness,' is used both in referring to loveliness of countenance and in referring to the ethical requirement for 'being fair,' 'playing fair,' and 'fair distribution'" (*On Beauty and Being Just*, 91). Although the two senses of the word can be employed in isolation, they are actually interconnected. Scarry is convinced of the almost self-evident character of the argument, to wit, that "beautiful things give rise to the notion of distribution, to a lifesaving reciprocity, to fairness not just in the sense of loveliness of aspect but in the sense of 'a symmetry of everyone's relation to one another'" (*On Beauty and Being Just*, 95).

30. See Rudolf Otto, *The Idea of the Holy: An Inquiry into the Non-Rational Factor in the Idea of the Divine and Its Relation to the Rational* (trans. John W. Harvey; New York: Oxford University Press, 1958), 81. For discussion, see Cook, *2 Isaiah*, 24–25.

31. Mandolfo, "Response." By "overconfident" I mean that she is wary of any approach that might gloss over the depths of Daughter Zion's experience of torment. Thus, although this vision of healing is "poetic and lovely to be sure," she would hesitate to defend it "in the presence of the mothers in Lamentations who were forced to eat their children, or the children tossed in the ovens of Majdanek." I can only reply that the texts of Second Isaiah, such as Isa 49:14–21, which I am about to explore, do

let us reexamine the text. I submit that Isa 49:14–21, which Mandolfo considers in her book, exhibits just the sort of reverence-based, aesthetically based healing for Zion that I have outlined.

Judging the text to fail, Mandolfo does not see any epiphany of alien fairness that would match my description. She sees no beginnings of Zion's rebirth. Rather, she complains that Zion, having been permanently damaged, "does not respond to God's overtures" in this pericope.[32] As elsewhere in Second Isaiah, the divine attempts at reconciliation fall short and, sadly, leave Daughter Zion alienated. Somehow Mandolfo has missed the poem's healing dynamic, its progressive tearing at the seams of Daughter Zion's world of alienation. As we move through the poem, I will argue, Zion experiences a rising "fairness" in the double sense of the word, aesthetic fairness and ethical fairness. At the text's conclusion, Zion responds—not in verbal dialogue, but in wonder. Her words clarify that she has moved beyond the demand for a sensitive and repentant spouse. Her dismay is quieted; she has sensed the way of God's working.

As the pericope ends in verse 21, Zion is wrapped up in awe at God's otherness. Though a penniless, exiled mother, she is unnerved to discover herself restored with perfectly reared children. "Where on earth did these children come from?" Zion asks. She is enthralled at something beyond explanation, something manifestly greater than herself. By fronting the pronoun אלה ("these") twice, the poetry brings out how preternatural the children really are: "these—who has reared them?" and "these—where are they from?"[33]

In Isaiah's theology, God's sublime otherness inverts our world, giving us a completely new take on fairness. Even a glimmer of the haunting sublimity of God transports us away from our self-orientation, creating real healing as the center of concern shifts away from the ego to the wonder of the sublime. Once we have met the Holy, we find ourselves without ego and intensely desiring the surrender of our selves.

---

dare to offer this very mode of healing precisely to a Daughter Zion acknowledged to have experienced the incomparable suffering attested in Lamentations (see Isa 51:19–20). My interest lies in taking this proffered vision of healing as seriously as Second Isaiah itself does and exploring its intriguing inner workings.

32. Mandolfo, *Daughter Zion*, 123.

33. John N. Oswalt, *The Book of Isaiah: Chapters 40–66* (NICOT; Grand Rapids: Eerdmans, 1998), 309 n. 82.

A flashlight holds no interest in broad daylight. Before the Holy, the world waxes and wanes and then everything becomes new. In this new place, we experience genuine recovery and harmony. I submit that we see this healing phenomenon of de-selfing unfold in Isa 49.

Note first how the broken Hebrew syntax of verse 19 abruptly drops all concern with past tragedy. The beginnings of a statement about the waste and desolate places of Zion's past terminates in midcourse and drops off the pages of the text. An exuberant observation of Zion's new fecundity interrupts the initial thought, pushing all self-focus and despondency to the side. The authors appear to have experienced a healing vision of such beauty and power that they have allowed their emotions to rule their syntax.[34]

The emphatic syntax of verse 21 is even more significant, since Daughter Zion herself is quoted as speaking. The Hebrew wording of the verse draws our attention directly to Zion's ego-self in order to emphasize that this self is specifically no longer Daughter Zion's focus: אני נשארתי לבדי, "as for me, I was left alone by myself," she declares. This "I" had nothing to do with the new wonder that has emerged, and which now enthralls her. Previously wrapped up completely in the self (cf. v. 14), Daughter Zion now experiences this self decentered. "The miracle is not about me," Zion realizes. "I am amazed just to be a part of it!" "This is a new, gratuitous kind of fairness!"

Beyond ideas of justice, our English term *fairness* may conjure ideas of beauty, of looking "fair," and that helps us appreciate Second Isaiah.[35] Beauty is a key element of God's otherness in this corpus, and it figures centrally in God's algorithm of salvation. This poetry espouses a Deity of glorious visage who plans to bathe Zion in splendor (see Isa 46:13; 52:1; 60:7, 19; 62:3). The grant of splendor is nothing less than the poetic equivalent of salvation (46:13). To save Zion is to adorn Israel with beauty.

Pointedly, our passage in Isa 49 shows Zion donning her returned children like jewelry, decking herself with them as a bride (v. 18b). Putting on jewels, as if throwing a wedding, she basks in reckless fairness. God's fairness is all she sees as she looks up and looks well (v. 18a). This fairness turns out to be morally as well as aesthetically satisfying, more satisfy-

---

34. See Alec J. Motyer, *The Prophecy of Isaiah: An Introduction and Commentary* (Downers Grove, Ill.: InterVarsity Press, 1993), 395.

35. See my discussion in n. 29 above.

ing even than securing a promise from God to amend God's ways.[36] After all, can Zion really want God to disavow judgment as a "specious notion," remaking God's self as a lover of sinners and sin alike?[37] Can Zion realistically expect precision judgments from God, fully predictable? Are not God's third-party instruments in judging so blunt and uncontrolled that the use of them is inevitably mixed and tragic?

Permit me to unpack verse 18 in light of Elaine Scarry's little gem of a treatise, *On Beauty and Being Just*. Scarry shows how beauty like that in our passage has power to persuade us of life's fairness, power to liberate us from our claims on existence. It opens us to a more encompassing majesty in reality than we had previously apprehended. Before, we were preoccupied with our own subjectivity. But now, as with Odysseus standing on the beach before Nausicaa, "all unease, aggression, indifference suddenly drop back, ... like a surf that has for a moment lost its capacity to harm."[38] Matisse knew the truth of this theology, and worked to "make paintings so serenely beautiful that when one came upon them, suddenly all problems would subside."[39]

By opening us up to the throbbing aliveness around us, beauty actually breathes life into us. It quickens, adrenalizes, makes life worth living. "Beauty is for the beholder lifesaving or life-restoring," writes Scarry, "the floating plank that Augustine holds onto, the branch Noah sees flying through the sky." A beautiful person "may sponsor—literally—the coming into the world of a newborn."[40]

As the beautiful new jewels of verse 18 draw her focus, Zion finds that they "act like small tears in the surface of the world that pull us through to some vaster space."[41] She experiences new vision, new imagination, new birth. Her old world of pain and alienation folds up and her arteries throb with life. In the presence of a beauty that seems incomparable and unprec-

---

36. Mandolfo, *Daughter Zion*, 111, 124–25.
37. Ibid., 90, 110, 118, 126.
38. Scarry, *On Beauty and Being Just*, 25.
39. Ibid., 33.
40. Ibid., 24, 89–90.
41. Phraseology used by Scarry (*On Beauty and Being Just*, 112) in describing reflections by Simone Weil, "Love of the Order of the World," in *Waiting for God* (trans. Emma Craufurd; 1951; repr., Harper Perennial Modern Classics; New York: HarperCollins, 2000).

edented, Zion senses the "'newness' or 'newbornness' of the entire world."[42] She moves toward a stance of welcome and embrace.

Mandolfo will likely object to Isaiah's aesthetic theodicy. Since her methodology emphasizes the negative and harmful dimensions of male gazing at female beauty, questions will immediately arise for her. For many feminist critics, such gazing is symbolic of male assertion of harmful authority over women. It is part and parcel of a patriarchal system of power. Making Zion into a trophy bride surely reifies her, does it not? By hanging ornaments on Zion, is the text not objectifying her and stripping her anew of subjectivity? Does not such a presentation support male dominance by portraying the objectification of women as a universal given?[43]

Such objections have little traction here. Zion is enriched by God's beauty—fulfilled, not diminished.[44] True, others may now gaze upon Zion in her newly gifted beauty, but she need not find this a threat. As Scarry shows, far from putting the one beheld at risk, beauty tends to provoke an affirmation of the person's aliveness and sanctity. "The thing perceived, the beautiful object, has conferred on it by the beholder a surfeit of aliveness," Scarry observes. "Even if it is inanimate, it comes to be accorded a fragility and consequent level of protection normally reserved for the animate."[45] As perceiver and perceived welcome each other, a protective compact builds.

---

42. Scarry, *On Beauty and Being Just*, 22.

43. Mandolfo, *Daughter Zion*, 53, 58, 82, 85, 101 n. 25.

44. Scarry, *On Beauty and Being Just*, 76.

45. Ibid., 89. A major goal of Scarry's book is to fearlessly challenge contemporary political arguments against the appreciation of beauty, including the beauty of persons. Responding to papers at the 2008 SBL meeting, Mandolfo made clear how brazen Scarry's challenge may seem. She emphasized that many cultural studies have theorized about the inherent threat of the "male gaze," which sexually objectifies women. She stated: "As the likes of Laura Mulvey and Jonathan Schroeder ... have demonstrated, the notion of 'the gaze' signifies a psychological relationship of power, in which the gazer, by definition, exerts potentially harmful authority over the object of his gaze—an idea basic to feminist textual analysis" (Mandolfo, "Response"). See Laura Mulvey, "Visual Pleasure and Narrative Cinema," in *Issues in Feminist Film Criticism* (ed. Patricia Erens; 5th ed.; Bloomington: Indiana University Press, 1991), 28–40; Jonathan E. Schroeder, "Consuming Representation: A Visual Approach to Consumer Research," in *Representing Consumers: Voices, Views and Visions* (ed. Barbara B. Stern; London: Routledge, 1998), 193–230. I admit to being persuaded by Scarry's defense of beauty and the admiring of beauty. At the same time, I would not want to deny the troubling consequences of our culture's insulting and reductionist definition of female

An intense reciprocity unfolds itself as Zion lifts up her eyes and takes in God's beauty as it pours upon her (Isa 49:18). What takes place is not the reciprocity of shared dialogue—the reciprocity between peers that Mandolfo champions.[46] Rather, an aesthetically inspired reciprocity is what comes into view—an interconnection that Scarry calls "a reciprocal salute" to one another's aliveness, to one another's shared ground.[47] Zion experiences God's beauty as if it were designed to fit her, to fit her like a wedding dress. Soaking up the beauty, she finds her true self recovered, welcomed, and ennobled. She finds that her will and God's will naturally accord.[48]

For Zion to experience this beauty is for her to enjoy effortless fertility, miraculous progeny. Verse 18 leaves us with little doubt: beauty is actualizing itself as fecundity in this passage. As Zion recovers her true self, her new splendor and vitality are directly equated with a plethora of newborns. They are beautiful gems, worn like jewels on a bride. As John Oswalt notes, Zion is not actually getting married in this text but is glowing as if she were. Her glow comes from gathering her children, which makes her appear like "a bride gathering her finery around her."[49] Her glory is her children.

But Mandolfo does not see much of a miracle glow in this vision of fecundity. She will object, "Zion's [first] children are irrevocably lost." They are "not coming home."[50] The damage is done and nothing can reverse it. We must read Isa 49:21 as skepticism, as an expression of Zion's doubts about a pie-in-the-sky resurrection. Against Mandolfo, cross-references and *relecture* within Second Isaiah render such a reading implausible.[51]

---

beauty as essentially an instrument through which women gain access to power and wealth controlled by men. We must insist on other ways of understanding and presenting female beauty—ways that are readily available.

46. Mandolfo, *Daughter Zion*, 19.

47. Scarry, *On Beauty and Being Just*, 92. Compare how their shared life binds together the mother and the nursing child of v. 15.

48. Ibid., 25–26.

49. Oswalt, *Isaiah 40–66*, 307 n. 76.

50. Mandolfo, *Daughter Zion*, 109; but note the ambiguity of the phrase בְּנֵי שִׁכֻּלָיִךְ ("children of your bereavement") in Isa 49:20. One interpretation, found already in the LXX and in Rashi, understands the text to speak directly of the astonishing return to life of Zion's original children who had perished (cf. NAB, NJB, NASB, NJPS)!

51. An interpretation of v. 21 as an expression of skepticism does not fit the parallel scene in 54:1–3, where Daughter Zion breaks into singing and shouts of joy

For Mandolfo, the pericope as a whole is probably a mystifying cover for a hidden agenda. With all its emphasis on the mystery and awesomeness of God's salvation, Second Isaiah conceals a political preference for those who went into exile (the *golah*) and a glaring insensitivity to the pain of those who remained in the land (the group that had experienced the cannibalistic horrors recounted in Lamentations). The text's joy at Zion's new children is too rosy and diverts our attention from the threat to those who had remained posed by a return of exiles who might well wish to reclaim farms and properties now put to new use. Recall the facts on the ground, Mandolfo presses: "The children who are being urged to return to Judah might better be considered colonists.… Isaiah's rhetoric specifically privileges the *golah* community."[52]

In mounting such an interpretation, Mandolfo insists on reading "more plainly."[53] She reifies the text as bare politics and mundane history. In this she is true to the spirit of critical suspicion, but at the cost of the text's canonical and theological integrity. She unravels layers of canonical shaping, which are present to guide the reader in appreciating the pericope's spiritual witness, which transcends all bare readings. In her own

---

over her new children. As Brevard S. Childs states, the mood in both texts—49:21 and 54:1–3—is one of "utter surprise and incomprehension" (*Isaiah* [OTL; Louisville: Westminster John Knox, 2001], 428). When Isa 60 again repeats the scene, Zion's heart thrills and rejoices (v. 5) as she lifts up her eyes and looks around to see her new children (v. 4, repeating 49:18 verbatim). Joseph Blenkinsopp sees a definite re-presentation of Isa 49 here, "*relecture* within the Isaian tradition" (*Isaiah 40–55: A New Translation with Introduction and Commentary* [AB 19A; New York: Doubleday, 2002], 311).

52. Mandolfo, *Daughter Zion*, 109; cf. NLT. Interestingly, however, what Daughter Zion actually says is that *she* is the one who has suffered life as a *golah* (גלה, "exile," v. 21), not the miracle children who are returning to her. The translators of the LXX apparently found the image of Zion as an exile confusing and substituted phraseology taken from 47:8–9 (see John Goldingay and David Payne, *Isaiah 40–55* [2 vols.; ICC; London: T&T Clark, 2006], 2:192). The theological burden of the passage, however, is God's intention to reverse the alienation of *the whole* of God's people, as embodied in the figure of Daughter Zion. The text eschews privileging the interests of any one faction (see Oswalt, *Isaiah 40–66*, 305). Klaus Baltzer rightly understands our pericope as a document of unification, which aims to include a variety of groups—including the nonexiled, those who remained in the land—in an expansive Jerusalem cult community (*Deutero-Isaiah: A Commentary on Isaiah 40–55* [trans. Margaret Kohl; Hermeneia; Minneapolis: Fortress, 2001], 327–28).

53. Mandolfo, *Daughter Zion*, 109.

words, she is "peering behind the text," emphasizing "what is canonically hidden."[54]

Mandolfo overlooks the "anxiety of influence" experienced by the tradents of Second Isaiah, which functioned to challenge all ideological biases and to mitigate ever-present temptations to pursue a political agenda. A theological tradition firmly in place behind Isa 49 has constrained its tradents. Its deep, strong roots were able to withstand the forces of politics, vogue, and *Tendenz*. Its kerygmatic witness pushed forward into the era of Second Isaiah to meet the reader through our text, affording the Scripture a canonical leverage against all efforts to historicize and denature its spiritual power. I shall conclude this essay by identifying and elaborating on the tradition at issue, the tradition of God's creation-blessing.

Relying on their group Scriptures now preserved in the Priestly Torah (PT) source of the Pentateuch, the Second Isaiah community oriented much of their theological reflection around God's creation-blessing.[55] They trained their focus on the hoary divine intention to bless the world with fecundity, familiar to us in the repeating pentateuchal command, "Be fruitful and multiply" (פרו ורבו). Walter Brueggemann has deftly shown how this refrain forms the kerygmatic heart of PT. Reflection on the recurring command makes plain its blessing of both humans and nature (Gen 1:22, 28 PT), a blessing that most assuredly goes beyond a mere divine desire for primordial life to spread.[56]

---

54. Ibid. Note that in the canonical shape of Second Isaiah, Daughter Zion's new children are a specifically *spiritual* breed of progeny (Isa 44:3–5), the "offspring" of the Suffering Servant, who may even include foreigners and outcasts (see 53:10; 54:17; 59:21; 61:9; 65:23; 66:22; Motyer, *Prophecy of Isaiah*, 395; Childs, *Isaiah*, 430–31, 458, 504–5, 538). Mandolfo's idea that the birth of these children represents nothing more than the return of the Judean exiles, whose numbers had expanded while in Babylonia (cf. v. 20 in the NLT), simply does not do justice to the mood of astonishment at something preternatural that is plainly observable in vv. 20–21 (see my arguments in n. 51 above).

55. For an introduction to the PT strand and the Holiness School (HS) strand (discussed below), see Jacob Milgrom, *Leviticus 1–16: A New Translation with Introduction and Commentary* (AB 3; New York: Doubleday, 1991), 1–2, 13–42, 48; Israel Knohl, *The Sanctuary of Silence: The Priestly Torah and the Holiness School* (Minneapolis: Fortress, 1995); idem, *The Divine Symphony: The Bible's Many Voices* (Philadelphia: Jewish Publication Society, 2003). For arguments detailing how the theology of Second Isaiah is rooted in the Scriptures of PT, see Cook, *2 Isaiah*. In my monograph I chose to rename the PT source the "Reverence School" (RS).

56. Walter Brueggemann, "Chapter 6: The Kerygma of the Priestly Writers," in

As cinematographers well know, chills run up the backs of audiences when birds, ants, bees, or other creatures mass together. Far from innocuous, the creation blessing of PT is downright otherworldly. Its numinous energy entails both natural and spiritual fecundity. Animated by the otherness that characterizes the sublime, God's transmission of dynamic, teeming power to earth is both life-giving and soul-nourishing. Second Isaiah declares that by soaking up this energy, poured out in buckets by God, earth will one day sprout harmony, bloom right living (Isa 45:8).

Repeatedly in texts such as 45:8, the poetry of Second Isaiah interconnects preternatural fecundity and spiritual invigoration. Thus 44:3–5 correlates a hope for "water" on a "thirsty land" with a hope for "blessing on [Israel's] offspring." Poetic parallelism bars us from ignoring a transcendent dimension in the blessing. God's blessing on Zion's new offspring specifically entails a pouring out of the spirit (v. 3b). We cannot reify the hope being expressed as any mere demographic agenda of the *golah* community. Isaiah 56:3 confirms the point: Zion's new children include eunuchs! If profane concerns were at the top of the agenda, the text would speak of *ex*-eunuchs.

Second Isaiah's theological and sacred understanding of the creation blessing is no innovation. We find the same understanding already within PT. As PT's story unfolds, the creation blessing soon concentrates itself as a divine empowerment of God's chosen people. The blessing becomes their unique charism, vitalizing them in their sacral calling. By Exod 1:7 (PT) the descendants of Abraham are fruitful and have multiplied (פרו ... וירבו). They swarm and teem as God intervenes in history, directing its course toward a dawning of the holy. "I will multiply [רבה] you exceedingly," God had assured Abraham (Gen 17:2 NAB); "I will make you exceedingly fruitful [פרה]" (Gen 17:6). God's guarantee is that Zion's children will swarm upon earth as a witness to God's splendor. The selfsame guarantee is being fulfilled as Daughter Zion lifts up her eyes in Isa 49 and is enthralled to find herself teeming with miracle children.

A universe of eerie fecundity reveals itself to Daughter Zion, an alternative divine reality of untamed birth and growth. History has arrived at the extraordinary telos toward which God's primordial blessing had

---

Walter Brueggemann and Hans Walter Wolff, *The Vitality of Old Testament Traditions* (2nd ed.; Atlanta: John Knox, 1982), 101–13; cf. Cook, *2 Isaiah*, 56, 118.

directed it. In this new paradisiacal world that defies decay and death, children are never "irrevocably lost."[57]

Neither can self-concern—ego-centeredness—maintain itself for long. The new landscape exhibits effortless, self-producing fertility. New offspring appear without labor; they nurse and rear themselves; their multiplication is inexplicable. Here, in tune with the verdant energy of a teeming land, one lets go of the sweaty work of justifying oneself and directing one's destiny. Instead, buoyed by the unforced rhythms of the surroundings, one relaxes and revels in the gratuitous gift of abounding life.[58]

One learns to love what one cannot control, what flourishes of its own accord. Living into a new Edenic experience, one lives instinctually and reverently, powered by the energy of the landscape, growing in active respect for its untamed beauty and power. One learns to love selflessly and with abandon.[59] A state of shalom reigns, in which everyone and everything interacts in a mode of patience, balance, and mutual giving. As a result, efficient, joyful living reigns supreme.

In fleshing out the kerygmatic forces behind Isa 49, I have used words like *paradisiacal* and *Edenic* on purpose. The tradents of Second Isaiah believed that the telos of God's creation blessing was nothing short of Eden on earth. They say as much in 51:1–3, where God reminds the people how their future is powered by the creation blessing, especially as it has been focused on the family of Sarah and Abraham. God "blessed" and "multiplied" them, verse 2 reminds us (see Gen 17:2, 6 PT). Verse 3 then specifies that, as the goal of the blessing, God will transform the wilderness of Zion into "Eden," make her into the "garden of the Lord."

The creation blessing has the selfsame trajectory in Ezekiel. Ezekiel 36 has God assure Zion-land that it will see the special promise to Sarah and Abraham fulfilled. Verse 11 of the chapter declares that, in the ideal future, life on the highland shall be fruitful and multiply (ורבו ופרו). As

---

57. Cf. Mandolfo, *Daughter Zion,* 109.

58. Henri J. M. Nouwen captures the spiritual meaning of fecundity well: "The great mystery of fecundity is that it becomes visible where we have given up our attempts to control life and take the risk to let life reveal its own inner movements. Whenever we trust and surrender ourselves to the God of love, fruits will grow" (*Lifesigns: Intimacy, Fecundity, and Ecstasy in Christian Perspective* [Garden City, N.Y.: Doubleday, 1986], 65).

59. As Nouwen rightly affirms, "Fecundity brings forth … new, fresh, and unique ways: … a kind word, a gentle embrace, a caring hand, … a new communion among the nations" (ibid., 81).

Daniel Block writes, "The phrase *they will increase and be fruitful* is an obvious echo of the divine blessing of beasts in Gen 1:22 and humans in 1:28 as well as 9:1, 7. This new fertility will exceed anything the land has experienced in history."[60] A numinous fecundity will arise, which will both cause the population to mushroom (v. 10) and lay a paradise out before it.[61] Of its own accord, the highland will shoot out its branches; it will yield its fruit in welcome (v. 8).

The "garden of Eden" is in mind, as shown by the appearance of the specific phrase in verses 33–38.[62] Verse 35 declares that all who pass by Israel will now exclaim, "This land that was desolate has become like the garden of Eden" (cf. Isa 51:3, just discussed). The context is a recapitulation of God's promise of repopulating the land and transforming it into a garden—a sublime, archetypal garden. Again the telos of the ancient creation-blessing is paradise on earth.

Though also priestly, the theology of Ezekiel differs in nuance from Second Isaiah. It focuses on communal holiness and sanctification rather than on splendor and reverence (see, e.g., Ezek 20:12; 37:28). Instead of on PT, Ezekiel's book leans heavily on the HS source of the Pentateuch and its ideal of God dwelling amid the people (Lev 26:9), sanctifying them,

---

60. Daniel I. Block, *The Book of Ezekiel: Chapters 25–48* (NICOT; Grand Rapids: Eerdmans, 1998), 334; cf. Paul M. Joyce, *Ezekiel: A Commentary* (LHBOTS 482; New York: T&T Clark, 2007), 203. (Later Hebrew is known to flip the word order within traditional phrases.) More centrally in view than these Genesis references may be the occurrence of the same diction in the HS strand at Lev 26:9. Whereas Second Isaiah orients itself on the PT strand, Ezekiel orients itself on HS (see below).

61. As in Isa 49, the new population consists of miracle children. Verse 10's language of "the whole house of Israel," "all of it," signals the return of the lost populace of the northern kingdom alongside the exiles of Judah. Cf. Ezek 35:10; 37:21–22; see Steven Tuell, *Ezekiel* (NIBC; Peabody, Mass.: Hendrickson, 2009), 244; Moshe Greenberg, *Ezekiel 21–37: A New Translation with Introduction and Commentary* (AB 22A; New York: Doubleday, 1997), 720. Verse 11 removes all doubt about the numinous nature of what is happening by insisting that Zion's new fecundity will include the animal world. Block grasps the transcendent scope here: "The land will be like paradise itself, and thus proclaim the mystery and presence of the divine person" (*Ezekiel 25–48*, 334).

62. Verse 8 does not yet mention Eden, but it does evoke elements of the Eden story in Gen 2–3 (see Greenberg, *Ezekiel 21–37*, 719). A perduring tradition of Jewish interpretation sees the fecundity of v. 8 as the beginning of the messianic age (720). The consensus among commentators is that vv. 33–38 hark back to the foregoing verses and elaborate on them, filling in some gaps.

making them holy (Exod 31:13; Lev 20:8; 21:8; 22:32).[63] The differing perspective means that Zion's Edenic fecundity takes on an alternate coloring in Ezekiel. Ezekiel 36:37–38 pictures the fecundity as an electrifying phenomenon of ballooning holiness.

Verses 37–38 convey Zion's fecundity with an image of Jerusalem bustling with flocks for sacrifice during pilgrimage time. "Thus says the Lord GOD: I will also let the house of Israel ask me to do this for them: to increase their population like a flock. Like the flock for sacrifices, like the flock at Jerusalem during her appointed festivals." My international students from Africa tell me how invigorating it is to participate in the similar scene they experience at open markets. On such occasions, one soaks up the energy of human community and mutuality. One is electrified.[64] In the case of making sacrifice at God's ideal sacred temple, the voltage would be multiplied immeasurably by God's seeping holiness.

The Hebrew behind the NRSV phrase "flock for sacrifices" in verse 38, צֹאן קֳדָשִׁים, might better be rendered "consecrated flock" or even "sacred flock." Holiness adheres to these sheep (cf. Lev 11:44; 19:2; 20:7–8, 26 HS)![65] The tenor of the image is "flocks of people," of course, so the Hebrew conjures the thought of holy multitudes burgeoning and teeming across the land of Zion.

---

63. See Stephen L. Cook, "Cosmos, *Kabod*, and Cherub: Ontological and Epistemological Hierarchy in Ezekiel," in *Ezekiel's Hierarchical World: Wrestling with a Tiered Reality* (ed. Stephen L. Cook and Corrine L. Patton; SBLSymS 31; Atlanta: Society of Biblical Literature, 2004), 182–90.

64. The values of traditional lineage-based African society can parallel and illuminate biblical emphases, such as the dream of booming fecundity. In Africa the impulse toward begetting runs deep and entails a longing for something more profound than biological propagation alone. To quote one black African religious thinker, Matungulu Otene, S.J., the traditional African "does all in his power to leave behind him some offspring, whether he be married or not married, living the life of a prostitute or of enforced celibacy. All Africans desire to have children, sometimes by any means" (*Celibacy and the African Value of Fecundity* [trans. L. C. Plamondon; Spearhead 65; Eldoret: Gaba, 1981], 13–14). If this drive for offspring impels even virgins and celibates, the meaning of fecundity must extend well beyond individual fertility to encompass a goal of "begetting" larger and deeper forms and qualities of life within one's entire community. When Otene insists on speaking of a nonbiological, "spiritual fertility," which entails involvement in "human formation" and "awakening" persons to fuller forms of life, he is sounding chords highly resonant with understandings of Second Isaiah that I flagged above in n. 54 (Otene, *African Value of Fecundity*, 2).

65. Joyce, *Ezekiel*, 207; Block, *Ezekiel 25–48*, 365.

By his turn of phrase, Ezekiel is conveying an idea of holy fecundity (cf. Ezek 47:1–12). God's presence amid the ideal Zion seeps into Zion's new children, sanctifies them, and makes them bubble with life, abound in mutuality. The holiness swells, pushing out beyond Jerusalem's confines. Zion's waste and desolate places become filled to overflowing. Daughter Zion finds fresh, authentic life and eschatological ennoblement in the realization of her ancient, divinely promised destiny (Lev 26:9 HS).

The prophet Zechariah, who follows in Ezekiel's footsteps, picks up where Ezek 36:37–38 leaves off. In his third vision (Zech 2:1–5), the prophet speaks of a new Jerusalem too big for walls, because of the multitudes teeming within the city. As Zechariah gazes upon Zion's telos, he sees a glowing, bustling city electrified by God's glory, which is dwelling amid the people and encompassing them round about (v. 5). Zion has realized the potential that she always carried within her (see Lev 26:9–12; cf. Exod 29:45; 40:34–35, all HS). Her story and God's story about her have come together at last.

Daughter Zion: Metaphor and Dialogue in the Book of Lamentations

Mary L. Conway

A significant change occurred in Lamentations scholarship after 1990 when the traditional themes of suffering as punishment and the need for repentance began to be disputed. Ideological criticism became prominent, and resulted in either a rejection of that content and message or its significant reinterpretation in light of current social and political values. Between the years 2000 and 2002, five significant works were published that offered new interpretations of this complex book and contested the conclusions of traditional criticism.[1]

Carleen Mandolfo's 2007 monograph, *Daughter Zion Talks Back to the Prophets*, offers a provocative and challenging analysis of the book from a feminist and postcolonial perspective.[2] Mandolfo considers some interesting issues in her analysis; however, an alternative approach in several areas—the horizontal dialogue, the multivalent nature of metaphor, and the structure of the book as a whole—would give a different perspective on the character of Daughter Zion and her significance within not only the book of Lamentations but also the Hebrew Bible.

---

1. Tod Linafelt, *Surviving Lamentations: Catastrophe, Lament, and Protest in the Afterlife of a Biblical Book* (Chicago: University of Chicago Press, 2000); Frederick W. Dobbs-Allsopp, *Lamentations* (IBC; Louisville: John Knox, 2002); Nancy C. Lee, *Singers of Lamentations: Cities under Siege, from Ur to Jerusalem to Sarajevo* (BIS 60; Leiden: Brill, 2002); Adele Berlin, *Lamentations: A Commentary* (OTL; Louisville: Westminster John Knox, 2002); Kathleen M. O'Connor, *Lamentations and the Tears of the World* (Maryknoll, N.Y.: Orbis, 2002).

2. Carleen Mandolfo, *Daughter Zion Talks Back to the Prophets: A Dialogic Theology of the Book of Lamentations* (SemeiaSt 58; Atlanta: Society of Biblical Literature, 2007).

First, Mandolfo's earlier book, *God in the Dock*,[3] did much to raise awareness of the multivocal nature of many psalms. Its insights can be applied to Lamentations to great advantage, and Mandolfo has used dialogic analysis as the primary methodology in *Daughter Zion Talks Back to the Prophets*. Her focus, however, is on the verbal interaction between Daughter Zion and Yhwh. Since Yhwh is conspicuously silent in Lamentations itself, however, she draws intertextually on Hosea, Jeremiah, Ezekiel, and Isaiah to reconstruct God's side of an extended conversation. If one gave closer attention to the interaction of the primary speakers (Zion, the male voices, and the community) within Lamentations itself, however, a different understanding of the book might emerge.

Second, the Daughter Zion metaphor is central to any understanding of Lamentations,[4] and Mandolfo draws implications from the graphic representation of Zion as a whore. The metaphor is never a simple one-to-one correspondence, however, in which "Daughter Zion" equals "whore," nor indeed in which "woman" equals "whore." Allowing the complex, multivalent nature of the metaphor to impact the message of the text reveals other significant layers of meaning.

Finally, because her stated intention is to allow Daughter Zion to speak, Mandolfo limits her analysis primarily to the first two chapters of Lamentations, with some comparisons to the lament in chapter 3, which she treats as a separate poem.[5] Whatever its sources and redactional history, however, the poems of Lamentations in its canonical form were placed together to be read together, and reading the book as a whole reveals structural and thematic links that suggest an overall design and purpose.

In this article I will propose a new reading of the final canonical form of the book of Lamentations, based on poetic and dialogic analysis, which incorporates these three suggestions. It will validate lament as an articulation of very real pain and suffering, while acknowledging the reality of

---

3. Carleen Mandolfo, *God in the Dock: Dialogic Tension in the Psalms of Lament* (JSOTSup 357; London: Sheffield Academic Press, 2002).

4. Daughter Zion dominates the first two chapters, speaking in Lam 1:9c, 11c–16, 18–22; 2:20–22. Her persona is absorbed into that of the community in Lam 3, but specific references to her recur in 4:2 and 22, along with some feminine pronouns. References to the physical Zion occur in 4:11; 5:11, 18.

5. Mandolfo, *Daughter Zion Talks Back to the Prophets*, 68.

sin and punishment and the need to find a way forward.[6] I will argue for a commutual interaction of the genders, in which both Daughter Zion and the male personae (the Speaker and the *Geber*) play significant roles in leading the community through its suffering and along the first steps toward forgiveness and mercy. I will submit that Lamentations as a whole presents a unified message that progresses meaningfully from judgment to pity, from detachment to empathy, from suffering to hope, and from the corporate through the individual back to the corporate perspective once more as the suffering community seeks a way forward.

Expression of Suffering (Lam 1)

The implied author[7] communicates through four main voices in the book: the unidentified Speaker (Lam 1 and 2), the *Geber* (הגבר; Lam 3 and 4), Daughter Zion (בת־ציון; Lam 1 and 2), and the community (Lam 3, 5).[8] The first chapter of Lamentations can be divided into two approximately equal, although overlapping, parts in which the Speaker and Zion interact.

---

6. Lamentations is a graphic representation of a traumatic moment in the history of Israel: the destruction of Jerusalem and its temple. Theologically, many Israelites understood this tragedy as the disciplinary action of God, and traditionally this is how the book has been interpreted. Although no claim is made here that *all* suffering is Yhwh's punishment for sin, or that *all* suffering is purposeful and redemptive, Lamentations argues that the destruction of Jerusalem in 586 B.C.E. was. The reality of judgment, however, does not invalidate the expression of pain; indeed, the inclusion of numerous laments in the Bible endorses the expression of suffering, however caused, in the human experience. Verse is the ideal medium for this, as Lamentations immediately attests.

7. No claims are made here about the redactional history of Lamentations. In this article I deal with the implied author of the final canonical form of the book.

8. See Iain W. Provan, *Lamentations* (NCB; Grand Rapids: Eerdmans, 1991), 7. Note that there are also minor characters such as the passersby and Daughter Edom. Mandolfo states, "Dialogic reading practices highlight the Bible's multiple, conflicting, and complementary voices and thus insist on readings that refuse to privilege one point of view" (*Daughter Zion*, 26; see also 68), and yet states that "we are obliged to privilege Zion's story" (18). This interpretation attempts to listen to all the voices interacting within the book. Also, whereas Mandolfo focuses on "divine speech and human speech that is directed to, or speaks about, God" (27) in spite of the silence of God in Lamentations, I focus on the more dominant interpersonal speech at the human level.

THE SPEAKER DESCRIBES JERUSALEM (LAM 1:1–9B, 10–11B, 17)

The poem opens with an unidentified voice who speaks of the destroyed Jerusalem and its inhabitants objectively in the third person. Although the text offers no compelling reasons to conclude that the first speaker is male, the original audience in a patriarchal society would likely have drawn this conclusion and a gender contrast between the two voices would have resulted. Consequently, in this article I will use male pronouns for the Speaker. Although this speaker is often called "the Narrator," he is a construct of the implied author who fills a role that is nearer to that of a character in a poetic drama; thus he will be termed simply "the Speaker."[9] The Speaker exists within the world of the text and participates as a character in its events, and he can be informed or changed by these events—and by the words of another character.

The striking contrast outlined immediately in verse 1 between the expectation of multitudes and the realization of solitude suggests an arriving visitor or a returning resident giving a detached, albeit sympathetic, description. The opening איכה demonstrates shock and disbelief: "How could this happen?" Jerusalem was not only "great of people," she was "great among the peoples" (Lam 1:2).[10] No indication is given here that the Speaker "belongs" in Jerusalem and identifies with it, although he is probably Judahite. He perceives Zion's suffering as external to himself, for there is no expression of distress on his own behalf. Characterizing the Speaker's detachment and objectivity as coldness or even derision would be incorrect, however, for the mere fact that the Speaker personifies the city as a woman, as Daughter Zion, imbues it with the capacity to feel and suffer.

Since the personification of the devastated city of Jerusalem is the dominant image in Lamentations, it makes a tremendous difference whether the Zion metaphor indicates an adulteress, a rape victim, or a mourner in dialogue with the Speaker. Metaphors serve to organize the reader's understanding of the subject, attributing more significance to some elements of the metaphor than to others, which it suppresses.[11] Difficulties ensue when interpreters "choose to activate aspects of the meta-

---

9. He is not termed "Jeremiah," although he may indeed be that prophet; the determination of authorship is beyond the scope of the present work.

10. Unless indicated otherwise, the translations are my own.

11. Max Black, "Metaphor," in *Philosophical Perspectives on Metaphor* (ed. Mark Johnson; Minneapolis: University of Minnesota Press, 1981), 63–82, here 75, 78.

phor that were latent."[12] Misinterpretation results when minor, subsidiary nuances of the metaphor are exaggerated in importance and dominate the interpretation, or when a metaphor is anachronistically interpreted from a modern perspective.[13] Therefore metaphor must be interpreted within the genre, the historical context, the immediate textual context, the logical flow of thought in the pericope, and comparison to relevant parallel passages in the prophets.[14]

Jerusalem is represented throughout Lam 1 in two contrasting ways: positively and sympathetically as a mother, a grieving woman, and an isolated widow who is a victim of rape and suffering; but also negatively and judgmentally as a promiscuous woman, an impure woman, and a rebellious sinner who is a deserving recipient of suffering.[15] These contrasting images are inherent in the multivalent nature of metaphor itself and integral to the overall message of Lamentations, evoking judgment but also compassion.[16]

In Lam 1:1 the Speaker compares Jerusalem to a widow (כאלמנה), a term that immediately connotes implicit sympathy. In addition, the comparison between her former status as princess (שרתי) and her current state as a slave (למס) is an expression of shock rather than an act of gloating. Although the sentence in isolation could indicate mockery, sympathy is suggested later in verse 7 when he relates that "her adversaries looked at her, and they laughed at her cessation." The verbs here are third-person plural (ראוה צרים שחקו), not first-person plural, and imply that the

---

12. Mandolfo, *Daughter Zion*, 25. Mandolfo, however, declares that she intends to "emphasize those aspects of the people's identity, for example, that are repressed by the vehicle" (*Daughter Zion*, 24). See also 31 n. 3.

13. See William W. Klein, Craig L. Blomberg, and Robert L. Hubbard Jr., *Introduction to Biblical Interpretation* (Dallas: Word, 1993), 175; also, regarding worldview confusion, see D. A. Carson, *Exegetical Fallacies* (Grand Rapids: Baker, 1984), 105.

14. See Black, "Metaphor," 74.

15. Daughter Zion, however, does not represent "woman" as a gender. See also Elizabeth Boase, *The Fulfilment of Doom? The Dialogic Interaction between the Book of Lamentations and the Pre-Exilic/Early Exilic Prophetic Literature* (LHBOTS 437; New York: T&T Clark, 2006), 82, 90. See Leah Ceccarelli, "Polysemy: Multiple Meanings in Rhetorical Criticism," *Quarterly Journal of Speech* 84 (1998): 395–415, for an excellent discussion of metaphor.

16. Contra Mandolfo's interpretation of the metaphor, which is more univalent: "Daughter Zion, wife of YHWH, is cast as an adulterous woman, a degenerate 'whore' who deserves the wrath of her lord" (*Daughter Zion*, 15).

Speaker does not count himself among those who deride Zion. Numerous indications are apparent in the text that he sees and is moved by her misery, for example, in verse 2:

> She continually weeps in the night and her tears are on her cheek.
> There is no comforter for her from all her lovers.[17]
> All her friends have acted treacherously against her;
> They have become her enemies.

The opening emphatic use of the infinitive absolute stresses the extent of her wretchedness, and the specification in the second phrase from a generalized weeping to an awareness of the individual tears on her face indicates that the Speaker fully comprehends her anguish as representing each individual human person, not just a vague collective "other." The repetition of כל in noting that all her lovers and all her friends have become enemies demonstrates an understanding of her helplessness. The use of the root בגד, meaning to "act or deal treacherously, faithlessly, deceitfully,"[18] shows that he disapproves of their actions. In this context, the repeated phrase "there is no comforter for her" (אֵין־לָהּ מְנַחֵם, also vv. 7, 9, 17 with variations) must be an expression of sympathy and regret.

The Speaker is fully cognizant, however, that the suffering of Daughter Zion is the deserved consequence of sin.[19] His comment in verse 5, "Indeed, Yhwh has afflicted her because of her many transgressions," is an acceptance of her culpability and its consequences. The remark is a brief statement of fact, however, not a harsh judgmental accusation; there is no lengthy enumeration of sins, no graphic depiction of their horror.[20] Guilt is a "given," partly because the Speaker acknowledges that Daughter Zion

---

17. Or possibly "those who love her"; see Provan, *Lamentations*, 36; J. Andrew Dearman, *Jeremiah/Lamentations* (NIVAC; Grand Rapids: Zondervan, 2002), 443.

18. Francis Brown, Samuel Rolles Driver, and Charles Augustus Briggs, *Enhanced Brown-Driver-Briggs Hebrew and English Lexicon* (electronic ed.; Oak Harbor: Logos Research Systems, 2000), 93.

19. See Frederick W. Dobbs-Allsopp, "Tragedy, Tradition, and Theology in the Book of Lamentations," *JSOT* (1997): 29–60, here 35; Joze Krašovec, "The Source of Hope in the Book of Lamentations," *VT* 42 (1992): 223–33, here 223–25.

20. Boase (*Fulfilment of Doom*, 172) has analyzed the prophetic literature and concludes: "Broadly, the day of Yahweh texts are, on the whole, more concerned with the nature and impact of the day than on the naming of the sins that initiated the day." Lamentations reflects this emphasis.

has already experienced, and continues to experience, God's discipline for her transgressions.[21] He therefore can express sympathy without denying her responsibility for her faults.

Daughter Zion's sin is not minimized, however, and verses 8–9 expand on the initial statement "Jerusalem has sinned greatly" with imagery related to her "impurity" or "uncleanness" ([22]נידה and טמאה). This attribution of uncleanness is central to an understanding of Zion's role and her relationship with Yhwh and the Speaker. Jerusalem's uncleanness has been variously attributed to her status as idolater, promiscuous woman, menstruant woman, rape victim, and mourning widow.[23]

The ultimate significance of the impurity imagery lies, however, in the crimes of adultery—figuratively representing idolatry—and rebellion against Yhwh. Adele Berlin gives a relevant summary of the elements of the Israelite worldview that would have influenced their understanding of this imagery.[24] The "paradigm of purity," as she terms it, recognizes two different types of impurity—ritual and moral. Ritual impurity implies no moral sin, although the impure person is required to perform purification rituals; the personified Jerusalem's uncleanness due to her menstrual state and her contact with dead bodies is an example of this. Moral impurity, on the other hand, implies the culpability of the impure person and is caused by transgressions such as immoral sexual acts and idolatry. As Berlin notes, "Moral impurity degrades the sinner and defiles the land of

---

21. Contra Mandolfo (*Daughter Zion*, 73), who relegates the Narrator's comment to an "aside, certainly not as denoting she deserves Yhwh's choice of punitive response."

22. Some commentators relate לנידה to the root נוד rather than נדד, indicating derision or wandering rather than impurity. See the discussions in Berlin (*Lamentations*, 53–54) and Lee (*Singers of Lamentations*, 104–6). Boase (*Fulfilment of Doom*, 176) argues against this interpretation.

23. For idolater, see Lee, *Singers of Lamentations*, 104. For promiscuous woman, see O'Connor, *Tears of the World*, 22. For menstruant woman, see Lev 15:19; O'Connor, *Tears of the World*, 27; Delbert R. Hillers, *Lamentations: A New Translation with Introduction and Commentary* (2nd ed.; AB 7A; New York: Doubleday, 1992), 76. For rape victim, see Lee, *Singers of Lamentations*, 101–9; Berlin, *Lamentations*, 55. For mourning widow, see See Lev 21:1; Num 5:2–3; 6:6–7; 9:10; 19:16; Xuan Huong Thi Pham, *Mourning in the Ancient Near East and the Hebrew Bible* (JSOTSup 302; Sheffield: Sheffield Academic Press, 1999), 49.

24. Berlin, *Lamentations*, 19–21, on which some of the following comments are based. See also Roy Gane, *Cult and Character: Purification Offerings, Day of Atonement, and Theodicy* (Winona Lake, Ind.: Eisenbrauns, 2005).

Israel. It has no expiating ritual; only punishment brings it to an end."[25] Jerusalem's adultery, symbolizing idolatry in its violation of her covenantal relationship with Yhwh, which is metaphorically represented as a marriage, demonstrates moral impurity.[26]

The interpretation that Zion's uncleanness is a misogynistic reference to her menstrual state, inferred by the phrase "her uncleanness is on her skirts" (v. 9), is unlikely here since although menstruation results in ritual impurity, there need be no guilt or moral culpability attached to it.[27] That the primary reference here is to rape is also doubtful.[28] The allusion is more likely to her promiscuity, with the uncleanness "on her skirts" the result of adulterous sexual activity.[29] This interpretation is reinforced in this text by the phase that follows, "and she was not mindful of the outcome," which indicates reckless behavior, by references to her lovers in other parts of the chapter (vv. 2, 19), and by the cause-effect assertion in verse 8 that "Jerusalem has sinned greatly; therefore she has become unclean."

---

25. Berlin, *Lamentations*, 19.

26. See Leland Ryken, James C. Wilhoit, and Tremper Longman III, eds., *Dictionary of Biblical Imagery* (Downers Grove, Ill.: InterVarsity Press, 1998), 39–40. See also below under "Daughter Zion (Lam 1:9c, 11c–16, 18–22)."

27. See Gane, *Cult and Character*, 199: "Physical ritual impurities are not moral evils." As Gane points out, however, the line between ritual impurity and moral sin is somewhat fuzzy. Moral sins can result in ritual impurity. Also, Gane points out that willful neglect of the priestly rituals that deal with these impurities is defiant sin (204). These nuances, however, are not germane to this specific context since there is no evidence that even if menstruation is in view, purification rituals have been neglected. See also Berlin, *Lamentations*, 54.

28. Contra Lee, *Singers of Lamentations*, 107, 109; and Dobbs-Allsopp, *Lamentations*, 63–67. According to W. G. E. Watson (*Classical Hebrew Poetry: A Guide to Its Techniques* [JSOTSup 26; Sheffield: JSOT Press, 1984], 265–66), metaphors imply by their context that the reader should either reinforce or neutralize the various parameters of the comparison.

29. See Boase, *Fulfilment of Doom*, 176–77; contra Dobbs-Allsopp (*Lamentations*, 49, 56, 64), who consistently denies that adultery is even in view in his analysis of Lam 1. See Jer 2:20, which identifies Zion's sin as adultery and rebellion. Cf. Ezek 16. According to Leonard J. Coppes ("*ndh*," *Theological Wordbook of the Old Testament* [ed. R. Laird Harris, Gleason L. Archer, and Bruce K. Waltke; 2 vols.; Chicago: Moody, 1980], 2:556), "Metaphorically, the concept of the ritual impurity of the menstrual period was used by Ezekiel to describe the nature of Israel's sin (36:17).... It is applied to Israel's most heinous sins (Zech 13:1; Ezr 9:11; II Chr 29:5)."

In the broader conceptual world of the monotheistic Israelite community, Israel's continuing pursuit of foreign gods is equivalent to marital infidelity.[30] However, other nuances, albeit secondary, of the Daughter Zion metaphor, such as mourning and rape, may be simultaneously suggested in order to encourage a more sympathetic attitude toward her in spite of her sin.[31]

After the Speaker recounts Zion's guilt, she interrupts and speaks for herself for the first time (v. 9c). Some commentators think that the Speaker ignores her;[32] however, his remarks in verses 10–11 indicate that he has not only heard her, but is deeply moved by her pain. Although suggestions of rape are included in earlier verses, the most poignant illustration of Daughter Zion's sexual exploitation appears in verse 10, in which the Speaker describes how the enemy "enters her sanctuary," violating her most intimate sacred space and effectively blending the sexual and religious imagery.

Although Lamentations readily assigns guilt, it also validates the reality of suffering and evokes sympathy for the sufferer. The book does not imply that Yhwh takes any pleasure in this discipline or is insensitive to the pain that the discipline brings.[33] That both the sin and the discipline are represented by graphic sexual images underlines not only the serious nature and the serious consequences of sin, but also the heart-wrenching misery of the sufferers, both Yhwh and Zion. According to Tikva Frymer-Kensky:

> When the prophet imagines the nation as a girl, he can go beyond anger to express love and sorrow. The marital metaphor of God and the Wife enables us to feel deeply the agony of God as God is betrayed by his beloved.... The image of the young woman as victim focuses our attention on the vulnerability and perishability of the nation in God's eyes and allows the prophet and reader to express a sadness that goes beyond questions of justice.[34]

---

30. Contra Mandolfo (*Daughter Zion*, 76), who dislocates the metaphor from its social and religious context.

31. See Boase, *Fulfilment of Doom*, 177–78.

32. O'Connor, *Tears of the World*, 22.

33. So similarly Lam 3:31–33.

34. Tikva Frymer-Kensky, *In the Wake of the Goddesses: Women, Culture, and the Biblical Transformation of Pagan Myth* (New York: Free Press, 1992), 169.

The tension between the two images in verses 8–10, between her adultery and her victimization, reflects the tension between Yhwh's holiness and mercy.[35] Finally, in verse 11, the Speaker broadens his sympathetic view from the personal suffering of Zion to the desperate situation of "all her people," fighting for their very existence.

Daughter Zion (Lam 1:9c, 11c–16, 18–22)

Daughter Zion's lament takes over the dialogue in verse 11c, and the intensification is striking. Whereas the Speaker focused on the finality of destruction and death, Zion focuses more on pleas to Yhwh to see and alleviate the suffering of the living, using her misery and grief as leverage.

In light of the destruction of Jerusalem, its temple, and many of its inhabitants, it is not surprising that "the first and most central theme of Lamentations is mourning."[36] The Hebrew Bible attests to the function of women—perhaps professional— who lead in the dirges, laments, and postures of grief in a number of passages, including the book of Jeremiah.[37] Although the expression of mourning often occurs spontaneously, the rituals of mourning can also elicit such responses, acting in a causative/formative rather than a resultative fashion.[38] In Lamentations Daughter Zion fills this role of mourner, lamenter, and dirge singer and in so doing not only appeals to Yhwh but also significantly impacts the Speaker.

Daughter Zion twice cries out to God with the imperative "Look, O Yhwh!" (vv. 9c, 11c), interrupting the Speaker with her sense of pain and urgency. Although some commentators view the speeches of the Speaker and Zion as parallel, involving no direct interaction between the two,[39]

---

35. Cf. Mandolfo, *Daughter Zion*, 16.

36. Berlin, *Lamentations*, 15. See also Lee, *Singers of Lamentations*, 33, for an overview of dirge and lament. See Berlin, *Lamentations*, 24; Provan, *Lamentations*, 5; and Lee, *Singers of Lamentations*, 34–35, for dirge and lament in Lamentations.

37. Jer 9:16–17 (Eng. 17–19). See also 2 Sam 1:24; Ezek 32:16; 2 Chr 35:25. See Emanuel Feldman, *Biblical and Post-biblical Defilement and Mourning: Law as Theology* (New York: Ktav, 1977), 134–37; Saul M. Olyan, *Biblical Mourning: Ritual and Social Dimensions* (Oxford: Oxford University Press, 2004), 49–51; Lee, *Singers of Lamentations*, 18, 51; Pham, *Mourning*, 52.

38. See Olyan, *Biblical Mourning*, 8, 33; Gary A. Anderson, *A Time to Mourn, a Time to Dance: The Expression of Grief and Joy in Israelite Religion* (University Park: Pennsylvania State University Press, 1991), 3–9 and 95–96.

39. E.g., O'Connor, *Tears of the World*, 22–27.

the use of variations on the phrase "There is no comforter for her" in both speeches (Speaker: 1:2, 9, 17; Zion: 1:16, 21) suggests that they are responding to each other. The interweaving of their speech in verses 9–11 reinforces this as the Speaker's voice slows and stops while Daughter Zion's voice assumes prominence.

Daughter Zion is unapologetically subjective in her expression of suffering, forcing the Speaker to see and even experience the pain from her perspective. Her demands are more than a plea for notice—they are an impassioned appeal, imploring others to enter into her misery and to alleviate it (v. 12b). Daughter Zion actively confronts the sympathetic but detached attitude of the Speaker and calls on him to participate in and assuage her sorrow.

A variety of poetic and semantic strategies are used in this passage along with the subjective perspective to generate sympathy for Daughter Zion. An example is verse 12b: "Look and see whether there is any pain like my pain which he has inflicted on me" (הביטו וראו אם־יש מכאוב כמכאבי אשר עולל לי). The importunate, repeated demand to "look!" (ראה) and "see!" (נבט) compels the Speaker to fix his eyes on her plight. The repetition of "pain" drives home its impact, but even more so, the addition of the first-person singular suffix (מכאוב כמכאבי) shifts the accent to the sufferer, as in "pain like *my* pain." The use of the term עולל, "to act arbitrarily or severely,"[40] suggests that the pain may be excessive or out of proportion to the transgression and evokes pity for Zion. Finally, the phrase לי, "on me," once again focuses attention on the victim. Intense depictions of misery such as this do much to mitigate the tendency toward judgmental condemnation of Daughter Zion, in spite of her confessions of sin that follow, beginning in verse 14.[41]

Daughter Zion's success in her efforts to reach out to the Speaker is evident in verses 16–17. After summarizing Yhwh's discipline, she laments, and this time the Speaker is the one who interrupts Zion, deeply moved by her distress. The reference to Zion's gesture ("Zion spreads out her hands") indicates that he sees her; the repetition of her key words "comforter" (מנחם) and "enemies" (אויב) suggests that he hears her and responds to her.[42] The Speaker, however, is helpless to effect any practical aid for Zion.

---

40. BDB, 759.

41. See Boase, *Fulfilment of Doom*, 179.

42. See also Linafelt, *Surviving Lamentations*, 39, 51, for other examples.

Three times in the pericope Daughter Zion uses the terminology of "rebelling": "I have rebelled against his word" (כי פיהו מריתי, v. 18a), "for I have indeed been rebellious" (כי מרו מריתי, v. 20b), and "because of all my rebellion" (על כל־פשעי, [43]v. 22b). Any form of sin within monotheistic Israelite culture was equated with rebellion and treaty violation. Additionally, treaties between nations were often marriage alliances in the ancient Near East, and a number of examples are present in the Hebrew Bible in which even ordinary marriage is referred to as a covenant (ברית; Mal 2:14; Ezek 16:8; Prov 2:17).[44] Therefore the adulterous acts of Daughter Zion would in and of themselves be construed as treaty violations against Yhwh.[45] The confession of Daughter Zion—a particular woman who represents the sin of all Israel, both male and female[46]—to deliberate rebellion against Yhwh represents Israel's absolute rejection of her covenant rela-

---

43. See *HALOT* 3:981, "rebellion, revolt." Although BDB (833) says "transgression," "to rebel" is also given as a meaning of the corresponding verbal root.

44. Paul Kalluveettil (*Declaration and Covenant* [AnBib 88; Rome: Pontifical Biblical Institute, 1982], 79–83) points out that there are also covenantal contexts in which the actual word ברית is not used.

45. Some recent scholarship has challenged this emphasis on rebelling in a treaty violation context and has suggested that the natural family/clan contexts are more meaningful for the understanding of rebellion. However, whether the rebellion destroys the hierarchical relationship between vassal and overlord or between father and son or family and clan, the end result is similar. See Gordon Hugenberger, *Marriage as a Covenant: A Study of Biblical Law and Ethics Governing Marriage, Developed from the Perspective of Malachi* (VTSup 52; Leiden: Brill, 1994), esp. 280–338; Frank Moore Cross, *From Epic to Canon: History and Literature in Ancient Israel* (Baltimore: Johns Hopkins University Press, 1998), 3–21; Seock-Tae Sohn, "'I Will Be Your God and You Will Be My People': The Origin and Background of the Covenant Formula," in *Ki Baruch Hu: Ancient Near Eastern, Biblical, and Judaic Studies in Honor of Baruch A. Levine* (ed. Robert Chazan, William W. Hallo, and Lawrence H. Schiffman; Winona Lake, Ind.: Eisenbrauns, 1999), 355–72; Steven L. McKenzie, *Covenant* (Understanding Biblical Themes; St. Louis: Chalice, 2000), 11–12; Kalluveettil, *Declaration and Covenant*, 98–99, 130, 181.

46. Stressing only the generic "womanhood" of Daughter Zion at the expense of other aspects of the metaphor is misleading. She is an adulterous woman, not "Everywoman," and she represents the infidelity of both men and women to Yhwh. Cf. Mandolfo, *Daughter Zion*, 75: "the poet of Lam 1–2 preserves the metaphor of Israel as a woman, a metaphor that in the discourse of the prophets is meant to humiliate and dehumanize the people, and imbues it with pathos and subjectivity."

tionship with her Lord and Creator and results in serious discipline.[47] The consequences would be deportation or destruction.

Summary

Lamentations 1 consists of a dialogue between an objectively detached Speaker and a subjectively suffering Daughter Zion who appear to be aware of and respond to each other. Daughter Zion herself is presented both negatively as a sinner and positively as a suffering woman. The Speaker begins the journey, which continues in Lam 2, from a sympathetic but detached attitude toward Zion and her sin to a more compassionate understanding of her miserable situation.

From Judgment to Pity (Lam 2)

Whereas the complacency of the Speaker was shaken in Lam 1, in the second chapter his whole attitude undergoes a radical metamorphosis as he moves from an attitude of detached sympathy for Zion to intense empathy. As Mandolfo points out, "an I-thou relationship moves beyond mere explanation … to empathy and understanding."[48]

The Speaker (Lam 2:1–19)

Description of the Destruction (Lam 2:1–12)

No interpreter can escape the lengthy description of the wrath of God in verses 1–11. Jerusalem is brought low—physically, politically, emotionally, and spiritually. Kathleen O'Connor identifies the Speaker's dominant emotion as anger directed at Yhwh.[49] Although anger is one possible interpretation of the Speaker's vehement outburst, it is not the only one, for there is no clear evidence that the Speaker considers God's actions to be motivated by unjustifiable and abusive rage rather than justifiable disciplinary

---

47. Contra Lee (*Singers of Lamentations*, 123–25), who interprets Zion's rebellion as justifiably standing up to God's oppressive and excessive discipline.

48. Mandolfo, *Daughter Zion*, 2.

49. O'Connor, *Tears of the World*, 33; see also Lee, *Singers of Lamentations*, 116–17.

wrath; his distraught enumeration may also be motivated by shock, regret, anguish, or pity.

In considering the severity of the discipline, one must either conclude that Yhwh is indeed abusive,[50] or that the malignancy of the sin that provoked God's judgment demanded drastic measures because the ultimate harm that would result from the sin was greater than the punishment that curtailed it.[51] A third explanation, however, must also be considered, one that is obvious but often overlooked—Lamentations is poetry, which is overtly expressive rather than merely mimetic, and has a persuasive goal.[52] Hyperbole is a common and effective poetic device that assists in achieving these ends.[53] The recognition of hyperbole in no way trivializes the suffering of the people, but merely acknowledges the limitations of language in attempting to reproduce emotional reality for a reader. According to Tod Linafelt, the poet's task is to "attempt to translate into language the suffering he sees," even though "no speech is adequate as an explanation of such suffering."[54] The Speaker himself acknowledges this in verse 13: "What will I call as witness? What will I compare to you, Daughter Jerusalem?" Hence he uses graphic and disturbing images and pervasive hyperbole.[55] To interpret such passages with slavish literalness ignores the poetic nature of the text.

In light of the reality of Jerusalem's current desolation, the Speaker's transition from third-person description to first-person expression of grief in verse 11 is not surprising. It is significant that the Speaker expresses his pain in vocabulary that closely resembles that of Daughter Zion in Lam 1: "Because of these things I am weeping ... my entrails are fermenting [מעי חמרמרו]" (1:16, 20), as compared to "My eyes are spent with weeping; my

---

50. As do Lee, *Singers of Lamentations*, 35–36; Linafelt, *Surviving Lamentations*, 55; O'Connor, *Tears of the World*, 27, 33, 118; Dobbs-Allsopp, *Lamentations*, 82–84; Walter Brueggemann, *Theology of the Old Testament: Testimony, Dispute, Advocacy* (Minneapolis: Fortress, 1997), 359–62.

51. See Jer 30:14–15.

52. David L. Petersen and Kent Harold Richards, *Interpreting Hebrew Poetry* (Minneapolis: Fortress, 1992), 8–11.

53. See Provan, *Lamentations*, 6.

54. Linafelt, *Surviving Lamentations*, 53; see also Dobbs-Allsopp, *Lamentations*, 96.

55. See Watson, *Classical Hebrew Poetry*, 316–20, who remarks, "hyperbole was practically part of everyday language." See also Luis Alonso Schökel, who notes, "Hebrew poetry tends more to hyperbole than to sobriety" (*A Manual of Hebrew Poetics* [SubBi 11; Rome: Pontifical Biblical Institute, 1988], 168–69).

entrails ferment [חמרמרו מעי]" (2:11).[56] His interaction with Daughter Zion has caused him to move from detached sympathy to true empathy with her wretchedness.

Address to Zion (Lam 2:13–19)

The series of rhetorical questions in verse 13 demonstrates the Speaker's helplessness, for no healer is in view. The prophets have failed Zion, the passersby mock her, and her enemies gloat over her defeat—even Yhwh has yet shown no mercy. The passersby add insult to injury, for the people of Jerusalem would have easily recognized the quotation in verse 15 from Ps 48:

> Beautiful in its loftiness,
> the joy of the whole earth,
> like the heights of Zaphon is Mount Zion,
> the city of the Great King. (Ps 48:2 TNIV)

The bitter irony is inescapable. Since the psalm affirms that "God makes her [Zion] secure forever" (v. 8), the sense of abandonment by Yhwh would have equaled the physical suffering of the inhabitants. Deeply moved, but unable to help her, in verse 19 the Speaker urges Daughter Zion to continue crying out to Yhwh for deliverance.

DAUGHTER ZION (LAM 2:20–22)

Zion's final address to Yhwh is characterized by some commentators as expressing defiance and "unmitigated rage."[57] Certainly, Daughter Zion's lament in verses 20–22 creates one of the most graphic, shocking, and poignant pictures of Jerusalem's destruction in Lamentations, and it has provoked many critics to further indict Yhwh for these unjustifiable, abusive actions. The focus of their concern is usually the cannibalistic image of starving mothers eating their own innocent children.[58] They view this state of affairs as excessive, even sadistic punishment for their crimes,

---

56. See Linafelt, *Surviving Lamentations*, 52.

57. Mandolfo, *Daughter Zion*, 103. See also Dobbs-Allsopp, *Lamentations*, 99.

58. See, e.g., Edward L. Greenstein, "The Wrath of God in the Book of Lamentations," in *The Problem of Evil and Its Symbols in Jewish and Christian Tradition* (ed.

and consequently see Yhwh as the perpetrator and Zion as the victim of God's brutality. Verse 20 may be persuasive exaggeration; nevertheless, as discussed above, to discount it as mere overstatement would be unjust since the very use of hyperbole in literature is intended to convey the intense reality of an emotion or idea. The possibility exists, of course, that the statement is literally true. The curses invoked on those who break the covenant in Deut 28:53–57 forewarn of cannibalism, as does Jeremiah's prophecy (19:7–9).

Is Daughter Zion's emotion unambiguous rage, however? Lamentations does not give the reader the advantage of a narrative framework or stage directions, and these words could equally well express desperation, anguish, or hopelessness; the tone could be one of pleading or pathos. This outburst may be a cry for mercy and relief, but even when the judgment is inevitable or the discipline already enforced, lament serves as a means to express, endure, and eventually survive the suffering. This cry is not, as Dobbs-Allsopp suggests, "an experience of liberation,"[59] or "heroic defiance" of Yhwh.[60] Yhwh himself authorizes such lament, as illustrated by Jer 9:16–20 (Eng. 17–21). Mark Boda points out, "This lament is not to change the heart of God but to express the pain of God's certain judgment."[61]

Lamentations 2 contains scant reference to sin; and Nancy Lee, while admitting that Jerusalem has sinned, remarks that she has confessed, and consequently wonders what else God could reasonably expect before relenting.[62] Yhwh's holiness and justice, however, demand more; discipline is imposed and must run its course. The lack of true confession and contrition in Lam 2, and the continuing tendency to blame Yhwh rather than admit culpability, may be one reason that Daughter Zion fades from the book without reaching peace of mind and attaining hope. The role of the female voice of Zion is primarily to give voice to suffering and evoke sympathy, appealing to the mercy of God, whereas the male voices of the Speaker and the *Geber*, while honoring the expression of pain, are intended to emphasize the need to accept responsibility for suffering and to find a

---

Henning Graf Reventlow and Yair Hoffman; JSOTSup 366; New York: T&T Clark, 2004), 29–42, here 36.

59. Dobbs-Allsopp, *Lamentations*, 103.

60. Ibid., 79.

61. Mark J. Boda, *A Severe Mercy: Sin and Its Remedy in the Old Testament* (Winona Lake, Ind.: Eisenbrauns, 2009), 247.

62. Lee, *Singers of Lamentations*, 111.

way forward, propitiating the holy demands of God. Admittedly, in contemporary society this would appear as gender stereotyping; however, in the ancient world of the Israelites this would simply be an expression of disparate male and female roles in a patriarchal system.[63]

Summary

The reader hears directly from Daughter Zion for the last time in verses 20–22; she is a pathetic figure who has yet to experience true hope for her future.[64] She has, however, converted the Speaker from a detached, objective view of Zion's pain to an empathetic view that causes him to suffer for and with Jerusalem. In so doing, he moves the implied reader/listener to a similar empathy with the guilt and suffering of Jerusalem. The focus is in the process of moving from Daughter Zion, a corporate representation of the people of Jerusalem, and the Speaker, who interacts and empathizes with her, to the *Geber*, an individual who suffers in his own right, and his particular responsibility and response.

From Corporate to Individual (Lam 3)

Lamentations 1 and 2 evoke both censure and pity for Daughter Zion by means of the Speaker, an individual who empathizes with her but is ultimately unable to help her. In Lam 3, however, the implied author creates a new persona, the *Geber* (הגבר), an individual from among those in Jerusalem who are severely afflicted. The movement of the book is away from the mode of expressing suffering and toward the process of dealing with suffering, and the *Geber* personifies one who turns to God for mercy and forgiveness and finds redemption.

---

63. See Olyan, *Biblical Mourning*, 49–51, for the dominant role of women as mourners, especially professionally. This does not of course preclude the participation of men. The prevalence of men as religious leaders is evident throughout the Hebrew Bible, although some female religious figures, such as Huldah (2 Kgs 22:14), are mentioned.

64. She may later, however, as part of the community she represents. See below.

The *Geber* (Lam 3:1–41)

Transition (Lam 3:1–24)

In Lam 3 the *Geber* is totally involved with the suffering and fate of Jerusalem. He begins this pericope with the statement, "I am the man who has seen misery" (אני הגבר ראה עני). The verb "to see" (ראה) can also mean "to experience," and there is a deliberate play on words here.[65] The *Geber* is not just an onlooker but a participant. As Dobbs-Allsopp perceptively notes:

> The result is that the aesthetic distance between the discourse of the poem and the reader's experience of that discourse is suddenly collapsed. The use of the first person voice draws readers into the poem, makes them identify with the speaker, and invites them to experience vicariously the suffering and affliction that the poem figures.[66]

The *Geber*'s identification of himself as "the man who has seen misery" poetically balances the feminine imagery of Daughter Zion in Lam 1 and 2 and signifies the transition from expressing and validating pain to dealing with the consequences of guilt and finding a way to move forward.

The repeated syntactic pattern of third-person masculine singular active perfect verbs parallels the catalogue of destructive events in Lam 2:1–10 and helps to link Lam 2 and 3 together as a literary unit. And yet the *Geber*'s tone is different, more muted; the text suggests that he is defeated and exhausted ("He has destroyed my endurance," 3:18). He later advises his audience, "Let him sit alone and let him be silent" (v. 28); he realizes that the time for lament, personified in Daughter Zion, has passed; and he is now actively seeking a way forward.

This insight may explain the transition that occurs in verses 18–20 from defeat to hope. Verse 18 is usually translated in a sense similar to the NASB indicating that both his strength and hope have perished: "So I say, 'My strength has perished, And *so has* my hope from the LORD,'" which makes such a transformation seem unlikely.[67] However, there is actually

---

65. See BDB, 907.

66. Dobbs-Allsopp, *Lamentations*, 50.

67. Hillers translates: "I thought, 'My lasting hope in the Lord has perished.'" He explains, "Hebrew 'my enduring and my hope' is taken to be a hendiadys" (*Lamenta-*

no verb in the second half of the bicolon in the Hebrew (ואמר אבד נצחי ותוחלתי מיהוה), and the NASB assumes ellipsis. The second part of this verse, however, can be translated as a verbless clause: "So I said, 'He has destroyed my endurance, and/but my hope [is] from Yhwh.'"[68] The implication would be that all his own resources have been expended and his only remaining hope is in the gracious character of God. This would fit the context well, and prompt the famous expression of trust and hope that follows in verses 22–23.

Exhortation to the Community (Lam 3:25–41)

O'Connor rightly points out that Lam 3 is not a demonstration of unqualified hope: "Instead, the realities of suffering and death and of a God remembered rather than encountered repeatedly moderate and overcome hope."[69] She also draws attention, however, to the repeated references to "waiting" in verses 24, 25, and 26.[70] Although Yhwh's face is currently hidden, the *Geber* has a God who is not only remembered but also anticipated, and hope in the character and justice of Yhwh remains.

In verse 25 the *Geber* changes his discourse from first to third person, verses 28–30 include a series of jussives, and in verses 40–41 there are three cohortative verbs. In conjunction with the didactic content it is reasonable to assume that the *Geber* is instructing the community and exhorting them to collectively repent.[71] The imagery used here is that of humility: "endure the yoke," "sit alone," "be silent," "put his mouth in the dust," and "give the cheek to the one who smites him."[72] The need is to move from lamentation to penitence.[73] The *Geber* assures the people that just as Yhwh has been faithful to the covenant in the past, so Yhwh will

---

tions, 110, 114). Although this is a possible reading, it is not obligatory, and the verbless clause makes more sense in context.

68. Lam 1:2 illustrates a similar use of the ו + nonverb, in which there is a verbless clause following a verbal clause.

69. O'Connor, *Tears of the World*, 45.

70. Ibid., 50.

71. See Hillers, *Lamentations*, 129.

72. See Berlin, *Lamentations*, 94.

73. See Mark J. Boda, "The Priceless Gain of Penitence: From Communal Lament to Penitential Prayer in the 'Exilic' Liturgy of Israel," in *Lamentations in Ancient and Contemporary Contexts* (ed. Nancy C. Lee and Carleen Mandolfo; SBLSymS 43; Atlanta: Society of Biblical Literature, 2008), 81–101, here 68.

now have compassion on those who humble themselves, for "he does not oppress from his heart, does not grieve the children of humankind" (v. 33), reflecting once again the tension between the justice of a holy God and the mercy of a loving God.

The use of first-person plural beginning in verse 40 does not necessarily imply a new collective voice; the *Geber* is conveying his insights to the people as a leader among them.[74] After reiterating the faithfulness of Yhwh, he encourages them: "Let us search out our ways and let us examine them and let us return to Yhwh" (v. 40). It is grace that provokes the community to respond.

THE COMMUNITY CONFESSES AND LAMENTS (LAM 3:42–47)

In verse 42 the community does just this with the opening words of a prayer of repentance: "We have rebelled; we have been obstinate...." Suddenly, however, the tone seems to change: "... you have not forgiven." From this many conclude that God is unjust. However, if the community is unable to respond authentically to the call to repent and falters partway into their attempt, the continuing discipline would not be unjust. Once again the community dwells on the physical destruction (vv. 43, 47), the assault of the enemy (v. 52), the isolation from God (v. 44), and the scorn of the attackers (vv. 45–46).

THE *GEBER* (LAM 3:48–66)

The *Geber* Empathizes and Identifies with the People (Lam 3:48–51)

The *Geber*'s words in verse 48, "Channels of water go down from my eye because of the crushing of the daughter of my people," recalls the Speaker's in 2:11: "My eyes are spent with weeping; my entrails ferment. My liver has been poured out to the ground because of the shattering of the daughter of my people." As the Speaker previously empathized with the suffering Daughter Zion, now the *Geber* empathizes with the continuing suffering and frustration of the community that she represented, interceding on its behalf. When the *Geber* so identifies with the destroyed city that its pain

---

74. See Paul R. House, "Lamentations," in Duane Garrett and House, *Song of Songs, Lamentations* (WBC 23B; Nashville: Nelson, 2004), 267–473, here 404; Hillers, *Lamentations*, 123.

becomes his own, he provides a model for corporate identity, responsibility, and commitment. He has not forgotten his own individual plight, however, and recalls his own defeat by his enemies and discovery of hope as encouragement to the faltering community and as a model of redemption to emulate.

The Speaker's Address to Yhwh (Lam 3:52–66)

In Lam 3:52–66 the *Geber* summarizes the assault of the enemy and recalls his moment of greatest need, graphically described earlier in 3:1–19, when he found himself "in the pit" and concluded, "I am cut off" (נגזרתי, vv. 53–54), for Yhwh had not yet spoken. Although the Hebrew root גזר is often translated as "perish," as in the TNIV, it can also mean "cut off" as in the NASB, in the sense of "separated, excluded, from" God.[75] The *Geber*, however, has confessed, shown contrition, and repented.[76]

Now he recalls the process: "I called your name, O Yhwh, from the lowest pit. You heard my voice.…You drew near on the day I called out to you. You said, 'Do not fear'" (vv. 55–57).[77] These words are reminiscent of a psalm of lament in which, even though there is often no actual evidence in the psalm that the situation has changed, the psalmist may assert that God has heard his or her prayer (e.g., Pss 6:9–10 [Eng. 8–9]; 28:6).[78]

---

75. BDB, 160. See Pss 31:23 (Eng. 22); 88:6 (Eng. 5).

76. Evidenced in vv. 39–42 as the Speaker initiates and then begins to lead the community in prayer.

77. Contra Provan, who argues that the verbs in vv. 52–66 are precative perfects and require a future reference in this context ("Past, Present and Future in Lamentations III 52–66: The Case for a Precative Perfect Re-examined," *VT* 41 [1991]: 164–75, here 172); and Dobbs-Allsopp, who also interprets them as precative perfects with the force of imperatives (*Lamentations*, 126–27). In *Lamentations*, 103–9, Provan translates the perfects as imperatives that make requests for the future. He argues (pp. 81–83) that to translate the verbs in the past tense would require them to refer back to some other unknown situation of distress from which the *Geber* had been delivered, since the imperatives in vv. 56, 59, and 63 would refer to the present situation of destruction of Jerusalem. This is not necessary, however, since the past tenses could refer to the destruction of Jerusalem and the experiences of Daughter Zion and the *Geber* in 1:1–3:19 before he finds redemption and hope in 3:20–41, and the imperatives to his desire for the exile to end, the enemy to be punished, and the continuing suffering to be over.

78. See Craig C. Broyles, *The Conflict of Faith and Experience in the Psalms: A Form-Critical and Theological Study* (JSOTSup 52; Sheffield: JSOT Press, 1989), 48.

It may be that the one praying has received an oracle, a sign, or a word from Yhwh that moves him or her from lament to confidence. The *Geber* is finally assured that Yhwh has redeemed his life and that he can trust God to ultimately bring justice to him and judgment to the enemy (vv. 58–66).

Summary

By the end of Lam 3 the implied author has poignantly depicted the corporate suffering of Daughter Zion, has shown the Speaker's transition from a judgmental attitude to an empathetic but helpless one, has depicted the *Geber* assuming a sense of individual culpability and responsibility, and shown him actively leading the community from within toward finding a resolution to their distress. The movement of the focus from the collective to the individual, and the subsequent establishment of the individual as leader of a collective voice, serves to draw the implied readers into the poem so that they also experience the insights and emotions of the personae.

From Individual to Community (Lam 4 and 5)

In Lam 4 and 5 individual voices recede and a communal voice of lament rises as the *Geber* leads the community to cry out to God corporately as he did individually. After the intensity of Lam 1–3, chapters 4 and 5 seem anticlimactic.[79] Daughter Zion's voice is no longer heard, and even the *Geber*'s voice is gradually overtaken by that of the community. This change in tone and style is appropriate, however, for Zion, the Speaker, and the *Geber* have accomplished their tasks. The community voice does not make for such vivid characterization and compelling dialogue, but in this passage the literary imagery of the first chapter transfers to everyday reality in the lives of the Judahite people and its purpose is achieved.

The *Geber*: Aftermath of Destruction (Lam 4:1–15)

Lamentations 4 consists of three sections that can be identified by the point of view expressed in them and their content. In verses 1–15 the

---

79. See O'Connor, *Tears of the World*, 58; Provan, *Lamentations*, 110; House, "Lamentations," 434.

Geber gives a third-person view of the aftermath of destruction, contrasting Jerusalem's current pathetic state with her former glory. The camera seems to draw back from a close up on the individual, the *Geber*, as the necessary transition back to a corporate emphasis on the community is begun. He describes a wide-angle view of the scene of destruction and famine, detailing the striking contrasts between her former prosperity and her present devastation.

The occasional reference to Zion and the "daughter of my people," combined with a smattering of feminine pronouns, recalls Daughter Zion from the first two chapters of the book, but now she does not speak. There is slippage in the metaphor, and the residual hints of her in the text suggest that she is losing her identity as an individual and merging with the population she once represented so vividly. This, and the switch of the *Geber* from first- to third-person speech, prepares the reader for the move from individual to corporate speech that follows.

The Community: Vain Help (Lam 4:16–20)

Here the people of Jerusalem recall the final days of the siege and the capture and deportation of the king. Whereas the *Geber* focused on the failure of the religious leaders, the priests and prophets, the community despondently remembers the failure of their political allies, perhaps from Egypt,[80] and leaders, including their own king, "the anointed one of Yhwh" (v. 20), on whom they had depended.[81] However, the only armies to arrive are those of the enemy.

The *Geber*: Justice (Lam 4:21–22)

The prospect is not all unqualified dreariness and defeat, however.[82] The *Geber*'s final contribution to the dialogue once again offers hope. Edom was a traditional enemy of the Israelites and, as such, personifies the enemy here;[83] however, having served as a disciplinary agent of Yhwh, she must now be held accountable for her own sins. The change in status is

80. House, "Lamentations," 446. See also Oded Lipschits, *The Fall and Rise of Jerusalem: Judah under Babylonian Rule* (Winona Lake, Ind.: Eisenbrauns, 2005), 78–79.

81. See House, "Lamentations," 448; Berlin, *Lamentations*, 112–13.

82. See House, "Lamentations," 434; Provan, *Lamentations*, 123.

83. Berlin, *Lamentations*, 113.

articulated fully in verse 22: Daughter Zion's sins have been paid for and her punishment will end; Daughter Edom's sins are now revealed and her punishment is about to begin.[84]

THE COMMUNITY LAMENTS (LAM 5:1–22)

Finally, in Lam 5, the community follows the lead of the *Geber* and turns to Yhwh in extended prayer, crying out for mercy and forgiveness. Paul House remarks, "There are no complementary or competing voices. Everyone wants the same thing."[85] This chapter is a variation on a communal lament, including most of the usual components.[86] The most significant missing element, of course, is the assurance of being heard—as many have noted, the voice of God is absent from this book.

Some components of true penitence are evident, however.[87] The people verbally confess their transgressions, "Woe to us, for we have sinned!" (v. 16). The people also acknowledge the need for repentance, for turning from evil to good: "Bring us back, O Yhwh, to you, and we will return" (v. 20).[88] A tone of submission and dependence on God indicated by the request, "Bring us back, O Yhwh," may also show a change in the inner affections, demonstrating a reliance on the mercy of God rather than their own self-righteous initiative.

The continuing silence of Yhwh may indicate, however, that their laments are not acceptable. This result can occur when the people continue in sin, when repentance is inadequate or insincere, when the option to repent has passed and the discipline must run its course, or, as the sup-

---

84. See Krašovec, "Source of Hope," 229–30.

85. House, "Lamentations," 456.

86. See Claus Westermann, *Praise and Lament in the Psalms* (trans. Keith R. Crim and Richard N. Soulen; Atlanta: John Knox, 1981), 52–70; Walter Brueggemann, *The Message of the Psalms: A Theological Commentary* (Minneapolis: Augsburg, 1984), 54–57. Cf. Ps 74.

87. Contra O'Connor, *Tears of the World*, 78–79. See Berlin, *Lamentations*, 116.

88. O'Connor's interpretation of this verse ("They ask for a turning around of God, for a conversion of God's heart back to them. They want God to turn from abandoning and rejecting them. And they themselves want to return to God.... But God's turning is what matters, for they have been turning to God throughout the book") is untenable based on the hiphil in the Hebrew השיבנו יהוה אליך, which implies that Yhwh is causing the people to turn back. In fact, O'Connor herself translates the verse: "Return us to yourself, YHWH, and we will return" (*Tears of the World*, 77).

plicants suggest, when Yhwh has totally rejected them. In these situations, lament serves only to express the pain of the discipline, not to avoid or alleviate it.[89] There is no way to know whether the community is truly repentant, and indeed the book ends on a very uncertain note: "For if you indeed reject us, you will be angry against us to excess" (v. 22).[90]

Summary

In Lam 4 the *Geber* leads the community to confront their own current helpless state, as he has done, and to return to God for aid; and in Lam 5 the people themselves finally cry out communally to Yhwh in prayer. Led by Daughter Zion, the suffering has been experienced and expressed; led by the Speaker, pity for Zion's miserable state has been evoked; and led by the *Geber*, the movement toward contrition, confession, and repentance has been initiated.

Conclusions

Through the structure and imagery of Lamentations, especially the voices of Daughter Zion, the Speaker, the *Geber,* and the suffering inhabit-ants, the implied author leads the implied readers to empathize with the anguish of the people, to accept responsibility for sin, to personalize the need for confession and redemption, and to participate in the religious life of the wider community as they seek to find a way forward. Significant here is the Daughter Zion metaphor complex itself, which evokes contrast-ing responses of both judgment and pity. Lamentations offers no facile answers or simplistic solutions, and Lam 3 is not so much the pinnacle of hope or the actualization of redemption as it is a watershed experience on the way toward hope and salvation. A primary purpose of Lamentations is to express and validate the suffering of Daughter Zion, in spite of her

---

89. See Mark J. Boda, " 'Uttering Precious Rather Than Worthless Words': Divine Patience and Impatience with Lament in Isaiah and Jeremiah," in *Lament: Israel's Cry to God* (ed. Mark J. Boda, Carol Dempsey, and LeAnn Snow Flesher; LHBOTS 552; London: Continuum, forthcoming).

90. For possible translations of this contentious verse, see House, "Lamentations," 453–54; Robert Gordis, "Conclusion of the Book of Lamentations (5:22)," *JBL* 93 (1974): 289–93; Tod Linafelt, "The Refusal of a Conclusion in the Book of Lamenta-tions," *JBL* 120 (2001): 340–43.

sin, as a personification of the Judahite people.[91] Too often Daughter Zion has been brushed off theologically, based on the view that she got what she deserved, but the essence of the multivalent Zion metaphor itself is to evoke *both* censure and sympathy in the reader. Mandolfo, however, in her effort to redress the balance, has tipped the scales in the opposite direction.

The overall movement of the book is from the corporate (the collective voice of Daughter Zion, and the Speaker's response to her) to the individual (the *Geber*) and back to the corporate (the community). The suffering of the people achieves its ultimate expression in the persona of Daughter Zion, who represents the physical city and its inhabitants; the Speaker empathizes with that suffering and evokes pity as well as judgment for the sinner, the individual *Geber* seeks a way through, forward, and back to Yhwh; and the broader exilic community, the Daughter Zion of Lam 4:22, is then led from within by the *Geber* along the first steps toward healing and reconciliation, although the ultimate realization of this goal remains in the future.

---

91. See Claus Westermann, *Lamentations: Issues and Interpretation* (trans. Charles Muenchow; Minneapolis: Fortress, 1994), 81, 86.

Yhwh as Jealous Husband:
Abusive Authoritarian or Passionate Protector?
A Reexamination of a Prophetic Image[*]

Brittany Kim

Analyzing Ezek 16 and 23, which express Yhwh's relationship with Jerusalem through the lens of the marriage metaphor, Carleen Mandolfo
describes the God depicted therein as "interested in little else than absolute domination," contending further that "with his wild mood swings
and blood lust, [he] seems nearly psychopathic."[1] Moreover, she finds
in these texts "extreme verbal abuse," vivid and even pornographic portraits of sexual violence, and a surprising absence of Jerusalem's voice,
resulting in a female city figure that is completely lacking in personality
and subjectivity.[2] Even in Isa 49–54, which appears to sound the note of
reconciliation between the divine husband and his estranged wife, Mandolfo claims that Yhwh "continue[s] to sidestep issues of divine culpability," rather than "explicitly admit[ting] that he failed in his duty as a
husband."[3] With these statements, Mandolfo expresses the reactions of
several feminist interpreters to the shocking and repugnant images generated by the prophetic use of the marriage metaphor in texts like Hos
1–3, Jer 2–3, and Ezek 16 and 23, leading these scholars to view Jerusalem

* This essay is a revised version of a paper presented to the Israelite Prophetic
Literature section at the annual meeting of the SBL in Atlanta in November 2010. I am
thankful for the insightful comments of Richard Schultz and the participants of the
biblical studies colloquium at Wheaton College on an earlier draft.
1. Carleen R. Mandolfo, *Daughter Zion Talks Back to the Prophets: A Dialogic Theology of the Book of Lamentations* (SemeiaSt 58; Atlanta: Society of Biblical Literature,
2007), 54, 50.
2. Ibid., 53, 50; cf. 47.
3. Ibid., 124.

as a helpless victim of domestic abuse and Yhwh as an abusive authoritarian. Like a domestic abuser, Linda Day argues, Yhwh is unreasonably jealous and possessive, engages in both verbal and physical abuse, blames the woman for provoking him, and exhibits a "dual personality" by showering the woman with gifts and affection when not overcome by rage.[4]

Judith Sanderson goes further and labels prophetic texts employing the marriage metaphor as dangerous, contending that "[t]o involve God in an image of sexual violence is, in a profound way, somehow to justify it and thereby to sanction it for human males who are for any reason angry with a woman."[5] After all, some feminist interpreters claim, identifying with the harlot Jerusalem is likely to prove intolerable for most

---

4. Linda Day, "Rhetoric and Domestic Violence in Ezekiel 16," *BibInt* 8 (2000): 205–30, here 218–24; cf. Renita J. Weems, *Battered Love: Marriage, Sex, and Violence in the Hebrew Prophets* (Minneapolis: Fortress, 1995), 73–78, 96–98; Julia M. O'Brien, *Challenging Prophetic Metaphor: Theology and Ideology in the Prophets* (Louisville: Westminster John Knox, 2008), 75; A. R. Pete Diamond and Kathleen M. O'Connor, "Unfaithful Passions: Coding Women Coding Men in Jeremiah 2–3 (4:2)," *BibInt* 4 (1996): 288–310, esp. 293, 310.

5. Judith E. Sanderson, "Nahum," in *Women's Bible Commentary* (ed. Carol A. Newsom and Sharon H. Ringe; rev. ed.; Louisville: Westminster John Knox, 1998), 236; cf. J. Cheryl Exum, "Prophetic Pornography," in idem, *Plotted, Shot, and Painted: Cultural Representations of Biblical Women* (JSOTSup 215; GCT 3; Sheffield: Sheffield Academic Press, 1996), 101–29, here 114; a slightly revised version of her earlier essay, "The Ethics of Biblical Violence against Women," in *The Bible in Ethics: The Second Sheffield Colloquium* (ed. John William Rogerson, Margaret Davies, and M. Daniel Carroll R.; JSOTSup 207; Sheffield: Sheffield Academic Press, 1995), 248–71, here 259–60; also Kathleen M. O'Connor, "Jeremiah," in Newsom and Ringe, *Women's Bible Commentary*, 178–86, esp. 181; Mary E. Shields, "An Abusive God? Identity and Power/Gender and Violence in Ezekiel 23," in *Postmodern Interpretations of the Bible: A Reader* (ed. A. K. M. Adam; St. Louis: Chalice, 2001), 129–51, esp. 146, 149–50; idem, "Multiple Exposures: Body Rhetoric and Gender Characterization in Ezekiel 16," *JFSR* 14 (1998): 5–18, esp. 18; Mandolfo, *Daughter Zion*, 125–26; Gale A. Yee, "Hosea," in Newsom and Ringe, *Women's Bible Commentary*, 207–15, who sees such a justification arising from forgetting "the metaphorical character of the biblical image"; on these texts' negative influence more generally, see Katheryn Pfisterer Darr, "Ezekiel's Justifications of God: Teaching Troubling Texts," *JSOT* 55 (1992): 97–117, esp. 115; Carol J. Dempsey, "The 'Whore' of Ezekiel 16: The Impact and Ramifications of Gender-Specific Metaphors in Light of Biblical Law and Divine Judgment," in *Gender and Law in the Hebrew Bible and the Ancient Near East* (ed. Victor H. Matthews, Bernard M. Levinson, and Tikva Frymer-Kensky; JSOTSup 262; Sheffield: Sheffield Academic Press, 1998), 57–78, esp. 77.

male readers, leading them to adopt instead the perspective of the "faithful husband."[6]

Other modern interpreters continue to follow the traditional (maledominated) approach to these texts, asserting that Jerusalem's punishment fits the crime and seeing Yhwh's violent response to the city as an outflowing of his love that aims to recapture Jerusalem's attention and cause her to turn back to him. To them, Yhwh is a passionate protector, who zealously seeks to restore Israel's life-giving relationship with him. These interpreters expect all readers, both male and female, to identify with the unfaithful wife.[7]

In large measure, these differences in interpretation derive from differences in interpretive approach. Before we even analyze the texts themselves, we are divided by our responses to such questions as: Should we read these texts in light of their near literary context, the book as a whole, and the canon, or should we analyze them by themselves? Should we read them with a prior assumption that they are authoritative or should we be open to critiquing them if we find their messages offensive or even dangerous? Should we try to discern, as well as we can, how the original audience might have understood these texts, that is, filling in the inevi-

---

6. Exum, "Prophetic Pornography," 123; Fokkelien van Dijk-Hemmes, "The Metaphorization of Woman in Prophetic Speech: An Analysis of Ezekiel 23," in *On Gendering Texts: Female and Male Voices in the Hebrew Bible* (ed. Athalya Brenner and van Dijk-Hemmes; BIS 1; 1993; repr., Leiden: Brill, 1996), 167–76, esp. 176; Shields, "Abusive God?" 150.

7. Daniel I. Block, *The Book of Ezekiel: Chapters 1–24* (NICOT; Grand Rapids: Eerdmans, 1997), 13–14, 467–70, 503–4; Moshe Greenberg, *Ezekiel 1–20: A New Translation with Introduction and Commentary* (AB 22; Garden City, N.Y.: Doubleday, 1983), 297–300, 305–6; Joseph Blenkinsopp, *Ezekiel* (IBC; Louisville: John Knox, 1990), 76–79; cf. the older commentaries by Walther Zimmerli, *Ezekiel: A Commentary on the Book of the Prophet Ezekiel* (trans. Ronald E. Clements; 2 vols.; Hermeneia; Philadelphia: Fortress, 1979–1983), 1:348–49; Walther Eichrodt, *Ezekiel: A Commentary* (trans. Cosslett Quin; OTL; Philadelphia: Westminster, 1970), 203–13. Other interpretive options exist, of course, and Sherwood's warning against viewing feminist biblical scholarship as homogeneous is well taken (Yvonne Sherwood, *The Prostitute and the Prophet: Hosea's Marriage in Literary-Theoretical Perspective* [JSOTSup 212; GCT 2; Sheffield: Sheffield Academic Press, 1996], 267–68; citing Alice Bach, "Reading Allowed: Feminist Biblical Criticism Approaching the Millennium," *CurBS* 1 [1993]: 191–215, here 192–93). I am not trying to set up a binary opposition but simply to lay out two well-supported and mutually exclusive readings to frame the discussion.

table gaps with assumptions culled from our knowledge of their literary and historical contexts? Or should we fill in the gaps with our own perspectives, reading the texts in line with our own cultural backgrounds or in whatever manner may be most useful for our current situation? In the midst of considerable hermeneutical debate, scholars on both sides can find themselves talking past one another with little hope that a sufficient bridge may be found to span the interpretive breach. My aim in this essay is simply to stimulate helpful dialogue by addressing the question: If the original audience could hear and understand the feminist critique[8] and even recognize the validity of some of its concerns, how might they respond to its interpretation of these passages?

In an effort to grasp how the original audience might have understood these texts (with a special emphasis on Ezek 16), I will examine them against their literary and historical-cultural background. Toward that end, I will first focus on the anthropopathic motif of divine jealousy through an analysis of the usage of the קנא root in the Hebrew Bible. Second, I will compare these prophetic texts with pentateuchal legislation concerning adultery and spousal jealousy in order to consider whether the divine response to Jerusalem's "adultery" legitimizes a similar human response. Finally, I will explore how the marriage metaphor functions rhetorically in the prophets.

DIVINE JEALOUSY

THE USE OF קנא IN THE HEBREW BIBLE

Although studies of the prophetic marriage metaphor frequently discuss the use of the Hebrew root קנא,[9] they rarely ask what exactly it means to say that Yhwh is "jealous" or to what extent Yhwh's jealousy is similar to that of humans.[10] Moreover, they often assume certain popular con-

---

8. For the purposes of this essay, "the feminist critique (or interpretation)" refers to the particular reading described above, which intersects with the concerns of many (though certainly not all) feminist interpreters of these texts.

9. קנא appears in the HB in verbal (piel [30x] and hiphil [4x]), nominal (קנאה [43x]), and adjectival forms (קנא [6x], קנוא [2x]).

10. In a 1979 article, Berg notes that there have been few in-depth discussions of Yhwh's jealousy (Werner Berg, "Die Eifersucht Gottes: Ein problematischer Zug des alttestamentlichen Gottesbildes?" *BZ* 23 [1979]: 197–211, here 197). This state-

notations of the English word that may or may not fit the biblical usage. Based on my own study of the relevant biblical texts, I contend that קנא may be classified into three primary categories: (1) envy (that is, the desire for a possession or quality belonging to another person),[11] (2) jealousy *of* another, and (3) jealousy *for/on behalf of* another. Only occurrences in the second and third categories are attributed to Yhwh and so necessitate further discussion.

Category 2: Jealousy of

While "jealousy" is often used in common parlance for cases of envy, I will define *jealousy of*[12] more narrowly as a three-party situation in which subject *S* desires to be favored (in a particular respect *P*) by person *O* (= object) but is concerned that *O* seems instead (or in cases of desired exclusivity, *O* seems also) to be favoring rival *R* in respect *P*.[13]

---

ment is not less applicable today. Aside from dictionary articles (e.g., H. G. L. Peels, "קנא," *NIDOTTE* 3:939), the only substantive study focused on Yhwh's jealousy that has appeared since Berg's article is Christoph Dohmen, "'Eifersüchtiger ist sein Name' (Exod 34:14): Ursprung und Bedeutung der alttestamentlichen Rede von Gottes Eifersucht," *TZ* 46 (1990): 289–304; though cf. K. Erik Thoennes, "A Biblical Theology of Godly Human Jealousy" (Ph.D. diss., Trinity Evangelical Divinity School, 2001).

11. This category includes eighteen uses of קנא: Gen 26:14; 30:1; 37:11; Job 5:2; Pss 37:1; 73:3; 106:16; Prov 3:31; 14:30; 23:17; 24:1, 19; Eccl 4:4; 9:6; Isa 11:13 (2x); Ezek 31:9; 35:11. A few of these are difficult to classify and may fit better into category 2 (jealousy *of*). The collocation piel קנא + preposition ב occurs only in this category (8x), though envy is also indicated by piel קנא + accusative object (with or without the direct object marker את, 3x) and the nominal form (6x). The collocation piel קנא + preposition ל is also used once for envy in Ps 106:16, which recounts how Korah, Dathan, Abiram, and their followers envied Moses and Aaron's position of status and authority over the community (cf. Num 16). Reuter suggests that ל is mistakenly used here instead of ב, noting that ל is elsewhere used with connotations of zeal (which corresponds to my category 3, jealousy *for*; Reuter, "קנא," *TDOT* 13:52–53).

12. Thirty-eight occurrences of the root fall into this category; human jealousy: Num 5:14 (4x), 15, 18, 25, 29, 30 (2x); Deut 32:21; Prov 6:34; 27:4; Song 8:6; divine jealousy: Exod 20:5; 34:14 (2x); Num 25:11 (2x); Deut 4:24; 5:9; 6:15; 29:19 [Eng. 20]; 32:16, 21; Josh 24:19; 1 Kgs 14:22; Pss 78:58; 79:5; Ezek 5:13; 8:3 (2x), 5; 16:38, 42; 23:25; Zeph 1:18; 3:8. Again, a few of these are difficult to classify. This category incorporates the broadest range of forms: the verb קנא in the piel (in both denominative, "to be jealous," and factitive, "to make jealous," senses) and hiphil (causative, "to make jealous"), the adjectives קַנָּא and קַנּוֹא, and the noun קִנְאָה.

13. This definition is similar in wording to the one given by Daniel Farrell, "Jeal-

Both in philosophical discussions of jealousy and in the Hebrew Bible, the paradigmatic case is sexual jealousy. The majority of references to human jealousy of another person occur in Num 5:11–31 (10x), a legal text discussing a case in which a husband (S) desires to be favored with sexual exclusivity on the part of his wife (O) but is concerned that she may also be having sexual relations with a rival (R, who is possibly unknown or even imagined). The husband's jealousy is here directed toward his wife (וקנא את־אשׁתו, v. 14), rather than toward the rival,[14] possibly since, as Aaron Ben-Ze'ev notes, "it is the mate who is shifting ... her preference to someone else."[15]

Yhwh's jealousy of Israel/Jerusalem appears most frequently in the Pentateuch (11x) and Ezekiel (7x).[16] Canonically the first reference is found in the Decalogue in the context of the commandment against idolatry (Exod 20:5; cf. Deut 5:9). Regardless of which of the texts depicting Yhwh's jealousy is the earliest and therefore potentially foundational for later occurrences,[17] the connection to idolatry portrayed in the Decalogue is clearly programmatic, appearing in almost every divine jealousy text.[18]

---

ousy," *Philosophical Review* 89 (1980): 527–59, esp. 530; cf. Robert C. Roberts, *Emotions: An Essay in Aid of Moral Psychology* (Cambridge: Cambridge University Press, 2003), 256–57.

14. Contra Peels, *NIDOTTE* 3:939; though Prov 6:32–35 describes a husband's fury and desire for revenge against the latter, cf. Reuter, *TDOT* 13:50.

15. Aaron Ben-Ze'ev, "Envy and Jealousy," *Canadian Journal of Philosophy* 20 (1990): 487–516, here 500; cf. Berg, "Eifersucht Gottes," 206.

16. Divine jealousy also occurs twice each in the historical books (Josh 24:19; 1 Kgs 14:22), Psalms (78:58; 79:5), and probably Zephaniah (1:18; 3:8; though these verses are difficult to categorize), for a total of twenty-four references.

17. Dohmen contends that Exod 34:14 is the earliest reference to Yhwh's jealousy in the HB and that the Decalogue is a further explication of it (Dohmen, "Eifersüchtiger ist sein Name," 297; cf. Reuter, *TDOT* 13:54).

18. Scholars debate whether the idols envisioned by the second commandment are images of Yhwh (so Mark E. Biddle, *Deuteronomy* [SHBC; Macon, Ga.: Smyth & Helwys, 2003], 108–9) and/or idols of other gods (so Brevard S. Childs, *The Book of Exodus* [OTL; Philadelphia: Westminster, 1974], 405). On the one hand, the latter is already addressed by the first commandment and so the second commandment would be somewhat redundant if understood as images of other gods. On the other hand, Yhwh's jealousy makes the most sense if understood in the context of other gods (Thomas B. Dozeman, *Commentary on Exodus* [Eerdmans Critical Commentary; Grand Rapids: Eerdmans, 2009], 482–83). Moreover, elsewhere in the HB, idolatry is almost always linked to worshipping other gods.

The basis for Yhwh's desire for (and expectation of) exclusive worship is the "covenant" (ברית), which is explicitly mentioned in about half of the eighteen divine jealousy passages. Although the context of the Exodus Decalogue contains no clear evidence of dependence on the marriage metaphor, it does depict the covenant as a similar kind of relationship.[19] Yet it offers a greater degree of subjectivity and privilege to Israel than ancient Israelite marriage practices often extended to wives. While the marriages of Israelite women were arranged for them by their fathers, Exod 19 portrays the Israelites choosing for themselves to enter into covenant with Yhwh (vv. 5–8). In the book's current form, the Decalogue functions as a response to this commitment, providing stipulations for the covenant (cf. Deut 5), which is ratified in Exod 24:3–8, again with the people's explicit agreement (v. 3).

Moreover, in the polygynous society of ancient Israel, sexual exclusivity was required only of wives; however, the covenant between Yhwh and Israel places expectations of exclusivity on both parties: Israel will be Yhwh's "treasured possession from among all the peoples" (Exod 19:5) and is called to worship Yhwh alone (20:3–5).[20] Deuteronomy 32:21 also suggests that expectations of exclusivity were mutual, stating that since Israel has made Yhwh jealous (piel קנא) with "No-god," Yhwh will respond with retributive justice by making them jealous (hiphil קנא)[21] with "No-people."[22] Despite Israel's rejection of him (vv. 15–18), Yhwh expects that

---

19. Cf. the link between marriage and covenant in Ezek 16:8 (Mandolfo, *Daughter Zion*, 47 n. 35).

20. Christopher Wright argues that the mutual exclusivity of the marriage metaphor in the prophetic texts indicates that monogamy was seen as the ideal in biblical thought, despite the common practice of polygyny ("Family," *ABD* 2:766). While Ezek 23 may seem to present a contrary perspective on Yhwh's exclusivity toward his people with its depiction of Yhwh's two wives, that passage is probably adapting the perspective of Deut 32, which focuses on the people of Israel as a whole, to reflect more clearly the situation of the divided monarchy (cf. Jer 3). For a compelling argument that Ezek 16 is a prophetic adaptation of Deut 32, see Jason Gile, "Ezekiel 16 and the Song of Moses: A Prophetic Transformation?" *JBL* 130 (2011): 87–108.

21. No distinction in meaning seems to exist between the piel and hiphil forms in this verse.

22. Cf. Deut 32:8–9: "the Most High … established the boundaries of the peoples according to the number of the sons of God. But the portion of Yhwh [here using the covenant name] is his people." Interestingly, despite the connotations of exclusivity, the primary metaphor in this context is not that of husband and wife but of parent and child (vv. 5–6, 18–20).

they still desire to receive his special favor and so will be jealous when he directs that favor toward another people.

Yhwh's claim to exclusive worship is predicated on his prior salvific action on Israel's behalf (cf. Exod 20:2). No other god has acted in Israel's history; only Yhwh has shown himself powerful, committed to Israel, and worthy of worship.[23] Furthermore, as Bernard Renaud points out, according to Israel's self-testimony, they are unique in that they were established as a nation at the same time as and for the express purpose of being established as the people of Yhwh.[24] Thus being the people of Yhwh is central to Israel's identity.

Yhwh's jealousy is explicitly linked to the marriage metaphor in only three texts.[25] Exodus 34:14–16 simply warns Israel against making covenants with the people of the land because their daughters "will whore after their gods with your sons."[26] The metaphor is much more prominent in Ezek 16, which describes how Yhwh found Jerusalem as an abandoned child, cared for her, and ultimately took her as his wife (vv. 1–14). Jerusalem, however, turned to other lovers, "whoring" (זנה, 21x!) after both idols and other nations. Ezekiel 23 focuses primarily on the "whoring" (זנה, 18x) of Jerusalem and Samaria after world powers, tracing their lewd behavior back to their early history of prostituting themselves to Egypt (vv. 19–21). In both texts Yhwh's jealousy, closely linked to his wrath and judgment (cf. 16:42; 23:25), prompts him to give his unfaithful wives over to their lovers for punishment (16:37–41; 23:22–29). Thus Yhwh's jealousy

---

23. Berg, "Eifersucht Gottes," 199–200.

24. Bernard Renaud, *Je suis un Dieu jaloux: Evolution sémantique et signification théologique de qine'ah* (Paris: Cerf, 1963), 67.

25. Surprisingly, the קנא root never occurs in Hosea or Jeremiah, where this metaphor plays a prominent role. While the absence of the word does not necessarily imply the absence of the concept, that Hosea and Jeremiah do not make use of the term is nonetheless significant. This analysis is focused on those passages that explicitly refer to Yhwh's jealousy, since they provide the strongest basis for defining the concept.

26. Dohmen sees this text as dependent on Hosea's use of the marriage metaphor to describe the relationship between Yhwh and Israel (Dohmen, "Eifersüchtiger ist sein Name," 297). See, however, Richtsje Abma, *Bonds of Love: Methodic Studies of Prophetic Texts with Marriage Imagery, Isaiah 50:1–3 and 54:1–10, Hosea 1–3, Jeremiah 2–3* (SSN 40; Assen: Van Gorcum, 1999), 4, who argues that זנה does not necessarily signify the marriage metaphor.

is in some sense an "affective acting and reacting" with respect to the faithfulness of his covenant people.[27]

Category 3: Jealousy for/on behalf of

Yhwh's *jealousy of*, however, is balanced by his *jealousy for*.[28] This final category of usage is the most difficult to define. Many of the occurrences in this category are frequently translated as "zeal." Yet if defined as "eagerness and ardent interest in pursuit of something,"[29] this meaning does not seem to go far enough in describing how the term is used, nor in connecting it with the other uses of the root. I contend that this category is best described as *jealousy for* or *on behalf of* another person, defined as a two- or three-party situation in which subject S is concerned that person or object O does not possess (or may lose to some personal or nonpersonal threat T) some possession or quality P (e.g., honor, well-being) that S thinks O should possess, leading S to perform action A on O's behalf.[30]

---

27. "[A]ffektives Agieren und Reagieren" (Dohmen, "Eifersüchtiger ist sein Name," 299).

28. This category includes twenty-nine uses of קָנָא; human jealousy: Num 11:29; 25:11, 13; 2 Sam 21:2; 1 Kgs 19:10 (2x), 14 (2x); 2 Kgs 10:16; Pss 69:10 (Eng. 9); 119:139; divine jealousy: 2 Kgs 19:31 (par. Isa 37:32); Isa 9:6 (Eng. 7); 26:11; 42:13; 59:17; 63:15; Ezek 36:5, 6; 38:19; 39:25; Joel 2:18; Nah 1:2; Zech 1:14 (2x); 8:2 (3x). On the verbal side, this category is marked by the distinctive piel קָנָא + preposition לְ, though the nominal form is also prominent. Also included are one occurrence of piel קָנָא + preposition אֵת (Num 25:11) and one of the adjective קַנּוֹא (Nah 1:2).

29. *Merriam-Webster's Collegiate Dictionary*, 11th ed., s.v. "zeal."

30. Although a number of philosophical essays and monographs seek to define and distinguish envy and jealousy *of* another person, I could find nothing dealing with this type of jealousy. Nevertheless, in biblical studies, there are a few hints in this direction. Thoennes offers two separate categories of human jealousy that use this terminology: "jealousy on behalf of God's honor" and "jealousy on behalf of another person." On the divine side, he also recognizes a category of "God's jealousy on behalf of his people," which occurs "when God is intensely concerned with, and takes action for, the well being [*sic*] of his people." Yet he does not explore this category more fully, since it does not accord with his formal definition of jealousy as "an ardent desire to maintain exclusive devotion within a relationship in the face of a challenge to that devotion." Thus he contends that the "more general definition of 'zeal'" is appropriate to these passages; however, in an appendix detailing the uses of קָנָא in the HB, he prefers the translation of "jealousy" to "zeal" for some of them (Thoennes, "Biblical Theology," 27, 26 n. 67, 368–73). John Oswalt contends that "Zeal and jealousy are two sides of the same concept.... [Jealousy's] better connotation depicts a consum-

Jealousy *for* is related to the pride we often feel in the possessions, qualities, or accomplishments of someone we are close to or associate ourselves
with. Like jealousy *of*, jealousy *for* O involves some kind of relationship
(real or imagined) between S and O. Yet in the latter case, what is threatened is not some aspect of that relationship (i.e., some particular favor
that S would like to receive from O) but rather something that relates to
O alone.

In the Hebrew Bible, humans are said to be *jealous for* both other
people and Yhwh. In Num 11:26–29 Joshua's concern that Moses (O) may
lose his unique status as a prophet (P) to the threat (T) of others who are
prophesying in the camp is described as jealousy for Moses (v. 29). The
paradigmatic example of jealousy for Yhwh occurs in Num 25—the Midi-
anites were drawing Israel into idolatrous worship of Baal of Peor, leading Phinehas to respond by killing Zimri and his Midianite wife, Cozbi.[31]
More frequently, however, Yhwh is the subject of this type of קנא.[32] His
jealousy for his people (Isa 26:11; and his land, which represents the
people, Joel 2:18; Zech 1:14; 8:2) expresses his concern that their well-
being or even survival is threatened by their adversaries. This leads him
to act either (1) by destroying their adversaries (sometimes described as

---

ing concern for the other's best and an unwillingness that anything should hurt or
destroy another" (*The Book of Isaiah: Chapters 1–39* [NICOT; Grand Rapids: Eerdmans, 1986], 248). Baruch Levine draws divine and human occurrences together on
the basis of the syntactic data, claiming that "*qinnē' l-* means: 'to express *qinʾāh* on
behalf of, on account of,'" though he translates *qinnē'* as "zeal, passion," and does not
define it further (*Numbers 21–36: A New Translation with Introduction and Commentary* [AB 4; New York: Doubleday, 2000], 289). Some of the modern English translations use "jealous for" in several of the relevant passages (e.g., ESV: Num 11:29; 25:13;
1 Kgs 19:10, 14; Ezek 39:25; Zech 1:14; 8:2).

31. Here Phinehas (S) is concerned that Yhwh (O) is losing the exclusive worship
he deserves (P) due to the threat (T) that the foreign wives have introduced into the
community with their worship of other gods. This leads Phinehas to remove the threat
he sees immediately before him by killing Zimri and Cozbi (A).

32. Interestingly, these occurrences emerge only in the prophetic literature,
with the sole exception of 2 Kgs 19:31, which reiterates Isa 37:32. Although there is
debate about whether this parallel section originated in Kings, in Isaiah, or as a separate source, the section seems more at home in Isaiah (cf. Christopher R. Seitz, *Zion's
Final Destiny* [Minneapolis: Fortress, 1991], 47–118). Since Yhwh's jealousy, leading to
action on Israel's behalf, occurs four other times in Isaiah and nowhere else in Kings,
this provides further evidence that the material fits better in Isaiah.

"his" adversaries) or (2) by restoring his peoples' fortunes (or in some cases by doing both).[33]

A final observation regarding the textual data is that Yhwh's jealousy *of* Israel and his jealousy *for* Israel are connected. Both are rooted in the covenant. As the Decalogue indicates, it is Yhwh's covenantal jealousy that leads him *both* to repay the iniquity of those who hate him *and* to pour out his steadfast love for countless generations of those who love him (Exod 20:5–6; Deut 5:9–10). His jealousy arises out of a concern to protect his relationship with Israel from threats both internal and external. When the threat is internal (e.g., idolatry), Yhwh is jealous *of* his people with regard to their worship of other gods. When the threat is external (e.g., Israel's enemies), he is jealous *for* his people with regard to their well-being. This jealousy *for* Israel, arising out of Yhwh's covenant love and promise, is unparalleled in the Hebrew Bible in cases of human marital jealousy.

Divine Jealousy and the Character of God

How does this analysis of the biblical portrayal of Yhwh's jealousy bear on its depiction of his character? In our contemporary culture, jealousy is generally viewed with suspicion if not outright disgust. Literature, film, and our own experiences of human relationships regularly remind us of the destructive power of jealousy.[34] Moreover, when looking at the biblical picture, passages like Ezek 16 and 23 testify that Yhwh's jealousy has a dark side, as portrayed by these texts' horrifically violent and explicit imagery. How might the original audience of these prophetic texts respond to modern condemnations of Yhwh's jealousy, as expressed, for example, by the claim of Mary Mills that it "implies a possessiveness which is far from healthy and which can stifle its object"?[35]

---

33. For example, when the priests cry out that Yhwh should spare his people from the threat of their enemies in Joel 2:17, the text states that Yhwh "became jealous for his land and took pity on his people," promising to send them good food, to take away their reproach, and to drive away their enemies (vv. 18–20).

34. Most recently, this has been brought to public attention by the haunting and disturbing music video for the song "Love the Way You Lie" by Eminem, who struggles with abusive tendencies, and Rihanna, a former victim of abuse in her tumultuous relationship with hip-hop artist Chris Brown.

35. Mary E. Mills, *Images of God in the Old Testament* (Collegeville, Minn.: Liturgical Press, 1998), 43.

First, the original audience might point out that the biblical portrayal of both divine and human jealousy is almost entirely positive, or at least morally neutral. Nowhere is jealousy condemned or viewed with suspicion.[36] Perhaps, however, this positive view of jealousy is simply a symptom of a patriarchal culture in which women were viewed as the property of their husbands. After all, the Hebrew Bible speaks only of the jealousy of men, never that of women.[37] If the original audience could recognize the power of the feminist critique of patriarchalism, would that change their perspective on Yhwh's jealousy?

In order to address this question, it may be helpful to take a look at the current philosophical debate. Despite the traditionally negative assessment of jealousy, several philosophers and ethicists have recently been developing a more positive view.[38] After all, as Peter Goldie points out, "occurrences of irrational or unjustifiable instances of jealousy are not sufficient to condemn jealousy outright as a type of emotion."[39] He argues further that it is not necessarily the case that the jealous person treats the object as a possession rather than as a person, since it may be that both parties have "mutually held *legitimate expectations* which do not involve treating the lover in an ethically unjustifiable way."[40] Certainly a marriage relationship in which both parties have pledged fidelity to each other entails a legitimate and (generally) mutually held expectation of sexual exclusivity. Even

---

36. Even Prov 6:32–34, which offers a warning about the destructive potential of jealousy, is directed toward the would-be adulterer and equates committing adultery with self-destruction.

37. The HB does, however, include at least one clear case of a wife experiencing jealousy according to the definition given above, though without employing the Hebrew root קנא: Leah is jealous with respect to Jacob's love for Rachel and, upon bearing his firstborn son, says, "now my husband will love me" (Gen 29:32). In the context of the polygynous culture, this is not exclusive sexual jealousy, but jealousy that Jacob is favoring Rachel with love instead of her.

38. For a defense of jealousy as a virtue, though based on an Aristotelian ethical framework that is in many ways foreign to the Bible, see Kristján Kristjánsson, *Justifying Emotions: Pride and Jealousy* (Routledge Studies in Ethics and Moral Theory 3; London: Routledge, 2002), 136–69.

39. Peter Goldie, *The Emotions: A Philosophical Exploration* (Oxford: Clarendon, 2000), 238.

40. Ibid., 237; for a different rejection of the necessary connection between jealousy and possessiveness, cf. Farrell, "Jealousy," 554–58; Kristjánsson, *Justifying Emotions*, 159.

those who are unfaithful often recognize that they have failed to fulfill their legitimate obligations toward their spouse.

Moreover, Ben-Ze'ev's definition of emotions may provide a helpful framework for conceptualizing jealousy: "Essentially, [emotions] are evaluative attitudes which reject or approve of a certain situation. Therefore, they have a motivational component which affects the desire to act accordingly."[41] Given the case of a wife's sexual infidelity (as in Num 5:11–31 and figuratively in Exod 34:14–16; Ezek 16 and 23), what sort of "evaluative attitude" on the part of the husband would be appropriate? I think most of us would agree that neither approval nor ambivalence would befit the husband; such reactions would probably lead us to question the depth of his love for and commitment to his wife.[42] In order to do justice to the value of the relationship, I would argue, the husband must reject the situation, and this attitude of rejection should be termed *jealousy*. (This understanding does not, however, justify all instances of jealousy, particularly those that are insufficiently provoked or disproportionate to the offense.)

This perspective seems to me to be in line with the understanding of jealousy reflected in the Hebrew Bible. In the patriarchal culture of the Hebrew Bible, there were undoubtedly unjustified cases of spousal jealousy involving a harmful possessiveness. Yet the evidence is not sufficient to conclude that such jealousy was the norm in biblical Israel nor that the Hebrew Bible's generally positive view of jealousy is dependent on its cultural framework of patriarchalism. Perhaps then the original audience would respond to modern feminist interpreters by saying that, for Yhwh, jealousy is an appropriate response to Israel's idolatry and may be justified on the basis of "mutually held *legitimate expectations*" of exclusivity. These expectations derive from Yhwh's covenant relationship with Israel, a relationship that Israel entered into voluntarily and that is in many ways reminiscent of a marriage.[43]

---

41. Ben-Ze'ev, "Envy and Jealousy," 498.

42. Cf. Goldie, *Emotions*, 240; David M. Buss, *The Dangerous Passion: Why Jealousy Is as Necessary as Love and Sex* (New York: Free Press, 2000), 47.

43. This view provides a context for understanding why the prophets equate disloyalty toward Yhwh with sin, an identification that Mandolfo calls into question (*Daughter Zion*, 76–77, 127–28).

Pentateuchal Legislation concerning Adultery and Spousal Jealousy

Even if jealousy is a justifiable response for Yhwh, however, that does not resolve the problem of his resultant angry action against Jerusalem. The biblical text itself may not emphasize the culpability of irrational and destructive jealousy, but human experience teaches that jealousy can have devastating effects on both subject and object when it is exaggerated or misguided. Surely, feminist interpreters argue, as Jerusalem's husband, Yhwh does not have the right to take matters into his own hands and punish her for her adulterous behavior.[44] Moreover, they express the further concern that this portrayal may encourage or at least legitimize human spousal abuse.

The Hebrew Bible, however, draws an important distinction between Yhwh and human husbands, as can be seen by a comparison of Ezek 16 with Num 5 and Deut 22:22–24. In Num 5, which addresses the case of a husband's suspicion that his wife has been unfaithful, the husband is instructed to take his wife to the priest, who makes an offering, gives the wife an innocuous potion to drink, and declares a curse. The matter is ultimately left to Yhwh to adjudicate by rendering the priest's curse effective or ineffective. The assumption is that only Yhwh is in a position to judge the woman, since no evidence of her misconduct has been found. Therefore, this law protects her from retribution on the part of her husband or the community.[45]

Deuteronomy 22:22–24 describes the cases of a married (v. 22) and a betrothed (vv. 23–24) woman caught in the act of adultery. In this text, both the woman and her adulterous partner are sentenced to death by stoning (v. 24; cf. Lev 20:10), a sentence typically executed by the community as a whole (as is suggested here by the fact that the punishment is enacted at the city gate).[46] Throughout these verses, the husband remains

---

44. See, e.g., Day, "Rhetoric," 222–23.

45. Jacob Milgrom, "Case of the Suspected Adulteress, Numbers 5:11–31: Redaction and Meaning," in *Women in the Hebrew Bible: A Reader* (ed. Alice Bach; New York: Routledge, 1991), 475–82, here 480; Herbert Chanan Brichto, "Case of the *Sōṭā* and a Reconsideration of Biblical 'Law,'" *HUCA* 46 (1975): 55–70, here 67.

46. See the immediately prior law concerning a wife guilty of fornication before her marriage in Deut 22:21; also Lev 20:2; 24:14, 16, 23; Num 15:36; Deut 13:10–11 (Eng. 9–10); 21:21. Deuteronomy 17:5–7 specifies that witnesses of a capital crime

entirely passive. Thus in neither Num 5 nor Deut 22 is a human husband permitted to take justice into his own hands and punish his wife.[47] Reading Ezek 16 and related texts against the background of Israel's legal traditions indicates that they would not have served to legitimize domestic abuse for ancient Israelite husbands, whose right of authority over their wives was limited by the law.[48]

These legal texts also suggest that Yhwh does not derive his authority to judge his unfaithful wife from his metaphorical role as her husband. The marriage metaphor has limits. As in all metaphors, there is both an *is* and an *is not*. Yhwh is like a human husband only in certain respects; when it comes to executing judgment, the metaphor breaks down. Thus the original audience might dispute the feminist interpretation by contending that, in Ezek 16 and related texts, Yhwh executes judgment against Jerusalem not because he is her husband, but because he is viewed as the supreme ruler and judge over all people, as is literally depicted in the case of the suspected adulteress in Num 5.

Rather than interpreting the prophetic marriage texts in light of Israel's legal tradition, Renita Weems reads in the other direction, contending that "[o]nly the marriage metaphor allowed audiences to glimpse the image of the impulsive volatile, ambivalent Hebrew man.... One gets the impression that ... considerable latitude was permitted husbands to avenge whatever damage adulterous wives might do to their honor and prestige."[49] Weems's approach, however, involves interpreting the clearer legal texts in

---

were to cast the first stones, followed by the rest of the community. Since the law requires at least two witnesses (cf. Deut 19:15), a woman could not be put to death on the basis of her husband's testimony alone.

47. Prov 6:32–35, mentioned above, does assume that an injured husband is likely to take vengeance against his rival. Here, however, we are concerned with the response of the husband toward his wife.

48. Cf. Tikva Frymer-Kensky, *In the Wake of the Goddesses: Women, Culture, and the Biblical Transformation of Pagan Myth* (New York: Free Press, 1992), 148–49, who mentions Num 5, as well as Deut 24:1–4, which permits a husband to divorce (but not to abuse) his wife if he finds in her ערות דבר ("something indecent," NIV; cf. ESV, NASB).

49. She does, however, cite Num 5 in an endnote, acknowledging that "measures were taken from time to time to protect wives from being falsely accused of adultery by jealous husbands" (*Battered Love*, 77, 141 n. 11); cf. Diamond and O'Connor, who adapt Mary Daly's oft-quoted maxim: "By making God a husband, it also elevates husbands to the role of God" (Diamond and O'Connor, "Unfaithful Passions," 309).

light of the more ambiguous prophetic texts and conflicts with the widely accepted cognitive linguistic theory of metaphor. According to this theory, in a metaphor characteristics of the source domain (in this case, associated commonplaces of ancient Israelite marriage) are mapped onto the target domain (here the relationship between Yhwh and Israel).[50] This process proceeds in a particular direction and is not reversible. For example, we tend to metaphorically conceptualize ideas as food ("half-baked ideas," "food for thought," "devouring a book"), but we do not turn the metaphor around and map our perceptions of ideas back onto the domain of food.[51] Similarly, we should not begin with the prophetic marriage texts and map all the characteristics of the relationship between Yhwh and Israel depicted therein back to the source domain of ancient Israelite marriage. Such a strategy is problematic, in part because the immediate context does not always clearly indicate where a metaphor begins and ends. Indeed, given the biblical authors' penchant for employing mixed metaphors,[52] readers should not assume that a metaphor evoked by certain verses underlies the whole of the passage.[53]

---

50. George Lakoff and Mark Turner, *More than Cool Reason: A Field Guide to Poetic Metaphor* (Chicago: University of Chicago Press, 1989), 38–39.

51. Zoltán Kövecses, *Metaphor: A Practical Introduction* (2nd ed.; New York: Oxford University Press, 2010), 7; cf. Hanne Løland, *Silent or Salient Gender? The Interpretation of Gendered God-Language in the Hebrew Bible, Exemplified in Isaiah 42, 46, and 49* (FAT 2/32; Tübingen: Mohr Siebeck, 2008), 35, 45–46. Some scholars assume that metaphors are bidirectional, following Max Black. Using the example, "man is a wolf," Black contends that while associated commonplaces of wolves filter and organize one's perception of man, "the metaphor [also] makes the wolf seem more human than he otherwise would" (Max Black, *Models and Metaphors: Studies in Language and Philosophy* [Ithaca, N.Y.: Cornell University Press, 1962], 44). Yet he never resolves the tension between his (unidirectional) image of filtering and his idea of a two-way interaction between tenor and vehicle (or in Black's terms, the principle and subsidiary subjects) by explaining *how* the vehicle is modified by the tenor (see Janet Martin Soskice, *Metaphor and Religious Language* [Oxford: Oxford University Press, 1985], 42).

52. Marc Zvi Brettler, "Incompatible Metaphors for Yнwн in Isaiah 40–66," *JSOT* 78 (1998): 97–120, here 118–20; Sarah J. Dille, *Mixing Metaphors: God as Mother and Father in Deutero-Isaiah* (JSOTSup 398; GCT 13; London: T&T Clark, 2004).

53. Responding to Fretheim's portrayal of God as at the same time husband and judge (Terence E. Fretheim, *God and World in the Old Testament: A Relational Theology of Creation* [Nashville: Abingdon, 2005], 160), Mandolfo questions, "isn't this image exactly the problem? Could such an image ever be a trope for a healthy rela-

Rhetorical Use of the Marriage Metaphor in the Prophets

In the context of ancient Israel, the marital relationship offered an ideal vehicle for depicting both the desired intimacy and the asymmetry of the relationship between Yhwh and Israel. Even if we reject the patriarchal background out of which the metaphor arose, that does not necessarily mean that we need to reject the metaphor itself. Ancient Israelite marriage may be an appropriate vehicle for understanding the relationship between a sovereign God and his people, even if we do not see it as a suitable model for human marriages today.[54] Moreover, narrative portrayals of patriarchy do not necessarily represent the ideal upon which the metaphor is based. The Hebrew Bible's "texts of terror"[55] may present sinful perversion of the cultural and religious norm, rather than the norm itself.[56]

Moreover, the marriage metaphor was not the only familial image used to depict Israel's rejection of Yhwh. They were also described as faithless and disobedient בנים ("children"), both in the plural, where the gender is ambiguous (Deut 32:5, 19, 20; Isa 1:2, 4; 30:1, 9; 63:8; Jer 3:14, 22; 4:22), and in the singular, where the male reference is explicit (Hos 13:13; Mal 1:6; note also the confusion between sg. and pl. in Hos 11:1, 10). Thus caution should be taken in asserting (following J. Cheryl Exum and Mandolfo) that the prophetic marriage metaphor signifies "an indictment of [the female] sex"[57] and results in "the divine [being] rendered male, while the female is aligned with sin."[58] As Robert Carroll argues, "If the biblical writers only used negative images of women and positive images of men, then I could see the force of the objections made by feminist readers of the

---

tionship? It does not seem too radical to observe that husbands should not be their wives' judges, they should be their partners!" (Mandolfo, *Daughter Zion*, 126). Yet her comment assumes that the prophetic marriage texts present a single metaphor of God as husband-judge, rather than two distinct metaphors interacting together to depict the complex reality of Yhwh's relationship with Israel.

54. Cf. J. Andrew Dearman, "The Family in the Old Testament," *Int* 52 (1998): 117–29, here 127.

55. Phyllis Trible, *Texts of Terror: Literary-Feminist Readings of Biblical Narratives* (OBT; Philadelphia: Fortress, 1984).

56. Cf. Daniel I. Block, "Marriage and Family in Ancient Israel," in *Marriage and Family in the Biblical World* (ed. Ken M. Campbell; Downers Grove, Ill.: InterVarsity Press, 2003), 33–102, here 41.

57. Exum, "Prophetic Pornography," 103; cf. 114.

58. Mandolfo, *Daughter Zion*, 32; cf. Yee, "Hosea," 207.

Bible. But that is not the case. The metaphorization processes represent negative *and* positive images both of women and men (as metaphors!)."[59]

Both Exum and Mandolfo discuss the male imagery for Israel in Jer 3:1–4:4, though following Mary Shields they argue that the passage exhibits a movement from female to male imagery that parallels its movement from condemnation to reconciliation.[60] As Shields herself notes, however, the rhetoric in this passage is complex. The text shifts back and forth between female (3:1–13 [or 14], 19–20) and male (3:14, 21–4:4) imagery, and its portrayal of Israel as sons is far from positive (cf. "faithless sons" in 3:14, 22).[61] Looking back to Jer 2, Mandolfo also observes that after describing the destruction of (male) Israel's land in verse 15, the text proclaims that this destruction "is what your [f.s.] forsaking YHWH your [f.s.] God is doing to you [f.s.]" (v. 17, Mandolfo's translation). Thus she contends that the female character of Jerusalem is blamed for what befalls male Israel.[62] Yet this statement overlooks the references to the overwhelming guilt of male Israel (both singular and plural) in verses 5–13. Therefore, the original audience might argue that just as the appalling portraits of Israel as faithless son(s) do not implicitly indict the male gender, neither do the prophetic texts utilizing the marriage metaphor contain a tacit indictment of the female gender.

In order to make that case, one would have to argue that the picture of Israel's lewd and adulterous behavior in these texts is intended to be understood as representative of women in general, an assumption made

---

59. Robert P. Carroll, "Desire under the Terebinths: On Pornographic Representation in the Prophets—a Response," in *A Feminist Companion to the Latter Prophets* (ed. Athalya Brenner; FCB 8; Sheffield: Sheffield Academic Press, 1995), 275–307, here 279; cf. 277–78, 288.

60. Exum, "Prophetic Pornography," 124; Mandolfo, *Daughter Zion*, 42–44.

61. Although Shields does argue that repentance is linked to the son metaphor (Mary E. Shields, "Circumcision of the Prostitute: Gender, Sexuality, and the Call to Repentance in Jeremiah 3:1–4:4," *BibInt* 3 [1995]: 61–74; cf. the fuller discussion in her published doctoral dissertation, Mary E. Shields, *Circumscribing the Prostitute: The Rhetorics of Intertexuality, Metaphor and Gender in Jeremiah 3.1–4.4* [JSOTSup 387; London: T&T Clark, 2004], esp. 133–35). The book of Isaiah demonstrates an opposite movement from the parent-sons metaphor to the marriage metaphor (on sons, see Isa 1:2–4; 30:1–9; 43:6; 45:11; 63:8 [which looks back to the past]; on wife, see 1:21; 50:1; 54:5–6; 57:3; 62:4–5). Again, the picture is somewhat complex, as both are used positively and both negatively, though on balance the marriage metaphor is more positive.

62. Mandolfo, *Daughter Zion*, 89.

by several feminist interpreters. For example, Exum takes issue with the perspective of Hos 1–3: "Given the carefully circumscribed social position of women in ancient Israel, it is hard to imagine a real woman getting away with such free and open behavior. I find it difficult therefore to see the bizarre exaggerated sexual appetite described here as anything other than a male fantasy of female desire."[63] The whole point of the prophetic rhetoric, however, is that Israel/Jerusalem's behavior is extraordinarily deviant. In the context of the prophetic critique, if the people of Israel are to be portrayed as Yhwh's wife, then they must be portrayed as the most villainous and disgusting wife that can be imagined. The prophetic rhetoric is not designed to engender in its audience the thought that Israel is like a woman and what vile creatures they are. Rather, the rhetoric is intended to shock its audience by depicting Israel as the kind of woman they have never seen the likes of (Ezek 16:16, 31–34).[64]

Finally, as Corinne Patton and others have pointed out, the judgment depicted in these texts is not simply a logical outflowing of the marriage metaphor. It is the historical realities of threatened or actualized military defeat at the hands of the Babylonians that prompt these descriptions of punishment.[65] With regard to Ezek 16, many have noted that the stoning of Jerusalem (v. 40) echoes the punishment for adultery in Deut 22:23–24, and some have tried to connect other aspects of the judgment in verses 37–41 to biblical and extrabiblical parallels dealing with adultery and divorce.[66] Peggy Day objects, however, that this does not account for the whole picture, particularly the role that Jerusalem's lovers play in executing the punishment, and thus argues instead that these verses depict the punishment for breaking the covenant. The involvement of the lovers then represents Jerusalem's defeat at the hands of foreign nations, as envisioned

---

63. Exum, "Prophetic Pornography," 104–5; cf. van Dijk-Hemmes, "Metaphorization of Woman," 175; Shields, "Abusive God?" 141; Sherwood, *Prostitute and Prophet*, 300; Diamond and O'Connor, "Unfaithful Passions," 309.

64. Cf. Block, *Ezekiel 1–24*, 469.

65. Corrine L. Patton, "'Should Our Sister Be Treated Like a Whore?': A Response to Feminist Critiques of Ezekiel 23," in *The Book of Ezekiel: Theological and Anthropological Perspectives* (ed. Margaret S. Odell and John T. Strong; SBLSymS 9; Atlanta: Society of Biblical Literature, 2000), 221–38, here 229.

66. E.g., Greenberg, *Ezekiel 1–20*, 286–87; Block, *Ezekiel 1–24*, 501–3. Note that the text itself describes the punishment as the judgment for adultery and murder (v. 38).

by the covenant curses.[67] Given this historical and religious background, the original audience might argue that viewing this text as a narrative of domestic abuse is too simplistic and does not account for its complex interaction between metaphor and reality.

CONCLUSION

Ezekiel 16 and related texts present a strong challenge to many modern interpreters who reject the patriarchal context out of which the prophetic marriage metaphor arose and are attuned to the tragic consequences of domestic abuse in the lives of so many women in our current society. Such concerns have prompted feminist readings that have opened our eyes again to the horrors of these texts, reminding us that we should be appalled and offended by them. If we are not, then perhaps we have become too comfortable with traditional interpretations and have not paid enough attention to the graphic and brutal imagery. These feminist readings have also helpfully asked about the texts' unspoken assumptions concerning gender and have considered how these assumptions might shape the minds of modern readers.

In the end, however, I do not think that the original Israelite audience would recognize their own texts in some of these readings. I think they might respond to the feminist critique by placing the prophetic marriage texts against the larger background of their religious heritage, legal traditions, and historical situation. Within this framework, they would likely present Yhwh as a God who is supremely concerned to preserve his covenantal relationship with his chosen people and so responds to threats from both inside (e.g., idolatry) and outside (e.g., foreign adversaries) the

---

67. Peggy L. Day, "Adulterous Jerusalem's Imagined Demise: Death of a Metaphor in Ezekiel xvi," *VT* 50 (2000): 285–309, here 303–8; idem, "The Bitch Had It Coming to Her: Rhetoric and Interpretation in Ezekiel 16," *BibInt* 8 (2000): 231–53, here 238–43. She may go too far, however, in failing to see any echoes of the adultery laws in these texts, arguing that that would involve taking literally what is meant metaphorically. It is true that Jerusalem is punished for metaphorical, not literal, adultery, yet the adultery metaphor may extend further than Day allows. Stoning, as the punishment for adultery, provides an appropriate metaphorical representation of the defeat of the city by foreign armies. In any case, Day's compelling argument provides an understanding of why Ezekiel's "rhetoric exceed[s] the demands of the law" against adultery and why Jerusalem is condemned for her sexual deviance, even though Yhwh sanctions the sexual violence perpetrated by her lovers (Mandolfo, *Daughter Zion*, 49).

covenantal community with the jealousy of a passionate protector and the authority of a divine judge, executing the terms of the covenant.

We must certainly acknowledge that the biblical text has been put to some horrific uses over the centuries—to support the bloody crusades of the Middle Ages and to justify the enslavement and barbarous treatment of one people group by another in the early history of the United States, to give just a couple of examples. Events like these should compel us to be vigilant and not allow such atrocities to be committed in the name of God and the Bible. Yet the original audience of the prophetic marriage texts would not have viewed these passages as providing justification for men to abuse their wives. Indeed, both male and female hearers would have been compelled to identify with the adulterous wife, not the faithful divine husband who is at the same time supreme God and judge.[68] This identification would have forcefully impressed on such hearers how reprehensible it would be to abandon the God with whom they had entered into a marriage-like relationship, challenging both men and women to respond in humble repentance, not domination.

---

68. Cf. Patton, "Should Our Sister," 232–38, who highlights the rhetorical power of this identification.

Zion's Plea that God See Her as She Sees Herself: Unanswered Prayer in Lamentations 1–2

John F. Hobbins

In *Daughter Zion Talks Back to the Prophets*, Carleen Mandolfo sets out to do what Harold Bloom refers to as a "strong misreading" in which "the mighty dead return," but "they return in our colors, and speaking in our voices."[1] With respect to Daughter Zion of the book of Lamentations or Eicha, Mandolfo succeeds in her intent. In her undoubtedly strong reading, Zion speaks in a voice of her devising, not Zion's own. Zion is put on stage, but Mandolfo dresses her up in a costume that suits our time and place, not hers.

The irreducible strength of Mandolfo's avowed misreading of biblical discourse, and of Lam 1–2 in particular, is that she puts her finger on precisely those areas in which the "religious episteme" of the Bible and the book of Lamentations[2] is in strident contradiction with our own. The

---

1. Carleen R. Mandolfo, *Daughter Zion Talks Back to the Prophets: A Dialogic Theology of the Book of Lamentations* (SemeiaSt 58; Atlanta: Society of Biblical Literature, 2007), 28 n. 49. The phrases in quotes are cited by Mandolfo from Harold Bloom, *The Anxiety of Influence: A Theory of Poetry* (New York: Oxford University Press, 1973), 141. Mandolfo's monograph is a breath of fresh air, a cogent attempt to grapple with issues biblical discourse presents to the modern reader. Nonetheless, I will not downplay my disagreements in this essay. I have seen Mandolfo in action at SBL meetings. I know she delights in spirited debate. Furthermore, I was taught by more than one teacher that frankness is the ultimate sign of respect. Disagreement is offered in that spirit. Throughout this article, translations from the Hebrew, ancient and modern, are my own.

2. Following Kwok Pui-Lan, Mandolfo avers (*Daughter Zion*, 77 n. 38) that postcolonial readings of the Bible must take care not to leave the Bible's "religious episteme intact." Mandolfo is quoting Kwok, *Postcolonial Imagination and Feminist Theology* (Louisville: Westminster John Knox, 2005), 139–40. (Note that Kwok Pui-Lan in the

contradictions are deep and wide. Most of us, regardless of location on the current continuum—radical, liberal, conservative, uncommitted—need the sharp analysis of a relentless critic for it to hit home. Mandolfo speaks from a radical perspective, that of postcolonial criticism. Feminist and postfeminist theories are central to her reflection. Her hermeneutic, broadly speaking, is Bakhtinian. In this essay, I speak from an opposing viewpoint. I seek to enable the return of Zion in her own colors. I fight to allow her to speak in her own voice—not mine, not Mandolfo's, but hers.

The case can be made that Bakhtinian hermeneutics does not protect a text or the authors of a text from the violence of its readers (in Bakhtin's scheme, coauthors). To the extent that Mandolfo follows Bakhtin, not only is the vision of the author(s) of Lamentations submerged in her coauthoring "surplus of vision" (Barbara Green's terminology) but also the perspective of Zion herself. The promise and peril of the "surplus of vision" is that the vision allows the interpreter, according to Green, to "see some facets of the others that they cannot see of themselves."[3] The super-vision of which the Bakhtinian hermeneut goes proud is also a type of *supervision* by which she maintains control. The fundamental persona of Lam 1–2, a city personified as a widow whose loss is limitless, is suppressed by Mandolfo in favor of another persona, an avowedly strong reader, *herself*. The terms of this suppression are discussed below.

Zion's prayer in Lam 1–2 is that God[4] see her as she sees herself. She makes her request with insistence, four times: 1:9, 11, 20; 2:20. In the economy of the book, her prayer goes *unanswered*. Those who await her salvation, the fulfillment of the promises that regard her, have wept for and with Zion ever since.[5] So long as she remains a shadow of her promised self, a

---

bibliography and author index of *Daughter Zion* correctly shows up under Kwok, her "last name" by Western reckoning.)

3. Barbara Green, *Mikhail Bakhtin and Biblical Scholarship: An Introduction* (SemeiaSt 38; Atlanta: Society of Biblical Literature, 2000), 41, and passim; quoted by Mandolfo, *Daughter Zion*, 18 n. 31.

4. "God," not "god," is the right diction from the point of view of the author(s) of Lam 1–2 and of the persona Zion in the poems. Mandolfo is right to note that Zion shared "the patriarchal, monotheistic, retributive worldview" of the biblical prophets (*Daughter Zion*, 83). Zion's protest is inscribed within that worldview. But then the gravity of Zion's plaint is diminished if it is "god" she challenges. She challenges "God," the one who gives and takes away, the arbiter of her future, her Lord.

5. The vitality of this tradition has been underscored by William S. Morrow, "The Revival of Lament in Medieval Piyyuṭīm," in *Lamentations in Ancient and Contempo-*

wineglass is broken in her honor at Jewish weddings the world over, by the groom on the most joyous day of his life and that of his bride.

Jesus wept over her (Luke 19:41–44). Paul expected that the Deliverer would come from her (Rom 11:26–27). Christians since, with few exceptions, have abandoned her. They have widowed her all over again, literally and figuratively.

Some people weep with her and for her still, and some have, literally and figuratively, repopulated her. Those who see themselves as her alter ego, who have suffered as she has, have always had a stake in seeing her as she sees herself in Lam 1–2.

Zion is a *populated* place, in more ways than one, not just a persona. Whenever Zion is treated as a nonentity, she is the target of violence all over again. Zion *continues* to exist between Lam 1–2 on the one hand and Isa 1:21–26 and 2:2–5 on the other.

Zion is also, I dare say, the little shepherd girl of which Dahlia Ravikovitch has spoken in "Hovering at a Low Altitude."[6] After providing a translation, the poem in Hebrew follows.

> I am not there.
> I'm on the fissures of eastern mountains
> dappled with patches of ice
> in a place where grass doesn't sprout
> and a broad shadow is released on the slope.
>
> A little shepherd girl with a herd of goats
> —black ones—

---

rary Cultural Contexts (ed. Nancy C. Lee and Carleen Mandolfo; SBLSymS 43; Atlanta: Society of Biblical Literature, 2008), 139–50; idem, *Protest against God: The Eclipse of a Biblical Tradition* (Hebrew Bible Monographs 4: Sheffield: Sheffield Phoenix, 2006). Tod Linafelt exemplifies it in *Surviving Lamentations: Catastrophe, Lament, and Protest in the Afterlife of a Biblical Book* (Chicago: University of Chicago Press, 2000). The "canonical" tradition of lament for and with Zion is often overlooked. Cf. Joseph B. Soloveitchik, קינות מסורת הרב *Eicha, Kinot, Tefilot for Tisha b'Av: The Complete Tisha b'Av Service with Commentary by Joseph B. Soloveitchik* (bilingual Hebrew/English ed.; ed. Simon Poser; trans. of *Kinot*: Tzvi Hersh Weinreb and Binyamin Shalom; trans. of *Tefilot*: Jonathan Sacks; Jerusalem: Koren, 2010).

6. For another translation, see Dahlia Ravikovitch, *Hovering at a Low Altitude: The Collected Poetry* (trans. Chana Bloch and Chana Kronfeld; New York: Norton, 2009), 174–76; I thank Jonathan Paradise for help in refining my translation.

burst forth there
from an unseen tent,
she won't bring her day to a close, that girl,
in the pasture.
…

The little girl rose early just so, to stand guard in the pasture.
Her neck is not outstretched,
her eyes are not lined with kohl, not done up with mascara,
she doesn't ask, "From whence cometh my help?"

I am not there;
I've been in the mountains for a long time already;
the light will not scorch me. *Me* the frost will not touch.

Nothing any more is able to batter me with amazement.
Worse things than these I've seen in my life.

I gather up my dress and hover
very close to the ground.
What was she thinking, that girl?
Wild in appearance, unwashed,
for a moment she bends down, knees flexed.

Her cheeks soft like silk,
frostbite on the back of her hand,
distracted in thought, seemingly,
intent, is the truth of it.
She still has a few hours left.

I don't mull the situation over.
My thoughts cushion me with a cushion of down.
I've found a very simple method,
not a foot-breadth away, not moving a wing,
I hover at low altitude.

Even so, while the midday stretched on,
many hours
after sunrise,

that man went up the mountain,
a simple mountain climber.
The girl is very close to him,
no one is there except them.
If she tried to hide, or cry out—
there was no place of refuge in the mountains.

I am not here.
I'm on top of precipices
of savage, awesome mountains
in the extremities of the East.
A matter on which there is no need to elaborate.
It's possible with a hard twirl
and a hovering motion
to circle with the speed of the wind.
It's possible to get away and reassure myself:
I didn't see a thing.
…

But the little one, her eyes
just bulged from their sockets
her palate dry as a potsherd,
when a hard hand held her hair tight
and gripped her
without a shred of pity.

אֲנִי לֹא כָּאן
אֲנִי עַל־נְקִיקֵי הָרִים מִזְרָחִיִּים
מְנוּמָּרִים פִּסּוֹת שֶׁל קֶרַח
בִּמְקוֹם שֶׁעֵשֶׂב לֹא צָמַח
וְצֵל רָחָב נָטוּשׁ עַל־הַמּוֹרָד

רוֹעָה קְטַנָּה עִם־צֹאן עִזִּים
שְׁחוֹרוֹת
הֵגִיחָה שָׁם
מֵאֹהֶל לֹא נִרְאָה
לֹא תוֹצִיא אֶת־יוֹמָהּ הַיַּלְדָּה הַזֹּאת
בְּמִרְעֶה

וְהַקְּטַנָּה הַשְּׁכִּימָה כֹּה לָקוּם אֶל־הַמִּרְעֶה
גְּרוֹנָהּ אֵינוֹ נָטוּי
עֵינֶיהָ לֹא קְרוּעוֹת בַּפּוּךְ, לֹא מְשַׂקְרוֹת
אָנָה שׁוֹאֶלֶת, מֵאַיִן יָבוֹא עֶזְרִי

אֲנִי לֹא כָּאן
אֲנִי כְּבָר בֶּהָרִים יָמִים רַבִּים
אוֹר לֹא יִצְרְבֵנִי. הַכְּפוֹר בִּי לֹא יִגַּע.

שׁוּב אֵין לִי מַה לְלַקּוֹת בְּתַדְהֵמָה.
דְּבָרִים גְּרוּעִים מֵאֵלֶּה רָאִיתִי בְּחַיַּי.

אֲנִי אוֹסֶפֶת שִׂמְלָתִי וּמְרַחֶפֶת
סָמוּךְ מְאֹד אֶל־הַקַּרְקַע.
מַה הִיא חָשְׁבָה לָהּ הַיַּלְדָּה הַזֹּאת?
פְּרָאִית לְמַרְאֶה, לֹא רְחוּצָה
לְרֶגַע מִשְׁתּוֹפֶפֶת בִּכְרִיעָה.

לְחָיֶיהָ רַכָּה כְּמֶשִׁי
פִּצְעֵי קוֹר עַל־גַּב יָדָהּ,
פְּזוּרַת דַּעַת כְּבִיכוֹל
קְשׁוּבָה לַאֲמִתּוֹ שֶׁל דָּבָר.
וְעוֹד נוֹתְרוּ לָהּ כָּךְ וְכָךְ שָׁעוֹת.
אֲנִי לֹא בְּעִנְיָן הַזֶּה הִגַּעְתִּי.
מַחְשְׁבוֹתַי רְפָדוּנִי בִּרְפִידָה שֶׁל מוֹךְ
מְצָאתִי לִי שִׁיטָה פְּשׁוּטָה מְאֹד,
לֹא מִדְרַךְ כַּף רֶגֶל וְלֹא מָעוֹף
רְחִיפָה בְּגוֹבַהּ נָמוּךְ

אֲבָל בִּנְטוֹת צָהֳרַיִם
שָׁעוֹת רַבּוֹת
לְאַחַר הַזְּרִיחָה
עָלָה הָאִישׁ הַהוּא בָּהָר
כִּמְטֻפָּס לְפִי תֻמּוֹ.
וְהַיַּלְדָּה קְרוֹבָה אֵלָיו מְאֹד
וְאֵין אִישׁ זוּלָתָם.
וְאִם נִסְּתָה לְהִתְחַבֵּא אוֹ צָעֲקָה
אֵין מִסְתּוֹר בֶּהָרִים.

אֲנִי לֹא כָּאן
אֲנִי מַעַל רִכְסֵי הָרִים
פְּרוּעִים וְאָיֻמִּים
בְּפַאֲתֵי מִזְרָח.
עָנָן שֶׁאֵין צְרִיכִים לְהִתְעַכֵּב עָלָיו.
אֶפְשָׁר בְּטַלְטֵלָה עַזָּה
וּבִרְחִיפָה
לָחוּג בִּמְהִירוּת הָרוּחַ.
אֶפְשָׁר לְהִסְתַּלֵּק וּלְדַבֵּר עַל־לֵב עַצְמִי:
אֲנִי דָּבָר לֹא רָאִיתִי.

וְהַקְּטַנָּה עֵינֶיהָ
רַק חָרְגוּ מֵחוֹרֵיהֶן
חִכָּה יָבֵשׁ כַּחֶרֶס,
כְּשֶׁיָּד קָשָׁה לָפְתָה אֶת־שְׂעָרָהּ
וְאָחֲזָה בָּהּ
לְלֹא קוֹרְטוֹב חֶמְלָה
כל השירים עד כה , עמ' 221–219

The eastern mountains of which the poem speaks are those of Nepal, a hip vacation destination of young Israelis. I reapply the figure of the shepherd girl to Zion of Lam 1–2; Isa 2:2–5; 14:32. The primary reference in the poem is to the Palestinian people.

THE UNSPEAKABLE TRUTH ABOUT ZION

The problem with a method of interpretation that seeks to return the mighty dead and endow them with our voices is that the voices of the dead are thereby squelched. The distinction between the voices of the dead and our voices is lost. In the case at hand, Mandolfo effectively devoices Zion insofar as Zion's self-understanding contradicts the postcolonial perspective she adopts. This plays itself out in her suggestion that in Lam 1:18, "Zion is not admitting to 'rebellion' at all"[7]:

Yhwh is in the right,	צדיק הוא יהוה
for I defied his word.	כי פיהו מריתי

---

7. Mandolfo, *Daughter Zion*, 93.

According to Mandolfo, "Lexical, grammatical, and contextual factors converge to suggest a[n] ... ironic intent."[8] That is far from clear: the reading assumes that Zion's quoted words were intended to contradict her own elsewhere (1:14, 22) and the words of the voice that introduces hers (1:5, 14). That does not seem likely.

Furthermore, the enormity of Zion's complaint is *diminished* by suppressing Zion's confession that (a) Yhwh is righteous, and (b) she is guilty. Since (c) the punishment she bears is unbearable, it is (d) God's righteousness that is unbearable.[9] The startling conclusion cannot be drawn if premises (a) and (b) are suppressed.

In place of Zion's self-recrimination in Lam 1:18, a sovereign and responsible act that empowers her as she challenges the maker of her destiny, Mandolfo claims that Zion maintains her innocence.[10] But the implausibility of a claim of innocence from a polis is fierce. Prouder and greater ancient cities may have pled innocence or privilege, from Babylon to Tyre. Nonetheless, a metropolis not built on bloodshed and oppression is unbelievable (Isa 1:21–23; Hab 2:12). In Lam 1–2 Zion does not pretend otherwise.

Zion's self-recrimination matters. The discovery of Luther, that the subject before God (*coram Deo*) is simultaneously in the right and in the wrong (*simul iustus et peccator*), remains beyond the grasp of self-understanding that begins and ends with awareness of being a victim. Zion, a figure in which the political is personal, is a Lutheran subject *ante litteram*.

---

8. Mandolfo, *Daughter Zion*, 93–94. See further Nancy C. Lee, *The Singers of Lamentations: Cities under Siege, from Ur to Jerusalem to Sarajevo* (BIS 60; Leiden: Brill, 2002), 132–34. Lee calls the confession "sarcastic." So far as I know, Mandolfo and Lee are alone in thinking that Zion's confession is not genuine.

9. The watchword of victimism: "you are the cause of all my problems," an improvement over Carl Rogers's mantra, "I'm okay, you're okay." A more discerning mantra is: "I'm not okay, you're not okay, we are still going to get through this." Zion, I suggest, pushes for a resolution on that basis. But her plea to God is met with silence. That is the peerless achievement of the book of Lamentations: the silence of God is reported and *never* justified.

10. Mandolfo (*Daughter Zion*, 18) seeks "to avoid the mistake of dismissing out of hand God's assessment of Zion simply because it is not her assessment. In light of their long history together, YHWH has a surplus of vision with regard to daughter Zion that positions him advantageously to assess her." But it is "their long history together" that underlies Zion's assessment of Yhwh in Lam 1:18, and Zion's corresponding self-assessment.

The Zion of Lam 1–2 does not converse with Mandolfo's mutable, all-accepting God,[11] but confronts a God understood to kill and bring to life. Zion's political and personal identity is *constituted* in that confrontation.

The reality Zion grapples with is that, as she sees it, her crimes called forth punishment beyond her ability to bear. She responds, not by denying her culpability, but by asking God to be moved by her desolation. The voice that introduces hers talks back to the prophets, as Mandolfo would have us understand Zion to do. But that voice talks back to the prophets of Zion because they *failed* to do what Jeremiah and Ezekiel did: they did not expose her iniquity (Lam 2:14). There are no textual clues that suggest that readers are to understand Zion and the voice that contextualizes her speech to be in conflict.

Yhwh is in the right, according to Zion, in the following sense. She defied his word. Zion does not defy her Lord yet again by invoking privilege or pretending otherwise. Her punishment is nonetheless unbearable, and she will not cease in her protest to that effect.

As Zion sees it, the consequences of her transgression dwarf beyond all reckoning the transgression itself. The consequences amount to nothing less than a descent into hell.

That descents into hell occur is carved into the bedrock of existence. Never once is it suggested, in the Law, the Prophets, or anywhere else, that it is inappropriate to scream bloody murder to God when one's life and health are compromised. On the contrary, the task of the believer is to advocate on one's own behalf and on behalf of others to God's face in the teeth of distress, regardless of the degree to which the distress is one's own fault or the fault of the person on whose behalf one intercedes. Zion is not out of line in her protest. She is doing what she thought God expected her to do.

"She weeps and weeps in the night, her cheek wet with tears. Not one of all her friends comforts her" (1:2). Not one.

Nor does it end there. The faithful interpreter of Zion's plaint must stand between her and the one who would comfort her. She had irreduc-

---

11. Ibid., 20. See further idem, "Talking Back: The Perseverance of Justice in Lamentations," in *Lamentations in Ancient and Contemporary Cultural Contexts* (ed. Nancy C. Lee and Carleen Mandolfo; SBLSymS 43; Atlanta: Society of Biblical Literature, 2008), 47–56, here 56.

ible cause to be inconsolable. The "struggle to find better responses to her suffering"[12] is to be resisted.

Precisely because the book of Lamentations forgoes "better" responses, it speaks like no other to the despairing heart of the sufferer whose integrity is violated by every attempt to console her. It is only in the context of a material reversal of her situation—presupposed, for example, in Isa 1:27–28; 34–35; and 40–66—that a better response has a place.

Reversal, renewal, reversal again: Not only then but now, Zion cannot be comforted. The endless sense of loss of the heirs of Zion calls to mind a further difficulty I have already touched on, one that nips at the heels of a great deal of interpretation of the book of Eicha: *the bracketing out* of Zion, the mourners of Zion, and Zionism, historically considered, in engagement with the text. The bracketing out is inexcusable.

Almost without exception, modern interpreters of Lamentations are party to the suppression of the community of reception through whom the book of Lamentations reaches us: the Jewish people. If they know something about the Zionism of the Jewish people, one of the most powerful forces in its history, a sign spoken against in the world today, most modern interpreters hide it from their readers.

Nonetheless, "Zion and weeping" have not ceased to flow together, especially on Tishah-b'Ab. A terrible consequence: every day ploughshares are traded in for swords. The productivity of the collocation remains beyond the pale of most academic treatments of Zion. *Sehnsucht* for Zion to which the promises attach is nonetheless evoked by Yehuda Amichai, in "Jerusalem Is Full of Used Jews."[13]

> Jerusalem brims with Jews
> worn out by history,
> second-hand Jews,

---

12. Mandolfo, *Daughter Zion*, 124. I agree that "Some suffering, what [Wendy] Farley calls 'radical suffering,' is both guiltless and simply too great to be justified by Christianity's expiatory and eschatological understanding of history" (Mandolfo, *Daughter Zion*, 126). Nonetheless, Zion's suffering is of another type. It is not guiltless. It is like the suffering that ensues when a parent drives intoxicated and kills her own children in a car accident.

13. For another translation, by Chana Bloch, see Yehuda Amichai, *Poems of Jerusalem and Love Poems: A Bilingual Edition* (Riverdale-on-Hudson: Sheep Meadow Press, 1992), 109.

gently used, great values.
And the eye stands watch for Zion all the time.
And all the eyes
of the living and the dead
are cracked like eggs
on the lip of the bowl, to make the city
rich and fat and fluffy.

Jerusalem is filled with tired Jews;
they are whipped incessantly
for days of remembrance and recurrence
like dancing bears on aching legs.

What does Jerusalem require?
She doesn't need a mayor,
she needs a ringmaster, with whip in hand,
to tame prophecies, to train prophets to gallop
around and around in a circle,
to teach her stones to arrange themselves
in a bold, audacious pattern for the grand finale.

Thereafter they spring down, on the ground,
to the sound of applause and wars.

And the eye stands watch for Zion, and weeps.

Modern ex≈egesis skillfully elides Jewish exegesis of Zion.[14] The over≈sight prolongs a history of oppression and a teaching of contempt that has characterized non-Jewish exegesis from time immemorial.[15] But

---

14. The symbol ≈ identifies instances of double entendre for the reader.

15. It would be churlish to suggest that Amichai the author; Zion, a persona and a place; and the Jews of whom he speaks, are not actual, in art and in life. It is likewise the case that Eicha is a document whose authors and personae are alive to this day. When this is forgotten, the contradictions in which the parties are entangled go forgotten as well. In the name of something they desire more than life, those who weep for Zion cause suffering to others, as people have always done, from John Brown to Ariel Sharon to Osama bin Laden. Authors of Zion, like Zion herself, are not guiltless. I am not charging anyone in particular with being a cog of structural anti-Semitism. I

ex≈egesis on behalf of Zion lives on. It blooms with every spring. Today no less than yesterday, there are those who mourn with and for Zion. The eye stands watch for Zion, and weeps.

The lament voiced in Eicha is an unquenchable fire.[16] The same lament, *not another*, finds expression in *Eicha Rabbah*, the *Kinot* and *Tefilot* of Tishah-b'Ab, the poetry of Nahman Bialik, and beyond. On the basis of what understanding of justice does one comment on Eicha without plumbing the tradition of lament the book has nourished through the ages? In Mandolfo's presentation, the place that tradition might have had is dis≈placed by engagement with feminist and postfeminist theory.[17] Without wishing to downplay the gain, the loss is irreparable.

---

am pointing to a history and a practice that coauthors us all, a history and a practice that deserves to be denounced.

16. Mandolfo (*Daughter Zion*, 83) is cognizant of Jewish tradition, but she sidesteps sustained engagement with it. Her adopted point of view is inimical to the pivotal concepts of that tradition: *monotheism*, in which the world is thought of in monological terms; a *hierarchical* understanding of the relationship of God and believer, who is constituted in an a priori "you"-plural addressee called into existence by that same Sustainer of all that is and Principle of *retributive* justice. In the entire arc of modernity, orthodox Jewish tradition has remained homeless. Said tradition has no place to rest its head in Mandolfo's *Republic* either. Instead, Mandolfo promotes a reading of the twenty-fourth *petichta* of *Eicha Rabbah* that de≈liberately transcends its terms. Justice on this reading is a zero-sum game that consists of shifting the blame from humanity onto God. The orthodox Jewish answer, in accord with the witness of the Tanak, is another: protest in the teeth of God's justice and confession of sin go hand in hand. The post-Holocaust theology of Eliezer Berkovits, the single example Mandolfo (*Daughter Zion*, 124) voices, is rigorous in its development of an explanation of divine withdrawal that prescinds from an affirmation of human culpability (*Faith after the Holocaust* [New York: Ktav, 1973]). In contrast to the language of the siddur, Berkovits's defense of God's justice in the aftermath of the Holocaust shies away, in the midst of unrelenting loss, from self-recrimination. The tension with tradition is enormous. Nonetheless, Berkovits's defense of holy unbelief is confident enough to allow for a concomitant defense of holy *belief*. Berkovits's monograph is misunderstood unless it is heard against the background of the siddur. It is not a replacement thereof.

17. Critical feminist theory has plenty to offer. It stands to be enriched by engagement with a voice like that of Zion in Lam 1–2, precisely because that voice is *radically other* vis-à-vis modern feminism. In place of that engagement, Mandolfo conflates her voice with the voice of Zion.

ZION THROUGH THE LOOKING GLASS

This is the dilemma that the interpreter of Eicha overlooks at her peril: Zion will be consoled if and only if her chosen partner-in-dialogue, the one she simply and nakedly calls *my Lord* and *Yhwh*, sees her as she sees herself. If Yhwh saw her as she sees herself—even better: if Yhwh saw *himself* as she sees him—the assumption is that Yhwh would reverse course and heed her plea post haste.

Zion, one might say, has gone through the looking glass. God continues to hide his face. The result, if a singular analogy be allowed: "'You know very well you're not real.' 'I am real!' said Alice, and began to cry.'"

The correct response to Zion's lament is not to offer oneself as a substitute for the dialogue partner Zion has chosen. Zion is interested in the response of the arbiter of her future. She is real in fact, because she stakes out a position *over against* her arbiter. The proper response of friends and peers to her protest is audition, silence, and participation in her pain.

Shared silence is what Job's friends offered, for seven days, in a situation of analogous desolation (Job 2:11–13). Nonetheless, in the wake of Job's protest, beginning with Job 3, they broke their silence. Any chance of healing was lost from that point on.

The coauthoring approach to interpretation is a power play. It has its place over against a powerful author. Coauthoring has no place vis-à-vis a Job or the personae of Lam 1–2. Something Job's friends did not understand, something coauthors do not understand: the *only* proper response to a desolated sufferer is audition and silence.

The author(s) of the book of Lamentations, despite Mandolfo's affirmation of the principle of dialogic interpretation, is not her concern. She pays primary attention to the speech of biblical personae, not the wordless speech of the author(s) thereof.[18] Much can be said for the epistemological modesty of said approach. Nonetheless, as already noted, Mandolfo reconfigures the persona of Zion for her own purposes. In place of Zion of Lam 1:18 who puts her God in the right and herself in the wrong, Mandolfo offers a Zion who puts herself in the right and her God in the wrong.

This unwillingness to allow Zion to be penitent, angry, and inconsolable at the same time is unnecessary. Nor is it necessary to paint Zion's Deity as an ogre because he responds to her on her terms.

---

18. Mandolfo, *Daughter Zion*, 27.

Mandolfo contends that the only explicit request Zion makes of God in Lam 1–2 is a call for retribution (1:22).[19] To be sure, in light of Lam 1:22, Ps 137, and many other passages, it is patent that Zion and her citizens were hopeful that what goes around, comes around. No one who has lost her son to a murderer is foolish enough to think that the murderer's incarceration or capital punishment will bring her son back. Nonetheless, a kind of symmetry in terms of consequences is the least one can wish. This understanding of justice is almost universal. In Mandolfo's deconstruction of the message of Second Isaiah, we read the following:

> In a gruesomely insensitive response to the cannibalistic horrors she was forced to witness (Lam 2:20), YHWH proclaims that her "oppressors will eat their own flesh and be drunk with their own blood"—all this so she might come to know that YHWH is indeed her savior and redeemer ([Isa] 49:26).[20]

The divine response, on the contrary, fits the circumstances. As much as we might wish otherwise, Yhwh's promise is a mirror image of Zion's request. There is nothing insensitive about it. In Lam 1:22 retribution of this kind is exactly what Zion calls for.

It is Mandolfo, not Zion, who cannot countenance a retributive God.[21] The concept of closure and the role retribution has in the attainment of closure—for example, in cases of murder in which surviving kin are given a say as to when the convict in question should come up for parole—have no identifiable place in her political and theological project. Given the abuse of the principle of retribution on the one hand, and teaching that goes in the opposite direction on the other, that is hardly surprising. It is impossible to disagree with Mandolfo on this score. Yet disagree one must, if one is to make room for Zion's call for retribution, and her Deity's acquiescent response.

Isaiah 49:26 would have been a gruesomely insensitive response to the Zion of Lam 1:22. So long as children in Zion were starving (2:12), so long as God hid his face so completely from Zion, any promise from God's side

---

19. Ibid., 105. Mandolfo overlooks Zion's fourfold request that God see her as she sees herself, the subject of this essay.

20. Ibid., 109.

21. Ibid., 90 and passim.

would have been hateful. Promises from God are not reported in Lam 1–2. They had no place under the circumstances.

For the same reason, the pregnant promise of Isa 49:14–26, the repopulation of Zion by children she never knew, foreign-born sons and daughters of displaced citizens, is absent from Eicha's horizon. A promise to that effect was perverse so long as children in Zion were starving. Even when the worst could be spoken of in retrospect, the assumption in Lam 3–5, hope remained muted. The time for hope had not yet come.

The absence of hope from Lam 1–2 must be respected. In the aftermath of her breach, the violation of her holy of holies, the exile, flight, and starvation that decimated her ranks, she asks first and foremost for her loss and shame to be re≈dressed. She is not dignified with a reply. The mood is improved in Lam 3–5, but not by much.

Between the implied occasions of Lam 1–2 and Isa 40–55, a generation came and went. Roughly fifty years, under the bridge. Thereafter and only thereafter, her God no longer on a trip to a far country, could Zion be comforted. That is the occasion of Second Isaiah's message. In that context, Zion's Deity seconds her call for retribution. He promises to accomplish it at some point in the future. In the meantime, he busies himself with her repopulation.

Thus far the message of Second Isaiah. Nonetheless, over the long duration, it is hard to avoid the conclusion that the repopulation, historically considered, has taken place on the metaphysical plane in inverse proportion to its realization on the physical plane. Alongside the "literal" Zionism of Ezra and Nehemiah and the songs of Zion in the Psalms, the dis≈placed Zionism of Ezekiel, Bar 4–5, and Tob 13:9–17; the "work of pain" of Tishah-b'Ab; and the re≈membrance of the temple service on Yom Tov—has been more productive of wholeness. Perhaps it is not too paradoxical to say that the presence of Zion in her absence is the flip side of her absence in her presence.

Jews and Christians honor teachings that give wide scope to the principle of returning good for evil (Exod 23:4–5; Lev 19:17–18; Jer 29:7; Prov 25:21–22; Matt 5:38–48; Rom 12:17–21). Nonetheless, in biblical discourse, these teachings are found side by side with affirmations of the principle of retribution. Retribution is retained as the touchstone of justice. Mandolfo's god, "who interpenetrates human beings without coerciveness and with unconditional love," apparently does without this touchstone. All well and good, unless someone is penetrating you against your will. In that case, one will demand a coercive power to remove, restrain, and punish the aggressor—the more coercive, the better. A noncoercive god creates more problems than it solves.[22] Zion's call for coercive redress makes sense in that context.

PORTRAIT OF ZION AS A YOUNG WOMAN

If we were to ask to what end the poems of Lam 1–2 were composed, the answer, as always for a text whose author is no longer extant,[23] would have to be inferred from clues and cues within the composition against the background of proximate media. I would contend that the near context of Lamentations is not the marriage metaphor from Hosea to Jeremiah to Ezekiel, Mandolfo's chosen point of comparison, in which Judah/Israel and/or Zion/Samaria is Yhwh's wife, but the metaphor of Zion as refuge of the poor and bulwark against the mighty that finds expression in several psalms and in Isa 1–39. In this metaphorical frame of reference, Zion is an indomitable force to be reckoned with. We hear her voice in Isa 37:22–23:

> Fair maiden Zion
> despises you,
> she mocks you!
> Fair Jerusalem
> wags her head after you!
> Whom have you blasphemed and reviled?
> Against whom have you raised your voice?

בזה לך
לעגה לך
בתולת בת־ציון
אחריך ראש הניעה
בת ירושלם:
את־מי חרפת וגדפת
ועל־מי הרימותה קול

---

22. For cogent reflections on the nature of god—uncapitalized by Mandolfo—see ibid., 20–23, in particular, nn. 33–39. I quote from n. 34.

23. I argue above in n. 15 that Zion's authors *are* extant. But her original authors are not.

Zion holds her oppressor in contempt. She tars her attacker's co-opting and slighting of her God (Isa 36:10, 20) for what it is: blasphemy, a reflex of hubris that violates everything in sight.

Zion is a warrior, like Deborah, Jael, and Judith. She is not afraid to contend with her enemies, which she has in abundance. She is a thresher, new and sharp, with many spikes (Isa 41:15). Fearless and awesome, she corresponds to the ideal type of the daughter of Israel described in Cant 6:10:

Who is she that leans out	מי־זאת הנשקפה
like the dawn,	כמו־שחר
beautiful as the moon,	יפה כלבנה
brilliant as the sun,	ברה כחמה
awesome as bannered armies!	אימה כנדגלות:

Her praises are sung in many places, for example, Ps 48:13–14:

Go around Zion, encircle her;	סבו ציון והקיפוה
count her towers!	ספרו מגדליה:
Take note of her wall,	שיתו לבכם לחילה
scale her bastions,	פסגו ארמנותיה
that you may re≈count	למען תספרו
to a generation to come.	לדור אחרון:

We understand her purpose from Isa 14:32:

And what will he answer the messengers of any nation?
That Yhwh established Zion;
in her, the needy of his people find shelter.

ומה־יענה מלאכי־גוי
כי־יהוה יסד ציון
ובה יחסו עניי עמו:

Her raison d'être is depicted in the frontier pastels of transhumance in Isa 33:20:

Look at Zion,
the gathering place of our assembly;

your eyes will see Jerusalem,
a habitat at ease, an immovable tent,
her pegs will not be pulled out, *for good*,
and none of her cords will snap.

חזה ציון
קרית מועדנו
עיניך תראינה ירושלם
נוה שאנן אהל בל־יצען
בל־יסע יתדתיו לנצח
וכל־חבליו בל־ינתקו:

To what end did the author(s) of Lam 1–2 give voice to ravaged Zion? The answer is analogous to the one we would give with respect to why there are psalms full of forlorn plaint and grim hope of revenge. Not just Lam 1–2 but compositions Adele Berlin refers to as "Jerusalem laments" showcase a datum of *nonreconciliation*: Pss 44, 74, and 137.[24] In these laments, hope for a resolution is decidedly forlorn. Bitterness rules.

The datum of nonreconciliation points to an irreducible truth. It cannot and should not be harmonized with a higher truth. Mandolfo knows this—she is wary of monological tendencies—but she does not stand her ground on that lonely rock.

If she had, she would not have seconded Kathleen O'Connor's claim that when Zion finds her voice in Lamentations, she recovers her life and acquires moral agency.[25] On the contrary, Zion is not party to a happy end in Eicha. She does *not* recover her life. She is as unrestored to her former health at the end of Eicha as she is at the beginning.

Zion does not reacquire moral agency when she finds her voice. Rather, she is a responsible agent before, during, and after her experience of destruction and horror. The moral agency she retains is nonetheless of no use to her. Within the confines of the book, it gets her exactly nowhere. To suggest otherwise is to sugarcoat the text.

24. Adele Berlin, *Lamentations* (OTL; Louisville: Westminster John Knox, 2002), 22–26, esp. 25.

25. Kathleen M. O'Connor, *Lamentations and the Tears of the World* (Maryknoll, N.Y.: Orbis, 2002), 83, cited in Mandolfo, *Daughter Zion*, 81 n. 3.

To what end did the author(s) of Lam 1–2 give voice to ravaged Zion? Reading a text first and foremost involves identification of genre.[26] To be clear, attention to genre inevitably shifts the axis of interpretation in the direction of the authors of a text, away from its readers and would-be coauthors. To pursue the question I pose in this paragraph is tantamount to swimming against the Bakhtinian flood. It means a return to Mandolfo's starting point, the point at which she identifies Lam 1–2's key features of form and content.

If nothing else, Lamentations is a "form" of lament, sharing such elements as subject, values, mood, style (to some degree), task (to some degree), attitude, and occasion (i.e., threat).[27]

These conclusions are programmatic. They beg for elaboration. What are the values Eicha vehiculates? What is its task?

The Politics and Ethics of Lamentation

The research of ethnographers and classicists on the politics and ethics of lamentation deserves to impact the world of biblical studies. A strength of Helene Foley's research is her concomitant attention to examples of lament in Greek tragedy on the one hand and studies of lament by ethnographers on the other.[28] Here are some sample quotations:

> Lamentation is traditionally performed as an antiphonal dialogue between single lamenters and a chorus of other lamenting women. This is the case whether we are speaking of Greek tragedy and epic or the modern Greek village. As modern studies of rural Greece by Seremetakis and others have shown, lament thus creates social unity through the force of shared emotion, shared moral inference, and shared memory.[29]

---

26. On the importance of genre identification, see John Barton, *Reading the Old Testament: Method in Biblical Study* (rev. ed.; Louisville: Westminster John Knox, 1996), 8–19, and passim.

27. Mandolfo, *Daughter Zion*, 55–77, here 67. The conclusions are cautious. Like Frederick W. Dobbs-Allsopp ("Darwinism, Genre Theory, and City Laments," *JAOS* 120 [2000]: 625–30), Mandolfo is careful to note differences, not only commonalities, that emerge on comparison of Lam 1–2 to Mesopotamian city laments.

28. Helene P. Foley, "The Politics of Tragic Lamentation," and "The Ethics of Lamentation," in *Female Acts in Greek Tragedy* (Martin Classical Lectures; Princeton: Princeton University Press, 2001), 19–55, 145–71, respectively.

29. Ibid., 152; cf. C. Nadia Seremetakis, *The Last Word: Women, Death, and Divi-*

In the modern context, another singer or the chorus will take over to reintegrate the mourner into a supportive and caring group and rescue her from self-inflicted violence. The intervention is often made at a lower pitch, and can sound somewhat like a lullaby.... Male onlookers can also intervene to revive overwhelmed mourners.[30]

[D]eath rites and lamentation in tragedy [in non-Western and rural Mediterranean contexts] ... are often political events, opportunities to foment revolution, resistance, or revenge under the cover of one of the few mass events that those in authority do not feel comfortable in suppressing altogether.... In nineteenth- and early twentieth-century India ... "state power ... attempted to stamp out visible signs of grief (articulated by women) ... which sought, through this banning to have direct control over forms of community justice, vendetta, and lines of inheritance, all of which could be mediated by lament."[31]

The political articulation of grief by women according to routinized social templates is extremely well attested cross-culturally. Those familiar with the pertinent research will formulate, almost as a matter of course, a working hypothesis regarding, at a minimum, the first three chapters of the biblical book of Lamentations, for example:

- Lamentations 1 is a dialogue in which (a) a chorus of lamenting women provide a context for the voice of (b) a single lamenting woman speaking in the voice of Zion: (a) = Lam 1:1–11 except for 1:9c and 11c; (b) = Lam 1:9c, 11c, 12–22.
- Lamentations 2 is a dialogue between two lamenting women: (a) a lamenter who speaks of and to Zion, and (b) a lamenter speaking in the voice of Zion: (a) = 2:1–19; (b) = 2:20–22. On this understanding, one of "the maidens of Jerusalem" referred to as a lamenter in 2:10 is the speaker throughout

---

nation in the Inner Mani (Chicago: University of Chicago Press, 1991).

30. Foley, Female Acts in Greek Tragedy, 156 n. 55; she refers to Seremetakis, Last Word, 119, 111; and Gail Holst-Warhaft, Dangerous Voices: Women's Laments and Greek Literature (London: Routledge, 1992), 29.

31. Foley, Female Acts in Greek Tragedy, 2, quoting Parita Mukta, "The 'Civilizing Mission': The Regulation and Control of Mourning in Colonial India," Feminist Review 63 (1999): 1.

2:1–19; note in particular 2:11–12 with its focus on children and mothers.

- Lamentations 3, with 3:51 construed as suggested in the excursus below, is the monologue of a lamenting woman, a female citizen of her city, who gives voice to the grief and hopes of an entire community in the persona of an "everyman."

The default assumption of virtually the entire field of scholarship on the book of Lamentations is the opposite: Lam 1–5 is the product of male performer-poets.[32] But that is not the natural assumption if one is familiar with anthropological research and/or the classical tradition. In the otherwise excellent *Lamentations in Ancient and Contemporary Cultural Contexts*, interaction with the titles listed in the bibliography below finds no place.[33]

THE ETHICS AND POLITICS OF LAMENT:
AN INTRODUCTORY BIBLIOGRAPHY

Lila Abu-Lughod, *Veiled Sentiments: Honor and Poetry in a Bedouin Society* (Berkeley: University of California Press, 1986); Margaret Alexiou, *The Ritual Lament in Greek Tradition* (2nd ed.; rev. by Dimitrios Yatromanolakis and Panagiotis Roilos; Greek Studies: Interdisciplinary Approaches; Lanham, Md.: Rowman & Littlefield, 2002); Angela Bourke, "More in Anger than in Sorrow: Irish Women's Lament Poetry," in *Feminist Messages: Coding in Women's Folk Culture* (ed. Joan Newlon Radnor; Urbana: Illinois University Press, 1993), 160–82; Charles L. Briggs, "Personal Sentiments and Polyphonic Voices in Warao Women's Ritual Wailing," *American Anthropologist* 95 (1993): 929–57; idem, "'Since I Am a Woman, I Will

---

32. Exegetes have never had a problem assuming that a male author wraps himself in the guise of a female persona, Zion, in the relevant passages in Lam 1–2. Why is it problematic to assume the reverse in Lam 3? Why assume that a male is the implied author of the speeches in Lam 1–2 in the first place? To be sure, a distinction has to be made between the poet-performer and the scribe. Just as we do in the case of prophecy (prophets and prophetesses, already at Mari). Just as we assume in the case of the song of Deborah. Just as we best do in the case of Song of Songs. Once that distinction is made, the working hypothesis I propose becomes plausible. I wish to thank Chris Brady for conversations around this point.

33. Nancy C. Lee and Carleen Mandolfo, *Lamentations in Ancient and Contemporary Cultural Contexts* (SBLSymS 43; Atlanta: Society of Biblical Literature, 2008).

Chastise My Relatives': Gender, Reported Speech, and the (Re)Production of Social Relations in Warao Ritual Wailing," *American Ethnologist* 19 (1992): 337–61; Anne Pippen Burnett, *Revenge in Attic and Later Tragedy* (Berkeley: University of California Press, 1998); Anna Caraveli, "The Bitter Wounding: The Lament as Social Protest in Rural Greece," in *Gender and Power in Rural Greece* (ed. Jill Dubisch; Princeton: Princeton University Press, 1986), 169–94; idem, "Bridge Between Worlds: The Greek Women's Lament as Communicative Event," *Journal of American Folklore* 368 (1980): 129–57; Ernesto De Martino, *Morte e pianto rituale: dal lamento funebre antico al pianto di Maria* (Torino: Boringhieri, 1975); Helene P. Foley, "The Politics of Tragic Lamentation," and "The Ethics of Lamentation," in *Female Acts in Greek Tragedy* (Martin Classical Lectures; Princeton: Princeton University Press, 2001), 19–55, 145–71; Gail Holst-Warhaft, *Dangerous Voices: Women's Laments and Greek Literature* (London: Routledge, 1992); Elizabeth L. Johnson, "Grieving for the Dead, Grieving for the Living: Funeral Laments of Hakka Women," in *Death Ritual in Late Imperial and Modern China* (ed. J. L. Watson and Evelyn S. Rawski; Berkeley: University of California Press, 1988), 135–63; Tullia Magrini, "Women's 'Work of Pain' in Christian Mediterranean Europe," *Music and Anthropology* 3 (1998); Judith Mossman, *Wild Justice: A Study of Euripides' Hecuba* (London: Bristol Classical Press and Duckworth, 1999); Parita Mukta, "The 'Civilizing Mission': The Regulation and Control of Mourning in Colonial India," *Feminist Review* 63 (1999): 25–47; Charles Segal, "The Ethics of Antiphony: The Social Construction of Pain, Gender, and Power in the Southern Peloponnese," *Ethos* 18 (1990): 481–511; idem, "The Gorgon and the Nightingale: The Voice of Female Lament and Twelfth Pythian Ode," in *Embodied Voices* (ed. Leslie C. Dunn and Nancy A. Jones; Cambridge: Cambridge University Press, 1994), 17–34; C. Nadia Seremetakis, *The Last Word: Women, Death, and Divination in Inner Mani* (Chicago: University of Chicago Press, 1991); Batya Weinbaum, "Lament Ritual Transformed into Literature: Positing Women's Prayer as Cornerstone in Western Classical Literature," *Journal of American Folklore* 114 (2001): 20–39.

As a first step in the direction of answering the questions posed—What are the values Eicha vehiculates? What is its task?—I will read Eicha through the prism of Helene Foley's already cited discussions of the ethics and politics of lamentation.

Sophocles' *Electra* presents its listeners with the endless and fiercely aggressive lamentation of one who sees revenge, per Anne Burnett's statements relative to revenge in the *Odyssey*, as the realization of a person's "ingrained right to retaliate," "an honorable imperative essential to preservation of order."[34]

Electra calls her men kin to avenge the death of her father. She stirs the women of the chorus, in Foley's words, "significantly called *polítides*, female citizens (1227)," to lament and incite along with her. If her men kin did not avenge her father's death, Electra would.

> According to Seremetakis, in the modern contexts, hearing and seeing "do not have the *passive* or purely receptive implications that" such terms have in English, but imply "an *active* role in the production of juridical discourse.... The act of hearing carries the value of the soloist's discourse. Hearing in the antiphonic relation is not external to speech but metonymical to it. *Hearing is the doubling of the other's discourse*."[35]

Zion, whose sons and daughters are dead, dispersed, or incapacitated, the very ones she grieves, calls on God to avenge her at the conclusion of Lam 1 (1:22). In Lam 3 an "everyman" lamenter builds up to a call for retribution (3:64–66). Chapter 4 winds up to a prediction of retribution (4:22). In the case of Electra, the chorus who takes up her cause, and the personae who speak in Lam 1, 3, and 4, lamentation "aims," as Foley puts it, "to provoke revenge through the awakening of shared pain."[36] Electra and the chorus succeed in their aim. Zion and the other personae of Eicha, within the limits of the book, do not. It is the "unansweredness" of Eicha that makes it powerful. An unanswered demand for justice, its relevance is perennial.

Zion's insistent request (1:9, 11, 20; 2:20) that the arbiter of her future see her as she sees herself discloses the goal of her discourse. She is asking her God to transit from a passive to an active role. Her self-presentation and her chastisement of God alike are meant to incite God and shame him into championing her cause. In the economy of Eicha's discourse nonetheless, God neither hears nor sees. The text-internal task of Eicha comes to naught. The meta-task of Eicha is to keep the memory of the request returned-to-sender alive, to throw it back in God's face for all eternity. In

---

34. Anne Pippen Burnett, *Revenge in Attic and Later Tragedy* (Berkeley: University of California Press, 1998), 38–42, cited in Foley, *Female Acts*, 154 n. 47.

35. Seremetakis, *Last Word*, 104, cited in Foley, *Female Acts*, 154 n. 47.

36. Foley, *Female Acts*, 151.

this confrontation, the identity of those who weep *with* and *for* Zion is constituted.

THE QUESTION OF THEODICY

Eicha is an anti-theodicy. It shares this quality with the books of Job and Qohelet, the psalms of grievance in the Psalter, and the storming of God's gates to be found in the intercessory prayer of Habakkuk and Jeremiah. Anti-theodicy is a pro≈phetic stance. For that reason it characterizes the intercessory prayer of Abraham and Moses in the Torah.

The various strands are witnesses to a single truth: the status quo cannot be challenged except from an anti-theodic point of view. Stated positively, biblical literature is strewn with examples of *anthropodic* discourse. Eicha is anthropodic discourse. Rather than take God's side, Eicha takes Zion's side. Its enduring value lies therein.

The strong misreading of greatest import in Mandolfo's monograph is the following: "In terms of divine self-expression, the Bible is always theodic."[37]

Not so. Theodic discourse *provokes God's anger* in the book of Job. In the book of Job, it is the sufferer who screams bloody murder from a location within God's jaws; it is the *screaming* sufferer who unlocks those jaws. Suffering, accusatory Job encounters divine favor. God commends him for having spoken sincerely about God.

It is not what you say. It is who you say it to, in what context. God, it appears, can take whatever a sufferer throws at him.

The sufferer, the one who inveighs against God from the viscera of her suffering, she alone is in a position to inter≈cede and inter≈pose on behalf of those who only know how to say nice things about God. The opposite is inconceivable.

The key lines that attest to these conclusions are found in Job 42:7–8:

Yhwh said to Eliphaz of Teman,
I am incensed at you and your two friends:
you did not speak about me sincerely
as did my servant Job....
Let Job, my servant, pray on your behalf!

---

37. Mandolfo, *Daughter Zion*, 117.

But I will favor him
by not treating you vituperatively.
For you did not speak about me sincerely[38]
as did my servant Job.

ויאמר יהוה אל־אליפז התימני
חרה אפי בך ובשני רעיך
כי לא דברתם אלי נכונה
כעבדי איוב: ...
ואיוב עבדי יתפלל עליכם
כי אם־פניו אשא
לבלתי עשות עמכם נבלה
כי לא דברתם אלי נכונה
כעבדי איוב:

The divine verdict in this passage is of a piece with the entire biblical discourse.[39] Wherever one looks in the Bible, the sincere words of
a sufferer, however incriminating, are acceptable in God's sight. If anything, the book of Job shies away from a blank-check acceptance thereof
by means of the Deity's cross-examination of Job out of the whirlwind. The
psalms of lament in the Psalter, *per contra*, are a witness to full acceptance.
Were it not so, God would not reply to the incriminations of the sufferer
with favor and mercy. The note of thanksgiving on which many psalms
of grievance end, psalms that are highly accusatory in the face of divine
mistreatment, psalms that do not in God's name accuse the supplicant in
turn—such psalms are an enduring witness to the experience of God as an
anthropodic, not a theodic, being. They document that, in concrete acts of
self-expression, Yhwh is a deity who takes up humanity's cause. In taking
up suffering humanity's cause, it might be said, he takes up his own. The
book of Job does not break the mold of the grievance psalms. It follows
their suit and complicates their plot.

Eicha is a book that "stands in the breach." Should it be the case that
there is no arbiter of the future to which humans can appeal, the book
might still make sense as a species of hopeless monologue and wish-pro-

---

38. Some translate "the truth" or "accurately."

39. To be sure, Job 42:7 has stuck in the craw of many an exegete in the history of
interpretation. For an example, Saadia Gaon, see Alan Mittleman's essay, "The Job of
Judaism and the Job of Kant," *HTR* 102 (2009): 25–50, here 32–33.

jection. But should it be the case that God is morally bound to respond as an acquiescing peer might respond, the book, which knows the Divinity's mouth to be the source of woes and weal (Lam 3:38), is nothing more than an enabler of oppression. Should it be the case that the book puts a God in the dock that does not exist, it covers for oppressors.

If instead the God of compassion is also the God of relentless anger, if the God who hides his face is the one who stands at the door and knocks, and if no one opens, blows the door down, then Eicha stands. Eicha witnesses to faith in an angry God with a capacious ability to embrace the anger of those who call to him in their distress—even if that embrace consists of stony silence, and the silence of the lambs.

Martin Luther, strangely enough, comes to mind in relation to the psalms of lament and the book of Lamentations. Yes, Luther, the one who caricatured Judaism with great avidity. Luther, because he defined sin as unbelief rather than transgression: Zion, and all penitents, are transgressors, but are still capable of belief. Luther, because he made a distinction between God's comprehensible and God's incomprehensible wrath, and never pretended the latter did not exist—an inveterate reader of the psalms, a man who saw demons—he knew better. Luther, because he knew "God as Devil," not only as good; because he knew that a "believing" human being is, by definition, simultaneously in the right and the wrong before the judge of which Scripture speaks. Luther's theology is anthropodic inside and out. It is devoid of theodicy. Oswald Bayer contemporizes Luther in this fashion:

> The question of theodicy cannot be answered actively with Kant or speculatively with Hegel. It can be resolved neither speculatively nor morally; it cannot be "resolved" in any way. We have to deal with it "practically" by experiencing it in meditation (through hearing and taking the Bible to heart), affliction, and prayer. The passive righteousness of faith does not conduct a dispute *about* God and God's righteousness, as does the natural, redeemed, or presumably already glorified reason before its own forum. It conducts a dispute *with* God in prayer and in lament.[40]

---

40. Oswald Bayer, *Living by Faith: Justification and Sanctification* (trans. Geoffrey W. Bromiley; Lutheran Quarterly Books; Grand Rapids: Eerdmans, 2003), 77. I made minor stylistic changes to Bromiley's translation. Theology *is* anthropology in Luther. A responsible human being is precisely the one who is justified—in the right before her Judge—by faith. Also according to Luther, faith, by God's grace, is the creator of divinity (*creatrix divinitatis*) in us (*in nobis*). Luther affirmed this without denying that

EXCURSUS: LAMENTATIONS 3:51

Lamentations 3:51 as it stands is a conundrum. Delbert Hillers notes that "the MT is corrupt and yields no acceptable sense."[41] Here is Lam 3:51 in context (vv. 48–51) as I would reconstruct it:

My eye streams with channels of water
over the disaster of my beloved people.
My eye is poured out and will not cease,
fits of inactivity disallowed,
until he lean out and see,
יהוה from heaven.
Misery was dealt my soul
beyond that of all other female citizens of my city.

פלגי־מים תרד עיני
על־שבר בת־עמי:
עיני נגרה ולא תדמה
מאין הפגות:
עד־ישקיף וירא
יהוה משמים:
<עָנִי עוֹלַל 42> לְנַפְשִׁי
כל בנות עירי:

On this understanding, עָנִי was misconstrued as עֵינִי, an assimilation to the preceding context (note עֵינִי in vv. 48 and 49 and וַיֵּרֶא in 50), the orthography filled out in consequence (or a plene עוֹנִי misread as עֵינִי), and the inflection of עולל adjusted accordingly. For the sense, compare Lam 1:12. The last line is literally: "more than (that of) all the (other) daughters of my city." מכל is "All the (other)," as in Gen 3:1.

_____

God is nonetheless also, and for our sake (*pro nobis*), beyond us (*extra nos*), radically other. See further Oswald Bayer, "Toward a Theology of Lament," in *Caritas et Reformatio: Essays on Church and Society in Honor of Carter Lindberg* (ed. David M. Whitford; St. Louis: Concordia, 2004), 211–20; idem, *Martin Luther's Theology: A Contemporary Interpretation* (trans. Thomas H. Trapp; Grand Rapids: Eerdmans, 2008).

41. Delbert R. Hillers, *Lamentations* (2nd ed.; AB 7A; New York: Doubleday, 1992), 118.

42. MT עֵינִי עוֹלְלָה, "my eye dealt."

Berlin sticks with what she calls the usual understanding of the text—
"my eyes have brought me grief more than all the daughters of my city"—
but admits that the text she renders is "less than intelligible."[43]

The NJPS proposes reading (1) עָנְיִי, "my affliction," instead of עֵינִי, and
(2) joining it to the preceding; (3) עוֹלַל, "he dealt," instead of עוֹלְלָה; (4)
and adding (apparently) יהוה. The result: "Until the LORD looks down
from heaven / And beholds my affliction / The LORD has brought me grief
/ Over all the maidens of my city."

Hillers reads עָנִי עוֹלַל לְנַפְשִׁי as I do, but understands it as a nominal
phrase that serves as the subject of a verb he reconstructs in the following
phrase, which he emends in more than one place to yield מְכַלֶּה בְּנוֹת עֵינִי,
"consumes my eyes."[44]

My proposal moves beyond the resignation of Berlin but is more
conservative than NJPS and Hillers. I posit a single misconstrual of a type
attested elsewhere (cf. 2 Sam 16:12, noted by Hillers), followed by a grammatical adjustment.

On my reading, in 3:1, at the onset of a larger whole, a female
lamenter explicitly casts herself as a male persona, an "everyman" (Hillers's
characterization,[45] developed brilliantly by Dobbs-Allsopp[46]) who gives
voice to a collective experience, only to allude to her particular identity in
3:51. In the poem's conclusion, 3:52–66, the singular "I" continues to be
used, but, as Dobbs-Allsopp notes, "it has become more inclusive."[47] As
she does throughout Lam 3, the lamenter concludes by voicing the grief
and hopes of an entire community.

---

43. *Lamentations*, 83.

44. Ibid., 118.

45. Ibid., 122.

46. Frederick W. Dobbs-Allsopp, *Lamentations* (IBC; Louisville: John Knox,
2002), 105–9.

47. Ibid., 107.

The Daughter of Zion Goes Fishing in Heaven

Michael H. Floyd

Father, forgive us for what we must do,
You forgive us, and we'll forgive you.
We'll forgive each other til we both turn blue,
Then we'll whistle and go fishing in heaven.
                                   —John Prine[1]

A number of studies have investigated the feminine personification of the city of Jerusalem, largely motivated by concerns about issues of gender in biblical interpretation.[2] Several of these studies have also been method-

---

1. "Fish and Whistle." Written by John Prine. © 1978 BIG EARS MUSIC (ASCAP) and BRUISED ORANGES MUSIC (ASCAP)/both administered by BUG MUSIC. All rights reserved. Used by permission.

2. Aloysius Fitzgerald, "The Mythological Background for the Presentation of Jerusalem as a Queen and False Worship as Adultery in the OT," *CBQ* 34 (1972): 403–16; idem, "*BTWLT* and *BT* as Titles for Capital Cities," *CBQ* 37 (1975): 167–83; Elaine R. Follis, "The Holy City as Daughter," in *Directions in Biblical Poetry* (ed. Elaine R. Follis; JSOTSup 40; Sheffield: JSOT Press, 1987), 173–84; Barbara Bakke Kaiser, "Poet as 'Female Impersonator': The Image of Daughter Zion as Speaker in Biblical Poems of Suffering," *JR* 67 (1987): 164–82; John F. A. Sawyer, "Daughter of Zion and Servant of the Lord in Isaiah: A Comparison," *JSOT* 44 (1989): 89–107; John J. Schmitt, "The Wife of God in Hosea 2," *BR* 34 (1989): 5–18; Mark E. Biddle, "The Figure of Lady Jerusalem: Identification, Deification and Personification of Cities in the Ancient Near East," in *The Biblical Canon in Comparative Perspective* (ed. K. Lawson Younger Jr., William W. Hallo, and Bernard F. Batto; Scripture in Context 4; ANETS 11; Lewiston, N.Y.: Mellen, 1991), 173–94; Tikva Frymer-Kensky, "Zion, the Beloved Woman," in *In the Wake of the Goddesses: Women, Culture, and the Biblical Transformation of Pagan Myth* (New York: Free Press, 1992), 168–78; Klaus Baltzer, "Stadt-Tyche oder Zion-Jerusalem? Die Auseinandersetzung mit den Göttern der Zeit bei Deuterojesaja," in *Alttestamentlicher Glaube und Biblische Theologie: Festschrift für Horst Dietrich*

ologically innovative, moving beyond conventional historical criticism. I share these concerns about gender, and I welcome this methodological innovation, but I find myself in disagreement with one of the key assumptions as well as one of the interpretive moves commonly made in these studies.

First, I would challenge the assumption that the phrase בת ציון and its variations characterize Jerusalem as a daughter. This is based on the claim,

---

Preuss zum 65. Geburtstag (ed. Jutta Hausmann and Hans-Jürgen Zobel; Stuttgart: Kohlhammer, 1992), 114–19; F. W. Dobbs-Allsopp, "The Syntagma of *bat* Followed by a Geographical Name in the Hebrew Bible: A Reconsideration of Its Meaning and Grammar," *CBQ* 57 (1995): 451–70; idem, *Weep, O Daughter of Zion: A Study of the City-Lament Genre in the Hebrew Bible* (BibOr 44; Rome: Pontifical Biblical Institute, 1993); Peggy L. Day, "The Personification of Cities as Female in the Hebrew Bible: The Thesis of Aloysius Fitzgerald, F.S.C.," in *Reading from This Place*, vol. 2, *Social Location and Biblical Interpretation in Global Perspective* (ed. Fernando F. Segovia and Mary Ann Tolbert; Minneapolis: Fortress, 1995), 283–302; Patricia Tull Willey, "The Servant of YHWH and Daughter Zion: Alternating Visions of YHWH's Community," *The Society of Biblical Literature 1995 Seminar Papers* (SBLSP 34; Atlanta: Scholars Press, 1995), 267–303; Mark E. Biddle, "Lady Zion's Alter Egos: Isaiah 47.1–15 and 57.6–13 as Structural Counterparts," in *New Visions of Isaiah* (ed. Roy F. Melugin and Marvin A. Sweeney; JSOTSup 214; Sheffield: Sheffield Academic Press, 1996), 124–39; John J. Schmitt, "The City as Woman in Isaiah 1–39," in *Writing and Reading the Scroll of Isaiah: Studies of an Interpretive Tradition* (ed. Craig C. Broyles and Craig A. Evans; 2 vols.; VTSup 70; Leiden: Brill, 1997), 1:95–119; J. Andrew Dearman, "YHWH's House: Gender Roles and Metaphors for Israel in Hosea," *JNSL* 25 (1999): 97–108; A. R. Pete Diamond and Kathleen M. O'Connor, "Unfaithful Passions: Coding Women Coding Men in Jeremiah 2–3 (4:2)," *BibInt* 4 (1996): 288–310; repr. in *Troubling Jeremiah* (ed. A. R. Pete Diamond, Kathleen M. O'Connor, and Louis Stulman; JSOTSup 260; Sheffield: Sheffield Academic Press, 1999), 123–45; Kathleen M. O'Connor, "'Speak Tenderly to Jerusalem': Second Isaiah's Reception and Use of Daughter Zion," *PSB* 20 (1999): 281–94; Marc Wischnowsky, *Tochter Zion: Aufnahme und Überwindung der Stadtklage in den Prophetenschriften des Alten Testaments* (WMANT 89; Neukirchen-Vluyn: Neukirchener, 2001); Mary Donovan Turner, "Daughter Zion: Giving Birth to Redemption," in *Pregnant Passion: Gender, Sex, and Violence in the Bible* (ed. Cheryl A. Kirk-Duggan; SBLSymS 44; Atlanta: Society of Biblical Literature, 2003), 193–204; Magnar Kartveit, "Daughter of Zion," *Theology and Life* 27 (2004): 25–41; Mary E. Shields, *Circumscribing the Prostitute: The Rhetorics of Intertextuality, Metaphor and Gender in Jeremiah 3.1–4.4* (JSOTSup 387; London: T&T Clark, 2004); Brad E. Kelle, *Hosea 2: Metaphor and Rhetoric in Historical Perspective* (SBLABib 20; Atlanta: Society of Biblical Literature, 2005); and Hyukki Kim, "The Interpretation of בת ציון (Daughter Zion): An Approach of Cognitive Theories of Metaphor" (M.A. thesis, McMaster Divinity College, 2006).

made in 1965 by William F. Stinespring, that this construct phrase should be understood grammatically as an appositional genitive.[3] In his view it does not mean that Jerusalem is a mother who *has* a daughter ("daughter of Zion") but that Jerusalem *is* a daughter ("Daughter Zion"). Elsewhere I have stated in detail my objections to Stinespring's view.[4] Here I will revisit some points of this argument in light of questions that have subsequently been raised by Andrew Dearman, and in relation to two studies of the sort described above, one by Carleen Mandolfo and the other by Christl Maier.[5]

In the process I would also like to challenge a commonly made interpretive move, particularly as it is evident in Mandolfo's work. This interpretive move is the tendency to conflate the various feminine roles into which Jerusalem is cast, just because they are feminine, and then to use this conflation of roles as an ideational construct with which to make generalizations about the social and theological aspects of gender in the Bible. In Mandolfo's case this tendency is evident on two levels. As she analyzes the feminine personification of Jerusalem in Lam 1–2, she conflates the role of the city herself and the role of בת ציון into the single role of Daughter Zion, and then she conflates this characterization of Daughter Zion with the prophetic characterization of the city as an unfaithful wife and prostitute. In her dialogic approach Mandolfo assumes that these are all one and the same feminine figure. In Hosea, Jeremiah and Ezekiel we meet her only as she is described from their patriarchal accusatory perspective, but in Lamentations the writer presents her more from her own perspective. My quarrel is not with the dialogic approach, but with the basis on which the feminine role in Lam 1–2 has been construed.

STARTING POINT

As a starting point I will take Dearman's critique of Mandolfo. He makes the same point that I have just made with regard to conflating the feminine

---

3. William F. Stinespring, "No Daughter of Zion: A Study of the Appositional Genitive in Hebrew Grammar," *Encounter* 26 (1965): 133–41.

4. Michael H. Floyd, "Welcome Back, Daughter of Zion," *CBQ* 70 (2008): 484–504.

5. J. Andrew Dearman, "Daughter Zion and Her Place in God's Household," *HBT* 31 (2009): 144–59; Carleen R. Mandolfo, *Daughter Zion Talks Back to the Prophets: A Dialogic Theology of the Book of Lamentations* (SemeiaSt 58; Atlanta: Society of Biblical Literature, 2007); Christl M. Maier, *Daughter Zion, Mother Zion: Gender, Space, and the Sacred in Ancient Israel* (Minneapolis: Fortress, 2008).

personification(s) in Lam 1–2 with what he calls "the figure of Wife Jeru-salem," which in Jeremiah and Ezekiel becomes the figure of an adulter-ous harlot-wife. He argues that these characterizations are not figuratively interchangeable:

> Each of [Jerusalem's feminine] roles has nuance and texture, and some may have distinct tradition histories. They are not easily interchangeable, even when there is some overlap and it is recognized that they depict the same character. And so one must differentiate among the female kin-ship roles as well as seek coherence in their ability to render Jerusalem. One should not, for example, collapse the figure of Wife Jerusalem into D[aughter] Z[ion]. This is essentially what Carleen Mandolfo does in her penetrating recent monograph on Zion's response to YHWH in the book of Lamentations. She takes the marriage metaphor between Jerusalem and YHWH in the prophets as background for the voiced pain of DZ in Lamentations, yet without discussion or even recognition that YHWH did not take "his" daughter as spouse. Although the poignant, accusa-tory voice of DZ is replete in Lam 1–2, the marital imagery is at best implicit and subsumed, if it is there at all. DZ is a dejected daughter and a deposed princess/queen, not a wife. She may be involved in promiscu-ous activity (Lam 1:19), but the language of adultery and divorce are not present in Lamentations as they are in Jeremiah and Ezekiel. Note, furthermore, that DZ does not occur in Jer 2–3, Ezek 16, 23, where the marriage and adultery metaphors are explicit. In those texts the kinship imagery associated with DZ may be implicit and subsumed, if it is there at all….
>
> Mandolfo's paradigm of reading would work better if the voice of DZ were seen more in response to judgment and punishment inflicted on the daughter of a household, rather than upon a spouse.[6]

Although Dearman rejects Mandolfo's conflation of the feminine personi-fication in Lam 1–2 with the prophetic figure of Wife Jerusalem, he main-tains that there is a single feminine figure in Lam 1–2 who can be charac-terized as "the daughter of a household." This counterproposal depends, in turn, on his reaffirmation of Stinespring's view that בת ציון is an apposi-tional genitive meaning Daughter Zion.

My argument will thus take the following form. First, I will respond to Dearman's position on the meaning of בת ציון, reasserting that this phrase should be understood to mean "daughter of Zion" rather than "Daugh-

---

6. Dearman, "Daughter Zion and Her Place," 156–57.

ter Zion." Second, I will show how Mandolfo's dialogic approach could be enriched by recognizing that there are actually several feminine figures in Lam 1–2.

DEARMAN'S ARGUMENT

Dearman makes three main points: (1) He objects to my claim that בת ציון can be understood as the singular form of the commonly attested plural expression בנות ציון, which refers to the feminine inhabitants of a city as her "daughters." He thus denies that the singular form בת ציון could collectively personify the female population of Jerusalem. (2) Based on the analysis of Christl Maier, Dearman maintains that in many contexts בת ציון has geographic and architectonic connotations, which make it necessarily refer to the city itself rather than to its human population. And (3) he objects that I do not give sufficient attention to variations on the formula represented by בת ציון, such as בת עמי and particularly to compound construct variations such as בתולת ישראל. He asserts that such phrases must be understood appositionally, just as בת ציון should be understood. I will take up each of these points in turn, but first I reiterate one of the pillars of my position that Dearman fails to address at all, namely, the grammatical question.

PROLEGOMENON: Is בת ציון AN APPOSITIONAL GENITIVE?

Although the very notion of a Hebrew appositional genitive remains problematic in some respects, it is not necessary to resolve all the linguistic niceties in order to see that sometimes the Hebrew construct phrase can indeed function like an appositional genitive. Thus the question is not whether there can be such expressions in Hebrew, but whether בת ציון is one such expression.[7]

I maintain that בת ציון cannot be understood appositionally because of a semantic restriction. The word בת denotes a familial relation, which is normally expressed with a construct phrase. No one would translate בת לאה as "Daughter Leah" (Gen 34:1). This phrase could only mean "the daughter of Leah." Similarly, no one would translate בת מטרד as "Daughter Matred" (Gen 36:39). This phrase could only mean "the daughter of

---

7. Floyd, "Welcome Back," 489–90.

Matred."[8] Why? Partly because of the genealogical contexts in which these phrases appear, but quite apart from considerations of context the phrase resists being understood appositionally because the terminology itself has genealogical implications. One is a "daughter" in relation to a parent, and this familial relationship is normally expressed through a construct phrase meaning "daughter of X." For similar reasons אחות צרויה would not be translated as "Sister Zeruiah" (2 Sam 17:25) but as "the sister of Zeruiah." Likewise אבי שכם is not "Father Shechem" but "the father of Shechem" (Gen 33:19).

In Stinespring's argument this problem was, in effect, obscured by his contention that בת can mean "young girl" as well as "daughter" and can thus function as a term of endearment. By suggesting that בת ציון could also be translated "Maid Zion" or "Dear Zion," he steered the discussion away from the semantic difficulties posed by בת being primarily a reference to a familial relationship. His argument that בת can mean "young girl" was based largely on a comparison with the Arabic cognate *bint*, together with a couple of doubtful examples from Biblical Hebrew. It is now generally recognized that this claim was an overstatement, and that בת scarcely has this secondary meaning.[9] Thus those who continue to affirm Stinespring's position have largely settled on "Daughter Zion" rather than the other sorts of translations he proposed. This, however, puts the semantic difficulties once again in sharp relief.

Following Stinespring's comparative lead, I considered the analogous question in Arabic. This is a particularly telling test case because Arabic has a true appositional genitive in the strict sense, and because the analogous term *bint* does mean "young girl" as well as "daughter." Despite this greater theoretical openness to the possibility of what Stinespring proposed, Arabic has the same semantic restriction. The term *bint* in construct relationship with a proper noun in the genitive case cannot be understood appositionally in Arabic either. It can only mean "daughter of X."[10] The same is also true of English. Although "the city of New York" can be understood appositionally as "New York City," and "Dublin's fair city" can similarly be understood to mean that the "fair city" in question is Dublin, it is difficult to imagine any context in which "the daughter of

---

8. The phrase בת ענה (Gen 36:2, 14) probably constitutes another similar case, but there is a text-critical problem here (see *BHS*).

9. E.g., by Dearman himself, "Daughter Zion and Her Place," 152.

10. Floyd, "Welcome Back," 491.

Mary" or "Mary's daughter" could be understood to mean that "Mary" is the daughter rather than the mother.

In sum, semantic restrictions prevent terms of familial relationship from being understood in the appositional sense proposed by Stinespring, and these restrictions apply across linguistic borders. Dearman and whoever else wants to argue that בת ציון can be understood appositionally to mean "Daughter Zion" need first of all to show that this is even a remote possibility by finding a clear example in some language of terms of familial relationship functioning in this way.

DEARMAN'S FIRST OBJECTION CONCERNING THE RELATION OF בת ציון TO בנות ציון

Now I turn to the first of Dearman's stated objections, his rejection of my claims about the relationship between the singular and plural forms of the expression in question. This part of my argument has three main points: (1) On the grammatical level בת ציון can simply be understood as referring to a single member of the group designated by בנות ציון. The plural form of the expression in question, בנות plus a place name, is a well attested way of describing the female inhabitants of that place. The singular form of the expression, בת plus a place name, would thus refer to a single female inhabitant of that place. (2) On the poetic-rhetorical level בת ציון generally serves as the personification of the city's women in a single feminine figure.[11] And (3) the cultural background of this poetical convention is the social role played by women as the leaders of public rejoicing and lamentation.

Dearman rejects these contentions, giving only one reason: "The 'daughters of Jerusalem/Zion/Judah,' as well as daughters of other geographic entities, are mentioned several times in the Hebrew Bible. For many of these plural references, however, one cannot easily substitute a singular 'synonym' (a daughter [of] ...)."[12] This statement is certainly true as far as it goes, but I cannot see what it proves.

Again, Dearman fails to address the grammatical question. When speaking of mountains, the singular form הר שמרון (Amos 4:1) would

---

11. I also argued that in some contexts it could refer, by extension, to the entire population (ibid., 492–94), but that corollary is largely irrelevant to the present argument.

12. Dearman, "Daughter Zion and Her Place," 146.

normally be understood as referring to a single member of the group designated by the plural form הרי שמרון (Amos 3:9). Similarly, when thinking in terms of the liturgical calendar, the singular form יום מועד (Hos 9:5)
would be understood as referring to a single member of the group designated by the plural form ימי מועד (Hos 12:10). When discussing the patriarch's children, the singular form בן אברהם (Gen 28:9) would be understood as referring to a single member of the group designated by the plural
form בני אברהם (1 Chr 1:28). The same would be true if the terminology
of sonship is being used figuratively. When ruminating about livestock,
the singular form בן בקר (Lev 9:2) would be understood as referring to a
single member of the group designated by the plural form בני בקר (1 Sam
14:32). When speaking of strangers, the singular form בן נכר (Gen 17:12,
22; Exod 12:43; Lev 22:25; Ezek 44:9) would be understood as referring to
a single member of the group designated by the plural form בני נכר (2 Sam
22:45–46; Neh 9:2; Isa 60:10, 61:5, 62:8; Ezek 44:7; Ps 144:7, 11).

The same goes for בת. When arranging a marriage for Isaac, the singular form בת לבן (Gen 29:10) would be understood as referring to a single
member of the group designated by the plural forms בנות לבן (Gen 28:2).
Thus, when describing the women of a particular place, why shouldn't
בת plus the place name be understood as the singular of בנות plus the
place name? Dearman and whoever else wants to argue that בת ציון and
בנות ציון are not related in this way need to give reasons why בת ציון is a
(unique?) exception to the norm represented by the foregoing examples.

As noted above, Dearman's claim that בת ציון cannot be understood
as the singular of בנות ציון operates more on the poetic-rhetorical than the
grammatical level. Drawing on examples from Song of Songs, he argues
that they are not interchangeable synonyms:

> This is the case with the several references to the "daughters of Jerusalem,"
> who are addressed in the Song of Songs. The "bride's" self-identification
> to them as "dark, but lovely" (1:5, NIV), makes sense as a comment to
> observant young women in the city, but would make less sense as an
> address to an otherwise unidentified "daughter of Jerusalem." The same
> logic applies also to the repeated adjuration to the "daughters of Jerusa-
> lem," elsewhere in the book.[13]

---

13. Ibid.

I would agree, but my agreement does not constitute a negation of my argument because I did not claim that the singular and plural forms are synonymous. I maintained that בת ציון is generally a personification of בנות ציון in the form of a single feminine figure. This does not imply that בת ציון could be substituted wherever בנות ציון occurs. The retention of the plural form "daughters of Jerusalem" in Song of Songs only shows that such personification is not appropriate in all contexts.

To illustrate this point in terms of a more recent example, Rosie the Riveter was a personification of the women who went to work in factories during World War II. She figured prominently in popular graphic art and music of the day.[14] This kind of personification, in which one woman doing one particular job stands for the whole female U.S. war-effort workforce, is appropriate in propaganda emphasizing that women can do such heavy factory work, and that they can do it just as well as the men who used to but are now serving in the armed forces. Personification of many workers as one would not be appropriate, however, in a

report from the War Department documenting how many women were doing such work, as well as the various kinds of jobs that women had taken over. For this purpose in this context, one could hardly substitute a single representative figure who only does one kind of work—riveting.

Similarly, in certain contexts it would make no poetic-rhetorical sense to personify the בנות of a place as the בת of that place. The examples from Song of Songs cited by Dearman constitute such a case. The feminine protagonist in this romance is addressing the women of her community—the בנות ירושלים—as if they were a kind of support group with which she can share her joys and frustrations in love. She cautions her companions about being too forward with their lovers, enlists them as go-betweens to communicate her affection to her lover, and describes him to them as an object of desire, and so on. The point of such description is to give an impression

---

14. E.g., "Rosie the Riveter," by Redd Evans and John Jacob Loeb (New York: Paramount Music Corporation, 1943).

of the companionship and solidarity that the female protagonist enjoys with those whom Dearman calls the "observant young women in the city."[15] For this purpose in this context one could hardly substitute the singular בת ירושלים for the group.[16]

When would such personification be appropriate? Here the third point of my argument, which concerns cultural background of the בת ציון figure, becomes relevant. As I pointed out, this symbolic convention is rooted in women's leadership of public rejoicing and public lamentation.[17] Personification of the בנות of a place as the בת of that same place would thus be poetically and rhetorically useful wherever connotations associated with this custom are being evoked. Even in these contexts, however, the personification of a city's בנות in a single בת would not be obligatory. Such personification is a poetic-rhetorical option that may or may not be exercised, depending on the writer's intention and the context.[18]

DEARMAN'S SECOND OBJECTION: בת ציון MUST REFER TO THE CITY AS A GEOGRAPHICAL ENTITY

Dearman reasserts one of the claims made by Stinespring, that because בת ציון is characterized in terms of the geographical and architectonic features of Jerusalem this must be a designation for the city itself rather than a prototypical inhabitant. I argued that בת ציון, as a personification of Jerusalem's women, is also a representative *of the city*. Given the nature of metaphorical language, there is no reason why she could not be described as having walls and gates, as in the examples cited by Stinespring (Ps 9:15 [Eng. 14] and Lam 2:8). Just because she is described in such terms, there is no reason to insist that she must be a personification of the city as a daughter. I cited the recurring phrase, "the gate of my people" (Ruth 3:11; Mic 1:9; Obad 13), to show that the physical features of a city could be figuratively described as pertaining to those who live in it.

Dearman grants the cogency of my point with regard to these few examples, but he wants to reopen the question on the basis of the wealth of

---

15. Dearman, "Daughter Zion and Her Place," 146.

16. The same goes for Isa 3:16–17, another example cited by Dearman (ibid., 147).

17. Floyd, "Welcome Back," 499–503.

18. The option is not exercised in the two examples cited by Dearman, Pss 48:12 (Eng. 11) and 97:8. ("Daughter Zion and Her Place," 146–47).

data presented in Christl Maier's recent study.[19] I too find Maier's analysis of the personification of Jerusalem in terms of spatial theory largely compelling. I do not agree with her assumption that בת ציון refers to Daughter Zion, but most if not all of what she says about the personification of the city as Daughter Zion could also be said, mutatis mutandis, about the city as represented by the daughter of Zion. I thus do not think that Maier's conclusions necessarily lead to the implication that Dearman draws from them. In any case, here is his take on the upshot of her work:

> With regard to the personified city, there is a wealth of textual imagery on her geography, architecture, and sacred space. For Maier, DZ/DJer represents the personified city of Jerusalem, and she shows that DZ's poetic portrayal fits handily within the broader corpus of texts personifying the city and employing gender-related imagery. Stated otherwise, personified Jerusalem and DZ have identical characteristics.[20]

In an attempt to substantiate this point, Dearman examines Zeph 3:14–20. He claims that in verses 14–16 בת ציון and its variant בת ירושלים are directly addressed in poetic parallelism with Zion and Jerusalem, as if they were all identical. Given this interpretation of who is being addressed here, the inclusion of Israel in verse 14, as part of the same series of vocatives, would seem to be anomalous. The people of Israel are obviously not geographically identical with the city of Jerusalem. Dearman attempts to get around this difficulty as follows:

> Israel is also addressed along with DZ and DJer in v. 14 and implored to shout with them. This is confirmation that they too are corporate entities, as they are used in parallelism with the covenant name of YHWH's people. The parallelism of the three entities in v. 14 includes, but is not limited to, geography, as the stress on returning people in vv. 18–20 confirms. Further confirmation comes with the consistent use of the feminine pronoun in 3:14–20, whose singular antecedent is the city (DZ, DJer, Zion, Jerusalem).[21]

This interpretation of the passage in question is problematic in two respects. First, as various studies of Hebrew poetry have shown, corre-

---

19. Ibid., 149.
20. Dearman, "Daughter Zion and Her Place," 149.
21. Ibid., 150

sponding terms in poetic parallelism are not necessarily identical.[22] Take, for example, Ps 96:11.

> Let the heavens be glad,
> Let the earth rejoice.

In this couplet the terms *heavens* and *earth* are corresponding in the sense that they are the two complementary realms of the cosmos, but they are not identical. Similarly, one could argue that in Zeph 3:14–16 בת ציון/ בת ירושלים and Zion/Jerusalem are corresponding, not because they are identical, but in the sense that they refer to two complementary aspects of the city. The first pair of terms personifies its population and the second pair of terms names the city as a geographical entity.

Furthermore, contrary to Dearman's analysis, the inclusion of Israel among the addressees does not confirm that they are all identical, but rather reinforces the impression that there is variation among them. He states that there is "consistent use of the feminine pronoun in 3:14–20, whose singular antecedent is the city (DZ, DJer, Zion, Jerusalem),"[23] but this is simply not true. In fact, Israel is implored to join the celebration with a masculine plural command, and second-person masculine plural pronouns are used throughout verse 20 (five times!). Of course, Israel is a "corporate entity," but that does not preclude that here Israel is addressed as a plurality. And, of course, בת ציון is also a "corporate entity," but this does not preclude her being addressed as a single figure personifying the people. There is nothing in this passage's pattern of direct address that requires בת ציון to be understood as identical with Zion. On the contrary, it gives the impression that they are related in precisely the way that the variation in the terms of address implies: בת ציון, "the daughter of Zion," personifies the population of the city; and Zion, the city itself, is thus her mother.

Starting from the same passage, Zeph 3:14–20, Dearman also launches another line of argument. He considers the attribution to בת ציון of geographic and physical details that to him seem incongruous when imagined in relation to a woman rather than a place. His main example is the statement addressed to Zion in Zeph 3:14, that Yhwh is "in your midst." He

---

22. E.g., Robert Alter, *The Art of Biblical Poetry* (New York: Basic Books, 1985); and James L. Kugel, *The Idea of Biblical Poetry: Parallelism and Its History* (New Haven: Yale University Press, 1981).

23. Dearman, "Daughter Zion and Her Place," 150.

goes on to list several texts in which various other things (soldiers, evil schemes, etc.) are said to be "in the midst" of בת ציון. Dearman takes this as a clear reference to geographical space within the city, and he cannot imagine that such things could be said about a "daughter" inhabitant of the city rather than the city itself: "Should a 'daughter of' Zion speak about [such things in] 'her midst,' the reference would imply a personal matter, not geography."[24] For the daughter of Zion to speak of "her midst" seems incongruous to Dearman because he is thinking literally rather than metaphorically, just as Stinespring did with respect to this same point.

If the nature of metaphorical language is taken into account, Dearman's objection loses its force. Mandolfo has given a wonderfully succinct summary of the theory of metaphor, as it relates to the personification of Jerusalem, and there is no need to repeat it here.[25] Suffice it to point out that when things are compared, things that are in some ways alike and in some ways not, the effect is to create a dynamic interplay among the similarities and differences. This interplay often develops through description of one of the things compared in terms of what makes it dissimilar from the other, as well as what makes it similar. Take, for example, the plant metaphor in "Thou are indeed just, Lord," by Gerard Manley Hopkins.

> Thou art indeed just, Lord, if I contend
> With thee; but, sir, so what I plead is just.
> Why do sinners' ways prosper? and why must
> Disappointment all I endeavour end?
> Wert thou my enemy, O thou my friend,
> How wouldst thou worse, I wonder, than thou dost
> Defeat, thwart me? Oh, the sots and thralls of lust
> Do in spare hours more thrive than I that spend,
> Sir, life upon thy cause. See, banks and brakes
> Now, leavèd how thick! lacèd they are again
> With fretty chervil, look, and fresh wind shakes
> Them; birds build—but not I build; no, but strain,
> Time's eunuch, and not breed one work that wakes.
> Mine, O thou lord of life, send my roots rain.[26]

---

24. Ibid.

25. Mandolfo, *Daughter Zion*, 23–26.

26. *Gerard Manley Hopkins, The Poems and Prose of Gerard Manley Hopkins* (Penguin Classics; Baltimore: Penguin, 1985), 67.

This poem is modeled on one of Jeremiah's complaints (Jer 12:1–4), and in some editions of Hopkins's works Jer 12:1 appears as an epigraph. The plant metaphor is introduced in the ninth line, after the initial contrast between the success of the wicked and the plight of the supplicant, as an image describing the way of wicked. They thrive like bushes and vines growing thick and green. Initially the metaphor functions abstractly, comparing the lushness of plant growth with the prosperity of the wicked. They are not said to be like plants in any substantial way. They do not have leaves or seeds, and so on. Comparison on this level introduces a note of fertility into the contrast, however, which is then contrastingly matched by a reference to the supplicant's sterility ("time's eunuch"). This extension moves the development of the metaphor away from the level of the purely abstract, more in the direction of the physical and material. Up until the very last line, plant-like qualities have been ascribed only to the wicked, as something that makes them dissimilar from the supplicant, and only in abstract terms. But the development of the metaphor culminates with the attribution of a material plant-like quality—roots needing rain—to the supplicant. The metaphorical terms in which the wicked were initially distinguished from the supplicant finally serve to characterize the supplicant himself.

Given that metaphorical language often works in the way just described, when either a city or its population is personified as a woman, we should not be surprised by the fact that the metaphor could develop in such a way that things pertaining to the city per se would be attributed to the feminine personification. In material terms a city is not very similar to a woman. The female body does not correspond in obvious ways to urban structures consisting of buildings, streets, public areas, fortifications, and so on. The personification depends primarily on the more abstract similarity between the way women typically nurture those that depend on them and the way cities serve as a matrix for the sustenance and enrichment of the human beings that live in it.[27] Once the comparison is established on the basis of such similarity, however, the dissimilarities can also come into play. The feminine personification can be characterized in terms of things that distinguish her body from urban structure. Thus בת ציון can have walls and gates, and so on.

---

27. This obviously does not exhaust the similarities, but it will serve as a basis for comparison and contrast.

The rhetorical purpose of personifying a city as a woman is precisely to efface, in particular ways, the distinctions between what Dearman calls "a personal matter" of the woman and the "geography" of the city. In light of this fact, one might ask why it is more problematic—as he claims—for the physical features of a city to be attributed to a feminine personification of the city's women ("the daughter of Zion") than to a feminine personification of the city itself ("Daughter Zion"). In either case the personification plays upon the incongruities a woman's body in relation to urban structures. This metaphorical dynamic does not in itself establish any probability about how בת ציון should be understood, one way or the other.

Moreover, in biblical poetry there are clear examples of metaphorical language being used in precisely the ways that Dearman would disallow. On the one hand, things can be said to be "in the midst" of the personification of a people rather than a geographical place. Take, for example, Isa 29:22b–23 (NRSV):

No longer shall Jacob be ashamed,
　　no longer shall his fact grow pale.
For when he sees his children,
　　the work of my hands in his midst,
　　they will sanctify my name.
They will sanctify the Holy One of Jacob,
　　and will stand in awe of the God of Israel.

Jacob is clearly a personification of all Israel as a social entity, not of the land or of any particular city. Here descendants of Israel are said to be engendered "in his midst." Yhwh too is said to be "in the midst" of his people when they are on the march from Egypt to Canaan, precisely when they are not yet settled anywhere in the land.[28]

As is evident in these examples, various things can obviously be described as "in the midst" of a people rather than a place, and also "in the midst" of the personification of a people. Why cannot things be similarly described as "in the midst" of "the daughter of Zion," who personifies the city in terms of its population rather than its physical space?

---

28. E.g., Exod 34:9 and Deut 21:8. Examples could be multiplied if we considered cases using תוך, which is virtually synonymous with קרב, even with respect to the בנות of a place (Ezek 15:63). But since Dearman limits himself to קרב, so do I.

On the other hand, the feminine personification of Wisdom, who clearly has nothing to do with geography, can have aspects of architectonic structure attributed to her. Wisdom has built a house that she opens to guests (Prov 8:1–6). They must decide whether to accept her dinner invitation or to go to the house of "the foolish woman." In terms of this figure, entering the house of Wisdom becomes emblematic of the decision to seek enlightenment. Wisdom lives in the house, and entering the house makes it possible to meet her. As the metaphor develops, entering the house becomes so closely identified with access to Wisdom that the points of entry are attributed directly to her as the one who dwells in the building, rather than to the building itself: "Happy is the person who meditates on wisdom,… who peers through her windows and listens at her doors" (Sir 14:20a, 23 NRSV). Compare Prov 8:34, where Wisdom says: "Happy is the one who listens to me, watching daily at my gates, waiting beside my doors." If the feminine personification of Wisdom can be metaphorically said to have windows, gates, and doors, why can בת ציון not be metaphorically said to have gates and walls?

Dearman's argument that בת ציון must refer to the city as a geographical entity is simply mistaken because he fails to consider the nature of metaphorical language.

DEARMAN'S THIRD OBJECTION: VARIATIONS ON THE בת ציון FORMULA MUST BE UNDERSTOOD APPOSITIONALLY

Dearman brings up the question of compound variations on the בת ציון formula, in which a third noun in construct relationship has been added to the construct phrase consisting of בת plus a place name. He claims that in these cases all three nouns must be understood to be in apposition. His first example is the phrase ישבת בת דיבון (Jer 48:18). He says that it "does not refer to 'a female dweller of the daughter of Dibon,' and is thus better understood as an appositional or explicative phrase."[29] His second example is בתולת בת ציון, of which he similarly says, "the longer construct chain should be interpreted appositionally or explicatively."[30] He would translate ישבת בת דיבון as "enthroned daughter Dibon," and בתולת בת ציון as "virgin daughter Zion."

---

29. Dearman, "Daughter Zion and Her Place," 148.
30. Ibid., 151.

In dealing with such phrases, Dearman presents a false either/or. He supposes that all three nouns must be in an appositional relationship, or that all three must be in a possessive relationship. This is not necessarily the case, however. In both of Dearman's examples the semantic restriction described above would require that בת plus the place name be understood possessively as "daughter of X," but there is nothing to prevent בת from being understood appositionally in relation to the initial noun. Such compound construct phrases combine a noun in apposition with the preceding noun and in a possessive relationship with the following noun. Thus ישבת בת דיבון should be translated as "the enthroned one, the daughter of Dibon," and בתולת בת ציון as "the virgin daughter of Zion."

In various other examples of compound construct phrases, semantic considerations similarly make evident that both appositional and possessive relationships are involved. Some geographic descriptions involving mountains have a structure similar to the one proposed just above:

Deut 1:2	דרך הר שעיר	"the road to Mount Seir"
Josh 8:33	מור הר גרזים	"the opposite side of Mount Gerizim"
Josh 15:10	כתף הר יערים	"the shoulder of Mount Jearim"
Judg 9:7	ראש הר גרזים	"the top of Mount Gerizim"

In all of these cases the noun הר is in an appositional relationship with the following proper noun, and in a possessive relationship with the preceding noun denoting a geographical feature. This is indicated not by the grammatical form itself, but by the semantics of the geographical terminology. A noun denoting a partial aspect of a mountain or an approach to a mountain cannot be in apposition with the noun denoting the mountain itself.

This phenomenon is not limited to geographic description. Following Stinespring, Dearman cites אשת בעלת אוב (1 Sam 28:7) as "another construct phrase that should be interpreted appositionally," in the same way that he would interpret בתולת בת ציון and ישבת בת דיבון.[31] In this phrase, however, all three nouns cannot be related appositionally. The first noun, אשת ("woman"), is indeed in apposition with the second noun,

---

31. Ibid., 151 n. 16.

בעלת ("mistress"), but the relationship with the third noun, אוב ("ghost"), is possessive. The woman in question is not a ghost, she is the "mistress" or summoner *of* a ghost.[32]

Parallel examples of compound construct phrases thus do not support Dearman's argument that if all three nouns cannot be understood possessively, then all three must be understood appositionally. On the contrary, they show that in such phrases nouns can be related to one another both appositionally and possessively, in precisely the way that I initially proposed to analyze בתלת בת ישראל and its variations.[33]

Dearman's Third Objection (continued): The Case of בת עמי

This particular variation on the בת ציון formula poses somewhat different problems. On the one hand, once it is clear that there is no reason to understand בת ציון as an appositional genitive, this implies that there is also no reason to understand בת עמי that way. On the other hand, however, there are some obvious differences between בת עמי and the other variations on בת ציון. In the other cases בת is in construct relationship with a proper noun that is also a place name, and the expression is entirely in the third person. But in this case בת is in construct relationship with a common noun (עם, "people") that is also modified by a first-person singular pronoun ("my"). These differences give rise to two questions: (1) To whom does the first-person singular pronoun refer? Whose people are described by this phrase? And (2) how does the answer to the first question affect the question of whether the phrase is to be understood appositionally ("my daughter people") or possessively ("the daughter of my people")?

When the phrase בת עמי occurs, Yhwh is sometimes the speaker (e.g., Jer 8:11 and 9:6 (Eng. 7)), and the people in question are obviously then his. But does the phrase refer appositionally to them as his daughter ("my daughter people") or possessively to one who is their daughter ("the daughter of my people")? In such cases the semantic restriction discussed above does not clearly apply, and either interpretation is perhaps conceivable. In the majority of cases, however, Yhwh is not the speaker, and the appositional alternative seems highly improbable (Isa 22:4; Jer 8:19, 21, 23; Lam 2:11; 3:48; 4:3, 6, 10). Take, for example, Jer 6:26:

---

32. As Dearman's own translation states, but in a way that is inexplicably inconsistent with his argument about the syntactic analysis.

33. Floyd, "Welcome Back," 491–92.

בת עמי, put on sackcloth,
    and roll in ashes;
make mourning as for an only child,
    most bitter lamentation:
for suddenly the destroyer
    will come upon us.

Here the people are obviously Jeremiah's, not Yhwh's, and the concluding first-person plural pronoun shows that the prophet identifies with his
people in their distress. In this context if בת עמי were taken to mean "my
daughter people," Jeremiah would also be characterizing himself as the
father of his people, which is hardly conceivable. I cannot think of any
context in which a prophet addresses or describes the people as *his* children. Similar problems arise with regard to the narrator in Lamentations,
though his may not be a prophetic voice strictly speaking. He can hardly
be the father of the people either. Although בת עמי is more semantically
ambiguous than the other variations on בת ציון, the way it is used in most
cases shows that it must be understood as "the daughter of my people,"
taking this figure as a personification of the women of the people—who
can be described as the people's "daughters" (cf. Ezek 13:17)—in the form
of a single woman.

CONCLUSION OF THE RESPONSE TO DEARMAN

I find none of Dearman's arguments compelling. On the contrary, they
only continue to beg the question. If Jerusalem is a daughter, as Stinespring proposed, then who is her parent? It is difficult to understand why
something would be characterized as a daughter unless this implied some
metaphorical line of descent, but the Bible nowhere describes Jerusalem
explicitly as anyone's daughter. Both Maier and Dearman argue that Zion
is metaphorically and implicitly the daughter of Yhwh, and Hugh Williamson has invoked the concept of a "dead metaphor" to explain how
the characterization of Daughter Zion could retain currency without any
explicit reference to who the father is.[34] Of course, Yhwh does have meta-

---

34. Maier, *Daughter Zion, Mother Zion*, 92; Dearman, "Daughter Zion and Her
Place," passim; Hugh G. M. Williamson, *Isaiah 1–5* (ICC; London: T&T Clark, 2006),
67–70.

phorical progeny, and dead metaphors do exist. The question is whether בת ציון is best explained in such terms.

The problem is that the argument is utterly circular. The only reason to suppose that Jerusalem is characterized as a daughter is the interpretation of בת ציון as an appositional genitive, and the only reason to suppose that בת ציון should be interpreted as an appositional genitive is conjecture about the possible significance of Jerusalem's hypothetical daughterliness. I have tried to break this vicious cycle by interjecting some grammatical, rhetorical-poetical, and sociocultural realism. On the grammatical level בת ציון cannot be understood as an appositional genitive. This phrase metaphorically refers to a daughter whose mother is the city of Jerusalem. On the rhetorical-poetical level this figure personifies the women of the city in particular, and the people of the city in general. This personification generally represents the people's expression of grief in bad times, or conversely the people's expression of exultation in good times. On the sociocultural level, this personification reflects the social role of women as leaders of civic lamentation and rejoicing.

When בת ציון is interpreted in this way, there is no need to invoke the hypothetical but never mentioned paternity of Yhwh, or to fall back on the concept of a dead metaphor. There are explicit descriptions of Jerusalem as a mother and its people as her children, and the part assigned to her daughter is a well-defined and well-documented role played by Israelite women.

The success of Stinespring's proposal is a notable example of the way in which a scholarly theory can be proposed, and then readily assumed, repeated, and built upon without being adequately tested. Why have so many scholars been so taken with the notion of Daughter Zion that they misrepresent or overlook the evidence to the contrary that is right before their eyes? Their doing so is a mystery that lies well beyond the scope of this essay. I can only note here that this is what has happened, and again suggest that it is now time to return to a more solidly grounded understanding of בת ציון as "daughter of Zion."

Rereading Mandolfo's Interpretation of Lamentations 1

In this section I will show how the recognition of בת ציון as "daughter of Zion" would affect Mandolfo's interpretation of בת ציון in Lamentations. Her reading is based on the assumption that the text features a single feminine figure (Daughter Zion), and it is driven by the desire to find an alternative to Jeremiah and Ezekiel's characterization of Jerusalem as Yhwh's adulterous harlot-wife. Mandolfo therefore focuses on those aspects of the text that counter the pejorative view expressed by Yhwh, as the aggrieved husband, speaking through these prophets. The result is a theodicy in which Yhwh is admittedly right but blamed for overreacting, and Jerusalem refuses to be comforted, unable to imagine any terms on which the relationship might be restored. My reading will be contrastingly based on the assumption that the daughter of Zion and Jerusalem are related but not identical, and that—as Dearman has rightly noted—Yhwh is not presented here as Jerusalem's husband. Many of Mandolfo's points will be reaffirmed rather than negated, but in a modified or relativized form, and the outcome will be a theodicy of a very different sort.

In the present discussion I have the limited goal of showing what difference it makes to recognize that בת ציון is "daughter of Zion" rather than "Daughter Zion." I do not pretend to offer an exhaustive commentary. For the sake of argument I will generally assume Mandolfo's solutions for text-critical and other such problems, and I will follow translation options taken by standard English versions without further discussion. Mandolfo deals with both chapters 1 and 2 of Lamentations, but for the sake of economy I will deal here only with chapter 1. In this regard it should be noted that in these two chapters the roles of בת ציון are very different. In chapter 2 she is the main character, but in chapter 1 she plays a relatively minor role.

The main character is chapter 1 is Jerusalem herself. As the result of the city's destruction she has experienced a traumatic reversal of status. She is now like a widow and a dethroned princess (v. 1). The text does not say who her husband was, but as the description unfolds her widowhood is evident in the lack of the protection and support that would have been conventionally provided by husbands in ancient society. The men have all been killed or taken captive. Thus there are food shortages (vv. 11 and 19), and "there is no one to help her" (v. 7).

Yhwh could not be Jerusalem's husband. If he were, given that she is a widow, then he would have to be among the casualties. But he is very much alive. Indeed, he is the cause of the destruction. He has made Jerusalem suffer (v. 5), inflicted sorrow upon her (v. 12), and handed her over to more powerful enemies (v. 14). The agents of Yhwh are the enemy forces, but in verse 13 their actions—burning, entrapping, repelling, and so on—are described as a quasi-theophanic manifestation of Yhwh's own power. Here Yhwh is characterized not as the divine aggrieved husband but as the Divine Warrior, and Jerusalem's reversal of status includes a reversal in his role, from her military defender to her attacker (v. 15).

As a dethroned princess, Jerusalem has experienced changes in her international standing. The destruction extends well beyond the city limits to the entire kingdom of Judah, over which she used to rule (v. 3). She now submits to those from whom she once exacted tribute (v. 1). Her former allies have betrayed her and have become her enemies (vv. 2 and 19). Her royal splendor is a thing of the past, as are the princes that formerly made up the king's court (v. 6). The humiliation of public nudity, to which exiles were typically subjected, has turned admiration into derision (v. 8).

As a holy city, where the royal temple was located, Jerusalem has also been profaned. Worshippers no longer make pilgrimages there, and the priesthood is decimated (vv. 4 and 19). Foreigners have violated the purity of her sanctuary (v. 10), so that she is now covered with impurity and is commonly regarded as something unclean (vv. 9 and 17).

Why has this horrendous state of affairs come about? The narrator says that this is Yhwh's retribution for Jerusalem's wrongdoing (v. 5; cf. v. 8). And when he allows Jerusalem to speak for herself, she admits her complicity. She has "rebelled" against Yhwh (vv. 18 and 20) and committed many "transgressions" (vv. 14 and 22), for which Yhwh is justly angry. But this is not the end of the matter. Jerusalem also suggests that Yhwh's retaliation is out of all proportion to the sins she has committed, particularly as it affects the innocent children of the next generation. And this is where בת ציון comes in.

A prominent leitmotif in the description of the destruction is its effect on the children. They are left desolate (v. 16). Even the little ones have been taken captive (v. 5), as well as the youths (v. 18). The young women are left grief-stricken (v. 4). In this context the text describes the plight of two feminine figures personifying two groups of women directly affected by what has happened to the children, the daughter of Zion (בת ציון) personifying the women of Jerusalem in particular (v. 6) and the virgin daughter of Judah (בתולת בת יהודה) personifying the women of Judah in general (v. 15). Along with Zion's young women (v. 4) and children (v. 5), the daughter of Zion has been left grief-stricken and homeless by the loss of her regal status (v. 6). And just as Yhwh has "crushed" the young men of Jerusalem, he has "trodden" the virgin daughter of Judah (v. 15). This is another case in which the generational connotations of the בת ציון formula are foregrounded.[35] This figure is an integral part of the imagery describing the tragic fate of Mother Jerusalem and Mother Judah's children.[36]

What, then, is the point of using such personification only in these two instances, while mostly describing the impact on the children without resorting to this device? What is the effect of this contrast? As noted above, the figure of בת ציון connotes the traditional role of women as leaders of public lamentation. In this context its use is connected with another leit-motif that surfaces repeatedly: Jerusalem is left "with no one to comfort her" (vv. 2, 9, 16, 17, and 21). The main function of women's lamentation is to console the survivors of catastrophe, and because of what has happened to בת ציון and בתולת בת יהודה such consolation is no longer possible. The personification thus serves to associate the children's misfortune with the demise of this feminine tradition and the consequent lack of consolation.

The personification of בת ציון and בתולת בת יהודה thus forms part of a web of associations that serve to define the issue of theodicy, as it is presented here, and to frame it in the most pathetic terms. Is it right to punish children for the sins of their parents? Some biblical texts affirm that Yhwh characteristically does so (Exod 20:5, 34:7; Deut 5:9; Num 14:18; Jer 32:18), while other texts affirm that he does not (Jer 31:29–30; Ezek 18:1–4). Whether or not he has been true to character, in this case Yhwh is implicated in the brutalization of Zion's children to an extent that they scarcely deserve, and in her grief Mother Jerusalem insists on holding him accountable.

This takes the form of repeated petitions directing Yhwh to "look" and "see" what he has done (vv. 9, 11, and 20). The implication is that Yhwh may not realize just how excessive he has been, but that on second glance it will dawn on him. Passersby are also asked to "look" and "see" that the sorrow inflicted by Yhwh is much greater than might be reasonably expected (v. 12), as if the more objective perspective of disinterested third parties will help to keep Yhwh's perceptions honest.

Mandolfo cannot imagine that this would have any effect on Yhwh because she has miscast him in the role of the enraged cuckold, who seeks reconciliation only on his own terms—a role that he indeed plays in other texts, but not here. If we instead see Yhwh in the role to which this text

---

35. See also Floyd, "Welcome Back," 502–4.

36. Mandolfo also notes that "Zion morally reorients the rhetoric by focusing on herself as bereaved nurturer" (*Daughter Zion*, 89).

has assigned him, as the overzealous Divine Warrior, there are hints of an outcome involving a more mutual give and take.

The chapter concludes with Jerusalem's petition that Yhwh subjects her enemies to the same reversal of status that she has suffered (vv. 21–22). In the style of many complaint psalms, Jerusalem expresses confidence that Yhwh has already decreed a response to what she has asked, implying that something along these lines will surely come to pass. On the one hand, this suggests that Yhwh recognizes the validity of her claim. Because his enemy agents have excessively mistreated Jerusalem's children in his name, justice demands that they be punished too. On the other hand, it also suggests that Jerusalem suspects that Yhwh may not be entirely responsible. He did indeed send his enemy agents to punish her, but then they arrogantly took matters into their own hands and did more damage than he intended. Thus Yhwh will judge them too (cf. Isa 10:5–19). When Jerusalem's enemies undergo the same fate as Jerusalem, this will not bring back the children who have died. It will, however, make it possible for the children held captive in exile to return home (cf., e.g., Isa 43:5–6; 60:4; Bar 4:30–36). Jerusalem will still be grieving, but the daughter of Zion will at least be there to comfort her.

With wry humor John Prine has described the kind of theodicy in which neither side wins, but both give in to get along ("you forgive us and we'll forgive you").[37] He does not make light of or mitigate the agony ("we'll forgive each other til we both turn blue") but he still leaves room for hope ("going fishing in heaven"). Lamentations 1 is a theophany of this sort, which is why Christian tradition has interpreted it as a prefiguration of Christ's passion. In such a typology, the daughter of Zion represents the way in which deep suffering can sometimes give birth to even deeper consolation. It would be interesting to put the enraged, cuckolded Yhwh and the adulterous harlot-wife of Jeremiah and Ezekiel in a dialogic exchange with the Divine Warrior Yhwh accosted for being overzealous, Mother Jerusalem, and the daughter of Zion of Lam 1. They could have a conversation while fishing, all together in the same boat, in heaven.

---

37. See the epigraph.

Ezekiel 16—Shared Memory of Yhwh's Relationship with Jerusalem: A Story of Fraught Expectations

Mignon R. Jacobs

Ezekiel 16 is an instance of shared cultural memory using figurative lan-guage to portray the Yhwh-Israel relationship. The constitutive images in the memory reveal perspectives about the relationship partners. Funda-mental to the portrayal is that the Deity's character "authors" the female character and thus constructs her identity. As both author and character, the Deity presents a complex portrayal of the failed relationship. Does the female/Jerusalem behave as she does independent of the quality of the rela-tionship with the Deity? How does the nature of the relationship impact the behavior? The shared memory suggests that the female behavior is contrary to the quality of the male-female relationship; that the male (Deity) is more favored than the female (community/Jerusalem); that the female behavior is deplorable while the male behavior is somehow commendable. In this article I propose that the portrayal uses memory as a tool and with that use presents competing perspectives (counterclaims) regarding the relationship and the identity of the characters. These competing perspectives within the text constitute its dialogical nature that both affirms and challenges the dominant perspective within Ezek 16. Without these counterclaims the pri-mary characters are not seen, heard, or perceived in the same way. Recog-nizing that these are prevalent interpretive tendencies among other viable possibilities, in this study I build on a few methodological observations.

First, I contend that the use of metaphor defines the text and the inter-pretive process. Utilizing the interactive approach for understanding the metaphor,[1] I further argue that the use of figurative language gives the

---

1. History of interpretation informs the statement regarding the interactive

text its particularity—namely, the overlapping images. Here I use "overlapping" to define the interplay of the relational elements drawn from different relationship domains—including, spousal, parental, rescuer—noting that the discourse filters these elements through the marital metaphor. The dynamics in these domains constitute the background for understanding the perspectives within the text. Yet as interpreters, decoding the dynamics would mean having access to the relationships. That access is especially difficult for modern interpreters who are situated at a distance from the text (chronologically, socially, ideologically, etc.). Nonetheless, the nature of the metaphor (its multivalence)[2] allows such access, not necessarily to a static entity behind the text but to the dynamic process inherent in the metaphor and the discourse it constructs and serves.

Second, I argue that the depiction betrays the nature of the relationship and thus presents competing perspectives regarding it—a "behind the scenes look" at the relational dynamics. Included in this argument are: the examination of the extended marital metaphor; endorsement of the multivalence of the metaphor wherein lies the potential to explore aspects

---

approach to metaphor; cf. I. A. Richards, "The Philosophy of Rhetoric," in *Philosophical Perspectives on Metaphor* (ed. Mark Johnson; Minneapolis: University of Minnesota Press, 1981), 48–62; Max Black, *Models and Metaphors: Studies in Language and Philosophy* (Ithaca, N.Y.: Cornell University Press, 1962); Paul Ricoeur, *The Rule of Metaphor: Multi-disciplinary Studies of the Creation of Meaning in Language* (London: Routledge, 1978). The present study is indebted to S. Tamar Kamionkowski (*Gender Reversal and Cosmic Chaos: A Study on the Book of Ezekiel* [JSOTSup 368; Sheffield: Sheffield Academic Press, 2003], 30–57) for the insightful and clear presentation of theories of metaphor and the place of metaphor in biblical studies. See also Julie Galambush, *Jerusalem in the Book of Ezekiel: The City as Yahweh's Wife* (SBLDS 130; Atlanta: Scholars Press, 1992), 4–10.

2. This aspect of the metaphor has been labeled "ambiguous," or according to Galambush, the "indeterminacy is a prime source of the power of metaphor; a metaphor does not make a single statement (or, to the extent that it does, that statement is always literally false) but provokes the reader to see connections where none had been seen before" (*Jerusalem*, 5). See also Antje Labahn, "Metaphor and Inter-textuality: 'Daughter of Zion' as a Test Case: Response to Kirsten Nielsen 'From Oracles to Canon'—and the Role of Metaphor," *SJOT* 17 (2003): 49–67, for a discussion of the metaphor's ability to create a world of meaning. He proposes: "The making of sense created by a metaphor happens rather between the text and its reader. The making of sense happens in a specific situation envisaged by the author of the text. The metaphor itself acts in a way of reader-response dialogue and raises reality in collaboration with a reader or hearer of the text" (50).

other than the primary claim of the discourse; and the identification of counterclaims, that is, the by-product of the primary claim that are nonetheless integral to the construction of the primary discourse/claim. In terms of memory, these counterclaims may be the suppressed aspects of the relational dynamics. Such suppressions and selection are parts of the natural process of memory construction that define the resultant portrait of agents depicted in the memory. With awareness of these counterclaims, the primary discourse is perceived differently.

In dialogue with Carleen Mandolfo's dialogical theology, I further contend that by their nature all readings privilege a perspective but do not in the privilege obliterate other perspectives.[3] Even so, Ezek 16 is one discourse about the relationship—a shared memory of the history and status of the relationship used to persuade its audience about the relationship and the partners/agents—but already disposed to negative images of the female agent.[4] Basic to this argument is recognizing the counterclaims inherent in the portrayal and not only those separate or distinct from Ezek 16. A counterclaim in this instance is any suggestion of an alternate reality implicit, explicit, inside, or apart from the text. So defined, the dialogic component need not depend on the existence of intertextual attestations to the portrayal for hearing counterclaims or countertestimony.[5] The existence of these counterclaims in other texts enhances the clarity of the counterclaims in Ezek 16.

Third, I identify Ezek 16 as shared cultural memory along with other memories and discourses about the nature of the Yhwh-Israel relation-

---

3. Carleen Mandolfo, *Daughter Zion Talks Back to the Prophets: A Dialogic Theology of the Book of Lamentations* (SemeiaSt 58; Atlanta: Society of Biblical Literature, 2007). Mandolfo contends, "Dialogic reading practices highlight the Bible's multiple, conflicting, and complementary voices and thus insists on readings that refuse to privilege one point of view" (26). I contend that the very suggestion presents a privilege for its argument, just as text in arguing for a point of view gives privilege to a perspective. At best, the dialogic reading juxtaposes the points of view; any attempt to systematize results in a privilege of a perspective or a cluster of perspectives.

4. For further discussion of the use of memory in presenting the relationship between Yhwh and Israel, see Adriane B. Leveen, "Variations on a Theme: Differing Conceptions of Memory in the Book of Numbers," *JSOT* 27 (2002): 201–21.

5. Walter Brueggemann, *Theology of the Old Testament: Testimony, Dispute, Advocacy* (Minneapolis: Fortress, 1997); contrast Mandolfo (*Daughter Zion*, 18), who terms this aspect of the text as "counterstory."

ship.[6] Aware of the portrayals of the cultural memory in Hos 1–3, Jer 2–3, and Ezek 23, I focus on Ezek 16 as a three-dimensional portrayal of the origin and status, including the prophetic voice, the Deity, and the personified community (Jerusalem). Although they are inextricably intertwined, the first and second dimensions coalesce—the voice of the prophet and the Deity being the same. The Deity is both author and character in the portrayal; accordingly, the portrayal of the Deity is as much a theological construct as a sociological one and has implications for understanding the identity and the designated roles in the shared memory.[7] These observations illustrate that the present study incorporates two distinctive yet interrelated methodological commitments: examination of metaphor and analysis of the phenomenon of shared cultural memory.

TEXTUAL INVESTIGATION: METAPHOR AND MEMORY

The text, a depiction of relationship, uses metaphor as its mode of shared memory to persuade its audience.[8] Both metaphor and memory suppress elements in order to feature a particular portrayal. According to the extended metaphor of Ezek 16, Yhwh observed Jerusalem when she was a child (v. 6). Jerusalem is accused of not remembering (זכר) the days of her youth (vv. 22, 43),[9] while the Deity remembers those days and honors the covenant (ברית) made at that time (v. 60). Does the perspective result in a conflict of memories? Did Yhwh care for Israel in her infancy? Were the days of her youth an idyllic stage of the relationship? Regarding care during infancy, are there differences between Yhwh's memory and other depictions of how the Deity cared for Israel (northern kingdom) vis-à-vis Judah/Jerusalem (southern kingdom)?[10] Ezekiel 16 is a three-dimensional

---

6. See Lyle Eslinger, "Ezekiel 20 and the Metaphor of Historical Teleology: Concepts of Biblical History," *JSOT* 81 (1998): 93–125. Eslinger explores how Ezek 16 represents cyclical mythologies (esp. 93, 99–100).

7. "Author" is used here to designated the inner level of the text—the voice of the text rather than the external composition or redactional aspects.

8. Cf. Walther Eichrodt, *Ezekiel* (trans. Cosslett Quin; OTL; Philadelphia: Westminster, 1970), 201, who identifies Ezek 16 as a story with similar persuasive methods as Judg 9, 2 Sam 12; 14:5–16; Jer 31; 47:6); Joseph Blenkinsopp, *Ezekiel* (IBC; Louisville: John Knox, 1989), 77, who also notes the persuasive methods of Ezekiel and 2 Sam 12.

9. The phrase is ימי נעורייך, "days of your youth."

10. Jerusalem's noted disregard for children is to be highlighted. The pattern of

portrayal constructed or authored from the vantage point of the Deity as both actor and observer.[11] While in this study I do not juxtapose the different portrayals of the relationship, one cannot ignore that the Ezek 16 portrayal is only one perspective and memory of the Yhwh-Israel relationship.[12] Juxtaposed to Ezek 23 and Jer 2–3, Ezek 16 is a competing witness or counterclaim to the relationship.[13] To illustrate the counterclaim, one notes that Ezek 23:1, 19, and 21 depict "the days of youth" as a time of "whoring" much like the adult stages depicted in Ezek 16. The presence of these intertextual claims validates the idea that memories are edited perspectives about the past that construct reality and identity through various filters (e.g., relational). Accordingly, filters define behaviors and expectations and are reflected in the memory about the agents and their respective behaviors, roles, responses, and evaluations. As the narrative of the Deity's memory, Ezek 16 is an attempt to persuade the community that she has not lived up to the expectations as defined by the covenant relationship.

CHARACTERIZATION OF JERUSALEM (FEMALE SPOUSE)

The text portrays the female agent, Jerusalem, through the use of metaphor and more specifically through its stance, descriptors, and noted responses. Many classify Ezek 16 on the basis of the female's behavior, for example, that she is unfaithful, ungrateful,[14] or even nymphomaniacal.[15]

---

learned behavior is helpful to understanding Jerusalem's actions—she was neglected/abandoned; she neglects and abandons others. For further mention of the noted abandonment, neglect, and/or violence against children in prophetic texts and Jerusalem practices, see Jer 2–3; Ezek 23.

11. For further discussion of "authoring" and the role in identity construction see, Mandolfo, *Daughter Zion*, 12–19.

12. Sharon Moughtin-Mumby (*Sexual and Marital Metaphor in Hosea, Jeremiah, Isaiah, and Ezekiel* [OTM; Oxford: Oxford University Press, 2008], 156–57) argues for variations with the "marriage metaphor and that Ezekiel 16 and 23 are two distinct stories with different characterization, plot, and interests." Similarly, Leveen ("Variations on a Theme," 203) notes the contradictory depictions of how memory functions in Num 32.

13. Another possibility for classifying the nature of the texts is Brueggemann's terminology of testimony and countertestimony to classify the perspectives and their dialectic nature (*Theology of the Old Testament*, 117, 122–24, 407–8).

14. Eichrodt, *Ezekiel*, 196; Ronald M. Hals, *Ezekiel* (FOTL 19; Grand Rapids: Eerdmans, 1989), 100, 105–6.

15. Blenkinsopp, *Ezekiel*, 76.

Yhwh constructs Jerusalem's identity using horrific images[16]—portraying her as sexually insatiable, playing the prostitute (זנה; cf. Ezek 16:26, 28, 29),[17] committing adultery (נאף, 16:32), stubbornly refusing to conform to Yhwh's expectations for her (16:43, 59; cf. Amos 4). So why does Yhwh want to sustain the relationship?[18] The narrative also speaks of Yhwh not necessarily in the most flattering light, and of Yhwh's efforts, not all of them conducive to positive interchange between those involved in the relationship. The manifestation of Yhwh's effort illustrates the inability to let go (although rejected). Even so, some traditional interpretations view the Deity's response as gracious;[19] to the contrary, I argue that the metaphor portrays a Deity desperate for the relationship. The Deity takes on the role of the jealous, overbearing, jilted lover; and the history of the relationship is filtered through those identity constructs. Accordingly, shared cultural memory constitutes the discourse within the metaphor regarding the developmental stages of the female character and hence the relationship with the Deity—her childhood, womanhood, independence, and comparison to other women. Notably, the first two are developmental stages while the second two are role-specific attributes associated with these stages.

HER CHILDHOOD

The multivalence of the metaphor generated the images presented and insights into the behaviors of the agents. Characteristic of the stage is the passivity of the female as compared to the parent's active neglect vis-à-vis the rescuer's initiative. First, regarding the female, her parents rejected her, abandoned her at a vulnerable stage at the beginning of her life, ignored

---

16. See below for discussion about the dualities.

17. Cf. Linda Day, "Rhetoric and Domestic Violence in Ezekiel 16," *BibInt* 8 (2000): 205–30; Fokkelien van Dijk-Hemmes, "The Metaphorization of Woman in Prophetic Speech: An Analysis of Ezekiel 23," in *On Gendering Texts: Female and Male Voices in the Hebrew Bible,* ed. Athalya Brenner and van Dijk-Hemmes (BIS 1; 1993; repr., Leiden: Brill, 1996), 167–76 [a slight variation of an earlier article in *VT* 43 (1993): 162–70].

18. Cf. Paul M. Joyce, *Divine Initiative and Human Response in Ezekiel* (JSOTSup 51; Sheffield: Sheffield Academic Press, 1989), 123. Joyce argues that the divine action is done out of love and "to preclude the possibility of a repeated pattern of sin and consequent profanation of the divine 'name.'"

19. Hals, *Ezekiel,* 106–7.

her, and showed her no compassion (Ezek 16:4–5).[20] In spite of this neglect, she exhibits signs of life, albeit basic—she flounders (בוס) in her blood (v. 6);[21] she is responsive and grows even within the wild environment (v. 7).

Second, the activity of the other agents also typifies the identity of those involved. The parents are labeled by their nationality—father Amorite, mother Hittite—not as a point of affirmation but rather as a stereotype and related expectations (16:45).[22] In saying that the child received none of the care due an infant, the author implicates the parents in the neglect and further portrays them as discarding the child (v. 5). The author highlights the abandonment motif, thus setting up a contrast between the parents and any who neglected the child vis-à-vis himself (rescuer) who noticed the child (v. 6).

Third, the male's (Deity) initiative toward the child is noteworthy for its brevity and its impact. Regarding its brevity the male observed (ראה) the child in its blood and commanded the child to live (חיה, vv. 6–7). This command challenges the expected consequence of being exposed in an open field, namely, death. Also profound is the responsiveness exhibited in the flourishing of one who was left to die. To live and grow is to beat the odds and to be indebted to the rescuer for the act of kindness. Even so, the child is left on her own to grow. There is a time gap between the observation and command to live and the second observation of the female's growth and physical maturity.

Her Womanhood

Characteristic of this stage is the physical growth of the female and the formalization of the marital relationship between the rescuer and the rescued. First, she is described in terms showing her physical maturation—the "time for love" (עת דדים, v. 8).[23] Although physically mature, she is naked (ערם, v. 7), retaining the characteristic by which she was first noticed. In

---

20. Blenkinsopp (*Ezekiel*, 77) notes that the neglect was an alternative to abortion and birth control.

21. The formulation ואמר לך בדמיך חיי occurs twice in 16:6—most likely an instance of dittography.

22. Cf. Mandolfo, *Daughter Zion*, 47, who notes that naming her origin was Ezekiel's indicator of her uncleanness.

23. Eichrodt contends, "she is won by her benefactor" and "taken out of her poverty and loneliness, and elevated to the status of wife and consort" (*Ezekiel*, 205).

her womanhood, however, the effect of her nakedness on the observer ensues in a marital relationship, a covenant initiated and formalized by the rescuer.[24] The move from abandonment to marriage is dramatic and defines the identity of the relationship partners. The rescuer/husband initiates a marriage with an otherwise unprepared, rescued female.

The second aspect of the womanhood stage is the female's lingering dependence and silence. She is taken as a covenant partner and thus becomes a wife. The action sequence highlights the relationship dynamics and the expected loyalty. After the covenant, the female is cleaned up, anointed, clothed, adorned, and fed (vv. 8–13).[25] The sequence raises the questions regarding the Deity's choice of partner and the rationale for that choice. These questions are the underlying counterclaims of the memory— that the choice was predicated on matters that could not be sustained in the relationship between such different characters.

The third aspect of the stage is the attention on the male's (*I*) activity toward the female (*You*) (vv. 8–13).[26] Noted in the benevolence is the focus on basic survival elements—clothes and food. With the possible exception of feeding her, everything done on her behalf focuses on accessorizing the external with the best of the best—that is, with gold, fine linen, and so on. As the object of Yhwh's activity, the beautified female became renowned.

The fourth aspect of the womanhood stage is the attention to beauty. The male (Deity) articulates that the female (Jerusalem) is exceedingly beautiful (יפה) and worthy of royal status, a worth associated with the ornamentation for which the male takes credit (vv. 13–14). As in the

---

24. With Day, "Rhetoric and Domestic Violence," 208, I argue that this is not language of adoption leading to a father-daughter relationship; cf., e.g., Galambush, *Jerusalem*, 93–94; Malul Meir, "Adoption of Foundlings in the Bible and Mesopotamian Documents: A Study of Some Legal Metaphors in Ezekiel 16.1–7," *JSOT* 46 (1990): 97–126.

25. For a discussion of the adoption process see Malul, "Adoption of Foundlings." Malul's explanation raises further questions about a father-daughter relationship in light of the descriptions of the female as adulterous and bearing the children of her male partner. Cf. Day, "Rhetoric and Domestic Violence," 208, for her concern about the adoption motif.

26. Note the sequence "I-You" pattern formed by the first common singular verbs and the second-person feminine singular object suffix—e.g., "I bathed you" (וארחצך); "I clothed you" (ואלבישך); "I bound you" (ואחבשך); "I adorned you" (ואעדך). A variation of the "I-You" pattern continues in 16:12 to describe the Deity's action on Jerusalem's behalf.

note regarding her origin, here too is the suggestion that expectations are attached. The portrayal is of a stage when the female is still under the male's control, the male being the focal point of her existence (exclusive loyalty). Also characteristic of this stage is the transition signaled by the growth of her fame "among the nations" (בגוים), namely, the transition and transformation from the abandoned and marginalized to the adorned and famous.[27]

HER INDEPENDENCE

The transition from dependence to independence originated in displayed trust (בטח)—in her beauty (יפה, v. 15). To the hitherto passive female is attributed a series of behaviors signaling her initiative toward herself and toward others. Regarding the behaviors toward herself, she replicated the actions that the Deity did on her behalf as if to suggest learned behavior. Yhwh focused on ornamentation and Jerusalem also focused on ornamentation; she did with images what the Deity had done for her. Yet the actions were outside the realm of expected and acceptable behavior. The metaphor conveys the active city/community choosing her relationship partners outside the covenant relationship with Yhwh.[28] The tension in the shared memory is that Yhwh accused Jerusalem of not remembering the days of her youth; but her behaviors toward the passersby suggest the opposite— that she remembered those days. In contrast to those who see her as forgetting, thus embracing the Deity's claim and silencing the counterclaim,[29] I contend that Jerusalem's memory informed her behavior—that is, the memory seen in her inclination to remember and to remain formed by the days of her youth.

Regarding the behaviors toward others, here too Jerusalem is depicted as having learned from the Deity. Yhwh, a "passerby" (עובר), related to her by entering into a relationship with her and giving her gifts. Similarly, she enters into relationship with other passersby and gives them gifts (vv. 31–34). Consequently, Jerusalem's relationship with Egypt, Assyria, and

---

27. Although it is compelling to argue that female Jerusalem is the temple rather than the community (cf. Mandolfo, *Daughter Zion,* 47), the multivalence of the metaphor also allows one to see the community as the point of focus.

28. Note Galambush's discussion of the OT's use of the marriage metaphor to include the city's infidelity (*Jerusalem,* 26–27).

29. E.g., Blenkinsopp, *Ezekiel,* 78; Eichrodt, *Ezekiel,* 207.

Babylon is viewed with suspicion and forms the basis of repeated accusations against her for prostituting (זנה) herself with the nations. She does not wait to be found; she seeks out her lovers. She does not receive gifts (נדה), she gives gifts to her lovers—or perhaps lavishes them in the way gifts were lavished upon her. We miss the point, however, when we see only the claim regarding her acting like a prostitute. The portrayal of paying her lovers may also be seen in terms of power. She is treating them like prostitutes—these powerful men (nations) are her sexual liaisons, at her disposal—she gives them payment (אתנן). The interpretation of the metaphor may be extended to include the nature of the behavior and not just the label assigned to the behavior. The nature of the behavior is independence, which was not obliterated but thrived after the Yhwh-Jerusalem covenant was initiated. These depictions heighten the awareness of Jerusalem's self-determinance; Yhwh's attempt to remake her is only partially effective. She does not embrace the identity of exclusive relationship partner constructed for her.

Rather than concealing her presumed indiscretions or seeing them as part of her vitality, Yhwh attempts to shame Jerusalem by describing her as being worse than the worst nations, for example, Philistines, Arameans, even Samaria and Sodom (cf. vv. 46–56). Yhwh humiliates Jerusalem in order to dominate her and secure her compliance. Yhwh in Ezek 16 may forgive only when Jerusalem becomes totally dependent on Yhwh (i.e., reverts to her childhood dependence). The humiliation juxtaposed to the willingness to take her back suggests her lack of viable options for a wholesome relationship. Clearly Yhwh's memory of her origin overshadows the reality of her adult independence.

The use of shame as a method of coercion is also attested elsewhere. Thus the text betrays the Deity's reasoning that Jerusalem would return to Yhwh after playing the prostitute (cf. Jer 3:7, 19–20). In these instances Yhwh is proven wrong about Jerusalem. Regarding the nature of the counterclaims, the Jeremiah passages enhance what is perceivable in Ezek 16:43–47. The female (Jerusalem) is characterized as failing to remember (זכר) her youth (נער); and the failure is the basis of the Deity's rage (v. 43). Highlighting the lack of memory conveys an associated expectation that remembering would promote awareness of identity within the relationship. But memory in this instance would serve as a method of control in as much as it compels static relationship dynamics. The time of youth (נער) for the female was a time of dependence, marginalization, and intense need. Yet this is the time when Yhwh made the covenant with her. The expectation is that she would be true to the covenant (v. 60), but Yhwh (the adult) was aware of her juvenile identity when making a covenant with her. So in a sense the Deity is demanding that the female take on the behavioral traits of the Deity—to remember in the way that the Deity remembers and to remain loyal to the covenant. Such demand to remember is an expectation that fails to embrace the knowledge of the female's identity and misses the point of the beautification—that accessories change outward appearance without bringing about internal transformation.

The voice of the narrative belies Yhwh's claimed shame and feigned ignorance by using the Deity's perspective placed in the words of observers—"Like mother, like daughter" (v. 44). Thus in verses 44–47 the toxicity of stereotypes emerges—"you are the daughter of your mother; … your mother was a Hittite and your father an Amorite" (v. 45; cf. v. 3); "your elder sister is Samaria … your younger sister is Sodom" (v. 46). The family resemblance is highlighted and used as a way of defining Jerusalem's identity. In this segment of the shared cultural memory, stereotypes perpetuate the perspective that descendants of particular ethnic groups are predisposed to particular wanton behaviors. Jerusalem therefore is seen to be like her parents and siblings—nothing else should be expected of her. Yet the counterclaim is that the Deity expected something different, perhaps owing to her being abandoned and rescued, not necessarily to her family legacy. Even so, the Deity seems to ignore Jerusalem's childhood, a time of abandonment—formative years when she was free of the relational structure demanded within a covenant. Any learned behavior supplements but does not replace the behaviors learned in the days of her youth. For her, to remember would be to act free of the relational constraints.

Comparison to Other Women

To shame a person or a group is a public matter, and the discourse in Ezek 16 employs shaming through its comparison of Jerusalem to others.[30] Nonetheless, Yhwh claims that the female's behavior comes as no

---

30. Cf. Saul M. Olyan, "Honor, Shame, and Covenant Relations in Ancient Israel and Its Environment," *JBL* 115 (1996): 204–6, regarding the expectation of reciprocal honor (cf. 1 Sam 2:30) and the fact that reciprocity is not always made explicit in the relationship. The loss of honor or diminishment is also public and usually accompa-

surprise. Consequently, two sets of comparisons are presented here: family and gender. First, Jerusalem exhibits the behaviors typical of her family. In addition, Jerusalem's behaviors are evaluated as worse than Sodom and Samaria's (vv. 47, 51). Thus the comparison is part of the portrayal and process of humiliating Jerusalem. In this comparison, the sibling relationship is used as a basis of constructing identity—Jerusalem is the worst of her family and her family is the worst of the worst.

Second, Jerusalem indulges in prostitution like other females, but unlike other females, she pays the male for sexual favors (vv. 32–38). Setting up the comparison, the voice of the Deity articulates the standard operating procedures of prostitutes. At this point in the discourse the metaphor is intensified by the inclusion of details and the clear connections with reality. Getting lost in the discourse and forgetting that a metaphorical process has perhaps become commonplace to the reader are easy tendencies.[31] Nonetheless the comparison highlights Jerusalem's learned behavior—she behaves toward her lovers like Yhwh behaved toward her, thus taking on attributes in the prostitute-client relationship usually associated with the male client.[32]

Characterization of the Deity (Male)

Language typical of prophetic literature introduces the portrayal of the relationship between the Deity and the community. As with the portrayal of the female Jerusalem, the memory portrays the male agent, Yhwh, through its use of metaphor and more specifically through its stance (I-You), descriptors, noted responses, and an added component: evaluation of the behaviors and responses. To the extent that the community accepts Yhwh's version of the shared memory, she legitimizes the negative representation of the community. On the other hand, the prophet, a human agent and medium of the communication, is directly connected to the portrayal of Jerusalem and the Deity. The voice of the prophet is the voice of the privileged perspective, the dominant perspective endowed with the power to speak, label, and characterize others.

---

nied by rituals and a loss of social status (cf. Isa 16:14; 23:9; Jer 46:12; Hos 4:7; Lam 1:6, 8).

31. For discussion of the process of a dead metaphor, see Galambush, *Jerusalem*, 36.

32. Compare Kamionkowski, *Gender Reversal*, 7, 9.

The prophet crafts the narrative, chooses the images and metaphor, and as such reflects the rhetorical and ideological context of the portrayal. Fundamental to the metaphorical representation of the Deity is that the male begins his story as an adult, whereas the female begins the story at her birth. Already the groundwork for the relationship dynamics is set in portraying the power differentials of the adult male and juvenile, maturing female.[33] From the perspective of the differentials three elements regarding Jerusalem are discernible.

Choice of Jerusalem

The adult male chose the female and exercised the freedom to select her and to bestow upon her a specific identity and role as wife. The choice may be conceived in multiple stages corresponding to the female's development. First, the Deity selected the female while she was in a state of abandonment. Second, the Deity selected the female when she was at the onset of womanhood. Third, the Deity selected her when she was asserting her freedom as a woman. The third selection stage represents the discord in the relationship because it is in this stage that the choices diverge. In stages one and two, the juvenile female is dependent on the male; she is young and presumably grateful or at least compliant to her rescuer. By portraying the Deity's choice the narrator leaves open questions about the wisdom of the choice. Although not a developmental stage as much as a psychological state of awareness, Yhwh chose one whose heritage the Deity did not embrace but rather condemned. Included in this choice is a suspicion about the female's ability to be loyal (a thought included in the stereotypes regarding her heritage). Also challenging is the concept of remembering in so far as the Deity wants Jerusalem to remember in the Deity's way, which suppresses part of Jerusalem's memory. Yet the history of being abandoned informed the Deity's choice of Jerusalem and should by implication inform the expectations of Jerusalem's behavior.

Expectations about Jerusalem

The expectations are communicated in the depiction of her behavior and evaluation of her and them. As a discourse about the origin and status of

---

33. See also the section below on tensions/contrasts.

the relationship, Ezek 16 shapes the portrayal of the female and the Deity. Fundamentally, the expectation is that Jerusalem would be loyal to the relationship. Avoiding shame would mean that Jerusalem would honor her relationship partner or at least do nothing to bring shame to her partner. But what is the source of such an expectation? Is the expectation for the reciprocity of honoring and not bringing shame? Or is the expectation perhaps the exclusive nature of the relationship? The expectation seems to build on power dynamics and not necessarily on the quality of the relationship commitment. Yhwh made a commitment, and at the very least the young Jerusalem assented to it—the choice between untamed yet free existence and sustained protection and nurturing. On the Deity's part, the duration of the commitment seems to be perpetual. The same cannot be said for the female Jerusalem. The counterclaim would be that for her the commitment was a temporary arrangement or perhaps one without the promise for perpetuity. The duration of the commitment constitutes a conflict of expectations. The start may not necessarily dictate the course or destination. The male rescuer saved a life; the turn of events happened when the rescuer transformed the relationship from the rescuer-rescued to the lover-beloved relationship. The discourse says nothing of the female's investment in the commitment; rather it portrays her lack of commitment to the relationship.

PLAN FOR SECURING JERUSALEM'S RESTORATION

The male is portrayed as one caught up in his own power of choice and desire. The moment we recall that this is a memory and metaphorical representation of the Yhwh-Jerusalem relationship we may be more inclined to hear the possible readings of the story. To humiliate Jerusalem into compliance is one of the Deity's methods seen in the language used to speak of her: she is a whore, an adulterous wife, a practitioner of child sacrifice, a murderer, and—implicitly—ungrateful. Part of the humiliation was to strip her of her possession (publicly; Ezek 16:41–42). Another way was to restore the fortunes to humiliate her through benevolence (v. 53).

Still another way of restoring the relationship was to remove the objects of her wanton behavior (v. 37). This idea seems to have been hatched in a vacuum and oblivious to behavioral tendencies. The expectation behind removing the lovers (turn the lovers against her) was to stop Jerusalem's prostitution; but the removal takes away only the specific object of the behavior. To remove the lovers only means that she may seek other lovers. The removal does not return loyalty or trust and may result in a temporary restoration only until another lover is found. Here, however, the named lovers are important to the idea of stopping her behavior. By turning the lovers against her, the presumption may be that she would experience the pains caused by disloyalty; however, the depiction of her behavior (her bribing lovers) already displays her disregard for loyalty—a nonessential part of relationship. The female in this instance seems more aware of human behavior than the Deity.

Similarly, the Deity threatens to "uncover her nakedness" (v. 37). As graphic as the description and threat of exposure are, the threat seems misdirected because Jerusalem has already been sexually exposed. How is that a negative or a threat to one who was used to being naked and sexually exposed (in various forms)? Granted, the choice to be exposed is part of the behavioral appeal. Perhaps taking the choice away constituted the humiliation since the assertion of independence is what the Deity was trying to suppress.

The final restoration strategy was to punish Jerusalem like any other woman who had committed prostitution (v. 38), including raging against her in anger (being abusive toward her, v. 42) and other forms of punishment. In this plan, the Deity threatens to forget her covenant status and treat her like other women. The shared memory is that she is like other women biologically and sexually; she is unlike other women in terms of relationship identity to the Deity. Fundamentally, the plan was to humiliate her into conformity (v. 63), including exposing her deeds to others and forgiving her, not as a gesture of love but as a ploy to shame and silence her. The Deity thus planned to shame Jerusalem and to redirect the shame of the failed relationship from the Deity onto Jerusalem.

Relational Dynamics (Claims and Counterclaims)

In considering the dialogical nature of the discourse, two presuppositions are noteworthy regarding the text and the interplay between the text and the reader.

First, the text's implicit and explicit aspects constitute its method to persuade. "A common tendency is to identify with the voice of the text and its representation of the relationship without adequate consideration"[34] of

---

34. Mignon R. Jacobs, "YHWH's Call for Israel's 'Return': Command, Invitation, or Threat," *HBT* 32 (2010): 17–32, here 26.

constructed identities of the other agents, their voices, their behaviors, and their responses. "The readers' identification with the voice of the Deity often results in the acceptance of the characterization of Israel and insufficient examination of the *meta*-issues involved in the text's characterization of the Deity whose voice is the instrument used to define the relationship."[35] Even as the text portrays Jerusalem as its primary object, by constructing Jerusalem's identity (however negative), the text also gives identity to the voice—the male Deity. In other words one cannot define another's identity apart from also defining one's own identity. Consequently, "if one trusts the voice of the Deity in characterizing Israel then one must also trust the portrayal of the Deity inherent in the mode of characterizing Israel because the depiction of Israel is as much about Israel as it is about the Deity."[36]

Second, the reader determines the significance of the image for understanding the whole, and that choice is dependent on the interplay of factors that both text and reader contribute to the interpretation.[37] The interpreter's perception defines the theological construction done on the basis of the text. In this phase of perception, the metaphor connects with the reader and pulls on the elements with which the interpreter is already acquainted. That connection brings the impression and regulates what may be perceived. Consequently, some interpreters, based on their experiences, may be more apt to perceive certain images. For example, in the interpretation of Ezek 16 many interpreters do not perceive the detrimental aspect of the relationship between the female (Jerusalem) and the male (Deity); yet these interpreters identify with the voice of the Deity and attribute negative behaviors to the female (Jerusalem).[38] Others, while rec-

---

35. Ibid.

36. Ibid.

37. Labahn ("Metaphor and Inter-textuality," 51) proposes that "the meaning of a metaphor is first raised when it is perceived by anyone. That means, interpretation of a metaphor is erected through perception. The power of the metaphor to generate an impression of what the text might wish to express has to be taken seriously."

38. For example, Blenkinsopp, *Ezekiel*; William H. Brownlee, *Ezekiel 1–19* (WBC 28; Waco, Tex: Word, 1986); Ronald E. Clements *Ezekiel* (Westminster Bible Companion; Louisville: Westminster John Knox, 1996); Hals, *Ezekiel*; Walther Zimmerli, *A Commentary on the Book of the Prophet Ezekiel, Chapters 1–24* (trans. Ronald E. Clements; Hermeneia; Philadelphia: Fortress, 1979). For a discussion of how each of these deals with the dominant male image in Ezek 16, see Day, "Rhetoric and Domestic Violence," 225–28.

ognizing the metaphor, try to connect the descriptors to specific historical occurrences,[39] thus missing the dimension of memory as a construct of reality with all of the poetic licenses employed to persuade.

PATTERNS OF BEHAVIORS (NARRATIVE AWARENESS)

In Ezek 16 the Deity is involved in a segment of shared memory about the relationship with the community, the personified city. This memory appears to dominate Yhwh's perspective about the Yhwh-Jerusalem relationship and about the Jerusalem-nations relationship, that is, how others should relate to the community.[40] The memory uses figurative language to facilitate negative images and thus to construct the community's identity. The dynamic nature of the language (especially the metaphor) is important to the portrayal of the relationship in that it exhibits patterns of behaviors.

First, the text's focus constitutes the patterned attempt to persuade about the nature of the relationship. Accordingly, the portrayal of the relationship partners promotes the relational tensions and thus attempts to persuade the audience to side with the Deity, the author of the shared memory and the dishonored relationship partner, over against Jerusalem, the unfaithful and ungrateful partner. Those siding with Yhwh would be a varied group depending on how they interface with the metaphor and dialogue with the agents, especially the author of the memory identified therein. Gender, while a factor in shaping readers' interface with the portrayal of both divine (male-I) and human agents (female-You), may not be the determining factor. Both male and female readers may side with the Deity (I-male); likewise, they may both side with the human (you-female).[41]

---

39. Among those who attempt to connect the description to specific historical events are Eichrodt, *Ezekiel*; Blenkinsopp, *Ezekiel*.

40. Some may refer to this as a master narrative with its fluidity, e.g., Mandolfo, *Daughter Zion*. I prefer to conceptualize the phenomenon as memory to reflect the adaptability to new contexts and uses and the maintenance of core features, as in the case of the marital metaphor. Even so, with Moughtin-Mumby (*Sexual and Marital Metaphors*) I argue that the marital metaphor is not a static element but evidences fluidity in its adaptability.

41.Generally, most male writers side with the Deity, e.g., Blenkinsopp, *Ezekiel*; Clements, *Ezekiel*; Zimmerli, *Ezekiel*. By comparison, Daniel I. Block (*The Book of Ezekiel, Chapters 1–24* [NICOT; Grand Rapids: Eerdmans, 1997], 467–70) notes the challenging images and the implications of siding with the male voice over against the

To side with one character is to endorse, embrace, or resonate with the depicted behavior of that character over against the other characters. On the other hand, a holistic view of the metaphor sees the portrayal as part of a dynamic process, seeing it for what it is, not only for what it is said to be. A holistic view presumes the multivalence of the metaphorical language and accepts the ensuing portrayals as generative forces that also define reality. Consequently, what one person perceives as mercy someone else may perceive as aggression. Thus a holistic reading calls for examination of all sides—privileging neither the Deity (I-male) nor the community (you-female) but hearing the claims and counterclaims about each.[42]

The second pattern is the Deity's anger characterized by a strong undercurrent of unforgiveness and a persistent bubbling up of anger toward the community. In this portrait of the relationship one hears the Deity's voice via the prophetic voice, but not the community's voice. The silent community and the incessant, negative nature of the depiction may signify a domineering stance toward the community.[43] Accordingly, the portrayal itself emerges as the voice of one embittered by the memories. Although the goal is to restore the relationship, the language used about the community signals a relationship fraught with anger, abuse, and an attempt to activate a prescribed normativity, including a particular relationship, behaviors, and perceptions. In this respect, the community's silence signifies the suppressed element of the metaphor, those elements that generate the counterclaims.

Yhwh's anger is neither new nor rare. Salient about the Deity of Ezek 16 is the language used to rationalize and hence to portray the anger. The Deity characterizes Jerusalem as undesirable and neglected, thus denoting the characteristics that defined her existence before and after he selected her—that is, cleaned her up and "made a covenant with her." After the cleanup, the Deity characterizes her as beautiful. She is made to look like a queen (because of how she is adorned), focusing on outward appearance.

---

negative female image. Some female writers side with the female character, including those who point to the apparent misconception in how the text has been interpreted, e.g., Peggy L. Day, "The Bitch Had It Coming to Her: Rhetoric and Interpretation in Ezekiel 16," *BibInt* 8 (2000): 231–53.

42. Cf. Kamionkowski, *Gender Reversal*, 41–42.

43. Even with this, some propose that Yhwh, who is the voice of the portrayal, is caring (e.g., Swanepol, "Ezekiel 16," 87). With Kamionkowski (*Gender Reversal*, 39) I argue that the language of the text portrays rage rather than compassion or care.

Clearly, the transformation is superficial. She is not more appealing to the passersby; nonetheless, she is more active in relating to these passersby. That mode of relating to the passersby angered Yhwh because of the perceived disloyalty to the covenant relationship. Furthermore, the negative portrayal of the community as a prostitute, facilitated by the "*I* (male)-*You* (female)" dichotomy,[44] indicates disparity within the relationship. The dichotomy suggests an appeal to persuade, that is, to be heard, to be sided with, to be affirmed as right, and ultimately to be justified in the portrayal of the community.

Third, this narrative metaphor constructs Jerusalem's identity: to the nations she is undesirable; in her own eyes she is unwanted, cared for by only one, and ungrateful. The shared memory uses patterns of behavior to portray Jerusalem, choosing to identify her by behaviors rather than by her name, which appears only twice in Ezek 16 (in vv. 2 and 3). According to the descriptions, others neglected Jerusalem even in her prostitution. Verses 33–34 characterize the behavior as a role reversal in that Jerusalem seeks out her sexual partners and she compensates them rather than being sought and being compensated for her services.[45] Contrary to the claim regarding her famed beauty, the female personified Jerusalem remained undesirable to others, except perhaps to the Deity. Others took the services but disregarded the provider (as would be characteristic of an encounter with a prostitute). Outside the pattern was Yhwh's act of transforming a temporary encounter with a marginalized, abandoned female to a permanent commitment. The Deity made the lovers pay not by having them give gifts to Jerusalem but by subjecting them to punishment because of their associations with Jerusalem.

CONCEPTUAL TENSIONS OF THE RELATIONSHIP DYNAMICS

Affirming that the sociological characteristic of domestic violence is part of the portrait displayed and those relational images convey the fractured relationship,[46] my concern has been to examine the textual portrayals and the constitutive nuances. Here the main duality is the claims and counterclaims; even so, the portrayals evidence conceptual tensions especially

---

44. The dichotomy is constituted by: *I* (Deity/male) the positive side (speaker) versus *You* (human/female), the negative side (silent partner).

45. See, e.g., Judah seeks Tamar (Gen 38); Kamionkowski, *Gender Reversal*.

46. Day, "Rhetoric and Domestic Violence."

in the dualities/polarities they suggest. Among these dualities are honor-shame, protection-exposure, and commitment-abuse.

HONOR-SHAME

This duality is fundamental to the discourse presented in Ezek 16 in that the Deity is humiliated by the female's behavior. The narrative is a claim about the loss of honor in a relationship that the Deity presumed to be safe. "Safe" is defined as the absence of viable relationship options for the female partner, resulting in loyalty and gratitude toward the male dominant partner. In the Yhwh-Jerusalem relationship, the rescuer/husband took on an abandoned, marginalized (weak, dependent) female as wife and expected fidelity and gratitude as a demonstration of loyalty. Although the text does not give voice to the community or the onlookers and passersby, its construction of their identities raises the question about the nature of the fractured Yhwh-Jerusalem relationship. The Deity's claim to shame is that Jerusalem behaved horribly—prostitution (vv. 15–16), child sacrifice/murdering her children (vv. 20–21), adultery (v. 32).[47] But the counterclaim might also be that the Deity failed in the relationship. The Deity's honor consists of the acts done on behalf of the female—namely, the Deity assisted the infant, adorned her and married her (undesirable as she was), beautified her and raised her status. By noting the female's response, the shared cultural memory focuses attention on the Deity's role.

Presumably the honor to the female would be status elevation and relationship with the powerful, benevolent, male figure. But therein lies the potential for shame, that is, if the female breaks the bonds of the relationship. This analysis is as appropriate for the marital images as it is for the patron-client relationship,[48] in which Yhwh failed to maintain the relationship according to the standards of a patron. Portrayed in Ezek 16, Yhwh's effort to maintain the relationship may be fruitful to the extent of restoring the relationship. Accordingly, the effort may be unfruitful in so far as the restoration did not secure mutual respect and commitment.

---

47. Ezek 16 presents these using the second-person feminine forms ("you sacrificed," v. 16; "you slaughtered," v. 21; "you prostituted," vv. 26, 28, 29; "you committed lewd acts," v. 43; cf. also v. 47).

48. T. R. Hobbs, "Reflections on Honor, Shame, and Covenant Relations," *JBL* 116 (1997): 501–3.

Jerusalem would continue to defy Yhwh and Yhwh would continue to vie for her love and loyalty in order to prevent further shame.

PROTECTION-EXPOSURE

The memory of the relationship's origin begins with the male protecting the female against the elements when not even her parents cared for her. But as powerful an image as it is, the image leaves an ambiguous portrait of the male figure. Included in the memory are a few exposures. First, if the infant was helpless and left to die, assisting but leaving her is also questionable (vv. 6–7). The counterclaim here is that the male did not complete the task of rescuing the abandoned child.[49] By leaving her to grow up on her own, the male figure exposed her to various influences. Likewise, leaving her on her own allowed her to develop coping mechanisms suitable for the environment where survival was paramount.

The second exposure is to the rescuer's ways. He responded to her when she was exposed (naked). He offered protection. He lavished her with gifts. She learned from him how to relate to passersby because her rescuer/husband was a passerby. The third method of exposure is the discourse about her behavior. A husband would presumably have options of concealing the behavior if the behavior was not already known. Here the shared memory rehearsed the characterization of Jerusalem and further exposed her as a prostitute (זנה). The exposure thus became part of the cultural memory and constructed identity—Jerusalem the unfaithful, Yhwh the faithful devoted. The exposure is also itself a means of shaming Jerusalem into being loyal to the Deity.

COMMITMENT-ABUSE

The expectations for Jerusalem are defined by the commitment resulting from the covenant (ברית) between the Deity and Jerusalem (vv. 8, 60–62).[50] In the portrayal Yhwh attempted to but did not control Jerusalem; the commitment and the attenuating behavioral framework appear to be from both sides of the relationship. On Jerusalem's side the commit-

---

49. Day, "Rhetoric and Domestic Violence," 207.

50. Note the recurrence of the reference to the covenant (ברית). In the midst of figurative language, the discourse introduces language and images of the commitment and thus signals the reality of the commitment.

ment failed to result in behaviors appropriate for the type of relationship; instead, she behaved as if there was no commitment, that is, as if she was in an open relationship. She behaved as a free agent, free to choose relationship partners, free to relate to them as she saw fit. On Yhwh's side, the failed commitment is manifested in the Deity's attempts to control and to restore the relationship. The Deity uses the lack of control as a justification for anger and retaliation. Rather than celebrate the independence of the female (Jerusalem) who was once completely dependent and needy, the Deity opts to stamp out the independence, the independence that signals her adulthood.

Some elements of the characterization are more salient than others, for example, the noted actions, responses, and evaluation vis-à-vis the choice of action and the rationale. That the Deity would choose to restore by intimidation and humiliation is noteworthy. By comparison, the methods used to restore are abusive. Here abuse is defined as the attempt or success at suppressing an agent's personhood or vitality to participate in his or her choices and to live within or without the relationship where such suppression is present or threatened. Keeping in mind that the Deity is authoring it (according to the prophet), the memory identifies the Deity's choice of a persuasive method based on the commitment to the failed relationship. This interpretation of the dynamics intends to raise the counterclaim about the covenant-based commitment (faithfulness) in which the male partner attempted to regain and maintain commitment by abusive practices. It is the latter that constitutes the main counterclaim in the portrayal of the relationship.

The commitment (faithfulness) to the relationship is fractured to the extent that Yhwh neglected Jerusalem. Whether or not she was a wanton woman, the commitment may have entailed protecting her well-being. By shaming her and pushing her to the brink of annihilation, the Deity demonstrated the conditional aspect of the commitment, a commitment that Jerusalem seemed to regard as insignificant at worst or null and void at best.

Also on the Deity's side is the commitment defined by the persistent behavior to regain control of a reluctant relationship partner. This commitment is dedicated to a particular outcome, which, though paramount, is at odds with the methods used to achieve it. Thus although Ezek 16 portrays the Deity actively seeking to restore a relationship, the narrative also highlights the fractures in the relationship and raises the questions about the health and vitality of the relationship and the true identity of the relationship partners.

CONCLUSION

In this study I have highlighted one of the texts that Mandolfo used to exemplify her dialogical model. By using one text, I illustrate the counterclaims inherent within a single text and thereby exemplify the conceptual tensions regarding the depicted relationship. Concerning the Yhwh-Israel relationship, Ezek 16 uses figurative language to portray relational images (spouse, lover, rescuer). The images constitute a perspective about each relationship partner and suggest a value system and the identities of the parties involved. Thus the text portrays relational dynamics and allows insights into the interplay of the behaviors of the agents involved. To facilitate understanding, the discussion of the portrayal of the failed relationship in Ezek 16 included an examination of the primary characters—the Deity and the female (Jerusalem)—as displayed in the relational metaphor, the shared cultural memory regarding the relationship, and the identities portrayed through the shared cultural memory.

Zion's Body as a Site of God's Motherhood in Isaiah 66:7–14

Christl M. Maier

In *Daughter Zion Talks Back to the Prophets,* Carleen Mandolfo uses Mikhail Bakhtin's idea of dialogic discourse as a heuristic device for interpreting Zion's voice in Lamentations.[1] She argues that Zion's heartfelt accusations against God, whose punishment has gone beyond all measure, challenge the prophetic charges of her behavior. Reading Lam 1–2 dialogically with Zion passages in Jeremiah, Ezekiel, and Second Isaiah, Mandolfo portrays Daughter Zion as defying the dominant voice of God and his prophets, the voice that is based on the idea of divine retribution. In my book on Zion, I trace the female personification of Zion in three Zion psalms, Lamentations, and the Prophets, trying to mark out a tradition history of this concept and paying special attention to the spatial aspects of the female city.[2] This article demonstrates my approach by means of Isa 66:7–14, a particularly interesting passage that connects the female city with a feminization of the Deity in the maternal role. After introducing my understanding of personification, of space and the female body, I will interpret Isa 66:7–14 with regard to its contents, especially the reworking of earlier oracles. Then I will analyze the function of the passage within the context of Third Isaiah and briefly review the motif of Zion as a mother city in later writings. In my conclusion, I will comment on some arguments of Mandolfo.

---

1. Carleen Mandolfo, *Daughter Zion Talks Back to the Prophets: A Dialogic Theology of the Book of Lamentations* (SemeiaSt 58; Atlanta: Society of Biblical Literature, 2007).

2. Christl M. Maier, *Daughter Zion, Mother Zion: Gender, Space, and the Sacred in Ancient Israel* (Minneapolis: Fortress, 2008).

A Theoretical Inquiry into Space and Body

In the last few decades, the concept of space has gained new attention in scientific and cultural inquiry including that of scholars in Bible or religion who analyze spatial concepts in ancient texts and archaeological remains.[3] In my own work on Zion texts in the Hebrew Bible, I use the epistemology of space of the French Marxist sociologist Henri Lefebvre (1901–1991). Lefebvre focuses on the interrelatedness of the geographical dimension of space, the cultural evaluation of space, and the human experience of space. He argues that space is socially produced and can be evaluated by three perspectives that are intrinsically intertwined. First, space is *perceived*, as physical space, the mere materiality of space (*l'espace perçu*): it is space produced by a spatial practice (*pratique spatiale*), for example, by architecture, urban planning, and daily life. The second perspective is *conceived* space (*l'espace conçu*), space as depicted by language and metaphor as well as by maps and drawings. In spatial terminology, conceived space offers "representations of space," the results of a social process of planning, naming, and inscribing significance. According to Lefebvre, this process of knowledge production tends toward a system of verbal signs and mirrors a certain political strategy in society. Thus conceived space is the "dominant space in any society."[4] The third perspective is space as *experienced* or *lived* (*l'espace vécu*), "*lived* through its associated images and symbols, and hence the space of 'inhabitants' and 'users.'"[5] As the result of a production of meaning, this space of the everyday activities of users is perceptible, hence "subjective."[6] The spatial terminology for lived space is

---

3. In a lecture in 1967, Michel Foucault already proclaimed the beginning of "a new epoch of space"; see idem, "Of Other Spaces," *Diacritics* 16 (1986): 22–77, here 22. Anthologies of the work on space by scholars in Bible and the history of religion are provided in David M. Gunn and Paula M. McNutt, eds., *"Imagining" Biblical Worlds: Studies in Spatial, Social, and Historical Constructs in Honor of James W. Flanagan* (JSOTSup 359; Sheffield: Sheffield Academic Press, 2002); Jon L. Berquist and Claudia V. Camp, eds., *Constructions of Space I: Theory, Geography, and Narrative* (LHBOTS 481; New York: T&T Clark, 2007); idem, eds., *Constructions of Space II: The Biblical City and Other Imagined Spaces* (LHBOTS 490; New York: T&T Clark, 2008).

4. Henri Lefebvre, *The Production of Space* (trans. Donald Nicholson-Smith; Malden, Mass.: Blackwell, 1991), 39.

5. Ibid.

6. See ibid., 362.

"spaces of representation,"[7] which refers to something different, often non-verbal, namely to symbols, communal values, traditions, dreams, and last but not least to collective experience. Lefebvre uses the plural to point out that there may be several simultaneous representations since lived space is open to different, even contradictory experiences; for example, night-time urban space may be perceived as liberating to burglars, or frightening to lone women. Interestingly, Lefebvre's starting point for his trialectic theory is the body: "each living body *is* space and *has* its space: it produces itself in space and it also produces that space."[8]

Using more conventional terminology, one might say that Lefebvre describes and explains the interrelatedness of topography—the geographical dimension of space—with its cultural evaluation or ideology and with the human experience of space. Lefebvre's tripartite epistemology allows comprehending textual Jerusalem as a social space produced by a specific society at a certain time. I hold that any space described in biblical texts is not only classifiable as conceived space produced by metaphor and ideology, but comprises all three dimensions of space: its materiality/topography, its ideology, and the experience of living in it. The third dimension, experience of space, covers also any use of space that challenges the dominant ideology and thus counteracts fixed spatial patterns (e.g., by staying overnight in lecture rooms a lot of students opposed the reorganization of study programs in Germany last year).

Besides using Lefebvre's theory of space, my exploration of the female personification of the city is based on feminist studies on the female body, especially on an idea of the theologian and ethicist Paula M. Cooey that she develops in *Religious Imagination and the Body*.[9] Cooey focuses on the potential of the body as a cultural artifact and its relation to the imagining subject, who also has a body. She attributes to the body a major epistemological role as a medium in art and texts, a role that is ambiguous because it is twofold: "Its ambiguity lies in its double role as site and as sign. Viewed as site, 'body' focuses conceptually upon sentience as a field of pain and pleasure, experienced by imagining subjects. Viewed as sign, 'body' forces the attribution or denial of agency to another, and therefore serves as a

---

7. I prefer this term to the translation "representational spaces" used by Nicholson-Smith; the French reads: "les espaces de représentation."

8. Lefebvre, *Production*, 170.

9. Paula M. Cooey, *Religious Imagination and the Body: A Feminist Analysis* (New York: Oxford University Press, 1994).

building block in the social construction of subjectivity."[10] Cooey's exploration of agency at the margins of the dominant ideology correlates to Lefebvre's search for *lived space* that resists *conceived space*. Cooey includes the viewer of art or reader of texts and thus explores the function of body in the production of meaning within the reception process. The key words *sentience, agency,* and *subjectivity* relate Cooey's theoretical work to the political goals of the feminist movement, which strives to establish as political subjects women who are marginalized because of their sex, race, class, age, and so on.

The link between women and space in female personifications such as the nation, the city, and the home has long been a topic of feminist analysis.[11] The female personification of a city is based on a general analogy between the role of women and the role of cities, at least in a patriarchal perspective: Cities, like women, can be desired, conquered, protected, and governed by men. A city provides the main sources of life such as food, shelter, and a home for its inhabitants, as a mother does for her children. Thus the female gendering of the space is primarily based on ideas about its use and usefulness for human habitation. In biblical texts, personified Jerusalem consists of a space and at the same time embodies its population. When addressed by God, she often represents her inhabitants, but sometimes she is opposed to her people. Thus the literary device of personification, a subcategory of metaphor, allows the creation of relationships between the city, its population, and the Deity; it also allows viewing these relations from different angles.

ZION AS MOTHERLY SPACE IN ISAIAH 66:7–14

The last chapter of the book of Isaiah offers a collection of passages introduced by different prophetic rubrics, which scholars analyze as containing

---

10. Ibid., 90.

11. Cf. Sigrid Weigel, *Topographien der Geschlechter: Kulturgeschichtliche Studien zur Literatur* (Reinbek: Rowohlt Taschenbuch, 1990); Linda McDowell, *Gender, Identity, and Place: Understanding Feminist Geographies* (Minneapolis: University of Minnesota Press, 1999). Cf. also the anthologies: Elizabeth Grosz and Elspeth Probyn, eds., *Sexy Bodies: The Strange Carnalities of Feminism* (London: Routledge, 1995); Nancy Duncan, ed., *Bodyspace: Destabilizing Geographies of Gender and Sexuality* (London: Routledge, 1996).

three to seven pericopes.[12] Since Isa 65–66 share key words and topics
with Isa 1, a deliberate framing of the book by the last editors can be plausibly assumed, although the extent of editorial revisions is debated.[13]

Isaiah 66:5 introduces a new unit with a call to listen to God's word
addressed to those "who tremble at his word" (החרדים אל־דברו). This
group is opposed to another called "brothers who hate you and expel you"
and "his [i.e., God's] enemies" (v. 6). In verse 7 the subject matter changes
abruptly with a saying about Zion (vv. 7–9) that is the starting point for
a call to an unnamed audience to rejoice over her (vv. 10–14a). In verses
14b–17 the distinction between the enemies of God and the other group
now called "servants of Yhwh" is resumed in an announcement of divine
wrath over those who purify themselves to go into the gardens and eat
unclean animals. The interpretation of verses 7–14 hinges on the range
of verses that scholars assume belong together.[14] If one considers verse
14b as an integral part of verses 7–14, then verses 5–6 belong to the unit,
since verses 5–6 and 14b frame the universal outlook of the passage about
Zion giving birth (vv. 7–14a) by distinguishing two groups and harshly
condemning one of them. Thus it is necessary to analyze the flow of arguments in verses 5–14.

5   Hear the word of Yhwh, you who tremble at his word:

---

12. Cf. the list of scholarly divisions in Joseph Blenkinsopp, *Isaiah 56–66: A
New Translation with Introduction and Commentary* (AB 19B; New York: Doubleday,
2003), 292.

13. For a concordance of terminological parallels between Isa 1 and 65–66 see
Willem A. M. Beuken, "Isaiah Chapters LXV–LXVI: Trito-Isaiah and the Closure of
the Book of Isaiah," in *Congress Volume: Leuven 1989* (ed. John A. Emerton; VTSup
43; Leiden: Brill, 1991), 204–21, esp. 218–19. Odil Hannes Steck attributes Isa 66:5–
24 to the last book redaction (*Studien zu Tritojesaja* [BZAW 203; Berlin: de Gruyter,
1991], 263–65). Brevard S. Childs (*Isaiah* [OTL; Louisville: Westminster John Knox,
2001], 542–45) argues that Isa 56–66 shape the entire book into a coherent whole.
For an overview on these scholarly theses and a comparison of modern and ancient
readers of Isaiah, see David M. Carr, "Reading Isaiah from Beginning (Isaiah 1) to
End (Isaiah 65–66): Multiple Modern Possibilities," in *New Visions of Isaiah* (ed. Roy
F. Melugin and Marvin A. Sweeney; JSOTSup 214; Sheffield: Sheffield Academic Press,
1996), 188–218, esp. 196.

14. According to Beuken and Blenkinsopp, Isa 66:7–14 forms an epilogue to Third
Isaiah and in this function corresponds with Isa 54:1–17 that concludes Isa 40–54. See
Beuken, "Isaiah Chapters LXV–LXVI," 204–21; Blenkinsopp, *Isaiah 56–66*, 293.

Your brothers who hate you and expel you for my name's sake
have said,
"May Yhwh appear in his glory,[15] so that we may see your joy";
but it is they who shall be put to shame.

6   A voice of uproar from the city! A voice from the temple!
The voice of Yhwh, dealing retribution to his enemies:

7   Before she was in labor, she gave birth;
before birth pangs came upon her, she delivered a male.

8   Who ever heard the like? Who ever saw such things?
Can a land come to birth in one day? Can a nation be born in one
moment?
Yet as soon as Zion was in labor, she gave birth to her children.

9   Will I open the womb and not bring to birth? says Yhwh.
Will I, who brings to birth, shut the womb? says your God.

10 Rejoice with Jerusalem, and be glad for her, all you [masc. pl.]
who love her.
Be very joyful with her, all you who now mourn over her;

11 that you may suck and be satisfied at her consoling breast;
that you may drink deeply with delight from her glorious bosom.

12 For thus said Yhwh:
Behold, I am extending prosperity to her like a river,
and the wealth of the nations like an overflowing stream that you
may suck.[16]
You will be carried on the hip and dandled on the knees.

13 Like someone whom his mother comforts, so I will comfort
you;
and in/through Jerusalem you will be comforted.

14a Then you will see, and your heart will rejoice;
your bones will flourish like grass.

14b Then it will be known that Yhwh's hand is with his servants,
but he will scold his enemies.

---

15. MT offers a qal form of the verb, whereas the ancient versions OG, Syriac, and
Vulgate translate a niphal form, which is preferable; cf. *BHS* and Blenkinsopp, *Isaiah
56–66*, 292.

16. So with MT and the masoretic structuring of the verse. 1QIsa[a] and OG offer a
noun and differing genders in the following two verbs; their reading, which results in
changing the subject of v. 12b into "their sucklings," may be influenced by Isa 49:22;
60:4. The MT should be retained since it is the shortest and less complicated variant.

The passage is a mixture of prophetic speech (vv. 5–6, 7–8, 10–11, 14b) and citations of the divine voice (vv. 9, 12–14a). Out of context, one may read verses 7–9 as an independent saying that is commented on in verses 10–14a since the latter passage presupposes the announcement of Zion's motherhood.[17] Yet verses 5–6 serve as an introduction to verses 7–9 and therefore the plural imperatives in verse 10 are directed to those who tremble at God's word (v. 5) and are opposed by "his enemies" (v. 14b).

In verses 7–9 Zion is clearly personified as a mother of newborns. Within the book of Isaiah, the idea that Zion gives birth to new children is unique to these verses.[18] Zion, however, is not like a normal woman, since she delivers without labor or pain. The verb מלט in verse 7b is unusual in this context; מלט I is commonly translated "to flee to safety" (niphal), "to rescue, bring away" (hiphil).[19] Yet for the hiphil form in 66:7b "to bear, give birth to," seems more appropriate; this meaning is supported by the use of a piel form of the verb in 34:15 with regard to a bird laying eggs.[20] The choice of this verb may be influenced by 49:24–25, where מלט is used twice in the niphal.[21] Zion's birth without pain is a counterimage of the "woman in labor" metaphor that often appears in prophetic writings to express a situation of war and inimical attack (e.g., in Jer 4:31, a verse that likens Daughter Zion to a woman crying of birth pangs and anguish).

The description in Isa 66 vividly focuses on Zion's body, especially those parts that define a mother: the womb, breasts full of milk, as well as a bosom, hips, and knees as places where newborns are carried or caressed. The group of people addressed in verse 10 is characterized as persons who love Zion or mourn over her. In the following verses this group takes the

---

17. Klaus Koenen (*Ethik und Eschatologie im Tritojesajabuch: Eine literarkritische und redaktionsgeschichtliche Studie* [WMANT 62; Neukirchen-Vluyn: Neukirchener, 1990], 196–97) takes vv. 7–9 and 10–14a as two independent sayings.

18. Helen Schüngel-Straumann argues that the birth imagery denotes the new situation of Zion and marks the distinction from a mere rehabilitation ("Mutter Zion im Alten Testament," in *Theologie zwischen Zeiten und Kontinenten: Für Elisabeth Gössmann* [ed. Theodor Schneider and Schüngel-Straumann; Freiburg: Herder, 1993], 19–30, esp. 27).

19. *HALOT* 2:589.

20. See the cross-reference in ibid.; cf. also *DCH* 5:299.

21. So with Ulrich Berges, *Das Buch Jesaja: Komposition und Endgestalt* (HBS 16; Freiburg: Herder, 1998), 524, who further argues that Zion's birth of the community of servants symbolizes their deliverance by God.

role of the newborns who are breast-fed and satisfied with nourishment and comfort.

The relationship between God and Zion is not explicitly stated, yet verse 9 characterizes the Deity as master of the womb in the role of a midwife who assists at a smooth birth. Interestingly, God is not named as either the father of the infants or the husband of female Zion. Zion's ability to feed her children even resembles God's ability to provide food since both verbs used in 66:11 to denote how Zion's breast satisfies and delights her children, namely שׂבע, "to be satiated," and ענג hitpael, "to take delight in," describe also Yhwh's feast of wine and milk in 55:1–2.[22]

Isaiah 66:7–14 is replete with intertextual references to passages in Second Isaiah and other Zion texts. For example, the mother metaphor of Zion refers to the first two chapters of Lamentations and to the message of Second Isaiah. In pairing the images of human mothers and the metaphorical mother Zion, the book of Lamentations presents an embodied Jerusalem as "mother" who in her destruction joins the experience of her children and their dirge. In Lam 1:16 personified Zion laments the desolate state of her children, whereas in Lam 2:11–12 the poet envisions children dying in the bosom of their mothers. As Patricia Tull Willey has convincingly claimed, the salvation oracles collected in Isa 40–55 directly answer to passages in Lamentations.[23] In Second Isaiah, Zion is only once explicitly named "mother" (Isa 50:1). Yet her personification as a desperate, even inebriated mother bereft of her children (51:17–20) is the starting point for Second Isaiah's message of Zion's restitution as queen and glorious city (49:20–23; 54:1–17). According to 49:21, Zion is ignorant of the whereabouts of her offspring during exile and does not know who cared for her children during the time of her devastation. In this situation, 49:22–23 aim at comforting Zion by the promise that her children will return to her:[24]

22. Cf. Mary Callaway, *Sing, O Barren One: A Study in Comparative Midrash* (SBLDS 91; Atlanta: Scholars Press, 1986), 79. Besides, ענג hitpael in Isa 58:14 indicates delight that comes from Yhwh.

23. Patricia Tull Willey, *Remember the Former Things: The Recollection of Previous Texts in Second Isaiah* (SBLDS 161; Atlanta: Scholars Press, 1997).

24. The allusion to Isa 49:22–23 has been noted by many scholars, e.g., Callaway, *Sing, O Barren One*, 78–79.

22 Thus said my lord Yhwh:
I will lift up my hand to the nations
and raise my signal to the peoples;
they will bring your [fem. sg.] sons in the bosom
and your daughters will be carried on the shoulder.
23 Kings will be your keepers, and their queens your nurses;
with their faces to the ground they will bow down to you
and lick the dust of your feet.
Then you will know that I am Yhwh;
those who wait for me shall not be put to shame.

This passage also imagines Zion's children as infants who have to be carried in the bosom or on the shoulder. Thus 66:7–14 has a double reference to 49:20–23: the role of Zion as mother and as comforter of her babies. With regard to the source text, however, Isa 66 intensifies Zion's maternal role. While 49:22 highlights the homecoming of Zion's children, 66:7 envisions Zion giving birth again. While in 49:23 foreign monarchs nurse Zion's children, in 66:11–12 it is Zion herself who breast-feeds her newborns and dandles them on her knees. With this newly conceived role of Zion, 66:11 also alludes to the promise in 60:16 that Zion herself will suck the milk of nations and the breast of kings. Again, 66:11 updates the prediction by changing Zion's role from addressee to mediator of the promise.[25] Furthermore, Zion's miraculous childbearing responds to the promise of a blessed offspring for the servants of Yhwh in 65:13.[26]

Another intertextual reference can be found in 66:12 in the motif that Jerusalem will be filled with wealth and prosperity. The vision of a stream of wealth pouring into Jerusalem combines 60:9 and Ps 46:5.[27] This Zion psalm portrays Jerusalem as surrounded by life-giving waters, while Isa 60:9 announces that foreign nations will bring Zion's children home together with wealthy gifts. The merging of both statements in Isa 66 into

---

25. Cf. Berges, *Jesaja*, 525.

26. Cf. Willem A. M. Beuken, "The Main Theme of Trito-Isaiah: The 'Servants of Yhwh,'" *JSOT* 47 (1990): 67–87, esp. 83.

27. Judith Gärtner argues that the stream of wealth in Isa 66:12 alludes to passages throughout the book of Isaiah (*Jesaja 66 und Sacharja 14 als Summe der Prophetie: Eine traditions- und redaktionsgeschichtliche Untersuchung zum Abschluss des Jesaja- und des Zwölfprophetenbuches* [WMANT 114; Neukirchen-Vluyn: Neukirchener, 2006], 316–17).

the metaphor of the river of prosperity adds spatial aspects to the female personification of Zion.

Through these intertextual references Isa 66:7–14 opens up a dialogue with other texts, especially former oracles of salvation. Thus I adhere to the thesis that Isa 56–66 are not the sayings of a prophetic individual,[28] but subsequent expansions written by a circle of scribes who aimed at actualizing the message of earlier oracles for the postexilic community in the Persian province Yehud.[29]

Compared with the salvation oracles in Second Isaiah and Isa 60–62, Isa 66 not only expands the vision but also increases the significance of Zion as a mother city. The function of 66:5–14 is to reassure a group of people who continue to mourn over Jerusalem and await the full restoration of their fate. What seems to be impossible for humans was possible for God, namely to help Jerusalem give birth to a whole people in one moment. The miracle is even convincingly expressed, if the time period "on a single day" (ביום אחד, v. 8) can be explained as an allusion to 47:9 that announces Babylon's loss of her children and her husband on a single day.[30] Thus the authors' intention is to persuade a consistently desperate audience that their Deity is close to them and can change their fate in an instant. In this light, the empathetic and loving Mother Zion offers a role model for Yhwh because it reinforces the idea of a compassionate and life-

---

28. This is argued by Koenen, *Ethik*, 215–21; and Seizo Sekine, *Die Tritojesajanische Sammlung (Jes 56–66) redaktionsgeschichtlich untersucht* (BZAW 175; Berlin: de Gruyter, 1989), 182, 230. Paul A. Smith attributes the bulk of Isa 60–62 to the prophet Trito-Isaiah (TI₁) and suggests another single author (TI₂) for 56:1–8; 56:9–57:21; 58:1–59:20; 65:1–66:17 (*Rhetoric and Redaction in Trito-Isaiah: The Structure, Growth and Authorship of Isaiah 56–66* [VTSup 62; Leiden: Brill, 1995], 24, 185).

29. The German term for such additions is *Fortschreibung*. A complex development of redactions and subsequent *Fortschreibungen* to the book as a whole is argued by Odil Hannes Steck, *Bereitete Heimkehr: Jesaja 35 als redaktionelle Brücke zwischen dem Ersten und dem Zweiten Jesaja* (SBS 121; Stuttgart: Katholisches Bibelwerk, 1985); idem, *Studien zu Tritojesaja*. Wolfgang Lau traces innerbiblical allusions and literary parallels of Isa 56–66 to other texts in Isaiah resulting in his assessment that Isa 56–66 is the work of scribes; see *Schriftgelehrte Prophetie in Jes 56–66: Eine Untersuchung zu den literarischen Bezügen in den letzten elf Kapiteln des Jesajabuches* (BZAW 225; Berlin: de Gruyter, 1994). Similarly Johannes Goldenstein, *Das Gebet der Gottesknechte: Jes 63,7–64,11 im Jesajabuch* (WMANT 92; Neukirchen-Vluyn: Neukirchener, 2001).

30. Cf. Koenen, *Ethik*, 197 n. 238; Blenkinsopp, *Isaiah 56–66*, 305; Goldenstein, *Gebet*, 219 n. 311.

giving Deity.[31] The personified city not only provides a space for communication with God, but also brings to mind a loving sentiment and atmosphere by her female gender and motherly role. Zion's body in 66:7–14a functions as a *site* and a *sign* of imagination. As a *site*, the fertile body of Zion underlines the notion of *perceived space*—a city full of people and merchandise, an ideal space for humans to live and prosper. The *site* aspect also covers Zion's motherly role, which mediates Yhwh's compassion and care and forms an element of *conceived space*. In reminding the audience of their own experience of motherhood and in evoking the sentiment of maternal love, 66:12–14 announces what has not yet been experienced: life in a secure habitation with abundant food and the feeling of protection. This vision transcends *lived space*, the actual experience of living in Jerusalem, insofar as some people continue to mourn over the present condition of the city (v. 10). As a mother who feeds her children well, Zion offers agency, a purposive role, to an audience that still awaits the flourishing of their own bodies (v. 14). For this audience, Zion's fertile body functions as a *sign* for their own salvation, which is said to be near. It is striking that the voice of Yhwh from the temple (v. 6) focuses on the city's body as the place of encountering divine care so that the sanctuary as a place of communication with God recedes to the background.

Although verse 13b may be a gloss (i.e., a late ad hoc comment by a scribe), the sentence draws an obvious conclusion from the passage that intertwines Zion's and God's motherhood by providing a double meaning of בירשלים. While most translations assume localization, reading "you will be comforted *in* Jerusalem," the preposition can also be interpreted as instrumental insofar as the comfort will be mediated *by* or *through* the personified Mother Zion.[32] Thus Zion's maternal body, not the temple, becomes the mediator of divine blessing and salvation. While 66:7–14a seem to offer a universalistic view of Zion's motherhood to a whole people, the passage can hardly be separated from its present context, which presupposes a schism among the inhabitants of the city. Therefore, an analysis of the context is required in order to identify those who claim to be Zion's newborn children.

---

31. Similarly, John J. Schmitt, "Motherhood of God and Zion as Mother," *RB* 92 (1985): 557–69, esp. 560–63.

32. For this meaning of the preposition, see Joüon §133c.

A Spatial Reading of Isaiah 66:7–14a in Its Context

In the present context, 66:5–6 and 66:14b hinder any universalistic view of Zion's motherhood. Verses 5–6 juxtapose those "who tremble at Yhwh's word" with another group called "enemies" of God. Both groups reclaim the presence of Yhwh among them. From verses 1–4 one can conclude that "the tremblers" seem to have abandoned the temple cult, claiming that heaven is God's throne, while the latter offer the customary sacrifices. Verses 14b–17 reprise this distinction, calling the positively evaluated group "servants of Yhwh" and charging the "enemies" with cultic aberrations.

The key word "servants of Yhwh" takes up a title that is frequently used in Second Isaiah, where Israel/Jacob are called "servant" (41:8–9; 44:1–2, 21; 45:4; 48:20). Moreover, there is the anonymous servant of God in the so-called Servant Songs.[33] Willem A. M. Beuken has plausibly shown that the servants and their vindication is the predominant theme of Isa 56–66 and that the title in the plural builds on the singular renderings.[34] These servants consider themselves to be the true remnant of Jacob that suffers from oppression by fellow Judeans. The latter are described as leading circles in Jerusalem (56:9–12) who make the pious perish (57:1–2), act relentlessly against the hungry and marginalized (58:1–8), and engage in crime and deception (59:1–8, 13) as well as in illegitimate cults (57:6–13; 65:1–5).

In my view, an analysis that combines Zion's female and spatial aspects helps to clarify the situation of the text's authors. The birth of Zion's children is described with *qatal* forms of the verbs, that is, as a completed action. Thus the city's repopulation is presupposed. Verses 12–14 are formulated as an announcement that now God is starting to direct a stream of wealth into the city; this wealth consists of abundant food and makes the bodies of those who still experience deprivation flourish. The existence of two groups competing over the claim of being true children of Zion becomes obvious in the opposing portraits of "brothers" (vv. 5, 14b). With regard to Lefebvre's theory of space, one could distinguish in the portrait of Jerusalem two competing views that belong to two different perspectives of lived space, the experience of space. While both views presuppose

---

33. The servant songs comprise Isa 42:1–4; 49:1–6; 50:4–9, 52:13–53:12.
34. See Isa 56:6; 63:17; 65:8–9, 13–15; 66:14; and Beuken, "Main Theme," esp. 68.

Jerusalem's rebuilding and restitution as capital (*perceived space*) and its significance as a place in which God's glory dwells (*conceived space*), they diverge on their understanding of *lived space*, especially on the question of who are to be the real beneficiaries of Zion's nourishment and comfort. While the oracles of salvation in Isa 40–55 and their reinterpretation in Isa 60–62 portray Zion as the former mother of all returning from exile and as a dwelling place open to everyone from the postexilic community, in Isa 66 the marginalized group reclaims Zion's motherhood for itself and denies it to others who are associated with the temple. Significantly, the authors of 66:7–14 claim to be newborn children of Zion, a designation that opens up the possibility of including people of non-Judean descent within the group of Yhwh followers.

In contrast to the universal message of hope put forward in Second Isaiah, several passages in Isa 56–66 point to a sharp divide within the postexilic community. There are different suggestions as to the sociological setting of the group that is represented by these "servants of Yhwh."[35] Paul Hanson thinks of a prophetic group in the early Second Temple period that was silenced by the ruling hierocratic party of the Zadokites, who were willing to compromise with the ruling Persian authorities. After being defeated in the political arena, this prophetic group retreated from the world of politics and devoted itself to the belief that Yhwh would one day intervene to bring them their salvation.[36] While Hanson dates most of Isa 66 to the time of the rebuilding of the Jerusalem temple around 520 B.C.E.,[37] in my view the multiple allusions in Isa 66 presuppose earlier prophecies in Isa 40–55 and 60–62 and thus point to a later time in the postexilic period.

Joseph Blenkinsopp rightly argues that the designation חרדים/חרד, "the one/those who tremble," at the word/commandment of God is used only in Isa 66:2, 5; Ezra 9:4; and 10:3.[38] In the account on Ezra's failed attempt to divorce the foreign wives of *golah* members,[39] "the tremblers"

---

35. For an overview of scholarly theses see Emmanuel U. Dim, *The Eschatological Implications of Isa 65 and 66 as the Conclusion of the Book of Isaiah* (Bern: Peter Lang, 2005), 201–14.

36. See Paul D. Hanson, *The Dawn of Apocalyptic: The Historical and Sociological Roots of Jewish Apocalyptic Eschatology* (rev. ed.; Philadelphia: Fortress, 1979), 218–20.

37. See ibid., 172–73.

38. Blenkinsopp, *Isaiah 56–66*, 299.

39. The MT of Ezra 10:44 does not state that the *golah* members actually divorced

seem to support Ezra's rigorous interpretation of the law, and Ezra is described as a devout ascetic like themselves. Since Isa 65–66 does not mention mixed marriages but opposes temple sacrifice and cultic aberrations, Blenkinsopp surmises that after Ezra's measure failed, the accused priests and leading circles turned the threat of ostracism and loss of property on their former critics.[40] In Mal 3:13-21 he sees a similar rift between the devout and the reprobate. Another text that refers to strife between aristocratic groups and impoverished Judeans is Neh 5, in which the Persian governor Nehemiah praises himself for having enforced a relief of debts for those who had to pledge their property or children to Judean creditors. Ezra 9–10 and Mal 3 as parallels point to a later dating of the schism in the postexilic community, probably at the end of the fifth or the beginning of the fourth century B.C.E.[41] While the "tremblers" in Isa 65–66 may have been part of the *golah* group, the main criterion of their self-distinction is not or, more precisely, is no longer Judean descent but loyalty to Yhwh's word, be it delivered in the *torah* or through a reinterpretation of earlier prophecy.[42] In reusing the old Divine Warrior metaphor, they claim that Yhwh will side with the afflicted and oppressed and punish those who worship Yhwh among other deities.[43]

Their reworking of theological statements can also be seen in their use of the root כבד, "to be heavy" (qal), or "to appear in one's glory" (niphal),[44] as a key word in Isa 66:5–17. The demand that Yhwh may reveal his glory

---

their foreign wives. Many scholars thus follow 1 Esd 9:36, but the authors of Ezra 9–10 aim at repentance; see Hugh G. M. Williamson, *Ezra, Nehemiah* (WBC 16; Nashville: Word, 1985), 145, 159–62.

40. Blenkinsopp, *Isaiah 56–66*, 301.

41. While Dim (*Eschatological Implications*, 206–12) reproduces Blenkinsopp's arguments, he continues to date Third Isaiah to the end of the sixth century following the line of Hanson. Cf. also Smith, *Rhetoric*, 187–203. Smith advances many perspicuous arguments against Hanson's thesis. Yet he delimits four units in Third Isaiah (56:1–8; 56:9–57:21; 58:1–59:20; 65:1–66:17), which he dates to the time of the rebuilding of the temple. His main arguments for this dating are that 66:1–2 refer to this time of transition and that the significance of the temple is one of the most contentious issues within these units. Differing views on the temple, however, could also occur in a later period.

42. For a similar historical setting see Berges, *Jesaja*, 542–45.

43. For the Divine Warrior metaphor see Childs, *Isaiah*, 545–47; Blenkinsopp, *Isaiah 56–66*, 316–17. For a detailed eschatological interpretation see Dim, *Eschatological Implications*, 251–54; Gärtner, *Jesaja 66*, 63–66, 93–101.

44. Cf. *HALOT* 2:455. For the text-critical issue in Isa 66:5, see n. 15 above.

(v. 5) put in the mouth of the adversaries has a sarcastic tone and denies that Yhwh will actually appear. Yet the noun כבוד, "honor, glory, splendor," used to describe Zion's "glorious bosom" (v. 11) and the "wealth of the nations" (v. 12), connects Yhwh's glory with the treasures that Zion's children receive. Thus the followers of Yhwh will be able to experience his glory mediated through Zion. While in other texts in Isaiah Yhwh's glory (כבוד) is often related to his epiphany at the temple (4:5; 6:3; 24:23; cf. 60:1–3, 13), the alteration of the motif demonstrates a shift from a temple-centered view to an appreciation of Yhwh's word that causes fear and awe among his followers.[45] The altered motif also pertains to the prophetic vision of Zion being the new Mount Sinai from which Yhwh's *torah* emerges and teaches many nations to stop waging war against one another (2:2–4).

In sum, the portrait of Zion in Second and Third Isaiah shows that Zion's role as mother can be used both with a universalistic or particularistic intention. Later writings mention Zion as mother city mostly in a universalistic perspective. Psalm 87, for example, counts even non-Israelites among those who are born in this city, and the Old Greek translation awards to Zion the title "mother."[46] Among the psalms found in Qumran there is the so-called Apostrophe to Zion, 11QPs[a] XXII, 1–15, which extends to Zion many promises of Isa 40–66, and especially takes up the idea of 66:10–11 that those who yearn for her salvation will be nourished in her midst (lines 4–5, 8).[47] This song also distinguishes between the sons of Zion and her enemies, who are associated with falsehood and evil (lines 7–8, 13). The apocryphal book Baruch from the second century B.C.E. offers images of Jerusalem as mother weeping for her children but also comforting them with the message that God will rescue them from the hands of their enemies (Bar 4:11–20).

---

45. Gärtner (*Jesaja 66*, 25–32) rightly perceives a double movement in Isa 66:5–17: While the passage attests to an enlargement of God's domain from the temple precinct to the whole earth, the experience of his glory is limited to only one group within the community who see themselves as the true children of Zion. Gärtner, however, underestimates the role of female Zion within this new constellation.

46. Cf. Christl M. Maier, "Psalm 87 as a Reappraisal of the Zion Tradition and Its Reception in Gal 4:26," *CBQ* 69 (2007): 473–86.

47. James A. Sanders, *The Psalms Scroll of Qumrân Cave 11 (11QPs[a])[a]* (DJD IV; Oxford: Clarendon, 1965), 85–89.

The eschatological setting of Isa 66 with its differentiation between Yhwh followers and enemies of God may have influenced the distinction between Jerusalem on earth and the "new" or "heavenly" Jerusalem that appears in Jewish apocalyptic writings (e.g., *4 Ezra* 7:26; 10:27, 40–54; *1 En.* 90:28–39; *2 Bar.* 4:1–7; *2 En.* 55:2; *4 Bar.* 5:33). The distinction between the city on earth and a heavenly Jerusalem is also attested in the New Testament (Gal 4:26; Heb 12:22; 13:14; Rev 3:12; 21:9–22:5) and again insinuates that not all actual inhabitants are really worthy of being called children of the Holy City.

Thus the reception of Zion's role as a mother to different groups of "children" in Jewish and Christian sources transforms the city into a religious symbol, a sign and site of imagination. As a site of extreme religious significance, Jerusalem continues to play an important role in both Jewish and Christian liturgy today: Jewish prayers should be offered in the direction of Jerusalem, and many of them mention Jerusalem as the place of divine presence.[48] The Christian liturgy of the Holy Week emerged both from actual rituals in fourth-century Jerusalem and from local customs of pilgrims who came to the city.[49]

Conclusion

The female personification of Zion in Isa 66:7–14 intertwines both spatial and gendered aspects within the literary figure. In her role as a mother of newborns, Zion offers an abundance of nourishment and comfort to those who remain marginalized. In and through Zion, Yhwh takes the role of a consoling mother and offers hope that the human bodies will flourish again and that the city will be the mediator of divine blessing. While this glorious vision seems to offer a universal view of peace, its current context limits Zion's nourishment to one group of followers of Yhwh who rely on the divine word more than on the temple cult. In the eschatological context of the last chapter of the book of Isaiah, Zion's motherhood will be the

---

48. See Andreas Nachama, "Jerusalem und die jüdische Gebetskultur," in *Die Reise nach Jerusalem: Eine kulturhistorische Exkursion in die Stadt der Städte. 3000 Jahre Davidstadt* (ed. Hendrik Budde and Andreas Nachama; Berlin: Argon, 1995), 76–79; Stefan C. Reif, "Jerusalem in Jewish Liturgy," *Judaism* 46 (1997): 159–68.

49. See Paul F. Bradshaw, "The Influence of Jerusalem on Christian Liturgy," in *Jerusalem: Its Sanctity and Centrality to Judaism, Christianity, and Islam* (ed. Lee I. Levine; New York: Continuum, 1999), 251–59.

reward of Yhwh's servants only in contrast to the enemies of God within the Judean community who will be destroyed in the fire of his wrath.

The question of how this personification of Zion as motherly space may be evaluated from a feminist point of view leads back to Carleen Mandolfo's work. She made a good point in stressing a dialogic reading of texts, which is able to address our modern intricate questions of justice and representation. Mandolfo argues that Daughter Zion in Lamentations challenges the dominant prophetic view that she is a whore, guilty and defiled. In the book of Isaiah, however, it is difficult to trace the dominant voice. In consoling the exiled Judeans, the prophetic voice in Second Isaiah privileges the *golah* community over against those who remained in the land after the fall of Jerusalem in 587 B.C.E. As a response to this marginalization, another group in 66:5–14 claims its share in being consoled and naturalized as children of postexilic Jerusalem. The seemingly universalistic portrait of Zion's consoling breast and womb cannot be separated from the highly particularistic viewpoint of its authors, namely that her "milk" belongs to those who tremble at God's word. If one reads 66:7–14 within its current context, the voice of the marginalized, the voice of those who suffer from oppression and long for divine retribution, becomes dominant. While one would rightly call the image of the Divine Warrior in 66:15–16 patriarchal, the concern for the marginalized is a trait in the Hebrew Bible that feminist scholars normally cherish as a counterimage of divine justice over human power structures. Thus I would respond to Mandolfo that the dominant voice is not one and the same in all prophetic writings and that within one single book there is already a dialogue between different voices.

Mandolfo also argues that, from the perspective of Lamentations, not even Second Isaiah's consoling words and promises are adequate responses to Zion's lament, because God's kindness is still constrained by the demands of patriarchal hegemony.[50] This is a valuable critical reading of Second Isaiah, yet clearly a postmodern assessment. I would extend this critical notion to the maternal role of Zion. It is obvious that the personification of Zion in Isa 66 feminizes the space in order to mark it as habitable and even comfortable and thus displays its embedding in a patriarchal system of thought. At the same time, however, the personification demonstrates the life-giving power of women's bodies and the importance of the care of mothers for a community. God's helping hand is

---

50. Cf. Mandolfo, *Daughter Zion*, 117–18.

compared to the comfort a mother gives to her infants (Isa 66:13). From a feminist viewpoint, one may dismiss the portrait of Zion as mother as a patriarchal concept that narrowly defines women with regard to their sex and biological function. Yet one may also read Zion's motherly role as an acknowledgment of the procreative power of women and cherish the idea that an all-male role model of God is just not sufficient and cannot picture life in its fullness. The personification of Zion as breast-feeding mother fosters a sense of agency in a disheartened audience and supports the idea of a hospitable dwelling place. At least, the reception of Zion as mother in later Jewish and Christian writings and liturgies demonstrates the metaphor's positive potential to offer hope and comfort in a time of distress, especially to people at the margins. Thus I would like to keep feminist readings of Zion texts dialogical in two respects: first, in dialogue with other voices within the text; and second, in dialogue with competing interpretations that aim at different audiences.

Demonized Children and Traumatized, Battered Wives: Daughter Zion as Biblical Metaphor of Domestic and Sexual Violence

Cheryl A. Kirk-Duggan

"The bad guys, … everywhere, have figured out that if you can't afford guns and bullets, and you have a political or military objective, the most effective strategy to employ is sexual violence."[1] Betty Makoni, a Zimbabwean activist and rape survivor, who, while she knows at least seven hundred women who have been raped as acts of war and terror, senses the actual numbers are much higher. The shame that comes with such rape and the unwanted children produced from these rapes makes rape an effective weapon. Throughout the globe, war, massacre, and genocide forged the murders of between 180 and 200 million in the twentieth century. In the later twentieth century and now the early twenty-first century, rape as a weapon of warfare has increased. Women and children are constantly under threat of domestic and sexual violence. Such brutality occurs globally and domestically, in life, in cultural artifacts, and in Scripture. The stories of Jephthah's daughter (Judg 11) and the secondary wife, or concubine, of the Levite (Judg 19) signal premeditated murder and the dismemberment as divinely sanctioned behavior. FaithTrust Institute, a nonprofit organization founded by Marie Fortune, working to end domestic and sexual violence, notes that "religious teachings can serve as a resource or a roadblock in stopping violence."[2]

In this essay I explore the notion of Daughter Zion, prophetic marriage metaphor, as a catalyst for sexual and domestic violence. After pro-

---

1. Jocelyn Craugh Zuckerman, "Victims of Sexual Violence in Zimbabwe Say … We Must Stop the Rape and Terror," *Parade Magazine* (22 March 2009): 6.
2. http://faithtrustinstitute.org/index.php?p=About_the_Issues&s=3.

viding an overview of my methodology, I (1) give a snapshot of the impact and depths of sexual and domestic violence globally; (2) analyze the marriage metaphor in Hos 2; (3) analyze domestic and sexual violence in one film (*Diary of a Mad Black Woman*) and one novel (*The Color Purple*); (4) examine critical issues when preaching Hos 2; and (5) suggest a few ways to illumine and thus subvert the power these texts subliminally have in U.S. culture.

Through a Looking Glass: A Womanist Interdisciplinary Lens

How one reads (whether holding a text up to a mirror as in Alice's case, through a magnifying lens, or with bifocals), why one reads, and the intent with which one reads shapes the outcome of dialogical reading of a text. I read biblical, artistic, and biotexts or living texts from a womanist perspective. Womanist theory seeks to juxtapose and problematize traditional, postcolonial, and liberationist readings of texts toward new readings that expose all manner of oppression. Such a reading commits to challenging systemic, communal, and theological oppressions with suspicion, or to tempered cynicism to seek a helpful/harmful continuum, given complex cultures and individuals, and how marginalized peoples experience identity and displacement. Oppression and injustice include all violence, that which does harm, including and not limited to: sexism, classism, heterosexism, racism, ageism, ableism, and ecological concerns. Critical to identity is a sense of agency: who speaks, who speaks for those deemed "other," and the process of self-actualization. With courage and creativity, I question interpretations regarding divine will, punishment, and judgment amid innocence and nature, free will, and the problematic of theodicy.

With many biblical texts, and particularly those of Daughter Zion, people who speak often gain authenticity and power from the textual and contemporary community. The lines of innocence and guilt often become blurred, depending upon which voice one privileges in the text. One must also question matters of superiority, inferiority, and mutuality. One may not be able to equate appearances with reality or history. Because the text comes from Sacred Scripture, assumptions are often made that one needs to deconstruct. Commitment to justice seeking and discovery with candor exposes pathological oppressions masking control, manipulation, and hidden agendas. Notably with Daughter Zion and the marriage metaphor, one can take a cavalier attitude and view the horrific violence and humiliation as metaphorical, all the while ambivalent to the preponderance of global violence against those deemed "other," and the enormous amount of actual violence within marriages and intimate partnerships.

Curiosity and a need to discredit the sanctity of misinterpretations that imprison academicians and the faithful support the comedic, which frame my reading, keeping me simultaneously sane and challenged.[3] The work is bumpy and messy, often disconcerting, and ultimately satisfying. While difficult realities may not invoke simple answers, the most important step may be asking the paradoxical questions, a step that begins with qualifying terminology.

SEX, LIES, AND VIDEOTAPE: A GLIMPSE INTO DOMESTIC AND SEXUAL VIOLENCE

Steven Soderbergh's 1989 Cannes Film Festival classic *Sex, Lies, and Videotape* explores the sexual escapades and personal obsessions of its four main characters, revolving around a selfish lawyer who, supposedly in response to his wife's frigidity, has an affair with his wife's free-spirited sister. However, when the lawyer's college roommate pays an unexpected extended visit, the neglected wife surprisingly responds to his enticing hobby of videotaping women as they explain their sexual fantasies. *Sex, Lies, and Videotape* puts a distinctly different spin on the consequences of infidelity.[4] The ways we view Scripture, relationships, metaphorical language, and sexual and domestic violence frame our understanding and interpretations of reality.

Noted social activist and pastoral theologian Marie Fortune depicts sexual violence as sin. Sin objectifies or violates another's bodily integrity and personhood as well as one's relationship, and it includes acts of psychological and/or physical aggression and hatred. Biblical sexual violence includes rape, incest, and adultery. Dinah's rape (Gen 34) shows how people misunderstand and misattribute rape. Dinah's voice is silent and no one speaks for her. The text/narrator's concern focuses on the struggles between two families: victim/survivor, Dinah, daughter of Jacob; and Shechem, rapist, son of Hamor. The rape violates Jacob's property rights

---

3. Cheryl Kirk-Duggan, "Slingshots, Ships, and Personal Psychosis: Murder, Sexual Intrigue, and Power in the Lives of David and Othello," in *Pregnant Passion: Gender, Sex, and Violence in the Bible* (ed. Kirk-Duggan; SemeiaSt 44; Atlanta: Society of Biblical Literature, 2003), 40.

4. Steven Soderbergh, *Sex, Lies, and Videotape* (ASIN: 0767812158, 1989).

(his daughter), not Dinah's personhood. She is property. Further, her rapist wants to marry Dinah. The story resolves in more violence, the premeditated murder of Hamor and his sons.

The story of Tamar of the royal Davidic house is one of sexual violence involving incestuous battering. Tamar begged Amnon, her half-brother, not to attack her, because she would be shamed, and he would be a villain. Amnon plots, tricks, and rapes Tamar. Then he further maliciously betrays Tamar by shunning her and sending her away. Though the practice was later outlawed, Amnon could have asked David's permission to marry Tamar. In her culture, no longer a virgin, Tamar is unmarried, damaged merchandise and has no one to provide for her. For this property crime, her brother Absalom, like Dinah's brothers Levi and Simeon, exacts revenge through violence: death of the perpetrator.

Bathsheba's story reflects unequal power dynamics, and reveals how those with authority can overstep personal and sexual boundaries, resulting in sexual abuse. David not only takes advantage of Bathsheba, he has her husband Uriah murdered when he fails to leave his army and go to Bathsheba, so that David can get around the paternity matter of having impregnated Bathsheba. While he experiences familial losses, David remains king. Though he confesses to Nathan, after Nathan challenges his misdeeds of domestic abuse and violence, both Scripture and tradition herald David as Israel's greatest king, and in the lineage of Jesus Christ.[5]

Throughout global history, masculine privilege exerted power over the bodies of women and children. Such supremacy is apparent from the collapse of the Roman Empire, through the 1960s (*Our Bodies, Ourselves*[6]) and the sexual revolution, to sexual escapades of the rich and famous. Daily global and local deaths due to domestic violence reiterate the same. Most states in the United States have a coalition against domestic violence and a coalition against sexual assault and violence. Most cities have battered women's shelters because abused women and children need support, protection, and distance from abusive husbands/fathers. Just as people

---

5. Marie Fortune, *Sexual Violence: The Sin Revisited* (Cleveland: Pilgrim, 2005), 3, 6–12.

6. Boston Women's Health Book Collective, *Our Bodies, Ourselves* (New York: Simon & Schuster, 1973). This groundbreaking book concerns women's health and sexuality. Women spoke about their own bodies. The book was initially a thirty-six-page booklet called *Women and Their Bodies*, published in 1970 by the New England Free Press, and written by twelve Boston feminist activists.

acquiesce to the adage, "What happens in Vegas stays in Vegas," women have been secretive about their abuse. Only recently could women own property without their husband's signature. In many parts of the world, women are still viewed as property. Myths of male sexual prowess, rights to "his woman," belief in male superiority, and systemic oppression against women result in misogyny and patriarchy. Such a mind-set crosses categories of age, race, gender, class, and sexual orientation.

As art imitates culture and culture imitates art, film, television, and print media depict more brutality amid sexual violence. Nothing inherent to gender warrants universal, law-based commitments to men and particular, personal commitments to women. Violence is often an arbiter of social control and occurs on cultural, structural, individual, and institutional levels. Many religious and legal institutions nurture practices often hidden and invisible that justify, support, and depersonalize acts of violence. This violence involves myriad kinds of coercion, force, and abuse, used to control women and children. Too often, the courts, the church, and society blame victims of sexual abuse and violence for the crime itself. They must have done something to deserve what they received. Statistics and the depiction of sexual abuse and violence in popular culture, literature, mass media, and Scripture reflect the insidiousness and preponderance of sexual abuse, whether exacted by a family member or a stranger, as normal, desirable, and natural. Denial about such abuse fosters stereotypes about who the victims are and who the perpetrators will be.[7]

Fortune notes that the dominant culture posits particular components of male sexuality. Such actualized male sexuality needs to be in control, avoids rejection, and exercises predatory sexual propensities requiring a subordinate partner. The related emotional or erotic pleasure demands initiative and dominance, and never supports mutuality or requires personal sexual accountability. Disregard for the autonomy of others is normative. Not only can such male culture justify any predatory sexual acts, it also avoids intimacy by objectifying the other. The other must meet his needs exclusively; and his sexual partners must be pure, innocent, passive, subordinate, and powerless.[8] Adherence to this belief system fuels the propensity of domestic violence and abuse.

---

7. Cheryl Kirk-Duggan, *Misbegotten Anguish: A Theology and Ethics of Violence* (St. Louis: Chalice, 2001), 95–100.

8. Fortune, *Sexual Violence*, 20–22.

Domestic violence involves a pattern of coercive, aggressive behavior by one adult in an intimate relationship over another adult or child. Such abuse may include repeated severe beatings or subtle forms of psychological abuse, including intimidation and control. The U.S. Department of Justice claims that 95 percent of domestic violence victims in the United States are women; thus men can also be victims. Domestic violence occurs in 28 percent of all marriages, according to surveys from the United States and Canada, which is probably a low estimate, since most domestic violence incidents go unreported. The four basic types of domestic violence include: sexual assault, physical assault, psychological assault, and destruction or attacks against pets and property. While sexual violence is rarely a topic of discussion in religious settings, it occurs in private and public venues: at home, work, schools, and religious communities. That we fail to discuss sexual and domestic violence often contributes to stereotypes, myths, and misunderstandings around this abuse. Such misunderstandings can also result in people misusing sacred texts to rationalize sexual violence.[9]

According to the U.S. Department of Justice, between 1998 and 2002 49 percent of the almost 3.5 million violent crimes were against spouses; 86 percent of victims of dating-partner abuse were female, and 84 percent of spousal abuse were females. While wives made up half of all spouses in the population in 2002, they were 81 percent of all domestic violence homicide victims. Statistically, women tend to be victims of sexual violence more than men are: women are 78 percent of the victims of rape and sexual assault. Most perpetrators of sexual violence against women and against men are acts perpetrated by men. In 8 out of 10 rape cases in the United States, the rape victim knows the perpetrator. Of all the reported acts of sexual violence, an intimate partner raped, stalked, or physically assaulted 64 percent of women and 16 percent of men.[10]

---

9. See http://www.faithtrustinstitute.org/index.php?p=Q_%26_A&s=45; http://www.faithtrustinstitute.org/index.php?p=Sexual_Violence_and_Religion&s=32; Matthew R. Durose et al., U.S. Dep't of Just., NCJ 207846, *Bureau of Justice Statistics, Family Violence Statistics: Including Statistics on Strangers and Acquaintances, at 31–32 (2005)*, available at http://www.ojp.usdoj.gov/bjs/pub/pdf/fvs.pdf.

10. Matthew R. Durose et al., *Family Violence Statistics: Including Statistics on Strangers and Acquaintances* (Bureau of Justice Statistics; Washington, D.C.: U.S. Dept. of Justice, 2005; cited January 4, 2010; online: http://www.ojp.usdoj.gov/bjs/pub/pdf/fvs.pdf); Patricia Tjaden and Nancy Thoennes, *Full Report of the Prevalence, Incidence, and Consequences of Violence against Women: Findings from the National Violence against Women Survey* (Washington, D.C.: U.S. Dept of Justice, 2000; online: http://

Globally, issues of domestic violence are equally overwhelming. In 2000 the UN *Commission on the Status of Women* stated that at least one in three females experiences physical or sexual abuse during her lifetime; the kidnapping and false sharing of information about jobs results in the annual involvement of 4 million women and girls in sexual trafficking. The 2000 U.N. Study on the Status of Women found that at least 60 million girls from different populations, mostly in Asia, who would be expected to be alive are "missing" due to neglect, infanticide, or sex-selective abortions because sons are more desirable than daughters. Every year, thousands of young women die as the result of so-called honor killings, mainly in Western Asia, parts of South Asia, and North Africa. The World Health Organization's *Multi-country Study on Women's Health and Domestic Violence against Women, 2005,* records that slapping is the most common act of violence against women. Domestic and sexual abuse and violence, while occurring at different rates globally, are present in every country in the world.[11]

Domestically and globally, the data substantiate that domestic abuse and violence threaten human well-being. Threats to human welfare mean that the physical, mental, and emotional health of individuals and communities are under siege. Heightened global terrorist attacks, recent economic downturn, burgeoning growth of prisons as opposed to better early education, and a lack of commitment to rehabilitation signal increased violence. Notably, the use of sexual violence, particularly rape as an act of war by renegade groups, with the aforementioned violent acts compound the onslaught of violence against people and their communities. When sacred texts use metaphors that implicitly support such violence, and readers may not be conscious of the metaphor's role in that text, have we sealed the fate of the vulnerable and are we complicit in that violence? The use of the marriage metaphor in Hos 2 provides an opportunity to explore the beauty, cunning, and power of symbolic speech.

SPEAK NOW, OR FOREVER HOLD YOUR PEACE: MARRIAGE METAPHOR FRAMES DAUGHTER ZION

While the number of persons getting married seems to be declining, as more persons are living together and others are waiting before they get

---

www.ojp.usdoj.gov/nij/pubs-sum/183781.htmhttp://www.abanet.org/domviol/statistics.html#prevalence).

11. *Facts about Violence* (http://www.feminist.com/antiviolence/facts.html).

married, the marriage industry is big business. Sometimes people spend more time and energy around the rituals and festivities of the marriage ceremony itself than they do regarding working through issues of compatibility. For those who do decide to "jump the broom,"[12] most rituals in the United States continue to ask midway through the ceremony, whether casual or high church: "if there is anyone who knows any reason why this couple should not be married, speak now or forever hold your peace." Did women during the times of Hosea have any peace about their marriages? What about the experience of Daughter Zion in Hos 2?

Hosea, an eighth-century classical prophet, preached in the northern kingdom from the end of Jeroboam II's reign to just before the northern kingdom fell to Assyria (ca. 750–725 B.C.E.). The first prophet to use the marriage metaphor, where the Deity equals the husband and sinful Israel is the divine's adulterous wife, Hosea's account mirrors a culture of male privilege and female as object in ancient Israel. By framing his theology with this sociocultural perspective, Hosea portrays, justifies, and sanctions divine, male-spousal, physical violence against wife Israel. Unfortunately, some hearers forget the use of metaphor and view in tandem—and as normative—God's vengeance against Israel and a husband's physical violation of his wife. After Hosea experiences a tumultuous marriage with Gomer and they have the three children, which marriage the prophet likens to God and Israel's covenantal relationship in chapter 1, Hosea then envisions the covenantal relationship as a marriage in chapter 2. He equates Israel's idolatrous practices around Canaanite gods as adultery. The reconciliation between Yhwh and Israel posed in chapter 3 signals reconciliation between Hosea and Gomer.[13]

Hosea speaks of the relationship between Yhwh and Israel as a marriage. Carleen Mandolfo posits that the woman the prophet marries as a sign-act (Hosea as husband-deity, woman as Israel) is a *zonah*, which

---

12. "Jumping the broom" symbolizes sweeping away the old and welcoming the new, signifying new beginnings. Jumping the broom is a popular African tradition at many African diasporan weddings. Originating in Africa, the original significance and purpose of this tradition is lost. During U.S. enslavement, blacks were not permitted to marry. Those in bondage engaged in jumping the broom as a way to legitimize their marriage vows and covenant of domestic life together, under God. Online: http://www.africanweddings.com/jumping_the_broom.

13. Gale A. Yee, "Hosea," in *Women's Bible Commentary* (ed. Carol A. Newsom and Sharon H. Ringe; exp. ed.; Louisville: Westminster John Knox, 1998), 207–15, here 207–12.

should not be understood as a prostitute, whore, or cult prostitute. Rather, she is a woman whose actions bring shame to her family. The *zonah* experiences public shame. Her status as *zonah* places dishonor on her, not her husband, and protects the husband and family's honor. In Hos 2 God and the prophet's voice become one; the text portrays the woman as those who betray God. The children get caught in the middle between the contentious accusations of the Divine/prophet against the people/Gomer, the mother. The relationship shifts from that of Hosea and Gomer to Yhwh and Israel, the adulterous woman. Yhwh's wrath is now unleashed on the woman and her children, which could be read as overcompensation. God gives voice to the woman. This scenario makes it seem as if God tried to reconcile, but Gomer was resistant. Thus Yhwh's words about the woman make her seem guilty, and Yhwh betrays her—it is payback time. She shamed Yhwh, so Yhwh will shame her. After venting, the Deity turns to square things and reconcile, with a caveat: reconciliation happens as a condition of being able to control Zion's agency.[14]

What could have happened with this text if Mandolfo had further problematized the role or function of a *zonah*? Does the reader really hear a distinction between a whore who dishonors her family and a woman who dishonors herself? If a woman is the property of her husband, it seems her status would still affect her family in ancient culture, as family is not about individuality but about covenantal reality. Do we not need to criticize the text or Hosea for equating sinful Israel with a woman? Why not equate sinful Israel with a man, since men had the power of decision making by law? Ultimately, the text places shame on the *zonah*, whether attributed to her alone or to her family; she still becomes the problem. Conversely, if the *zonah* could speak for herself, would she be bold enough to not accept the role of shame the text and society seek to place on her? By the divine and prophetic voices being one in Hos 2, the odds are stacked against the woman, resulting in psychological abuse against Gomer and her children. How could Gomer ever experience healing? What is her shame? Was Hosea aware of her issues before marriage? Must the children also experience shame with their awful names? A womanist analysis seeks health and well-being for all, to love all, to seek justice. Both Gomer and Israel experience harsh treatment, and Hosea and Yhwh are above it all. Where

---

14. Carleen R. Mandolfo, *Daughter Zion Talks Back to the Prophets: A Dialogic Theology of the Book of Lamentations* (SemeiaSt 58; Atlanta: Society of Biblical Literature, 2007), 31–36.

is the justice for Gomer and her children? Is Hosea's history so pristine that he has no culpability in the process? Do not healthy, responsible husbands/fathers support and protect their families? The condemnation and divorce in ancient culture drain the life out of the family. What happens when literalists preach or study this text? Can they see beyond labels and blaming to the foundational issues and need to work together to resolve the conflict?

Hosea's story changes from one of hope (2:1) to one of condemnation, via a divine, legal indictment apparently addressed to Hosea's children Jezreel (God sows), Lo-ruhamah (Not pitied), and Lo-ammi (Not my people); the last signals a covenantal or marriage dissolution or divorce. After the tumultuous, abusive relationship and the husband's third punishment strategy, Yhwh/husband and the wife return to the wilderness, the place where the two first pledged to be in covenantal relationships; there they did enjoy marital ecstasy. The marriage metaphor expresses the divine-human relationship as no other metaphor can and supports Hosea's monotheistic agenda, as he frames his argument in matters of the woman's sexual exclusivity for the sake of paternity. In Hosea the marriage metaphor, the predator husband, adulterous wife, and domestic assault together press a monotheistic scenario that champions an abuse of power, creating a social and theological problem: the story of wife beating, minus awareness of the biblical metaphorical image, validates God's vengeance against Israel. Further, Gale Yee notes that institutions like the Vatican use this marriage metaphor to deny women the sacrament of ordination, for the church must be the female bride and the priest must be the male. She encourages us to use the study and interpretation of Hos 2 as pedagogical moments to explore several concepts. The study of metaphorical, religious language can help one determine how to find meaning. Analysis of the reversal of gender roles with Yhwh/husband and Israel/wife, along with other metaphorical, relational paradigms beyond the husband/wife model, is critical for understanding the impact of literary framing of relational matters that signify sin, judgment, and violence.[15] What is the prophetic impetus for them using metaphorical models?

Prophets used figurative language, like metaphors, to talk about themes often difficult to define. God's immanence and transcendence, mysteriousness, and ambiguity mean that the most accessible way to talk about God

---

15. Gale A. Yee, "Hosea," *NIB* 7:197–336, here 223–29.

is in the language of human relationships. The five significant metaphors prophets used to teach their audiences about divine-human relationships were parenting, marriage, imperial status, slavery, and legal standing. Use of these metaphors reveals that one can only know God in intimate relationship; that the Deity-human relationship is one of hierarchy, not mutuality; that the relationship involves mutual commitment and responsibilities; and that human failure to comply nearly guarantees retribution, discipline, or punishment. The marriage metaphor intends to rationalize the punishment and violence people experience, and to absolve God from any wrongdoing. When human beings fail to engage in covenantal responsibility, the prophets see that God is the victim, as Israel's/the wife's disobedience and poor behavior dishonor God. Metaphors then are effective because they help us reorganize how we think about and react to a particular subject.[16] Metaphors help us with interpretation and ascribing identity.

God, Daughter Zion's husband, constructs her identity. No one affords her subjectivity or agency, because no one allows her to engage in dialogue. The prophets reflect ancient sociocultural norms when they portray Daughter Zion—one of the marginalized—as a social outcast, whore, adulterous woman, whose master can justify abusing her. Prophetic Scripture finds women automatically inferior, and God determines what Zion knows and can do, and how it is she owes allegiance. Prophets represent her discourse indirectly and commit violent acts against her physical body. The course set forth for Daughter Zion reeks of troubled, relational misogyny (Hosea), hegemonic diatribe (Jeremiah), and an experience of absolute domination (Ezekiel). Mandolfo notes that in Lamentations, however, Daughter Zion creates a victimized persona, a mother, in juxtaposition to Jeremiah's villainous wife; here she portrays herself as nurturing mother. Daughter Zion reconstructs her story as she reacts to the metanarrative, woven by prophetic voices privileging the Divine. Following feminist and postcolonial scholars, including Kwok Pui-Lan, Nancy Lee, and Jon Berquist, who view Lamentations as a moving manifestation of existential anguish, distress, and betrayal, we are moved by the text to read with or alongside Daughter Zion, depicting the Divine/male as object. Mandolfo cautions that both Daughter Zion and God have issues; they both make mistakes and have a part of the truth to speak on their own behalf; and

---

16. Renita Weems, *Battered Love: Marriage, Sex, and Violence in the Hebrew Prophets* (Minneapolis: Fortress, 1995), 15–19, 23.

that those who compiled the text included Daughter Zion, which expands our reading from privileging only Yhwh's voice. While Yhwh often comes across as a bully regarding Zion, Zion gains her subjectivity through her own resistance. In colonial, prophetic discourse, human beings do not speak for themselves; divinely shaped discourse usually frames human speech, pressing a divine agenda.[17]

Mandolfo contends that the prophetic use of the marriage metaphor is a consummate depiction of Buber's I-It encounter. When God talks to people there is a major disconnect, as the communication happens at cross-purposes, around, over, and past each other. Reading Yhwh as a textual construct can possibly have ethical significance for dealing with human relationships that extend beyond the text. Mandolfo engages a dialogic, deconstructive, midrashic reading against the limits and intent of the particular text, while also opting to employ traditions for contemporary use. Such a process does not intend to replace one value system for another, but rather to hold various readings together in tension, while suggesting a minor correction, without any dialectic resolution. Using Mikhail Bakhtin's notion of authoring, Mandolfo posits that we help to shape and coauthor the lives of others; we help tell their story based upon what we know about them. Stories or narratives provide meaning, which helps us to build the identity of others.[18]

From a womanist perspective, questions arise as to power, access, and the way they affect how one reads the story, interprets it, and finds meaning. Not all readings are the same, as inclusive, or as just. Championing an I-It relationship is not helpful for fostering healthy relationships, for some would not, could not, hear anything for potential healing, when one who is automatically in a role of property has the status of an "it." That we help to interpret the story does not mean the interpretation is helpful. Mandolfo seems not to be mindful of how her revisioning is still problematic—how would a woman or child who lives with domestic violence possibly find that both Daughter Zion and Yhwh having problems is helpful for getting out of their oppressive situation? Spreading around the onus for problems does not necessarily provide a liberating message. The problems still exist.

Mandolfo further qualifies her reading of the marriage metaphor as prophetic. Mandolfo views the prophetic marriage metaphor (in Hosea,

---

17. Mandolfo, *Daughter Zion*, 3, 15–17, 27, 52–54, 79–90, 101.
18. Ibid., 2, 7–11, 23–26, 45–54, 81, 86.

Second Isaiah, Ezekiel, and Jeremiah) as a way to tell the story of God and Israel from the perspective of the husband; in Lam 1–2 the wife speaks back: Israel becomes God's adulterous wife. The marriage metaphor unfolds as one-sided where Yhwh has difficulty and often fails to listen, and the prophets blame the wife for not listening, resulting in violence. Reading how the text makes, manipulates, and controls meaning exposes the one-sided, third-person language depicting Israel as wife-whore. Sometimes Yhwh accuses Zion of associating with providers other than Yhwh. In some instances, one can gain a lot by rebelling against Yhwh, for example, when making offerings to the Queen of Heaven (Jer 44:15–19). Intriguingly, in Jer 2:18 Zion's rebellion is a result of Yhwh's tyrannical demands. Yhwh really does not provide for Zion in a way commensurate to the demands Yhwh makes regarding being worshipped (Hos 2; Jer 44:17–18).[19] Theologically, the metaphor works to defend Yhwh and answer Israel's queries regarding divine mystery, theodicy, and human suffering. Socio-rhetorically, the metaphor communicates well to an elite male audience, who can scapegoat women (an adulterous wife threatened ancestral linage and brought her husband social dishonor) to deal with their deepest anxieties and offer God acquittal regarding any injustice or weakness.[20] Even if one acquits God and understands how to speak to an elite male audience, those sensibilities still do not have enough power to make Daughter Zion or abused family members safe. Such awareness is important at the personal, familial, communal, and institutional level.

Two ancient Israel institutions affected by the marriage metaphor are marriage and family. Promiscuity would threaten patriarchal, social, and property codes. From a literary perspective, the metaphor has a powerful influence over contemporary notions of marriage, power, and gender roles. Prophetic portraits paint women as sexually dangerous, deviant, evil, forging an intersection between human sexuality, politics, and the Divine. Yet men of all kinds can have multiple wives and concubines, and still maintain respectability. Israel's betrayal of the covenant made between God and their ancestors shaped the prophetic sociopolitical use of brazen, vulgar, and promiscuous rhetoric.

Renita Weems notes that such a move was provocative and bold. The prophets wanted to make a powerful, moral statement condemning Israel's

---

19. Ibid., 1–2, 11–12, 29–31, 39–40, 83–84, 122, 125, 126.
20. Weems, *Battered Love*, 4, 41–43, 65, 71.

behavior. Weems presses us toward womanist biblical analysis when we ask what this type of language does to the marginalized, to persons who have been assaulted, raped, and battered. How can we rationalize using such Sacred Scripture that revels in the obscene humiliation and abuse of a woman? How can we be morally and ethically responsible in our exegetical processes so that we can glean how such texts challenge our greatest uncertainties and engage our noblest principles? Metaphors work when they can bring two distinct things into cognitive and emotional or expressive relation so that one cannot contemplate the lesser known without referring to the better-known one. The marriage metaphor communicates depravity and brazenness, not just irresponsibility and rebellion, and signals that human disobedience brought shame to both dominant and subordinate parties—the Divine and the human.[21] Simultaneously, we must be extremely careful when equating Israel's disobedience with that of a female prostitute. The power dynamics experienced by a lone female and a nation are not equal. The level of disobedience and the related consequences are also different, particularly given that most women had no substantive power to begin with. All matters of disobedience are ultimately theological.

In Hos 2 the theological problems that emerge have serious connotations for us today, given Hosea's use of the marriage metaphor, on a human and religious level. Yhwh/husband uses three strategies to bring the wife under control. Some of these strategies are key tools for sexual and domestic abusers in the twenty-first century. Just equating the Divine with the male human automatically privileges the male with even more authority than ancient Israel's society gave him by definition. First, Yhwh/husband separates wife/Gomer/Israel from others to make her totally dependent upon her husband. Separating Israel from her lovers (Hos 2) mirrors Hosea seizing and keeping Gomer in hiding (Hos 3). Second, Yhwh/husband uses physical and psychological coercion, withholds food, and totally physically and emotionally humiliates her by forcing her to be naked publicly before her lovers; he ends her laughter, her joy, and destroys her vineyards (2:9–12). Third, after Yhwh/husband literally and figuratively whips her into submission, he seduces her, takes her to the wilderness, and speaks to her with gentleness (2:14), which parallels the abuse-honeymoon cycle of many abusive marriages. Yee reminds us that as problematic as the marriage metaphor is, we must

---

21. Ibid., 2–9, 13, 25–30.

question our hermeneutics and intentionality in its use, and remember that 11:3–11 does offer another potential metaphor of parent/son, where the mother/father-God offers compassion, allows for the son to repent, and does not exact anger or destruction, though legally permitted.[22] The option for metaphorical use in Hos 11 cannot, however, mitigate the harshness found in Hos 2, despite Hosea's motives and concern that Israel becomes obedient.

Troubled by unstable national politics and perverted religious practices, perhaps it is not surprising that Hosea develops the marriage metaphor to speak about divine-human covenantal, cultic relations. According to Yee, in the past scholars have posited that Canaanite cultic prostitution involved an annual, mythic reenactment of coitus between Anat, Baal's sister-lover, and Baal, after Anat rescues Baal and brings him back to life. Previously Mot, the god of death and barrenness, had killed Baal, signaling the lack of rain from May through September. Passionate coitus between Anat and Baal signals the return of rain in October. Several more recent scholars have questioned the existence of cult prostitution in the wake of the absence of substantive, supporting archaeological or textual evidence for such an institution; ancient testimonies to the contrary are not reliable.[23] Yee further cautions against dubbing Gomer a harlot. The noun *zonah* comes from *zanah*, which pertains to having sexual relations outside marriage, including: prostitution, sex for hire; fornication, sex involving an unmarried sister, daughter, or widow under the levirate code; and adultery, a married person having sex with someone other than a spouse. Yee suggests that more precise labeling would be to call Gomer promiscuous.

The language of sexuality and marriage are critical because of Hosea's use of the marriage metaphor, steeped in ancient patrilocal, patrilineal kinship systems, framed by morality markers of honor and shame. Family name and inheritance and marriage arrangements all follow male lineage. A young woman comes to the hostile home of her husband, where such relationships are often based on building alliances with other households and clans. Sometimes she married into a polygamous family. Her ability to give birth to sons often shaped her destiny. Sons had more value than daughters as they did not leave the home and could inherit the land. In

---

22. Yee, "Hosea," in Newsom and Ringe, *Women's Bible Commentary,* 211–12.
23. Ibid., 208–10.

this culture that found value in honor and shame, along gender lines, male honor derived from his abilities to be courageous, manly, protect and provide for his family, and assert his masculinity sexually. The positive value of shame for women manifested within her reputation as she embodied submission to male authority, humbleness, diffidence, passiveness, and sexual purity. In this cultural, familial matrix, sexual behavior of women in the household greatly influenced male honor. If a woman—mother, wife, sister, or daughter—misbehaved sexually, the father, husband, or brother would publicly lose his standing, his honor. Then and now, there was a double standard regarding punishment for extramarital relations by a man versus a woman. Adultery was punishable by death or by being stripped naked and exposed publicly.[24]

In sum, this reading of the use of the marriage metaphor and Daughter Zion in Hos 2 champions an exploration of the impact of violence rippling through the text and the sociocultural realities of ancient Israel, and how those realities shape thinking today. Power in the hands of Yhwh/husband affords abuse toward Daughter Zion. The marriage metaphor makes certain the bond between God and Israel, husband and wife. One cannot avoid an awareness of marriage given Israel's ties to the covenant God made with Abraham (Gen 12:1–3), in which God promises land, relationship in perpetuity, and a son. Marriage is tied to land; only a son can inherit land. Even when the daughters of Zelophehad (Num 27:1–7) went to Moses to plead their case and were then rightfully given the land of their father after his death because he had no sons, once the women married, the land went to their husbands.

Can one's relationship with God, the import of marriage and family, ever justify, rationalize, and sanctify domestic violence? I think not. When people do not or cannot see the underlying violence in the text, can they have the capacity to ignore the abuse and understand that subliminally they are being programmed to view women as inferior, and to regard abuse against women as acceptable? Persons who claim that the violence does not affect them in some way, that they are only cognizant of God's love and compassion for us, remind me of persons who claim that they only pay attention to the beat, the pulse of music whose misogynistic, vulgar lyrics demonize women. What can we learn from other cultural artifacts about domestic and sexual abuse and violence?

---

24. Ibid.

CULTURAL ARTIFACTS CONVICT:
DOMESTIC AND SEXUAL VIOLENCE IN LITERATURE AND FILM

The Color Purple, Alice Walker's epistolary novel, opens as young Celie addresses God in her letters, which she writes over a twenty-year period. Raped and abused frequently by the patriarch, who she thinks is her father, Celie sees a lot of domestic violence and fears for her sister Nettie's life. Her "father" sells her into marriage with an older widow, Mr. _____, who has four children. (We only learn his name much later in the narrative when their relationship reverses, and they experience a friendship of mutuality.) Mr. _____ terrorizes and beats her, taunts her, and forces her to clean, cook, and look after his dirty and ungrateful children. Meanwhile, Mr. _____ yearns to be with Nettie, until she runs away and becomes a missionary. Celie eventually learns that her abusive husband has been keeping her sister's letters from her. The rage she feels, combined with the love and independence she experiences when she and her close friend Shug fall in love, pushes her toward an awakening of her creative and loving self; she learns to embrace her own body, sensuality, sexuality, and a liberating, loving experience of God.[25]

Celie, the protagonist, is scapegoat and suffering servant, as she experiences horrific violence, socializing control of domination, and the accompanying low self-esteem amid a rural, dysfunctional black family—a story that ultimately transcends its racial-ethnic, socioeconomic, and geographical context, for domestic violence occurs globally. People experience violence daily with gross victimization and scapegoating. Celie's story is one of encounter and torment that leads to self-actualization, freedom, and wholeness. Before achieving wholeness, one can view Celie as a "suffering servant," as a Christ figure. Celie is like many abused women in the Hebrew Bible. From the widowed Tamar of Genesis; to the violated, discarded princess Tamar of the household of David; to the dismembered, decapitated, unnamed secondary wife or concubine of Judg 19; and to the unnamed, sacrificed, young virgin daughter of the idiot Jephthah—they all know the horrors of human inflicted evil, of domestic violence. As metaphorical "suffering servant," dubbed to be the redemptive figure, Celie and Mr. _____ are both victims in this persecution text.

---

25. Alice Walker, *The Color Purple* (New York: Pocket Books, 1982).

Cultural anthropologist and literary critic René Girard views scapegoats psychosocially, as victims of unmerited discrimination or violence; groups in society may punish or blame them for the wrongs of others, any conflicts, tensions, or problems based on delusions. Thus Mr. _____ scapegoats Celie unconsciously, because the world has done the same to him. In this model, scapegoating is hidden, not obvious. Those who are unjust do not see themselves in this light. Yet the misogyny, sexism, and racism fuel myths, which authorize and authenticate crimes of sexual abuse and domestic violence. In Scripture, literature, and contemporary society, too often many women, and in other instances, children and those men who are victimized, accept that they are at fault. Somehow, it is their fault that the spouse, lover, or parent beats them physically and/or maligns them psychologically and spiritually. With the help of Shug, Celie is able to challenge Mr. _____'s control and domination over her. Like Gomer in Hos 2, Celie lacks male affirmation and thus in one instance stands outside the community, while yet being a marginal insider to the same community. Celie's metamorphosis through the love of others and a transformed sense of an outsider God, who does not condone patriarchal, misogynistic brutality, moves her from silence, from being her stepfather's incest victim and a spouse battered by her husband, to a woman of power and authenticity.[26]

As part of self-actualization, Celie chooses her God and frames her own existence as *imago Dei*. The novel espouses such a relationship and the notion of a good creation, reflecting a close intimacy with God. Aware of sin in a world that often does not afford people deemed "other" any options, sinners enjoy themselves—and in their minds please God by pleasing themselves. For those who finally can please themselves, this is not a destructive but a redemptive note. Though Celie rarely blames God for her suffering, sometimes she feels distanced from God. Her sense of God moves from that of a fat, male banker; through a wilderness experience where God is a distant, trifling, lowdown, forgetful man who fails to listen to poor black women; to a God who transfigures into the ultimate good that ever could have been or ever will be.[27] Where Daughter Zion does not speak, Celie speaks and embodies her truth that ultimately brings about salvific impetus for Celie, Mr. _____, and the entire community.

---

26. Kirk-Duggan, *Misbegotten*, 266–74.
27. Walker, *Color Purple*, 11, 96, 183, 198–200, 202; Kirk-Duggan, *Misbegotten*, 275–78.

Celie and Mr. _____'s lives intersected at points of pain; ultimately, they reconnect through love.

Mr. _____'s premeditated, horrific cruelty of physical, sexual, and psychological abuse reflects the depths to which some will go to control and manipulate women, children, and some men to be victims. Critics of the novel's discourse about violence set in a black community often fail to realize that this novel is not narrowly about violence of black males on black females. Walker focuses on the liberation of the entire community and on black women having agency, knowledge, and self-love; and the majority of the relationships move from systemic/personal dominance to beautiful harmony. Without harming others, Celie ends up whole, with a restored, new relationship with God, learns the truth about her real parents, is reunited with her sister Nettie, and knows love that includes and transcends sexuality.[28] Mandolfo's deconstructive, dialogic reading of Daughter Zion seeks to afford her the same liberative transformation that Walker gives Celie and other members of her community.

Situated in the rural south in the late nineteenth to early twentieth century, *The Color Purple* deals with extended family, domestic and sexual violence, community, theology, gender issues, and transformation. *The Diary of a Mad Black Woman*, a movie set in the urban, metropolitan, twenty-first century, ultimately involves similar issues, with class desires and perceptions intersecting with domestic violence.

In Tyler Perry's *Diary of a Mad Black Woman*, Charles, an attorney, and Helen, his devoted wife, seem to have everything: money, affluence, public visibility, and a beautiful mansion—the American Dream.[29] Yet, as Helen prepares to celebrate their eighteenth wedding anniversary, her life takes a surprising turn. The relationship is about appearances. The film opens with Charles being honored at a banquet, and he in turn gives attribution to his wife, claiming that he is who he is because of her. The couple reflects a veneer of success, which masks tremendous brokenness. She notes how with "every dime and every case, things change"; Charles particularly turns cold, mean, and volatile in private. Charles does what batterers, abusers, and domestic predators do: he helps to isolate her. And she is willing to do anything. Notably, Charles and Hosea are synonymous in their capacity and intent to cause Helen and Gomer pain. The next

---

28. Kirk-Duggan, *Misbegotten*, 278–85.
29. Zuckerman, "Victims of Sexual Violence," 6.

evening, Charles tells Helen the marriage is over and kicks her out of the mansion, ready to replace her with his mistress, with whom he has two sons. Thus the trappings of success do not create happiness. When commiserating about how things used to be, those realities are in the past. She does not want to leave and cannot figure out what she is supposed to do without Charles. He physically drags her out of the house and locks the door. As Hosea did with Gomer, Charles publically humiliates Helen. Charles demands that Helen leave, because she signed a prenuptial agreement and her name is not on the deed for their home. Like Gomer, someone other than God had become Helen's God.

Helen leaves in a van Charles rented for her, driven by Orlando, a person she does not know. In conversation with Orlando, she realizes that Charles successfully alienated her from her entire family. He also insisted that she place her mother in a retirement home, because she did not fit his idea of an American family. Helen finally goes to her grandmother's home (Madea). Initially Helen is fearful, enraged, and bitter. Her anger could shift to hate, out of her low self-esteem, her hurt. Persons in that setting often sabotage other relationships. Her mother reminds her that she should let go of being obsessed about Charles and their past, and not to put anyone before God. Helen learns that she can be a strong woman and can survive. Like Celie, she writes in her diary. In this process and with the love of others, Helen comes to love herself. After being nursed to health by Helen while recovering from a gunshot wound, Charles confesses to his many wrongs in the relationship, that he tried to destroy her; but she has a big heart. Conversely, Hosea does not confess any wrongs, though he does woo, seduce, and reclaim Gomer for his wife. Helen makes choices Daughter Zion apparently cannot make. Charles's experience does not end as smoothly Hosea's scenario.

During Sunday worship service, several problematic relationships begin to move toward healing. Charles joins the church. After worship, the extended family enjoys a Sunday meal at Madea's house. Clear that Charles is healing and that she has more than done her part, Helen walks away from the relationship. At the end of the meal, Helen signs the divorce papers and returns her rings. She goes to be with Orlando, recognizing that she no longer needs the trappings of success.

Unlike many victims of domestic abuse and violence, Helen is a survivor. After eighteen years of living with Charles's psychological abuse, she leaves. In comparison to Gomer's experience in Hos 2, some would think Helen had no reason to complain. She appeared to have a successful life. Apparently, Charles had not hit her before, though he had abused her emotionally. Some would argue that being given the cold shoulder and being emotionally distant was a small price to pay for all Helen received. But no one deserves emotional, physical, or spiritual abuse. Helen supported Charles as he stepped up the ladder of success. Not unlike some of the recent celebrity domestic violence and marital/sexual scandals in print and social media, from state governors to professional athletes and film/television celebrities, others knew about Charles's indiscretions. Others kept his secrets. "You are only as sick as your secrets" is a popular adage, which speaks volumes.

Domestic and sexual abuses are corrupting factors and cause harm to victim and perpetrator. The victim cannot be well, safe, and self-actualizing; the perpetrator steals one's personhood and causes great harm to the total well-being of his or her victim. By definition, perpetrators embody harm and are sick and more dysfunctional than the victim is. Keeping the perpetrator's secrets means one is an accessory after the fact and cannot live a life of spiritual, moral, and ethical integrity.

The beautiful, profound poetry of Hos 2 is equally scatological, particularly if one fails to recognize the power of metaphor. If one chooses to call Gomer/Israel a whore or harlot, if one buys into stereotypes that all women are inferior and property for hire via favors for sex, the result has to be domestic and sexual violence. For this reason, some pastors can preach this text about hope for Israel, profess faith in God, be married, have children—and sleep around with several parishioners. Those same pastors can preach and bring deliverance and challenges for wellness to congregations and then go home and beat their wives and be distant from their children. Psychologist and pastoral therapist Arthur Pressley notes that the two groups of people who most participate in domestic violence are pastors/preachers and police. The day when most domestic violence occurs is Sunday.[30] Some preachers choose not to deal with the ramifications of the metaphorical violence, and focus only on notions of salvific hope in their preaching.

---

30. Arthur Pressley, unpublished presentation on domestic violence, Society for the Study of Black Religion, Charleston, South Carolina, spring 2008.

A Word from the Lord? Hosea as Homiletics of Hope or Pain

Preachers, pastors, and scholars, across religious traditions, view homiletics and exegesis from different perspectives. Some recognize that the Hebrew Bible has its own history and tradition, and when preaching from it, they focus on the particularity of ancient Israel's traditions and on God's movement in that context. When preaching from the Hebrew Bible, some persons adamantly always connect it with the New Testament, including focusing on the cross. They do not believe one has preached if they do not close the sermon by focusing on Calvary and the cross. Some people preach by telling a story; some have one theme, others have a thesis and three points; some use the Hegelian method, with its thesis, antithesis, synthesis. Personal choice, training in preaching, and contextual realities notwithstanding, teaching and preaching from biblical texts as loaded as Hos 2 require clear attention to text and context, and the clear explication of biblical metaphor.

The worship or liturgical drama and the preaching or homiletics event are blasphemous, hypocritical, and downright sinful when we see brokenness and abuse in front of our eyes and we refuse to address such evil. Domestic violence infiltrates all of our communities. Physical, psychological, emotional, spiritual, and sexual abuses occur daily, as we often pretend that such acts do not exist. Some clergy preach about the seven deadly sins of pride/vanity, envy, gluttony, greed/avarice, lust, sloth, wrath/anger; they may get on their high horse about abortion and same-sex marriages because they believe they can make particular groups of people "other" and scapegoat them, since surely their members are not involved. Such belief systems allow them to rile up their audiences. Some preachers may even now focus on global warming because of fossil fuel usage, high gas prices, and recent meteorological anomalies—but fail to teach and preach to raise the awareness of a sin that eats away at the fiber of many parishioners' souls. The cancer of domestic violence is so potent that it cyclically infests and erodes, and slowly, painfully, egregiously effects homicidal destruction, generation after generation. Popular culture exposes the despicable nature of domestic violence, from novels and film to poetry, art, and television. All kinds of music, from opera and country to the blues, R&B, and even hip-hop decry the ghastly, revolting, repeated assault upon human bodies, minds, and souls. Nevertheless, the church tends to turn the other way, making victims voiceless shadows, championing predators as victorious sycophants, thus annihilating the gospel. How might a sermon on Hos 2 approach this situation?

Hal Brunson's sermon on Hos 2 connects with the New Testament and does not wrestle with the challenges around the marriage metaphor, Daughter Zion, and the violence included in the text as relevant to domestic and/or sexual abuse and violence. In "A Word of Hope," Brunson posits that one has to understand Hosea to understand Paul, particularly as Hosea uses Lo-ammi and Ammi. Incorporating the New Testament texts of 2 Pet 2, 1 Tim 3, and Revelation, Brunson claims one can play the whore physically and spiritually, by experiencing seducing spirits—the great whore of apostate religion. Without problematizing the marriage metaphor, Brunson states that divorce is a penalty, because God is a divorcee. For Brunson, both Hosea and the book of Ruth have metaphorical meaning for New Testament theology. He summarizes the book of Hosea by saying that 2:23, "in the place where it is said unto you, not my people, there shall you be called my people," is the crux of the meaning of the book; and then he juxtaposes being called "my people" with the cross. The closest Brunson comes to focusing on sexuality is around promiscuity. If one reaches after a lover, and experiences prevenient grace against one's rebellion, it signals one's salvation, thorns in Christ's crown, simultaneously juxtaposing sin, grace, and the suffering of Christ.[31]

Taking Mandolfo, womanist thought, and the realities of domestic violence seriously, one could preach Hos 2 and foreground the problems of domestic violence, using the title "When Covenant Gets Broken," or "It May Not Be What It Seems." Using a womanist liberative reading of this text involves ongoing intellectual, spiritual dialogue to prepare individuals to experience their own reality in a holistic manner. A womanist liberative theory embraces engendering mutuality and community amid the responsibility and stewardship of freedom, and honors the *imago Dei,* the image of God, the essential goodness and divine beauty in all persons, and engages texts held as authoritative with a careful, critical, creative reading.

One thesis of the sermon or homily would be: The use of commanding, authoritative texts can harm and/or transform people's lives at the most vulnerable or powerful times in their lives. One could use three points to undergird this thesis. Following introductory remarks on the book of Hosea itself, point one analyzes the context. Here one notes that, for Israel, religious pluralism and broken marriage represent the breaking of

---

31. Hal Brunson, "A Door of Hope," First Baptist Church of Parker Texas (preached 25 May 2005; http://www.sermonaudio.com/sermoninfo.asp?SID=52905145841).

covenant. One could develop this issue by exploring the divine command to Hosea, the abuse of Gomer, and the abuse of their children through their naming. Exploring the disobedience of Israel and the dynamics from this text on the spiritual and human level would help show the tension that unfolds and the complications of living in covenant then and now.

Point two, the circumstances, would explore how the dynamics of institutional sexism create problems that affect textual interpretation and the lives of real people. The threats within the text, the place of women as property in ancient Israel, and a review of domestic violence statistics locally and globally would show the pervasiveness of domestic violence. Further, one could examine the danger of viewing Yhwh as husband and Gomer as unfaithful Israel, for there are some things that God can do that a husband cannot. Questioning if one can in fairness lay the weight of a nation on the shoulders of a woman could help prod people to thinking about interpretation, sexism, and how laws and customs adversely affect people's lives and their understandings of the Divine.

Point three, the challenge, analyzes the import of critical thinking and dialogical engagement of life, where the use of texts and concretized belief systems can support domestic violence, to press people to examine their personal and communal lives. How much denial exists in the particular community around domestic violence? Have men or women in their lives used Scripture to control, demean, or harm? In response, one could then explore the equality of all people, regardless, and the essential importance of giving love and respect to God, others, and self. While positing that there is no justification for domestic violence, Hos 2 provides an opportunity to talk about the importance of establishing healthy values, to explore conflict resolution, and to learn to agree to disagree without being disagreeable. Another challenge would be to break the mold of ethical dichotomy: in this culture we still have separate expectations and we teach distinctive gender-based morality, which continues to see women as inferior, physically, socially, spiritually, and economically. Herein exists an opportunity to value Daughter Zion just as much as biblical texts historically value David. Hosea 2 provides an opportunity to talk about faithfulness and obedience and to decry the abhorrent practice of domestic violence. Here is an opportunity to stress the vital nature of understanding when and how to use metaphorical language—carefully, providing clear, thorough explanation as to what is at stake.

Where do we go from here in the second decade of the twenty-first century? We can no longer keep domestic and sexual abuse and violence secret or hidden. The violation of every human being is personal and communal, and is an assault against God. Tempered cynicism requires that we examine the continuum of violence, the tensions surrounding it, the use of power and manipulation, and work to do more preventative education. Working through a variety of ways of engaging Hos 2 gives us an opportunity to see how elite and marginalized persons experience identity and displacement, and how all people need to avoid being victims or perpetrators of violence. New readings such as those suggested by Mandolfo help expose various levels of oppression, showing both the subtlety and the ultimate pain of it all. A choice to avoid privileging Yhwh in this prophetic text makes for interesting use of one's prophetic imagination.

Naming the violence and giving Daughter Zion voice and agency can help persons see the import of self-actualization and personal agency. Using courage and creativity as tenets of one's attitude amid analysis, we can see how connections between violence, marriage, and faith can destroy one's soul. Reading prophetic texts through the lens of literature and film afford different insight into divine-human relations, where sometimes divine will feels more punitive, and sometimes people really are quite resilient. Foregrounding Daughter Zion reflects how others can come to authenticity and power from the textual and contemporary community. Depending upon how one reads Hos 2, both God and Daughter Zion can be victim or victor. In ancient and contemporary societies, questions of superiority, inferiority, and mutuality must be addressed. Commitment to justice seeking and discovery with candor exposes pathological oppressions that can arise when one forgets, dismisses, or is unaware of the impact of the marriage metaphor. With Daughter Zion and the marriage metaphor, to take a cavalier attitude and dismiss global domestic violence is to be reckless and to move in ways antithetical to justice and decency. Curiosity pressed a reading of a sermon that moves from a totally different context to see what one could learn from such a treatment of Hos 2. An awareness of the comedic has afforded a great deal of insight on the power of written and artistic texts, the pain of violence, and the hope that new ways of reading will help us better communicate, help us be better scholars and better people.

Mission Not Impossible:
Justifying Zion's Destruction and
Exonerating the Common Survivors

Kim Lan Nguyen

Carleen Mandolfo's analysis of the narrator's position in the book of Lamentations contains a couple of comments that, despite their passing nature, are of great significance in the discussion of Zion's sin and identity. Mandolfo gives us the idea that Zion's sin is not within the focus of the narrator, whom she calls the Didactic Voice (DV), when she remarks: "Even when the DV alludes to Daughter Zion's transgressions it comes across as no more than an aside, certainly not as denoting she deserves YHWH's choice of punitive response."[1] Arguing that the DV in Lamentations does not defend Yahweh's goodness or justice as its counterpart in the lament psalms does, but rather understands Zion's situation from her perspective, Mandolfo also seems to substitute the suffering humans for Zion in her rhetorical question: "What does it mean, theologically, when the voice traditionally representing the divine position, the voice of authority, speaks against its own interests and from the perspective of suffering humans?"[2]

Is it true that mention of Zion's transgression is an aside in the book of Lamentations, and is the identification of Zion with the survivors after the fall of Jerusalem correct? These questions confront us with the issue of the enigmatic nature of Zion's identity and sin. First, Lamentations never defines who Zion is in concrete terms; and second, although the charge of her guilt is repeated several times, not much explanation of it is given.

---

1. Carleen Mandolfo, *Daughter Zion Talks Back to the Prophets: A Dialogic Theology of the Book of Lamentations* (SemeiaSt 58; Atlanta: Society of Biblical Literature, 2007), 73.

2. Ibid., 74.

Scholarly opinion is divided as to what this vagueness means. Some scholars have concluded that this vagueness indicates the author's attempt to express that the punishment of Zion is way more than she deserves.[3] In support of their conclusion, these scholars always adduce the suffering of Zion, as seen in the children and infants dying on the streets. In asserting that the narrator's allusion to Zion's transgression is no more than an aside and certainly not denoting that Zion deserves her punishment, and in casually exchanging the name Zion with suffering humans, Mandolfo in effect takes the same approach as the above scholars. Other scholars, however, think that the vague nature of Zion's sin perhaps signals that her sin is more serious and deep-rooted than the combination of specific acts of sin. These scholars conclude, more often than not, that through Zion's confession, the surviving remnant acknowledges that they suffer for their own sins.[4] I think we do not have to choose between these two positions. Furthermore, I suggest that both of these positions misread the meaning of the vagueness in Zion's identity and the nature of her sin. In this paper, I seek to establish that the vague nature of Zion's identity and sin is the author's strategy to suggest a new theological paradigm that justifies the city's destruction and exonerates the common survivors at the same time. I will substantiate my thesis by demonstrating the following points: (1) the vague nature of Zion's sin is not an indication of the author's protest; (2) Zion is not the equivalent of the surviving people; and (3) the historical reality of the destruction of Jerusalem in 587 B.C.E. demands a modification of the Deuteronomic paradigm.

---

3. See Frederick W. Dobbs-Allsopp, "Tragedy, Tradition, and Theology in the Book of Lamentations," *JSOT* 74 (1997): 36–38; Edward L. Greenstein, "The Wrath at God in the Book of Lamentations," in *The Problem of Evil and Its Symbols in Jewish and Christian Tradition* (ed. Henning Graf Reventlow and Yair Hoffman; JSOTSup 366; New York: T&T Clark, 2004), 27–42, here 35.

4. See Norman Gottwald, *Studies in the Book of Lamentations* (SBT 1/14; London: SCM, 1962), 68–69; Claus Westermann, *Lamentations: Issues and Interpretation* (trans. Charles Muenchow; Minneapolis: Fortress, 1994), 135–36; Paul House, "Lamentations," in Duane Garrett and House, *Song of Songs, Lamentations* (WBC 23B; Nashville: Nelson, 2004), 267–473.

The Vagueness of Zion's Sin Is No Indication
of the Author's Protest

I am surprised that no one seems to see the vague nature of Zion's sin as characteristic of the Hebrew lament genre.[5] Concerning the confession of sin in the psalms, Sigmund Mowinckel comments, "It is quite characteristic of the psalms that they do not deal very much with concrete sins. It is the natural result of their being psalms for general use in the cult, that they have to speak in general terms."[6] He is quite correct. Reading through the psalms one quickly realizes that the nature of sin is not specified whenever sin, guilt, transgression, or iniquity is confessed. Confession of sin in these various terms is found in the communal laments of Pss 79, 85, 106; in the individual laments of Pss 25, 31, 38, 39, 51, 69, 130, 140, 141; and in the individual thanksgiving of Ps 32.[7] In all these texts, apart from Ps 106, no attempt is made to specify what kind of sin is committed. An example of a communal lament illustrates the point:

> Do not remember against us the iniquities of our ancestors;
> let your compassion come speedily to meet us, for we are brought
> very low.
> Help us, O God of our salvation, for the glory of your name;
> deliver us, and forgive our sins, for your name's sake. (Ps 79:8–9
> NRSV)

Psalm 106 is an exceptional case, where the rebellious acts of the ancestors are enumerated with details. Yet even here, while the poet confesses both the sins of his generation and the ancestors (v. 6), he provides an exhaustive list of the sins of the ancestors (vv. 7–39), but says literally nothing about those of his generation.

> Both we and our ancestors have sinned;
> we have committed iniquity, have done wickedly.

---

5. See, e.g., Dobbs-Allsopp, "Tragedy, Tradition, and Theology," 36–37; Greenstein, "Wrath at God," 34–35; Gottwald, *Studies*, 68; House, "Lamentations," 351.

6. Sigmund Mowinckel, *The Psalms in Israel's Worship* (trans. D. R. Ap-Thomas; 2 vols.; Oxford: Blackwell, 1962), 2:14.

7. The classification of these psalms is by Hermann Gunkel and Joachim Begrich, *Introduction to Psalms: The Genres of the Religious Lyric of Israel* (trans. James D. Nogalski; Macon, Ga.: Mercer University Press, 1998), 83, 121, 199.

Our ancestors, when they were in Egypt, did not consider your
    wonderful works;
they did not remember the abundance of your steadfast love,
but rebelled against the Most High at the Red Sea. (Ps 106:6–7
    NRSV)

Outside the Psalter we also find poetic confessions in the prophetic corpus
(e.g., Isa 38:9–20; 59:12–13; 64:4, 6, 8 (Eng. 5, 7, 9); Jer 14:7; Mic 7:9). Even
in the prophetic corpus, where all kinds of transgressions are described
within the contexts, the poetic laments themselves rarely enumerate specific sins (e.g., Isa 38:9–20; 64; Jer 14; Mic 7). Thus we may agree with
Mowinckel that the ancient Hebrew poets seldom discuss the detail of sin
in their laments.

Furthermore, confession of sin in the communal laments of the Psalter is a very rare phenomenon.[8] Of all the psalms Hermann Gunkel identifies as communal laments (Pss 44, 60, 74, 79, 80, 83, 89, 94),[9] confession
is found only in Ps 79. As we have seen, the confession in Ps 79 mentions
both עֲוֹנוֹת רִאשֹׁנִים, "the iniquities of our ancestors," and חַטֹּאתֵינוּ, "our
sins." Although one may argue that the meaning of עֲוֹנוֹת רִאשֹׁנִים is rather
ambiguous and that it might refer to "former iniquities," whatever that
means, it should be noted that the sufferers of Ps 79 are unmistakably portrayed not as a sinful but as a righteous people, according to verse 2:

They have given the bodies of your servants to the birds of the air
    for food,
the flesh of your faithful to the wild animals of the earth. (NRSV)

Even if the category of communal lament is extended to include all the
psalms that are identified as either communal laments, psalms with the

---

8. Ibid., 92–93; Mowinckel, *Psalms*, 2:214, 216; Paul W. Ferris Jr., *The Genre of
Communal Lament in the Bible and the Ancient Near East* (SBLDS 127; Atlanta: Scholars Press, 1992), 129; Richard J. Bautch, *Development in Genre between Post-exilic
Penitential Prayers and the Psalms of Communal Lament* (SBLABib 7; Atlanta: Society
of Biblical Literature, 2003), 119.

9. The chart prepared by Ferris (*Genre*, 16) informs that all these psalms, apart
from Ps 94, are identified as communal laments not only by Gunkel but also by S. R.
Driver, Mowinckel, Otto Eissfeldt, Westermann, Artur Weiser, and Leopold Sabourin.
Psalm 94 is identified by Gunkel, Driver, and Mowinckel.

communal lament theme, or very personal communal laments by either S. R. Driver, Mowinckel, Otto Eissfeldt, Claus Westermann, Artur Weiser, Otto Kaiser, A. A. Anderson, Leopold Sabourin, or Paul Ferris,[10] confession of sin is found only in Pss 69, 85, 90, and 106. Psalm 106 has been discussed above. Of the remaining three, Ps 85 mentions only the iniquity and sin that God has forgiven in the past, Ps 90 confesses the iniquity of humankind in general, and finally the confession in Ps 69 is coupled with the poet's claim of unjustified attack from the enemies (vv. 4–5 [Eng. 5–6]):

> More in number than the hairs of my head
> are those who hate me without cause;
> many are those who would destroy me,
> my enemies who accuse me falsely.
> What I did not steal
> must I now restore?
> O God, you know my folly;
> the wrongs I have done are not hidden from you. (NRSV)

The rarity of confessions in communal laments coupled with the desire to be vindicated shows that the poets who included a confession in their poems took it quite seriously. Otherwise, they could have easily omitted this minor element of the genre.[11]

Compared to the psalm laments, Lamentations says more, not less, about sin. In only three chapters (chs. 1, 2, and 4) sins are mentioned nine times using various terms: "transgressions" (פשעיה and פשעי; 1:5, 22), "sinned" (חטאה; 1:8), "rebelled" (מריתי; 1:18, 20), "iniquity" (עונך and עון; 2:14; 4:6, 22), and finally "sins and iniquities" (חטאת and עונות; 4:13). Confession with this level of concentration in poetic communal lament is not seen anywhere else in the Hebrew Bible.

---

10. Then the category of communal laments would include Pss 9–10, 12, 13, 14, 35, 42–43, 46, 55, 56, 58, 59, 68, 69, 77, 82, 83, 85, 90, 94, 102, 106, 108, 109, 115, 123, 124, 126, 129, 137, 142, and 144 (Ferris, *Genre*, 14, 16).

11. See Bautch, *Developments in Genre*, 119, 135, 156; and Mark J. Boda, "The Priceless Gain of Penitence: From Communal Lament to Penitential Prayer in the 'Exilic' Liturgy of Israel," in *Lamentations in Ancient and Contemporary Contexts* (ed. Nancy C. Lee and Carleen Mandolfo; SBLSymS 3; Atlanta: Society of Biblical Literature, 2008), 81–101, here 52. Both show that confession was not a required element of the communal lament, but became an essential one in the penitential prayer that emerged in the Persian period, e.g., Neh 9 and Dan 9.

In addition to a high level of concentration, the confession in Lamentations also exceeds the level of detail required by the communal laments of the Psalter, since the charge of particular sins to specific persons in a few places is stated explicitly. For instance, in Lam 2:14 the prophets are singled out as the perpetrators of false and deceptive visions:

> Your prophets have seen for you empty and tasteless visions
> They did not reveal your iniquity to restore your captivity
> But they have seen for you oracles worthless and misleading.

Again in 4:13 the nature of sin and the identity of the culprits are anything but ambiguous: the prophets and the priests are charged outright with shedding blood:

> Because of the sins of her prophets, the iniquities of her priests,
> Those who poured out in her midst the blood of the righteous.

Indeed, this specification is quite extraordinary and has no precedent in the Psalter. It can only be found in the prophetic corpus of the Hebrew Bible, especially in Jeremiah and Ezekiel.[12] So, against the backdrop of the Hebrew communal lament genre, it is clear that the confession of sin occupies a central place in Lam 1, 2, and 4. The conclusion that Zion's confession is merely conventional is simply without basis. Mandolfo is incorrect in stating that the narrator's allusion to Zion's transgressions (1:5, 8; 4:6, 22) is not more than an aside.

ZION IS NOT EQUAL TO THE SURVIVING PEOPLE

That the author never attempted to reveal the exact identity of the personified Zion is perplexing. That he overlooked the import of his omission is unbelievable, if repentance from those who needed to repent is assumed to be the implied aim of all the confession that Zion makes. When the poems were read in the hearing of the survivors, who would identify with Zion? Did they know the offenses they had committed against God and from which they needed to repent? Who is Zion in a concrete sense and whose

---

12. Jeremiah stresses the sin of the false prophets and Ezekiel the sin of the idolatrous priests.

sin is hers? I think these questions have not been accorded the importance due them by scholars as they often view the personified Zion as representing the people without further qualification.

To be sure, the admission of sin in Lamentations probably indicates that the community as a whole, the surviving remnant, confirms the prophetic pronouncement.[13] Lamentations indicates in various places that the survivors finally realized what previous generations had entirely rejected, that judgment day was inescapable because of Israel's collective sin (1:15b, 17b; 2:17ab, 21c, 22b; 3:37). It is equally clear that the magnitude of the collective sin, due to the scope of destruction, was finally acknowledged and agreed upon by them (1:5b, 8a, 14a, 18a, 20b, 22b; 2:14; 3:42; 4:6, 13, 22; 5:7, 16). That this realization was done by the surviving remnant is undeniable, since the different voices in Lamentations seem to speak with one accord. Contra Mandolfo's view, the narrator, in agreeing with the personified Zion, the "man" (גבר), and the community about the magnitude of Israel's sin, is far from speaking against the divine interest.

We need to note, however, that the agreement is only good as far as the collective sin of Israel is concerned, with "collective sin" referring to all the sin committed by the people of Israel through all of its historical periods. The problem comes in when this collective sin is treated as if it is unquestionably absorbed by the surviving remnant. Paul House, for instance, says that Lamentations "operates somewhat like the book of Job, but in reverse. It demonstrates that *those who suffer because of their own sins* may cry out to God as readily as innocent sufferers do."[14] Such a statement presupposes that all the survivors were guilty, a point that is quite contestable, to say the least.[15] The focus of my paper is on the confessions of the narrator and the personified Zion in Lam 1, 2, and 4. House's presupposition appears to stem from equating Zion and the survivors indiscriminately, since nowhere do we find an attribution of sin to the common populace.

---

13. Westermann, *Lamentations*, 224–25; Delbert R. Hillers, *Lamentations* (AB 7A; Garden City, N.Y.: Doubleday, 1972), xvi; Johan Renkema, *Lamentations* (trans. Brian Doyle; HCOT; Leuven: Peeters, 1998), 432; House, "Lamentations," 323–24; Gottwald, *Studies*, 6–9.

14. House, "Lamentations," 320, emphasis added.

15. For practical purposes, the wholeheartedness of the people's confession in Lam 5:16 cannot be discussed here, but I would like to suggest that it is much less likely than the opposite alternative, given the people's complaint about having to suffer for the sins of the fathers in 5:7. Likewise, I suggest that the confession in 3:42 does not reflect the complete sentiment of the common populace.

Indeed, with the exception of 2:14 and 4:13, which blame not the surviving people in general but only the religious leaders (i.e., the prophets and priests), both the narrator (1:5b, 8a; 4:6, 22) and the personified Zion (1:14a, 18a, 20b, 22b) attribute all sins to Zion herself.

Confessions by the narrator:

כי יהוה הוגה על רב־פשעיה

Because the LORD made her suffer for the multitude of her transgressions. (1:5b)

חטא חטאה ירושלם על־כן לנידה היתה

Jerusalem sinned grievously, therefore she has become impure.[16] (1:8a)

ויגדל עון בת־עמי מחטאת סדם

For the iniquity of the daughter of my people has been greater than the sin of Sodom.[17] (4:6a)

תם־עונך בת־ציון

The punishment of your iniquity is accomplished, O daughter of Zion. (4:22a)

---

16. Hebrew לנידה is a hapax legomenon, and I follow BDB (622) by taking it as a variant of the form נדה, "impurity," as in Lam 1:17. Others take it as from נוד, "move to and fro, wander, show grief." Adele Berlin (*Lamentations* [OTL; Louisville: Westminster John Knox, 2002], 42) and the NRSV translate it as "banished" and "mockery," respectively. But Bertil Albrektson (*Studies in the Text and Theology of the Book of Lamentations* [Studia theologica lundensia 21; Lund: Gleerup, 1963], 63–64) seems right to give more weight to BDB's understanding for two reasons. First, in the sense of mockery, the verb נוד is usually used with the word ראש, "head"; second, it makes more sense to take the word as "impurity" in connection with the word ערותה, "her nakedness," implying female impurity, in 1:8b.

17. Cf. NRSV: "For the chastisement of my people has been greater than the punishment of Sodom." See also Aloysius Fitzgerald, "*BTWLT* and *BT* as Titles for Capital Cities," *CBQ* 37 (1975): 167–83, here 174; Greenstein, "Wrath at God," 38; Frederick W. Dobbs-Allsopp, *Lamentations* (IBC; Louisville: John Knox, 2002), 131; Berlin, *Lamentations*, 99; see also NIV. I prefer the other sense of עון, "iniquity," and חטאת, "sin," here. See also JPS; ASV; Westermann, *Lamentations*, 194; Hillers, *Lamentations*, 75; Renkema, *Lamentations*, 508; and House, "Lamentations," 431.

Confessions by Zion:

נשקד על פשעי בידו ישתרגו

The yoke of my transgressions has been under watch;[18]
In his hand they intertwined themselves. (1:14a)

צדיק הוא יהוה כי פיהו מריתי

He, the LORD, is just, for I have rebelled against his mouth. (1:18a)

נהפך לבי בקרבי כי מרו מריתי

My heart is turned over within me, because I have been very rebellious. (1:20b)

כאשר עוללת לי על כל־פשעי

As you have dealt severely with me because of all my transgressions. (1:22b)

When House speaks of the people suffering because of their own sins, he apparently assumes that personified Zion and the survivors are somehow interchangeable.[19] Nothing in Lamentations warrants such an

---

18. The word נשקד is a hapax legomenon, the meaning of which is very doubtful. According to *BHS*, several Hebrew manuscripts have נשקד, "to be watched." The LXX further reads על as a preposition and thus renders, Ἐγρηγορήθη ἐπὶ τὰ ἀσεβήματά μου, "He watched over my transgressions." David Kimchi, followed by Gottwald, JPS, and NRSV, takes the MT as is and suggests the meaning "bind on" (BDB, 974). Other emendations have also been suggested. For example, נקשה על פשעי, "schwer gemacht ist das Joch meiner Sünden" ("the yoke of my transgressions has become heavy"), by F. Praetorius; and נקשו עלי פשעי, "schwer lasten auf mir meiner Sünden" ("my transgressions weighed heavily on me"), by Rudolph (cited by Albrektson, *Studies*, 73–74). Hillers emends to: עישף נשקד על, "Watch is kept over my steps" (*Lamentations*, 3, 11). To deal with the difficulty, Berlin chooses a neutral word to convey that a yoke is being made: "My yoke of transgressions was fashioned" (*Lamentations*, 43, 46). Since the renderings of the LXX and other ancient translations seem to reflect an effort to deal with the same textual difficulty facing modern interpreters, I incline to retain the MT as much as possible, reading only with the Hebrew variant to convey the idea of God making sure that the yoke stays in its place.

19. This assumption is rather obvious in his commentary. We find, for instance, comments such as: "Chap. 1 … also addresses why such disaster has befallen the chosen city. God has sent the day of the Lord on the people for their sins against his word (1:5, 8–9, 12, 14, 18–22)." Or, "The city's grief is compounded by the realization that it need not have happened. The people sense that their affliction is self-inflicted

assumption. Nowhere is Zion identified as the surviving people. To the contrary, the suffering people are always described in possessive terms in relation to Zion as follows:

כהניה	her priests	1:4
בתולתיה	her young girls	1:4
עולליה	her children	1:5
שריה	her princes	1:6
עמה	her people	1:7, 11
אבירי	my warriors	1:15
בחורי	my young men	1:15
בני	my children	1:16
בתולתי ובחורי	my young women and young men	1:18; 2:21
כהני וזקני	my priests and elders	1:19
מלכה ושריה	her king and princes	2:9
נביאיה	her prophets	2:9
זקני בת־ ציון	elders of daughter Zion	2:10
בתולת ירושלם	young girls of Jerusalem	2:10
נביאיך	your prophets	2:14
עולליך	your children	2:19

---

to an extent. God has punished their sin, just as the covenantal blessings and curse texts (see Lev 26; Deut 27–28) promised. They understand that the God who protected them in the past has forsaken this role because of their disobedience. Their wounds are their own fault" (*Lamentations*, 364–65).

בני ציון	children of Zion	4:2
נזיריה	her princes	4:7
נביאיה	her prophets	4:13
כהניה	her priests	4:13

If anything can be inferred from this exhaustive list, nothing would be more obvious than the distinction between Zion and the people. The suffering people are not Zion's equivalent, despite the fact that they belong to her.

House, of course, is not alone in casually restricting the people Zion represents to the surviving remnant. In fact, besides Mandolfo, Frederick W. Dobbs-Allsopp, Norman Gottwald, and Erhard Gerstenberger do more or less the same thing.[20] Fortunately, that Zion is to be distinguished from the surviving remnant does not escape other scholars' attention. Westermann asserts,

> The notion of "personifying" ... would be inappropriate if by that one meant nothing more than the equating of a some*thing* with a some*one*, of an object with a person. The essential point of the comparison [Lam 1:2–3] is that, through it, a history of a people is accorded a characteristic usually reserved for a personal story. A whole people acquires the traits of an individual, someone whose destiny involves the possibility of suffering.[21]

In terms of history, those who actually suffered after the fall of Jerusalem make up only a small portion of the people. Delbert Hillers correctly

---

20. Dobbs-Allsopp, *Lamentations*, 52. Gottwald (*Studies*, 69) states, "But one thing is sure: the sin is not laid solely at the door of the religious leadership, but is shared equally by the populace. This can be seen in the distinction that is made between the prophet's falsity and 'thy guilt' (2:14)." However, Gottwald does not seem to be correct in his interpretation of Lam 2:14. It is true that the narrator makes a distinction between the prophet's falsity and Zion's guilt, but that distinction does not necessarily exclude the prophet's guilt from Zion's guilt. Zion herself does not seem to differentiate between the prophets and priests from other groups of people. All are referred to as hers. See also Erhard S. Gerstenberger, *Psalms, Part 2, and Lamentations* (FOTL 15; Grand Rapids: Eerdmans, 2001), 472, 476.

21. Westermann, *Lamentations*, 124.

states, the one in anguish is "Zion, the city of God, the community of the elect, who in her historical being is not identical with those alive at any one time." When Zion refers to herself as "I," it is not the "I" of an individual, "even as the spokesman for the survivors, but of Zion herself."[22]

As we can see, Zion's identity is anything but concrete. I suggest that an ambivalent portrayal of her is necessary if both corporate and individual responsibilities are to be represented in her confession, and that the complexity of the situation after the fall of Jerusalem demands such a representation. The fall of Jerusalem constitutes a novel condition for which no adequate response can be obtained from extant theological paradigms. The fall creates an unprecedented theological crisis, and the resolution of it requires nothing less than a radical understanding of God and of the people in terms of their covenantal relationship. We need to understand the crisis as it occurs after the fall of Jerusalem before we can better understand the author's purpose in his portrayal of Zion.

The Reality of the Fall of Jerusalem Demands a Theological Revision

The fall of Jerusalem unquestionably created a colossal crisis. At the core of the crisis is what appears to be the nullification of the covenant God made with Israel. For the first time in Israel's history, the people lost all at once the possession of the land, the autonomy of the nation, and the Davidic kingship. The following factors further complicated the situation: (1) the breaking of God's promise to sustain the Davidic throne (which I will not treat in this essay); (2) the failure of the Deuteronomic tradition to put into effect the repentance occasioned by King Josiah's reform only two decades earlier; and (3) the brutality of a devastation that took a severe toll on the helpless and innocent people of the city. While some believe that the prophetic pronouncement of divine judgment was finally acknowledged by the people after the fall,[23] this belief seems too simplistic. For the survivors, the Deuteronomic tradition completely fails to explain the problem of innocent suffering.

The true extent of the failure of the Deuteronomic belief is often overlooked when personified Zion is equated with the people without the nec-

---

22. Hillers, *Lamentations*, 17.
23. House, "Lamentations," 364–65; Westermann, *Lamentations*, 224–25.

essary qualification. To be sure, scholars have correctly observed that the confession of sin in Lamentations is in keeping with the Deuteronomic faith as portrayed in the book of Deuteronomy and the prophetic teaching.[24] According to Deuteronomic faith, God controls history and thus historical events are attributed to his acts of benevolence or retribution. Political and economic prosperities represent God's blessing upon obedience, while calamities are sure signs of punishment for sin. The many confessions of sin in Lamentations testify to the fact that the author held a faith similar to that of the prophets who had relentlessly pronounced judgment on Jerusalem and called for repentance without success. Lamentations definitely stands in agreement with the prophets in directing attention to a guilt that has corrupted the whole people.

With that in mind, we need to consider what Gottwald calls the situational key to the theology of Lamentations, "the tension between Deuteronomic faith and historical adversity."[25] According to Gottwald, Lamentations "stands at the point in Israel's life where tension between history and faith is for the first time most sharply posed."[26] Indeed, the survivors would hardly comprehend why total destruction took place only a couple of decades after the nation's great religious reform rather than at another time, for instance, when the nation was led completely astray by its most evil king, Manasseh. The discrepancy between the historical optimism of the Deuteronomic reform and the cynicism and despondency evoked by the fall of the nation must have been pronounced. Despite the assertion made by the prophets Jeremiah and Ezekiel that all would die for their own sins (Jer 31:29–30; Ezek 18:1–4), bewilderment felt by the surviving people must have been strong and pervasive. Even while confessinng the sins of the past and present generations, the psalmist boldly claims that the dead were among the faithful:

They have given the bodies of your servants
to the birds of the air for food,
the flesh of your faithful to the wild animals of the earth. (Ps 79:2
NRSV; cf. vv. 8, 9)

---

24. Berlin, *Lamentations*, 17–22; Gottwald, *Studies*, 65–69; Hillers, *Lamentations*, 22, 28; House, "Lamentations," 351; Westermann, *Lamentations*, 224–25.

25. Gottwald, *Studies*, 50–53.

26. Ibid., 51.

Though a firm believer in the Deuteronomic faith, the author of Lamentations could not ignore exceptions where the interrelation between sin and punishment evidently fails. Granted that Lamentations has for its basic purpose the mastery of pain and doubt in the interests of faith, as Gottwald puts it,[27] that mastery does not necessarily mean sweeping under the rug anything that questions the insufficiency of the prevailing theological system. Lamentations represents the author's effort to deal with, or at the very least acknowledge, the discrepancy—the presence of innocent suffering.

While the prophets occasionally recognize that the righteous and innocent can suffer too (e.g., Amos 2:6; 5:12; Jer 2:34), that recognition is essentially drowned out by their judgment of the nation—they accuse *everyone* (e.g., Jer 6:11, 13; 9:1–5 (Eng. 2–6). In some places, Jeremiah and Ezekiel flatly deny the suffering of the innocent (Jer 5:1; Ezek 14; 18). Against the prophetic teaching of Jeremiah and Ezekiel, Lamentations affirms innocent suffering after the destruction.[28]

The claim of absolute justice by the prophets was probably made before the Day of Yahweh became a reality.[29] Since the primary focus of Jeremiah and Ezekiel was judgment, it is quite understandable that they did not give much thought about the death of infants or were not able to even imagine

---

27. Ibid., 52.

28. The response of Lamentations perhaps was not so much a challenge of the worthiness of traditional authority as an act of rectification. Study in the prophetic corpus shows that prophecies are not static but vary greatly from prophet to prophet and especially from one historical period to the next. While some variations are attributed to the prophets' individual characteristics, the theological ones are often due to change and development in historical circumstances. The author of Lamentations, even if he did not belong to the prophetic circle, might still legitimately be a participant in this prophetic phenomenon. As such, he could not help but reexamine even the most cherished theological principles in light of historical development. See John Bright, *Jeremiah* (AB 21; Garden City, N.Y.: Doubleday, 1965), xxiii; Joseph Blenkinsopp, *A History of Prophecy in Israel* (Philadelphia: Westminster, 1983), 227–29.

29. In its literary context, Jer 31:29–30 is a prophecy about the future that Yahweh commands Jeremiah to write down in a book (30:2). This took place perhaps toward the end of the reign of Zedekiah, when Jerusalem was besieged by the Babylonians (cf. 32:1–2). The date of the composition is controversial; I assume as the worst scenario that the idea originates from Jeremiah, since that would make the prophet himself responsible for the discrepancy between his teaching and the reality. Ezekiel 18:1–4 belongs to the section of prophecy spoken by the prophet in the sixth year of the first exile, which is ca. 591 B.C.E.

it.[30] Ezekiel 14 defends God's justice by referring to the evil ways and deeds of the exiled remnant rather than directly accusing the devastated Judean remnant, whose suffering the prophet never actually witnessed. Ezekiel 18 only justifies God's judgment upon people who have full capacity of making choices but does not take into consideration the fate of children who are too young to know the difference between good and evil.

The prophetic judgment saw its fulfillment only in the destruction of Jerusalem, when death did not seem to distinguish the old from the young or the wicked from the righteous. The reality as Lamentations sees it is that on the Day of Yahweh none survives or escapes (2:22), that children faint for hunger at the head of every street (2:19), that women eat their offspring (2:20), and that the young women and young men have fallen by the sword (2:21). The unquestionably innocent were the children who died from either hunger or cannibalism. Only extremely rigid adherents of the Deuteronomic faith would justify the suffering of children and infants, and Lamentations refuses to do so. Indeed, from the narrator's point of view, the children constitute the only legitimate reason to appeal to Yahweh.[31] Only for the sake of children does the narrator urge Zion to appeal to Yahweh in 2:19,

קומי רני בלילה[32] לראש אשמרות
שפכי כמים לבך נכח פני אדני
שׂאי אליו כפיך על־נפש עולליך
העטופים ברעב בראש כל־חוצות

Arise, cry out in the night, at the beginning of the watches.
Pour out your heart like water before the face of the Lord.
Lift your hands to him for the lives of your children,
who faint in hunger at the head of every street.

Interestingly, the narrator's advice to Zion in 2:19 is accompanied by a formal anomaly. Instead of having three lines like other stanzas in this

---

30. Jer 6:11 and 7:18 mention the punishment of children on the street, supposedly those who gather wood for their mothers to bake for the Queen of Heaven. These children are not quite like suckling infants.

31. The suffering of children is the cause of weeping for both the narrator (2:11) and personified Zion (1:16).

32. Read with the Qere; Kethib בליל.

poem, 2:19 includes a fourth line. That a similar deviation occurs in 1:7, which is often considered the result of a gloss, makes an immediate assessment of the significance of the formal deviation in 2:19 difficult.[33] Since

---

33. Albrektson, *Studies*, 62; Hillers, *Lamentations*, 9; Westermann, *Lamentations*, 112; Xuan Huong Thi Pham, *Mourning in the Ancient Near East and the Hebrew Bible* (JSOTSup 302; Sheffield: Sheffield Academic Press, 1999), 70–71; Berlin, *Lamentations*, 46; see also the critical apparatus of *BHS*.

In a poem of three-line stanzas, Lam 1:7 has four lines instead of three:

זכרה ירושלם ימי עניה ומרודיה
כל מחמדיה אשר היו מימי קדם
בנפל עמה ביד־צר ואין עוזר לה
ראוה צרים שחקו על־משבתיה

Jerusalem remembers, in the days of her affliction and wandering,
all the precious things that were hers in days of old.
When her people fell into the hand of the foe, and there was no one to help her,
the foe looked on mocking over her downfall.

Although the ancient versions (LXX, Peshitta, and Vulgate) also have four lines, given that these translations were much later than the original, the majority of scholars agree that one of the lines was a gloss. With the same assumption that this stanza should conform to the strict formal pattern of the poem, scholars differ on whether 1:7b or 1:7c should be stricken as a gloss. Most scholars take out 1:7b since it seems out of place if v. 7 is to be consistent with the rest of the context by referring to Jerusalem's remembering the time of her destruction. The Hebrew of 1:7a seems to support this conclusion with ימי עניה ומרודיה being the object of זכרה. Albrektson, however, is concerned that if this is the case, then the days of Jerusalem's affliction must be understood as something already past, which to him is obviously not the situation of the dirge. He therefore regards ימי עניה ומרודיה as a temporal accusative, "in the days of…," and deletes the third line, 1:7c (*Studies*, 62–63).

Theophile J. Meek seems to avoid making a decision by suggesting that 1:7 is a conflate text that contains two variant readings, 1:7b and 7c ("The Book of Lamentations," in *IB* 6:9).

Renkema questions the assumption that either 1:7b or 7c is a gloss. He correctly observes that "it is hardly imaginable that a glossator or copyist would not have noticed the interpolation of a marginal note that disturbed the evidently regular structure of three bicola per strophe" (*Lamentations*, 131). Appealing to structural analysis of the subcanto 1:7–11, he argues that both 1:7b and 7c function on a higher literary level within the song and concludes that it is possible that "the poets consciously employed literary irregularity in order to express the precise extent to which YHWH's aloofness had knocked Lady Jerusalem off balance" (131–32). Renkema's structural analysis, however, is not convincing. Nor does the suggested purpose of the poet seem to be

1:7 has been proven to contain a gloss, the same scholarly conclusion on 2:19 is hardly surprising.[34] In the case of 2:19, the last line seems to pose no new problem if deleted. As far as the content is concerned, it is recognized as a mosaic of bits from 2:11b, 12b; 4:1b; and formally it is the only line that does not open with the second-person volitive. Even so, I think it is worthwhile to reconsider the possibility and even probability of a theological irregularity signaled by the formal divergence of 2:19.

In contrast to 1:7, whose formal irregularity cannot be justified by a well-established significance in content, 2:19 signals a theological crux, a seeming failure on the part of Yahweh that urgently demands correction: innocent suffering. Nowhere does the narrator urge Zion to appeal to Yahweh except here in 2:19. Contrary to scholarly opinion regarding 2:19d as superfluous, I suggest that it is precisely what gives legitimacy to the appeal. Whereas 2:19c just begins to give a reason for the appeal "concerning the life of your children" (עַל נֶפֶשׁ עוֹלָלַיִךְ), 2:19d explains why it is a legitimate reason: "who are fainting because of hunger at the head of every street" (עֲטוּפִים בְּרָעָב בְּרֹאשׁ כָּל־חוּצוֹת). Verse 19d is not an unnecessary repetition of 2:11c or 12b as usually argued, but an important specification of who the children are in the narrator's view. By using the same terms, the narrator makes sure that these are the innocent infants who are dying in the bosoms of their mothers. Only by appealing to these, whose innocence no one can deny, can Zion possibly hope to change Yahweh's mind.[35] Let us note that, in urging Zion to appeal for the sake of the innocent children, the narrator by no means suggests that Zion does not deserve Yahweh's punishment, as Mandolfo seems to imply.[36]

Thus 2:19, in the entire book of Lamentations, marks the only issue that the Deuteronomic theology fails to explain: the suffering of the inno-

---

significant enough in either ch. 1 or in the entire book of Lamentations to justify a divergence from the strict pattern of the poem.

34. Albrektson, *Studies*, 119; Hillers, *Lamentations*, 40; Westermann, *Lamentations*, 146; Pham, *Mourning*, 109.

35. It is notable that the narrator's point of view is in sharp contrast to Zion's blurry vision in which the children are extended to include the entire populace. See 2:20–21: Look, O LORD, and consider! To whom have you done this? // Should women eat their offspring, the children they have borne? // Should priest and prophet be killed in the sanctuary of the Lord? // The young and the old are lying on the ground in the streets; // my young women and my young men have fallen by the sword; // in the day of your anger you have killed them, slaughtering without mercy.

36. See Mandolfo, *Daughter Zion*, 1–28.

cent.[37] The theological failure inherent in the Deuteronomic tradition but surfacing only in the aftermath of Jerusalem's destruction compelled the author of Lamentations to seek a new understanding, and the ambiguity about Zion became a crucial element in his strategy to achieve it.

Conclusion

Through Zion, both the justification of the city's destruction and the exoneration of the common people are achieved. First, that Zion, as a city stained by the sins of her inhabitants, deserves her punishment is clearly stated in Lam 1, 2, and 4. Her massive and unforgivable sin against Yahweh is admitted both quantitatively and qualitatively. Let us recall that the blame is profusely placed upon the personified city by both the narrator and Zion herself in these chapters. As a city, Zion legitimately represents all the people who live in her throughout her history. Since any group of people who live in Zion at any time can be called hers, their sins also become hers. At the same time, any group of people who live in Zion at any given time must necessarily participate in her history, or in the person she is, whether they are in her recovering present or in her depraved past. In terms of law and order, just as a person who has committed heinous crimes in her past cannot be acquitted even if she has become clean in the present, so Zion's past sins must be punished if justice is to be upheld. The collective sin accumulated by Zion's citizens through all generations has

---

37. If the argument for the author's intentional divergence at 2:19 has merit, then maybe we can proceed to suggest an explanation for how 1:7 got its fourth line. Hypothetically, if 2:19 originates from the author, then to a scribe or copier who does not discern that this irregularity is meant to signal something extremely important, the strictness of the formal pattern is weakened considerably. As Renkema points out, it would be unimaginable that a scribe or glossator would take the liberty to disrupt the strict pattern of the poem by adding a fourth line to 1:7 (*Lamentations*, 131). With the presence of the irregular 2:19, however, the situation is changed considerably. Now, having precedent, the glossator would be less restrained to add a line when he feels a pressing need to do so, unwittingly creating a problem for later exegetes.

Pham suggests that 1:7a cropped up because the glossator did not think it right for Zion not to remember the temple. The speaker in 1:4, 10, 11 is concerned not only about Jerusalem but also about Yahweh's honor and the proper worship of Yahweh, and Jerusalem seems to share this sentiment in 1:18a. Verse 7, without 7b, would suggest that Jerusalem only thinks about her own loss. Therefore the glossator corrected the picture by adding 7b (*Mourning*, 70–71).

made her totally corrupt and repulsive to Yahweh. It is this accumulated sin that might be said to be worse than the iniquity of Sodom and deserves every measure of punishment. With their sense of corporate responsibility, which accepts that the sin of one person might cause Israel to be susceptible to destruction, as Joel Kaminsky shows in his study of Josh 7,[38] the survivors perhaps understood very well the rationality of the fall of the corporate entity symbolized by Zion. Thus, through the profuse blame placed on the personified city, God's judgment on the city is fully justified.

Now, let us return briefly to the question modern exegetes raise against the justification of the destruction of Jerusalem. The suffering of the survivors usually prompts scholars to address the so-called excessive punishment of the city.[39] Gottwald offers one of the strongest statements regarding the matter: "In 2.20–22 there is a fierce indictment of God, spared from blasphemy only by the brutality of the circumstances it describes and by the relentless and callous God which the whole poem has portrayed."[40] Dobbs-Allsopp argues that the vagueness of Judah's sin indicates that in

---

38. Joel S. Kaminsky, "Joshua 7: A Reassessment of Israelite Conceptions of Corporate Punishment," in *The Pitcher Is Broken: Memorial Essays for Gösta W. Ahlström* (ed. Steven W. Holloway and Lowell K. Handy; JSOTSup 190; Sheffield: Sheffield Academic Press, 1995), 315–46, here 320. See also idem, "The Sins of the Fathers: A Theological Investigation of the Biblical Tension between the Corporate and Individualized Retribution," *Judaism* 46 (1997): 319–32; Mowinckel, *Psalms*, 2:42–44; Geo Widengren, *The Accadian and Hebrew Psalms of Lamentation as Religious Documents* (Uppsala: Almqvist & Wiksell, 1936), 171.

39. House seems to be the only one who equates Zion with the surviving remnant but affirms justice in her destruction. In House's view, the people in Lamentations consider their losses perhaps more than sufficient for the crimes committed ("Lamentations," 319), but the suffering of children does not provide a sufficient basis for questioning God's justice. His view is clearly betrayed in his critique of those who raise the question: "First, they do not note that the different speakers in Lamentations agree about what has happened to Jerusalem.… Every character agrees that Israel's sin has caused this pain, that God has brought this pain, and that the pain is severe. Second, they do not accept the book's own statements about the original context. That is, they do not fully believe the book's speakers when they state that all the book's sufferers are not innocent sufferers. Of course, they correctly observe how the speakers in Lamentations mourn the treatment of innocent children, and this issue deserves to be addressed. At the same time, it is more than an open question whether one should consider God abusive at this point or the Israelites the most negligent parents imaginable. The biblical testimony is that these parents ignored warning after warning before the Babylonians came" (323).

40. Gottwald, *Studies*, 58.

the mind of the author the sin of Judah was not equal to its suffering.[41] He suggests, "The gruesome images of children dying in the streets from starvation (2:11–12; 4:2–4) or being cannibalized by their mothers (4:10) stand as paradigms of innocent suffering for which there is no justification and for which Yahweh's actions are directly and indirectly responsible," and that the comparison with Sodom in 4:6 implicitly raises doubts about the rightness of Yahweh's cause.[42] Edward Greenstein echoes Dobbs-Allsopp, finding "Lamentations' focus on the cannibalization of the children a case of divine wrath gone to the extreme—a terrible excess of 'justice,' which is no justice at all," and "the idea that YHWH's punishment of Judah is way out of proportion is expressed as well in 4.6."[43]

From the above comments, one thing is obvious: the question of God's justice in his punishment of Jerusalem is tightly connected to the suffering of the survivors and based on the assumption that punishment rather than sin is the focus of 4:6. Such questioning involves not only an indiscriminate view of the punishment of the city and the punishment of the survivors, but also a questionable interpretation of 4:6, as already discussed. Once the personified Zion is recognized as the *personification of the city, a center of civilization with a history and a people,* I believe the question of the justice of her punishment cannot maintain its force. The destruction of Zion, with respect to her material culture, her institutions (political, religious, economic, social), and her mainstream population (the condemned by the prophets), is justified in the author's view.

While the objection against the treatment of Zion, the city, cannot be maintained, the protest against the suffering of innocent people rightly brings our attention to the great tension between the ideas of corporate and individual responsibilities that clearly surfaced in Jeremiah and Ezekiel (Jer 5; Ezek 14; 18).[44] Through Zion's ambiguous confession, the author of Lamentations could spare the surviving community from undeserved accusations and protest the measures of punishment placed on them. Even if the survivors, in the scheme of things, are relatively insignificant compared to the city, the author would not sacrifice their human integrity. Although Zion's representative nature makes it completely believable that the people as a whole has acknowledged that Yahweh is in the right, as

41. Dobbs-Allsopp, "Tragedy," 38.
42. Ibid.
43. Greenstein, "Wrath at God," 38.
44. Cf. Kaminsky, "Sins of the Fathers."

scholarly interpretation of Zion's confession amply shows,[45] in effect this is only half the picture. On the one hand, through the voice of Zion, the surviving community could confess the nation's sin and admit the horrendous magnitude of it. On the other hand, the popular proverb, "The parents have eaten sour grapes, and the children's teeth are set on edge," makes it doubtful whether the guilt placed upon Zion was necessarily felt by the survivors, except those who were singled out for reprimand, that is, the prophets and the priests. As a person who faces judgment for past crimes would not have difficulty understanding that her past behavior is responsible for punishment, the survivors probably had an idea which part of Zion exacted her judgment.

Theoretically, placing all the measures of punishment on one guilty generation can hardly be justified, let alone on one not so guilty. Although Lamentations does not explicitly affirm the existence of innocent survivors, we have enough evidence for understanding that it was the case. First, let us recall again that in Lam 1, 2, and 4, the blame is not even once placed on the common survivors. On the contrary, concrete crimes are charged directly to the prophets and priests. Second, as the existence of innocent suffering is firmly established in the children and infants who died from hunger,[46] the case can be extended to include the suffering of those Ps 79 calls the "faithful ones" (חסידיך, v. 2), those who were like the Rechabites,[47] whose obedience to their ancestors is commended by Yahweh (Jer 35:18), and the list could go on.[48] In fact, the people who were left in the land of Israel were the poorest and owned nothing (2 Kgs 25:12; Jer 39:10). They plausibly belonged to the category of the oppressed "innocent poor" (Jer 2:34) who had no means to escape to other countries during the war or

---

45. See above. It appears that all scholars think the *surviving remnant* confessed the sin of the nation through Zion.

46. See also Dobbs-Allsopp, "Tragedy," 38; Renkema, *Lamentations*, 271, 310; Yehoshua Gitay, "The Poetics of National Disaster: The Rhetorical Presentations of Lamentations," in *Literary Responses to the Holocaust 1945–1995* (ed. Gitay; San Francisco: International Scholars, 1998), 1–11.

47. The ethnicity of the Rechabites is somewhat perplexing. According to 1 Chr 2:55, they were descendants of Caleb. In the same verse, however, they were also called Kenites. The Kenites were not Israelites but associated with or lived among them according to Judg 1:16; 4:11; 1 Sam 27:10.

48. We can at least add those who were like Ebed-melech (Jer 38:7–13; 39:15–18) or Baruch (Jer 45), and those who died in battle after they had repented in the religious reform, like King Josiah (2 Kgs 23:28–29).

immediately after the destruction.[49] Third, 2 Kgs 22–23 indicates clearly that Josiah's reform was too late to ward off the Day of Yahweh (22:15–17; 23:26–27). Judgment had been sealed and the day had already been decreed, a fact that Lamentations certainly confirms (Lam 2:17; cf. 3:37). The destruction of Jerusalem testified to the hard fact that on judgment day none survived or escaped; both the guilty and the innocent suffered from hunger, hardship, and shame, if not death by the sword. To be sure, this would have been the reality whether the Day of Yahweh took place in 587 B.C.E. or not, because children and the innocent inescapably exist side by side with the wicked in every generation. Unless judgment on the city is revoked, innocent suffering becomes just a matter of fact.

A major concern of the author of Lamentations was the innocent portion of the populace and their undeserved fate.[50] To ask them to believe that they are being destroyed by God for their own sins or to confess in order to be forgiven is not just wrong—it is cruel and oppressive. With Zion's confession, the Judean survivors are not required to do so. More positively, their suffering is acknowledged by both Zion and the narrator as undeserved. Most importantly, they constitute the only reason why God must look and consider, the only reason for Zion's appeal. They are the only part to whom justice has not been done in Jerusalem's destruction. If the punishment inflicted upon Jerusalem is seen as unjust, on what basis can one appeal to a God who is unjust in the first place? But if Jerusalem's destruction can be seen as fully justified, God remains a just God. Consequently there is hope. Supposedly, a just God cannot overlook the suffering of the innocent; will he not eventually intervene and compensate for those who suffer because of a cause bigger than themselves? The answer we get from Lam 4:22a is affirmative. The suffering of the remnant

---

49. Hayim Tadmor states, "There can certainly be no doubt that a great many left Judea during the war or immediately after the destruction and fled in all directions—to Samaria, Edom, Moab, Ammon, or Egypt" ("The Babylonian Exile and the Restoration," in *History of the Jewish People* [ed. H. H. Ben-Sasson; Cambridge: Harvard University Press, 1976], 159–82, here 161–62). My personal experience of the fall of Saigon in 1975 confirms that while the wealthy have the option to leave or remain in the country before or after its defeat, the poor in general have no choice but to remain. They simply have no means to do otherwise.

50. Isa 2:3–4 seems to imply that the survivors in Zion are the pure, those who are left after purification has been done. If that is the case, then Lamentations brings to the surface what is only latent in the prophets.

depicted in 4:18–20 seems to be the basis for the community's hope of an imminent divine intervention in 4:22.

תַּם־עֲוֹנֵךְ בַּת־צִיּוֹן לֹא יוֹסִיף לְהַגְלוֹתֵךְ
פָּקַד עֲוֹנֵךְ בַּת־אֱדוֹם גִּלָּה עַל־חַטֹּאתָיִךְ

The punishment of your iniquity is accomplished, O daughter of
Zion;
he will no longer keep you in exile.
He will punish your iniquity, O daughter of Edom;
he will reveal your sins.

The situation after the fall of Jerusalem required a paradoxical theology that must acknowledge both the justification of the city's destruction and the presence of undeserved suffering. The fall of Jerusalem confirms that an ideal situation in which punishment affects only the wicked does not exist in reality, but the author of Lamentations clearly showed that one does not have to despair about that. In the presence of injustice, one can still believe in God's justice. Believing in God's justice does not have to blind one from recognizing injustice even if tradition teaches otherwise. The surviving generation does not have to choose between justifying God and condemning themselves or justifying themselves and condemning God. They can both recognize God's justice and show him their unde-served suffering,[51] believing that God will eventually correct the tragic situation. If the surviving generation can view their situation in this way, they may have hope for the future and be able to endure extreme adversity in the present. After all, the purpose of Zion's vague confession, if any-thing, is to give this downtrodden community relief from the heavy guilt placed on them by earlier prophetic pronouncements of judgment.

If the argument for my thesis has merit, then Mandolfo's assessment of the role of the narrator and her understanding of the identity of Zion need to be reconsidered. As I have commented throughout this chapter, the assumptions that the narrator's allusion to Zion's transgressions is an aside, that he speaks against the divine interest, and that Zion is identical with the survivors are basically incorrect and require further revision.

---

51. Although the people's suffering is expressed only indirectly as underserved in Lam 1, 2, and 4, where we encounter the personification of Zion, it is openly voiced in 5:7: "Our fathers sinned and are no more, and we bear their iniquity/punishment."

DAUGHTER ZION: CODEPENDENT NO MORE

LeAnn Snow Flesher

The Judeo-Christian writings, commonly referred to as the Scriptures, or the canonical text(s), have been read and studied for thousands of years by faith communities around the world in hopes of finding some inspiration, spiritual and otherwise, about a Divine-human relationship. While teaching these Scriptures in urban, multicultural, theological seminaries in New York, Berkeley, and around the world for over twenty years, I have encountered a variety of faith commitments and challenges. However, common to every local and culture are questions related to extreme suffering and injustice as well as questions related to God's role and participation in such events.

In *Daughter Zion Talks Back to the Prophets*, through a dialogical reading of the prophets and Lamentations, Carleen Mandolfo has raised numerous questions related to suffering, the human condition, the God relationship, theodicy, unresolved grief, and faith.[1] Her work is tremendously engaging, but not intended for the weak of stomach or the weak of heart. I have been at a loss as to where to begin to unravel the complexities that have surfaced as a result of reading her work. Her book is so stimulating I find my mind going numerous directions all at one time, so much so that I can barely contain the excitement that it stirs within me. She has asked us to engage some very difficult but tremendously important theological questions related to suffering and the Divine-human relationship.

At the risk of being tremendously reductionist, I want to state simply: the major idea in Mandolfo's work is related to a depiction of the Deity by the prophets (specifically Hosea, Jeremiah, Ezekiel, and Second Isaiah)

---

1. Carleen R. Mandolfo, *Daughter Zion Talks Back to the Prophets: A Dialogic Theology of the Book of Lamentations* (SemeiaSt 58; Atlanta: Society of Biblical Literature, 2007).

as a God who has been wronged by his covenant people and as a result is first angry, hurt, shamed, vengeful, and violent; then eventually, ultimately, forgiving, merciful, and reconciliatory. Conversely, the covenant people are depicted by the prophets, through the use of feminine metaphors, as being wanton, adulterous, sexually insatiable, and in general exhibiting shameless behavior as relates to their covenant God. As a result (according to the prophets) the unfaithful covenant people, hereafter referred to as Daughter Zion,[2] must be disciplined, and her shame must be exposed so that she can be brought to repentance. Yet it is not her act of repentance that brings reconciliation (according to the prophets), but God's choosing, in his mercy, to break the law of divorce (Deut 24:4) and to bring Daughter Zion back to himself. Meanwhile, we find in Lam 1 and 2 the voice of Daughter Zion loudly and incessantly proclaiming her lament of pain and suffering at the hand of the Deity, and she will not be comforted.

In this essay I attempt to track, with Mandolfo, the dialogue between Daughter Zion, God, and the prophets. As such, I begin with a summary of the conclusions Mandolfo has reached through her dialogical study of Hosea, Jeremiah, Ezekiel, Lam 1–2, and Second Isaiah, followed by a dialogical reading of the remnant theology found in Third Isaiah, specifically Isa 62–66, in conversation with Lam 5. First, some definitions. I have noted that Mandolfo's work is a dialogical reading of the prophets and Lamentations. Mandolfo leans on Martin Buber's definition of dialogue as "existential encounter, meaningful exchange of selves, reciprocal revelation." In other words, and Mikhail Bakhtin agrees here, an I-thou encounter must move beyond mere explanation to empathy and understanding. Buber understood such communication to take place between God and humanity in the biblical text. Mandolfo notes instances when this is true (e.g., in Gen 18 when Abraham engages God over the fate of Sodom), but goes on to suggest there are many more moments when God and the people are seemingly missing each other entirely.[3]

---

2. Mandolfo reads dialogically between Lam 1–2 and the prophets. In Lam 1–2 the city of Jerusalem is personified and as such is referred to as "daughter," "virgin daughter," "Zion," "widow," etc. In the first two chapters of Lamentations a personified Zion laments over the destruction of Jerusalem. Mandolfo calls her by name, Daughter Zion, throughout her book, in recognition of the identity formation that has taken place through the personification of the city. See ibid., 15.

3. Ibid., 2.

Reading the biblical text dialogically thus involves looking for voices of God, humanity, and the narrator in conversation with one another, and Mandolfo engages this method intertextually. Such an approach leads to a dialogic theology that provides humanity an avenue for speaking honestly to God.[4] Carol Newsom has noted that critical biblical scholarship was founded on the idea that the Bible is not monologic; rather the Bible is heterogeneous—filled with contradiction, disjunction, and multiple perspectives. In other words, the Bible is polyphonic, bringing together ideas and worldviews typically estranged from one another and forcing them to quarrel. In a polyphonic text one reads for dialogic play; a dialogic reading is a means of calling back and forth to kindred ideas from various epochs. To read for the dialogues is to participate in them.[5]

Walter Brueggemann finds biblical precedent for this:

> The lament psalms insist upon Israel's finding voice, a voice that tends to be abrasive and insistent. The lament psalm is a Jewish refusal of silence before God.… It is a Jewish understanding that an adequate relationship with God permits and requires a human voice that will speak out against every wrong perpetrated either on earth or by heaven.… I consider this matter of voice and violence not to be a theoretical issue but a concrete, practical, pastoral issue because we live in a violent, abusive society in which there is terrible conspiracy in violence that can only be broken when the silence is broken by the lesser party.[6]

LAMENTATIONS 1–2

Hear the lament of Daughter Zion after the destruction of Jerusalem as exemplified in this excerpt from Lam 1 and 2. The lament closes (2:20–22) with Daughter Zion's cry of anguish, which has not and cannot be comforted, and with her accusations of injustice.

> Look, O Lord, and consider! To whom have you done this? Should women eat their offspring, the children they have borne? Should priest and prophet be killed in the sanctuary of the Lord? The young and the old are lying on the ground in the streets; my young women and my young men have fallen by the sword; in the day of your anger you have

---

4. Ibid.

5. Carol Newsom, "Bakhtin, the Bible, and Dialogic Truth," *JR* 76 (1996): 290–306.

6. Walter Brueggemann, "Voice as Counter to Violence," *CTJ* 36 (2001): 22.

killed them, slaughtering without mercy. You invited my enemies from all around as if for a day of festival; and on the day of the anger of the LORD no one escaped or survived; those whom I bore and reared my enemy has destroyed.

The voice of God does not appear in Lam 1 and 2, only that of Daughter Zion and the narrator. To find the voice of God we must go to the prophets. We will walk through examples from the prophets one by one in chronological order: Hosea, Jeremiah, Ezekiel (Lamentations), and ultimately Second Isaiah.

Hosea

The book of Hosea opens with a call from God for Hosea to take a wife of whoredom and have children of whoredom as a sign. This is an act in which the prophet lives the experience of the husband/Deity by entering into a relationship with a *zonah*, a woman who shames her family through some form of sexual indiscretion. In Hos 2 the angry voice of God dominates, but simultaneously Daughter Zion is allowed two quotes found in verses 5 and 7. Hear the forceful, even violent language:

Plead with your mother … plead that she put away her whoring from her face, and her adultery from between her breasts, or I will strip her naked and expose her as in the day she was born, and make her like a wilderness and turn her into a parched land and kill her with thirst. Upon her children also I will have no pity, because they are children of whoredom. For their mother has played the whore; she who conceived them has acted shamefully. For she said, "I will go after my lovers; they give me my bread and my water, my wool and my flax, my oil and my drink." Therefore I will hedge up her way with thorns; and I will build a wall against her, so that she cannot find her paths. She shall pursue her lovers, but not overtake them; and she shall seek them, but shall not find them. Then she shall say, "I will go and return to my first husband, for it was better with me then than now." She did not know that it was I who gave her the grain, the wine, and the oil, and who lavished upon her silver and gold that they used for Baal. (NRSV)

Mandolfo interprets this text in accordance with the perspective of Yvonne Sherwood,

Alongside the picture of a self-assured deity who knows that Israel will return to him, the text presents a jealous and insecure husband who turns to violence in desperation. The tensions of the divine-human metaphor lead to a bizarre situation in which the deity who confidently asserts his superiority is also a rather pathetic figure who lashes out in anger.[7]

JEREMIAH

Terence Fretheim has noted that the books of Jeremiah and Isaiah each opens with a divine lament depicting God as in deep pain and anguish over the loss of an idyllic relationship with Israel and Judah.[8] Yet Jeremiah does not exhibit the hope for reconciliation found in Hosea. The God of Hosea seems sad, hurt, and jealous; the God of Jeremiah is wrathful and vengeful.[9] In Jer 2–3 we find Yhwh's voice sprinkled with quotes from Daughter Zion (here portrayed as a wanton-adulterous wife). In these chapters Yhwh is calling her to task for breaking her yoke of servitude (2:20), going after other gods (2:23–25), and harming the poor and innocent (2:34). Throughout these accusations Yhwh quotes her as declaring her innocence (2:23, 35). She is depicted as a wild animal in heat with unrestrainable lust (2:23–25). Her punishment is described elsewhere; in 13:20–27 God himself declares that he will "lift up her skirts" so she can be raped by her "allies." Her justification for her behavior is found in 44:15–19, where she rejects Jeremiah's word spoken in the name of the LORD and vows to continue to make offerings to the Queen of Heaven and pour out libations to her because ever since they have made these offerings they have had enough to eat. The dialogue is intense, with Israel/Judah accusing God of not adequately providing for their needs and God accusing them of being unfaithful.

Finally, in 3:22–25 we see a remnant of "faithless children" who return, repent, and are reconciled. The shift from feminine to masculine imagery is significant here—when Israel and Judah are spoken about as wanton adulteresses the imagery is feminine, but the returning remnant is referred to as children with all masculine pronouns. This shift is only emphasized by the fact that those called to the new covenant in Jer 31 are

---

7. Yvonne Sherwood, *The Prostitute and the Prophet: Hosea's Marriage in Literary-Theoretical Perspective* (JSOTSup 212; GCT 2; Sheffield: Sheffield Academic Press, 1996), 222–23. Cf. Mandolfo, *Daughter Zion*, 33–36.

8. Terence E. Fretheim, *Jeremiah* (SHBC; Macon, Ga.: Smyth & Helwys, 2002), 4–11.

9. Mandolfo, *Daughter Zion*, 87–98.

sons (31:18–20), virgin Israel (31:21), and faithless daughters (31:22); the adulterous wife is never mentioned.

EZEKIEL

As we move to the book of Ezekiel, we lose the voice of Daughter Zion— she is not allowed to speak anywhere in the book. Instead, we find in Ezek 16 and 23 severe, even violent, imagery describing her discipline from God and by God for her unfaithfulness. Chapter 16 opens with a description of God adopting Israel as a naked, abandoned baby, then clothing her with fine riches, feeding her, rearing her until she was of age, then marrying her. But as verse 15 states: "you trusted in your beauty and played the whore because of your fame, and lavished your whorings on any passerby." Her punishment is found in 16:37b–43a:

> I will gather them against you from all around and will uncover your nakedness to them, so that they may see all your nakedness. I will judge you as women who commit adultery and shed blood are judged, and bring blood upon you in wrath and jealousy. I will deliver you into their hands, and they shall throw down your platform and break down your lofty places, they shall strip you of your clothes and take your beautiful objects and leave you naked and bare. They shall bring up a mob against you, and they shall stone you and cut you to pieces with their swords. They shall burn your houses and execute judgments on you in the sight of many women; I will stop you from playing the whore, and you shall also make no more payments. So I will satisfy my fury on you, and my jealousy shall turn away from you; I will be calm, and will be angry no longer. (NRSV)

The language of the NRSV in fact cleans up the Hebrew a bit. Excerpts from Mandolfo's own translation of verses 35–40 more closely convey the harshness of the original: "Therefore, whore, hear the word of YHWH!... I will gather all your lovers ... against you from all around and ... [t]hey shall gang rape you and ... stone you and sever you up the middle with their swords."[10] The rhetoric exceeds the demands of the law; in general, only female sexuality is figured as offensive; the rapists are only tools in Yhwh's retributive scheme. In Ezek 23:24–35 the language and imagery is even more intense.

---

10. Mandolfo, *Daughter Zion*, 49.

In response to the Ezekiel monologues, hear the voice of Daughter Zion in Lam 2:20–22 once again.

> Look, O LORD, and consider! To whom have you done this? Should women eat their offspring, the children they have borne? Should priest and prophet be killed in the sanctuary of the Lord? The young and the old are lying on the ground in the streets; my young women and my young men have fallen by the sword; in the day of your anger you have killed them, slaughtering without mercy. You invited my enemies from all around as if for a day of festival; and on the day of the anger of the LORD no one escaped or survived; those whom I bore and reared my enemy has destroyed. (NRSV)

SECOND ISAIAH

Finally, we find in Second Isaiah a response to Lam 1 and 2. Except for a few references to a feminized Jerusalem, much of the first half of Second Isaiah is addressed to the "Servant," or a second-person masculine singular addressee that most assume is the Servant. It is not until Isa 49:14 that we hear Zion speak, "But Zion said, 'The LORD has forsaken me, my Lord has forgotten me'" (NRSV). Yet in 49:8–9 Yhwh has responded to a speech by the Servant:

> Thus says Yhwh:
> In an hour of favor I answer you,
> And on a day of salvation I help you.
> I created you and appointed you a covenant people,
> Restoring the land,
> Allowing anew the desolate holding,
> Saying to the prisoners, "Go free,"
> To those in darkness, "Show yourselves."

Then in verse 13:

> Shout, heavens, and rejoice, earth!
> Break into shouting, hills:
> For Yhwh has comforted his people,
> And has had compassion on his afflicted ones.

Immediately following this statement of jubilation come Zion's words: "Yhwh has forsaken me, my Lord has forgotten me." The contrast of Zion's short speech in verse 14 is stark when juxtaposed to the Servant's speech in verses 1–6 (vv. 5–6 quoted below):

> And now the LORD says, who formed me in the womb to be his servant, to bring Jacob back to him, and that Israel might be gathered to him, for I am honored in the sight of the LORD, and my God has become my strength—he says, "It is too light a thing that you should be my servant to raise up the tribes of Jacob and to restore the survivors of Israel; I will give you as a light to the nations, that my salvation may reach to the end of the earth." (NRSV)

Second Isaiah's speech privileges the *golah* (sojourner) community, those who have been colonized under Babylonian rule; it does not speak to the suffering of those who have been left behind in Judah, the probable creators of Lamentations.[11] Their children are not coming home—Zion's children are lost forever—having been eaten in desperation by their own mothers (cf. Lam 2:20). Time does not permit me to walk through the many parallels between Lam 1 and 2 and Second Isaiah,[12] but suffice it to say Yhwh and the prophet work hard in these chapters (chs. 49–54) to address the lament of Zion, and many commentators point out the correspondences.[13]

After Daughter Zion speaks in 49:14, we never hear from her again—although she is mentioned or addressed by name seven more times within Isa 50–52. Each address is a reference to Zion being comforted, the LORD returning to Zion, and Zion being restored. Yet in 54:11 we find mention again of one who has not been comforted: "O afflicted one, storm-tossed, and not comforted." After this allusion to Daughter Zion—followed by a description of how Jerusalem will be rebuilt—the chapter concludes

---

11. Frederick W. Dobbs-Allsopp, *Lamentations* (IBC; Louisville: Westminster John Knox, 2002), 4.

12. Examples include Lam 1–2 in relationship to Isa 49:1–14 and 54:7–11, 17.

13. Discussions of the correspondences between Lam 1–2 and Second Isaiah can be found in Kathleen M. O'Connor, *Lamentations and the Tears of the World* (Maryknoll, N.Y.: Orbis, 2002), 137–47; idem, "'Speak Tenderly to Jerusalem': Second Isaiah's Reception and Use of Daughter Zion," *PSB* 20 (1999): 281–94; Benjamin D. Sommer, *A Prophet Reads Scripture: Allusion in Isaiah 40–66* (Contraversions; Stanford, Calif.: Stanford University Press, 1998); Tod Linafelt, *Surviving Lamentations: Catastrophe, Lament, and Protest in the Afterlife of a Biblical Book* (Chicago: University of Chicago Press, 2000), 62–79; Norman Gottwald, "Social Class and Ideology in Isaiah 40–55: An Eagletonian Reading," *Semeia* 59 (1992): 3–71.

with, "this is the heritage of the servants of the LORD and their vindica-tion from me, says the LORD" (54:17b). Daughter Zion is not mentioned in this final verse; only masculine pronouns and servant language are used. The afflicted one and not-comforted one has disappeared and been subsumed by the servants of the LORD. The remainder of the book of Isaiah focuses on remnant theology—not all of Judah is restored, only the "faithful remnant." Some have been lost; they have not returned in faith to Yhwh.

INTERPRETATION

The observations noted above describe dialogic intricacies and details of considerable import. For example, each of the prophets handles Daughter Zion a little differently; while some allow her voice, one (Ezekiel) does not. Hosea, the earliest of the prophets, is addressing Israel's alliance with and eventual destruction by Assyria; Jeremiah and Ezekiel are address-ing Judah/Jerusalem's fraternizing with Assyria, Babylon, and Egypt; and Second Isaiah is responding to Daughter Zion's complaints in Lam 1 and 2. So the imagery is being used allegorically to refer to political alliances with foreign nations, behavior for which the prophets are chastising the political leaders since it has led to the eventual demise of the entire nation. The prophetic response to these crises is varied and intensifies as we move from Hosea to Jeremiah to Ezekiel. Second Isaiah, with its Suffering Ser-vant passages, is focused on bringing comfort and resolution to the breach between Yhwh and his people. Yet Mandolfo and several before her have made a significant and important observation for this conversation: that Second Isaiah personifies Jerusalem as servant and as Daughter Zion, and those who are reconciled to Yhwh are in alliance with the Servant (use of masculine pronouns), but Daughter Zion is never reconciled (use of femi-nine pronouns) to Yhwh.[14] Indeed, she is left hanging, just as Daughter Zion is not to be comforted in Lam 1 and 2. The surfacing and empha-sizing of this reality is perhaps the greatest contribution (at least in my mind) that Mandolfo's work provides. This brings us to the question of theodicy. What Mandolfo has noted over and over in her book is that, in contrast to the prophets, in Lam 1 and 2 Daughter Zion or the group that

---

14. Mandolfo, *Daughter Zion*, 45.

she represents is nontheodic (i.e., not willing to justify God).[15] This is true even for Second Isaiah, in which the faithful remnant is associated with the Suffering Servant and the voice of Daughter Zion is depicted as the "other." What we are left with, then, is a voice "crying in the wilderness" who cannot, will not, be reconciled to God and insists on calling God to account for implementing a punishment too extreme, too severe, for the sins committed.

What exactly are the sins that have been committed? For Hosea, Israel's sin is that she looked to another for sustenance (Hos 2:5, 8); for Jeremiah, there are hints of much the same (Jer 44:15–19), but also suggestions that Yhwh's demands have been unreasonable and oppressive (2:20), causing Judah to break free from its yoke of service; in Ezekiel, Judah is accused of wrong political alliances, idolatry, and even infanticide (see esp. Ezek 16:15–29). All of these prophetic responses are dealing with an underlying concern of Yhwh's potency. Is God truly able to provide, deliver, and sustain? The people have not seen evidence of this and have turned to building alliances with obviously powerful nations in order to have their needs met. But in the end this worked against them, since instead of becoming equal political players in the world of the ancient Near East, they became powerless vassals that experienced increasingly more extreme expectations and demands from their overlords until they ultimately rebelled, and were consequently forced into submission militarily and taken into exile. The prophets are critiquing these political choices by claiming that the national leaders did not remain faithful to Yhwh and the covenant, resulting in their own demise. The military takeover is then viewed as Yhwh's disciplinary action; Daughter Zion's response is to say this discipline is too extreme and too severe, whereas the Suffering Servant's response is to accept the discipline and build toward reconciliation with God in hopes for eventual restoration of the nation.

Hence the voice of Daughter Zion in Mandolfo's work comes to represent the voice of the "other," the voice of the powerless, the voice of the population that refuses to remain colonized—but chooses instead, shame and all, to break free from the socioreligious mores that have sustained her to this point. Daughter Zion dares to face the shame of her position and the accusations brought against her, dares to reassess these socio-religio-cultural norms, and call God to account for his wrath-filled reactions to

---

15. Ibid., 111–18.

her covenant-breaking behavior that cross over the line of discipline into abuse. Therefore, she will not be comforted, she will not reconcile, and she will call the God she has known to account.

THIRD ISAIAH AND LAMENTATIONS 5

The numerous correspondences between Second Isaiah and Lam 1 and 2 have already been acknowledged. Similar correspondences can be found between Third Isaiah (esp. chs. 62–66) and Lam 5. As we move through Isa 62–66 we encounter, once again, a dialogue between God and the people. In 62:1 the voice of God declares, "For Zion's sake I will not keep silent [חשה] … until her vindication shines out like the dawn and her salvation like a burning torch." "The nations shall see your vindication" (v. 2a); "you shall be called by a new name" (v. 2b). "You shall be a crown of beauty in the hand of the LORD" (v. 3a; cf. Lam 5:16). "You shall no more be termed Forsaken" (v. 4a, *Azubah*; see Lam 5:20b), "and your land shall no more be termed Desolate" (v. 4b, *Shemamah*; see Lam 5:18), "but you shall be called My Delight is in Her" (v. 4c, *Hephzibah*), "and your land shall be Married" (v. 4d, *Beulah*). Verse 5 continues with the marriage theme, noting that God will rejoice over Daughter Zion (see Isa 62:11) as a bridegroom rejoices over his bride. Isaiah 62:5 is certainly a recasting of the marriage metaphor that we have seen played out in Hosea, Jeremiah, and Ezekiel. Now, after the discipline has been given, Zion is being brought back as the bride of God. And God rejoices over his bride. Verses 6 and 7 emphasize the language of verse 1a; God will establish a sentinel that will not keep silent (חשה) and will not allow God to rest (דמי; 2x) until he establishes Jerusalem. In verses 8 and 9 God promises to never again give Jerusalem's grain as food for the enemy or wine as drink for the foreigners (see Lam 5:4, 9–10). In verse 10 the prophet calls for the preparation of the highways for the return of the people to the gates of Jerusalem (see Isa 49:8–12), followed by a declaration: "Say to daughter Zion, 'See, your salvation comes.'" Finally, in verse 12, they (the people) are called "The Holy People, The Redeemed of the LORD"; and Jerusalem is "called Sought Out, a City Not Forsaken" (NRSV).

In Isa 63:1–6 the tone shifts considerably. While in Isa 62 God proclaims his salvific intentions to Daughter Zion (i.e., Jerusalem) as a collect that includes those who come through her gates (see v. 10), the first six verses of Isa 63 appear to be a revisiting of God's past anger and resultant discipline and vindication. The language is extreme in describing the discipline of the people, this time through the image of trampling grapes in a winepress, a significant metaphorical shift away from the rape language found in the earlier prophetic writings. Verse 6 provides a summary: "I trampled down peoples in my anger, I crushed them in my wrath, and I poured out their lifeblood on the earth" (NRSV; see Lam 5:22). One cannot help but hear the allusion to the Cain and Abel story (Gen 4) and Job 16:18 in the use of this language; but given the context and the speaker, this usage is a reversal. In the Genesis and Job passages the lifeblood poured out upon the earth is a cry to God for vindication; in this usage the lifeblood poured out upon the earth is a sign of God's vindication having been achieved by God's own hand.

Given the covenant relationship between God and the people, certain expectations are present on both sides. God expects total allegiance and faithfulness from the people, and in return the people can expect sustenance and protection. The covenant relationship is in reality a reciprocal relationship, albeit clearly hierarchical. When one party of the covenant does not fulfill its role, the other party experiences shame.[16] The speech of Isa 63:1–6 notes that God, who has been shamed by the unfaithfulness of his people, has had to work his own vengeance, as a helper was nowhere to be found (see v. 5). While Isa 62 emphasizes God's magnanimous salvific agenda for Zion, 63:1–6 reminds us of the reason for her current state. While in the earthly realm Jerusalem has been destroyed by her human enemies, God is taking credit for the "punishment" and owning it as his own vindication. In 63:7–64:11(Eng. 12) we find the communal response to this God-speak.

---

16. In her commentary on Ezekiel, Margaret Odell has noted: "Like all emotions, shame is invested with cultural meanings. While most westerners experience shame as a profound feeling of inadequacy, that is probably not its primary connotation in the biblical texts. More likely, the primary experience of shame in the Hebrew Bible occurs in contexts where one is affected by others' failures. In many of the contexts where shame language appears, one person has pledged loyalty to another in exchange for that person's recognition, protection, or security (see Judg 18:7; 1 Sam 25:7, 15). When that person fails to deliver what is expected of him, then the other person feels shame. It is the one who is wronged not the wrongdoer, who suffers shame" (*Ezekiel* [SHBC; Macon, Ga.: Smyth & Helwys, 2005], 196).

Isaiah 63:7–64:11 (Eng. 12)

Through the use of particular grammatical forms (God[thou]-lament, accusatory questions and negative petitions), of language charged with indifference and complicity, of idiomatic expressions (סתר פנים with ענה), and of the father metaphor, the author of Isa 63:7–64:11 (Eng. 12) has created a communal lament filled with accusations against God, as outlined in the table below.

Category	Evidence
Grammatical	second-person singular forms
	God(thou)-laments (63:17; 64:4, 6 [Eng. 5, 7])
	accusatory questions (63:15, 17; 64:11 [Eng. 12])
	negative petitions (64:8 [Eng. 9])
Semantic	סתר פנים hide the face (64:6 [Eng. 7])
	ענה answer (64:11 [Eng. 12])
	קצב anger (64:4, 8 [Eng. 5, 9])
	זכר remember (64:8 [Eng. 9])
	חשה be silent (64:11 [Eng. 12])
	שוב turn (63:17)
	עד forever (64:8 [Eng. 9])
	עד־מאד exceedingly (64:8, 11 [Eng. 9, 12])
Idiom	סתר פנים with ענה
Metaphor	אב father (63:16 [2x]; 64:7 [Eng. 8])

The God(thou)-lament, one of three types of laments,[17] is evidenced by pronouns and verbs in second-person singular forms. In the commu-

---

17. Craig Broyles has noted that Westermann's idea of the threefold lament (the complaint against God, the complaint against the enemy, and the lament of one's current adverse circumstance) can be identified by the grammatical subject of the sen-

nal lament of 63:7–64:11 (Eng. 12) these constructions are found in three verses (63:17; 64:4c, 6 [Eng. 5c, 7]). In 63:17 God is asked why God causes the community to stray from God's ways and why God has hardened their hearts. The verbs used are תעה (to wander) and קשׁח (to make hard). Both verbs are in the hiphil with God as subject and the community as object. The first of these, תעה, when used to refer to a mental or moral state/condition is translated, "cause to err, mislead." The second, קשׁח, when used with the noun לב (heart), as in this context, is translated "make hard." It seems the verse ought to be read as causal, as the NRSV translates: "Why, O LORD, do you make us stray from your ways and harden our heart?"[18] While the people acknowledge they have strayed (see 63:10), they accuse God of having turned away from them by causing them to lose hope and faith and to look to another for sustenance and protection.

In 64:4c (Eng. 5c) the verb קצף is a qal perfect, translated "you were angry," immediately followed by חטא qal imperfect + *waw* conversive, "and we sinned." The construction does not necessitate a causal relationship, but does not exclude it. Unfortunately, the remainder of the verse is corrupt and so the full sense of the verse cannot be determined with

---

tence: I/We-lament, Thou(God)-lament, and the They(foe)-lament (*Conflict of Faith and Experience in the Psalms: A Form-Critical and Theological Study* [JSOTSup 52; Sheffield: JSOT Press, 1989], 37). I use these labels throughout this paper as simplified representative language for Westermann's original three categories of lamentation.

18. Richard Bautch does not address the grammar of this verse but does discuss the grammar of 64:4c and 64:6 ("Lament Regained in Trito-Isaiah's Penitential Prayer," in *The Origins of Penitential Prayer in Second Temple Judaism* [vol. 1 of *Seeking the Favor of God*; ed. Mark J. Boda, Daniel K. Falk, and Rodney A. Werline; SBLEJL 21; Atlanta: Society of Biblical Literature, 2006], 83–101, here 93–96). The causal idea is only clear in 63:17, but its presence here suggests that 64:4c and 64:6 should be read similarly. By not addressing 63:17 Bautch can argue for different grammatical interpretations of 64:4c and 6. Of the former he says, "Isaiah's verse has been read as legal discourse whereby God's anger stands as the verdict against a sinful people" (p. 93), and he finds support for this in Delitzsch's interpretation of the grammar, mainly that the *waw* forms the imperfect consecutive, "… so we have then sinned." Others translate: "you were angry, we having sinned" (John Oswalt, *The Book of Isaiah: Chapters 40–66* [NICOT; Grand Rapids: Eerdmans, 1998], 619); and "You grew angry, and yet we sinned" (R. N. Whybray, *Isaiah 40–66* [NCB; repr., Grand Rapids: Eerdmans, 1981], 264). All of these translations ignore 63:17 as causal and therefore setting the tone, and seek to prioritize penance at the exclusion of lament. The result is an either/or mentality that is not necessary. It is not either penitential prayer or lament, but both/and.

any confidence.[19] Finally, in 64:5 (Eng. 6) the phrase פנים סתר (you have hidden your face; hiphil perfect second masc. sg.) is initiated with a כי clause, suggesting a causal relationship with what has come before, "There is no one who calls on your name." The verse ends with the ותמוגנו ביד־ עוננו (you have melted us into the hand of our iniquities).

Commentators, including Claus Westermann, have noted these constructions, but the dating of the lament,[20] coupled with the confessions of sin within it, have clouded their conclusions. Westermann, R. N. Whybray, and Joseph Blenkinsopp, to name a few, temper the God(thou)-lament by emphasizing the confession of sin. Westermann states, "Thus, the affirmation of their iniquity gives the charge brought against God its quietus."[21] These commentators are reading with God here (as we have all been trained to do) and not with the people; thus the voice of the community that Daughter Zion represents has been deemphasized and deemed irrelevant. But if we choose to read with the lamenting community of Isa 63–64 and listen to her accusations and complaints, we will draw some very different conclusions.

Added to the second-person God(thou)-lament constructions are the accusatory questions found in 63:15, 17 and 64:11 (Eng. 12). After

---

19. Isa 64:4c (Eng. 5c) ends with בָּהֶם עוֹלָם וְנִוָּשֵׁעַ. Of the various possible solutions to this textual problem, two are of particular interest. The NASB reads: "We continued in them a long time; and shall we be saved?" The NASB translation presupposes that a word has dropped out and provides one (in italics) in order to make sense of what is found in the Hebrew. The NRSV translates "because you hid yourself we transgressed," which evidences considerable reconfiguration of the Hebrew with the end result that the entire v. 4c is causal. The NASB comes closest to honoring the current state of the Hebrew by translating the pronominal suffix as a referent to the sins of the people, which must be deduced from the verbal form that precedes it. The NRSV reconfigures the Hebrew to create a causal emphasis that aligns with the translation found in 63:17 and 64:6 (Eng. 7). These two translations adhere to two important principles for dealing with textual corruptions: the NASB taking a minimalist approach, emending the text as little as possible; and the NRSV emphasizing a contextual approach, assuring the concluding translation fits with the surrounding context. Neither translation is completely satisfactory.

20. For a full explanation, see discussion under "Remnant Theology" below.

21. Claus Westermann, *Isaiah 40–66* (trans. David M. G. Stalker; OTL; Philadelphia: Westminster, 1969), 397. See also Whybray, *Isaiah 40–66,* 264–65; Joseph Blenkinsopp, *Isaiah 56–66* (AB 19B; New York: Doubleday, 2003), 266, although Blenkinsopp does acknowledge the tendency for biblical authors to charge God with indifference or even complicity (263).

a lengthy section of praise (63:7–9) and description of God's past saving deeds (63:10–14), the author petitions "Look down from heaven and see.... Where are your zeal and your might? The yearning of your heart and your compassion [רחם]?" (NRSV).[22] This question stands in sharp contrast to the previous verses that praise God for delivering the people safely through Sinai into Canaan. The interrogative איה is generally used rhetorically in poetry. Thus the expected answer is, "Nowhere."

In 63:17 the lamenting community questions, "Why [למה], O LORD, do you make us stray from your ways and harden our hearts so we do not fear you?" למה is an interrogative used in the laments to indicate something in the situation, as they saw it, was deeply wrong. Westermann noted that the complaint against God was dominant in the communal laments, especially in the reproaching questions "Why?" and "How long?"[23] Broyles has suggested that when למה is used the psalmist finds the current situation inexplicable.[24] The community cannot understand why God has turned away from them (see Isa 63:17c).

Finally, the communal lament of Isa 63:7–64:11 (Eng. 12) closes with a sentence that begins with an interrogative ה: "After all this, will you restrain yourself, O LORD? Will you keep silent, and punish us severely?" (NRSV). The preceding verses (64:9–10 [Eng. 10–11]) speak of the destruction and desolation of Zion and her temple, and, of course, the entire lament speaks of God's hiddenness and the people's sin. This concluding interrogative coupled with those that have come before (Where is your mercy? Why do you make us stray? Why do you harden our hearts?) carries a tone of accusation. God's mercy cannot be found, God's active involvement in the people's waywardness, the desolation of Zion and her temple—all of it is incomprehensible. Why would God remain silent? Why would God punish so severely (64:11 [Eng. 12])?

In 64:8 (Eng. 9) the author uses the negative petition (imperfect + אל), "Do not be exceedingly angry, O LORD, and do not remember iniquity forever." The negative petition, while more subtle than the accusatory

---

22. The penitential prayer is an appeal to God's mercy (רחם), and is in fact counting on God's mercy for forgiveness. But in 63:15 the one praying questions, Where is God's mercy?

23. Examples of "Why?" questions can be found in Pss 44:24–25 (Eng. 23–24); 74:1. "How long?" questions can be found in Pss 79:5; 80:5 (Eng. 4); 89:47 (Eng. 46); as well as in the prophets, Hab 1:13; Jer 14:8; Isa 58:3.

24. Broyles, *Conflict of Faith*, 80.

questions discussed above, is itself accusatory in that it functions to ward off impending doom. In this verse, the community describes the reality of God's anger and memory for sin, but petitions against the superlatives (that God would not be *exceedingly* angry, or remember sin *forever*) in an attempt to ward off such a finality.

Having exhausted the conversation around categories of grammatical forms, we move next to the list of words and phrases found in 63:7–64:11 (Eng. 12) that are common to psalms of lament. The first of these, סתר פנים (hide the face), always appears with God as the subject. The phrase is usually found in poetry, most often in the laments, where it is frequently coupled with the accusatory interrogative, and is thus viewed as unjustified. It is found in the prophets in relationship to judgment; the cause of God's hiding is always related to the sin of the people. The phrase is used idiomatically with ענה; thus when God is accused of hiding, God is often petitioned to answer, as in 64:11 (Eng. 12).[25]

God's anger (קצף) is associated with punishment for sin(s) committed. In the Psalms frequently the reason for God's anger is not expressed, but when it is, it is related to punishment for sin and is frequently protested as excessive (see Pss 6:4 [Eng. 3]; 80:5 [Eng. 4]; 85:6 [Eng. 5]; 89:47 [Eng. 46]). Psalms 6 and 38 begin with identical petitions that request that God not punish in anger. These introductory negative petitions do not request that discipline be held off, only that its severity and duration (see 6:4 [Eng. 3], "How long?") be moderated. Similarly the negative petitions of Isa 64:8 (Eng. 9) request that God not be exceedingly (עד-מאד) angry, or remember (זכר) forever (עד). A correlative petition for forgiveness is not found in the Psalms[26] or here in Isaiah.

God is frequently petitioned to not remain silent (חשה) in the lament psalms (see Pss 28:1; 35:22; 39:13 [Eng. 12]; 83:2 [Eng. 1]; 109:1), as in Isa 64:11 (Eng. 12). This petition addresses God's inactivity in time of distress. The petitioner is not looking for an audible response, but for an act of deliverance from enemies. This petition stands in stark contrast to God's promise found in 62:6–7 to take no rest (דמי; 2x) until Jerusalem is established.

---

25. See Pss 69:18 (Eng. 17); 102:3 (Eng. 2); and 143:7 for examples of סתר פנים used with ענה.

26. LeAnn Snow Flesher, "The Rhetorical Use of the Negative Petition in the Lament Psalms" (Ph.D. diss., Drew University, 1999), 55.

Finally, the conditions described above—God hiding, God's anger, God's silence—are frequently associated with a petition that God would turn (שׁוב). When God is hiding, angry, or silent, the sense is that God has turned away from the petitioner/community (i.e., God is shunning) and as a result adversity has come. Should God turn back (see Isa 63:17), deliverance and restoration are sure to be the result.

A review of the grammatical and semantic components of the communal lament of Isa 63:7–64:11 (Eng. 12) reveals language that accuses God of contributing to the rift between God and the people due to his hiddenness, declares the hiddenness and severity of punishment incomprehensible, resists a finality in the rift between God and his people, deems God's hiddenness as unjustified and God's punishment too severe, and ultimately calls God to account for his inactivity and shunning.

FATHER METAPHOR

Perhaps the most interesting and most convincing evidence for a connection between Lam 5 and Isa 62–66 is the appearance of the father metaphor (Isa 63:16; 64:7 [Eng. 8]; Lam 5:3). With regard to its use in Isaiah, Blenkinsopp has noted the reflection on covenant in Isa 63:8, "Surely they are my people," is an allusion to the formulaic "You will be my people and I will be your God" (Deut 29:12 [Eng. 13]; Lev 26:12; Jer 7:23), which would or could naturally move on a father-son axis. He also acknowledges that "the practice of addressing God as Father … developed significantly only in the post-destruction period."[27]

The use of the father image to refer to God is uncommon in the prophets,[28] and surprisingly we find it in Lam 5. In Isa 63:16 and 64:7 (Eng. 8) a significant part of the lamenter's argument is placed on the fact that Yhwh is their father. Commentators are not much help here, probably due to the infrequency of the use of the metaphor; but when compared to the use in Lam 5:3, the passage in Isa 63–64 makes more sense. In Lam 5 the community laments, "we have become orphans, fatherless." This particular expression of lament is found nowhere else in the Hebrew Bible.

---

27. Blenkinsopp, *Isaiah 56–66*, 260.

28. The metaphor of God as father is found only three times in Jeremiah (3:4, 19; 31:9), four times in Isaiah (8:4; 63:16 [2x]; 64:7 [Eng. 8]), and one time in Lamentations (5:3). Although the word *father* does not appear, one could also suggest the use of the parent metaphor (a mixture of father and mother images) in Hos 11.

If we presume the priority of Lam 5, and I believe Frederick Dobbs-Allsopp has given us warrant for that assumption,[29] and if we assume the voice(s) from Lam 5 and Isa 63:7–64:11 (Eng. 12) reflects the speech of a community that Daughter Zion represents, then the use of this metaphor in Isa 63:7–64:11 (Eng. 12) shows a shift in theological interpretation. In Lam 5 the emphasis is upon the idea that God has abandoned his people (i.e., "we have become orphans, fatherless," Lam 5:3), a metaphor that is ultimately followed up with a petition for restoration (v. 21) unless God has utterly rejected them (v. 22). The combination suggests a glimmer of hope. The language is accusatory—God has forgotten and forsaken for too long (v. 20)—yet the petition for restoration comes. The final verse suggests the community is not totally convinced God has deserted them forever, but the possibility looms. Thus the father metaphor is hyperbolic and rhetorical; it works in combination with the final petition (v. 21) and extreme expressions of rejection (v. 22) to heighten the implications and urgency of the current distress so as to persuade God to act.

In Isa 63:16, however, Daughter Zion states, "you are our father, though Abraham does not know us, and Israel does not acknowledge us, you, O LORD, are our father." There is no claim to orphanhood (to being fatherless) in Isa 63; instead we find a claim to being rejected by the community of Abraham/Israel. While the community continues to play the "father" card in 63:7–64:11 (Eng. 12) with its allusions to the covenant relationship, she now emphasizes her rejection by another group (Abraham/Israel) instead of her total rejection by God. We still find evidences of God's extreme discipline (64:8 [Eng. 9]) and hiddenness (64:6 [Eng. 7]), but the idea of total rejection is now related to those who come from Abraham/Israel. The word *father* is used three times in the lament of 63:7–64:11 (Eng. 12), and each time it is clearly asserted, "you are our father."

Given the rarity of the use of the God-as-father metaphor and the associations between Isa 62–64 and Lamentations outlined above, it is legitimate to suggest a dialogue between these two texts. However, the shift in emphasis from Lamentation's "we are ... fatherless" to Third Isaiah's "you are our father" raises a question about the nature of the community represented by each text. Do we have evidence of shifting theologies? Or are we seeing two different groups in dialogue with God? Thus far in

---

29. Frederick W. Dobbs-Allsopp, "Linguistic Evidence for the Date of Lamentations," *JANESCU* 26 (1998): 1–36.

this essay, following Mandolfo's lead, I have been addressing a conversation between two entities in Isa 62–64 and noting correspondences with Lam 5 as if the latter represents the same voice as that found in the lament of Isa 63:7–64:11 (Eng. 12). The distinctly different uses of the father metaphor in Isa 62–64 and Lam 5 suggests, however, two unique, but (perhaps) related groups. The determination of the identity of these groups is well beyond the bounds of this paper, but the possibility must be raised.

Renita Weems has helped us think about the significance of the father metaphor through her analysis of the use of female imagery in the prophets. Weems has noted that in ancient Hebrew culture part of the male's responsibility was to protect the sexual purity of the women in the household. Thus the males were obligated to protect all the women of their household—their wives, daughters, sisters, and even the widowed mothers. Male status and prestige could rise and fall according to a male's ability to protect the women in his household. Those men who were successful at this were honored, and those who were not were shamed.[30] This idea can easily be carried over to the entire household, so that the father is understood as protector and provider for all under his care.

Consequently, the focus on the covenant relationship between Israel and her God (Isa 63:7–9) coupled with the image of God as father work together to establish God's obligation to provide and protect. The language does not deny Israel's responsibility to be and remain obedient/faithful, as is evidenced by the confessions of sin (cf. 64:4–8 [Eng. 5–9]), but does highlight God's role in the covenant relationship.

The people have sinned and God has disciplined, but the duration of the discipline has gone on too long. The complaint is that for too long God the covenant maker, the father and redeemer from of old, has turned away, has hidden his face, and has shunned his people because of his anger. It has been a long time since the people have been under his care (63:19a). Because of the length of the discipline no one calls on God's name (64:6 [Eng. 7]), and so the negative petition appears: "do not be *exceedingly* [עַד־מְאֹד] angry, O LORD, do not remember iniquity *forever*" (64:8 [Eng. 9]; see Lam 5:22). Juxtaposed to this negative petition is a reminder, introduced by the demonstrative adverb הֵן, "Behold! We are all your people."[31] This is followed by a description of Zion and her

---

30. Renita Weems, *Battered Love: Marriage Sex and Violence in the Hebrew Prophets* (Minneapolis: Fortress, 1995), 42–43.

31. The negative petitions of 64:8 (Eng. 9) are surrounded on either side by this

temple in desolation (Isa 64:9–10 [Eng. 10–11]). The prayer concludes with a petition (64:11 [Eng. 12]), really a plea, embedded with the accusatory language of the major complaint, "after all this [הַעַל־אֵלֶּה] will you restrain yourself, O Lord, will you keep silent [תֶחֱשֶׁה] from answering [עֲנָה] exceedingly [עַד־מְאֹד]?" The use of עַד־מְאֹד seems a bit unusual here, but connects this final plea with the earlier negative petition against God being exceedingly angry (64:8 [Eng. 9]); its use is paralleled in Lam 5:22, "Restore us … unless you have utterly rejected us, and are angry with us beyond measure [עַד־מְאֹד]."

Remnant Theology

About fifty years ago Westermann concluded that the genre of biblical lament evolved into petitionary prayer after the exile. Specifically he stated that the lament, whose central nerve in the early period had been the complaint against God, receded into the background until it was finally reduced to a simple petition, while the complaint against God fell altogether silent. In addition he noted that the prevailing prayer in postexilic Israel arose out of praise (thanksgiving) and petition, and the lament remained silent—even in the New Testament.[32]

---

reminder; note also in v. 7 (Eng. 8) God is reminded that he is father and potter and all the people are the clay, the work of his hand.

32. Claus Westermann, *Praise and Lament in the Psalms* (trans. Keith R. Crim and Richard N. Soulen; Atlanta: John Knox, 1981), 213; trans. of *Lob und Klage in den Psalmen* (5th ed.; Göttingen: Vandenhoeck & Ruprecht, 1977). This paper is the by-product of a journey initially born out of a fundamental disagreement with Westermann's conclusion on the silencing of the prayer of lament in the Hebrew Bible. This disagreement has been tempered by engagement with the numerous papers presented throughout the three years of Consultation on Penitential Prayer at the national SBL meetings (2003–2005), now published as Mark J. Boda, Daniel K. Falk, and Rodney Werline, eds., *Seeking the Favor of God* (3 vols.; SBLEJL 21–23; Atlanta: Society of Biblical Literature, 2006–2008). After careful study of the materials presented at these meetings it has become clear that the postexilic writings do reveal a significant theological shift. Yet Westermann's claim has not been completely substantiated, for there are several evidences of "traditional" use of lament, albeit with some shifts in theological undertones, to be found late, after the exile and throughout the Second Temple era. Cf., e.g., Pss 51 and 89, each of which is a response to the destruction of Jerusalem and her temple. Psalm 51 is clearly a penitential prayer, but Ps 89 a God-lament. Broyles has defined "God-lament" as an expression of complaint regarding God's disposition or action, which the psalmists in their distress interpret as being indifferent or hostile

Samuel Balentine has noted that it was Westermann's "survey of the history of lament that provided the base line for the assessment of penitential prayers for approximately the next fifty years."[33] While Westermann did not speak of the rise of penitential prayer in place of lament (only petitionary prayer), his conclusions, as stated above, have become the starting point for many who work in the area of penitential prayer.

In 2005 the SBL Penitential Prayer Consultation participated in a joint session with the Biblical Hebrew Poetry group in which papers on the poetics of lamentation in the prophets and the rhetoric of lamentation in the book of Judith were presented, engaged, and discussed by participants from both groups. From this cross-pollination of ideas a preliminary categorization of theological tendencies between the two genres has been determined. Some of the theological observations most broadly embraced include:

Penitential Prayers	Biblical Laments
God is always righteous	God frequently the culpable party
Humans are the covenant breakers	Humans are frequently presented as innocent
Enemies are a tool of God's punishment	Enemies can be the guilty party
God's wrath brings punishment	God's wrath brings punishment
Punishment is shameful	Punishment is shameful
Need: God's wrath to shift to pity	Need: God's wrath to shift to pity
Confession averts God's wrath	Complaint + petition avert God's wrath[34]

(*Conflict of Faith*, 40). See also LeAnn Snow Flesher, "The Use of Female Imagery and Lamentation in the Book of Judith: Penitential Prayer or Petition for Obligatory Action?" in *The Development of Penitential Prayer in Second Temple Judaism* (vol. 2 of Boda et al., *Seeking the Favor of God*; SBLEJL 22; Atlanta: Society of Biblical Literature, 2007), 83–104, for an example of the "traditional" use of lament in Jdt 9.

33. Samuel Balentine, "I Was Ready to Be Sought by Those Who Did Not Ask," in Boda et al., *Origins of Penitential Prayer*, 3–6.

34. In the canonical laments the psalmist delivers either declarations of innocence, accusations that the punishment is too severe for the crime, or complaints that the punishment has gone on too long. These are coupled with the petitions to build a rhetorical argument in an attempt to get God to act on their behalf; or, to state it another way, in an attempt to assuage God's wrath and appeal to God's sympathies.

A comparative analysis of these genres beyond a mere stating of these general theologies is well beyond the scope of this paper except as it applies to Isa 63:7–65:25, to which we now turn. According to the theology of penitential prayers, God is always righteous and humans are the covenant breakers, whereas in the laments of the Psalter, God is frequently accused of being the culpable party and humans are frequently presented as innocent. Both penitential prayers and laments sought to avert God's wrath and turn God's heart to pity. The attempt to move the heart of God occurred through penitential prayer by means of confession of sin, and through lament by means of complaint coupled with petition(s). For the latter, the complaint frequently consisted of declaration of innocence (or a complaint of the inexplicable nature of the distress), a complaint that the punishment is too severe, and/or a complaint that the punishment has gone on too long. While the author of Isa 63:7–64:11 (Eng. 12) at no point suggests the community is innocent, he does ask the accusatory question "why": "Why … do you make us stray from your ways … and harden our hearts?" Given the statement concerning duration of time in 63:19a, the negative petitions in 64:8 (Eng. 9), and the plea in 64:11 (Eng. 12), this complaint seems to be connected to the severity and the duration of the distress/discipline.

Meanwhile, there is an implicit hope that the petitioner's complaint will be rectified given the negative petitions of 64:8 (Eng. 9) that ward off "God's exceedingly angry response that could go on forever." While the lament of Isa 63–64 clearly addresses the culpability of the people, it also establishes the culpability of God for a disciplinary response that is too extreme and has gone on too long.

ISAIAH 62–66 AS A LITERARY UNIT

Many scholars have noted the abrupt conclusion to the communal lament of 63:7–64:11 (Eng. 12). Most communal laments end with a statement of hope or confidence or an assurance of being heard, followed by a vow to praise once God has brought resolution. This lament leaves the reader hanging with a concluding complaint infused with an implicit petition.

In addition, there is a tendency to conclude that 63:7–64:11 (Eng. 12) represents the whole community as is noted or emphasized by the word כלנו found at the close of 64:7 and 9 (Eng. 8, 10).[35] The reference in 63:16 to

---

35. See, e.g., Oswalt, *Isaiah 40–66*, 629–30; and Paul Hanson, *Isaiah 40–66* (IBC;

the community having been rejected by Abraham and Israel points, however, to a distinct group that has been separated off from their ancestors.

As we leave the lament of Isa 63:7–64:11 (Eng. 12) and enter Isa 65–66, we experience yet another shift in voice, back to God. It has long been noted that Isa 65–66, with its emphasis on "my servant, ... but you ..." (e.g., 65:13–14), exhibits remnant theology. Given this shift in voice, genre, and theological perspective, scholars have tended to read the communal lament of 63:7–64:11 (Eng. 12) as separate from Isa 65–66, while noting the numerous connections between Isa 65 and 66.

Given the commitment to read dialogically and the connections that have surfaced between Isa 62–64 and Lam 5 as outlined above, as well as the manner in which these conclusions conflict with the post-destruction theology of God's righteous (i.e., inculpable) nature, I would like to suggest a rhetorical dependency between the communal God(thou)-lament of Isa 63:7–64:11 (Eng. 12) and the God-response found in Isa 65–66.

Using as a model Robert Alter's work on Gen 38 as an example of literary art,[36] one can find so many correspondences of language between chapters in Isa 62–66 that time and space do not allow for a full discussion. So I will limit my observations and comments to the comparison of language between the God(thou)-lament discussed in 63:7–64:11 (Eng. 12), Lam 5, and Isa 65 as outlined in the table below.

Evidence of God(thou)-Lament in Isa 63:7–64:11 (Eng. 12)	Corresponding Language in	
	Isa 65	Lam 5
Grammatical		
2nd-person singular forms		
God(thou)-laments (63:17; 64:4, 6 [Eng. 5, 7])		
Accusatory questions (63:15, 17; 64:11 [Eng. 12])		Accusatory questions (5:20)
Negative Petitions (64:8 [Eng. 9])		

Louisville: Westminster John Knox, 1995), 235–40, although Hanson does understand 63:16 as an alienation from kin.

36. Robert Alter, *The Art of Biblical Narrative* (New York: Basic Books, 1981), 3–5.

Semantic

סתר פני hide the face (64:6 [Eng. 7])	סתר 65:3; פני 65:16	נבט look (5:1)
ענה answer (64:11 [Eng. 12]	65:12, 24	
קצף anger (64:4, 8 [Eng. 5, 9])	עשן באפי 65:5	קצף anger (5:22)
זכר remember (64:8 [Eng. 9])	65:17	זכר remember (5:1)
חשה be silent (64:11 [Eng. 12])	65:6	
שוב turn (63:17)	66:15	שוב return (5:22)
עד forever (64:8 [Eng. 9])	עדי־עד 65:18	עולם forever (5:19)
עד־מאד exceedingly (64:8, 11 [Eng. 9, 12])	תמיד 65:3	עד־מאד (5:22) exceedingly/ beyond measure

Idiom

ענה with סתר פנים

Metaphor

אב father (63:16 [2x]; 64:7 [Eng. 8])	אב father (5:3)

Every word studied in 63:7–64:11 (Eng. 12) has a counterpart in Isa 65; the two texts function as a call and response; in 63:7–64:11 (Eng. 12) the community cries out to God, and in Isa 65 God responds. In 64:6 (Eng. 7) God is accused of hiding his face (פנים סתר) with the result that "no one calls on his name." In 65:3 God accuses the people of provoking him to his face continually (פני) by "sacrificing in gardens and burning incense on bricks." In 65:1 God claims he "was ready to be sought out by those who did not ask … to be found by those who did not seek." In other words, the people claim they did not call out to God (specifically Yhwh) because God had turned away from them; God was nowhere to be found. Conversely, Yhwh retorts by stating he was always present, waiting to be called upon, but instead the people were worshiping other gods right in front of his face.

In 65:16 God announces the former troubles will be forgotten (a response to the negative petition that God not remember sin forever, 64:8 [Eng. 9]) and hidden (סתר) from his sight, which can be understood as a variation on פנים סתר. Instead of God hiding, the sins of the people will be hidden. In 65:17 God is about to create new heavens and a new earth and the former things will not be remembered (זכר), after which the people are told to be glad and rejoice forever (עדי־עד, forever and ever, 65:18) at what God is creating. Just as God was petitioned to not remember iniquity forever (עד; 64:8 [Eng. 9]), the people are told to be glad and rejoice forever and ever (עדי־עד; 65:18). The promises of God are given only to a select group referred to as "my chosen and my servants" (65:9). According to God, "My servants shall eat, but you shall be hungry; my servants shall drink, but you shall be thirsty; my servants shall rejoice, but you shall be put to shame" (65:13). Who does the "you" refer to? Third Isaiah is continuing the servant language found in Second Isaiah (see 54:17). Those who are reconciled to God are deemed "my servants," while those who are not becoming reconciled are being addressed directly, thus the use of the second-person pronoun. The God speech of Isa 65–66 is responding directly to the accusations made in the communal lament of 63:7–64:11 (Eng. 12). Daughter Zion calls on God to not be exceedingly angry (עד־מאד; 64:8 [Eng. 9]) to which God replies: you are "a people who provoke me to my face continually" (תמיד; 65:3).

Chapters 65–66 are famous for their remnant theology, which is emphasized by who does and does not answer God (65:12; "when I called you did not answer, when I spoke you did not listen"), who God will answer (65:24; "before they call I will answer, while they are yet speaking I will hear"), and how God will answer (65:6; "I will not keep silent [חשה], but will repay … I will indeed repay their iniquities and their ancestors' iniquities"). God will repay those who are smoke in God's nostrils (באפי עשן; a parallel expression for קצף). The scales have been weighted in favor of the group called "my servants." Daughter Zion is told she did not answer when called (65:12), God says of "my servants": "before they call I will answer" (65:24). God will repay the iniquities of Daughter Zion and her ancestors (65:6), but will hide the sins of "my servants" (65:16).

Those who have called out to God saying, "You are our father, although Abraham does not know us and Israel does not acknowledge us," are being discarded. Those who accused God of a discipline that was too long and too severe (64:8, 11 [Eng. 9, 12]) will be destined to the sword, forced to bow down to the slaughter (65:12). Those who confronted God's hiddenness (63:17, 19 [Eng. 64:1]; 64:4 [Eng. 5]) have been told: "I was ready to be sought out.... I said, 'Here I am, here I am.... I held out my hands all day long'" (65:1–2).

I will stop here, as I have exhausted the correspondences to the language of communal lament listed thus far, but I could go on—even moving into Isa 66. Suffice it to say, Isa 65–66 responds to the complaints of 63:7–64:11 (Eng. 12) with remnant theology. No longer will "my servants" constitute those born into Israel, but those who are obedient and faithful. Thus the problem of divine culpability described in 63:7–64:11 (Eng. 12) has been resolved. God no longer shuns Israel; rather God redefines her. Humans are culpable, but not all of them—there is a faithful remnant. God is righteous and attentive; the covenant maker remains faithful to the promise, at least partially. God's heart has been turned away from anger to pity for the "faithful remnant," but God's anger still burns for the culpable human covenant breakers. In any event, the post-destruction theology of a righteous, inculpable God has been sustained, but only after Daughter Zion's communal God(thou)-lament has been addressed. Thus, logically, there is a rhetorical dependency between chapters in Isa 62–66, and resolution comes in the shift from communal to faithful remnant.

If we read with God or "my servants," as we have been taught to do, then all is well. Restoration and resolution have come. If we choose to follow our postmodern ideals of inclusivity, and choose ethically to continue to include the community that Daughter Zion represents in the conversation, then we have a problem. For the voice that called to God saying, "You are our father," also declared, "Abraham does not know us and Israel does not acknowledge us." In other words, they are the voice of the "other." The same voice has declared that God was nowhere to be found. If Dobbs-Allsopp is correct in determining that the book of Lamentations consists of writings from the community that was left behind after the destruction of Jerusalem in 587/586 B.C.E., then the voice of Daughter Zion that Mandolfo has tracked in her study represents that community. She was a community left to live within the devastation of the ruins of Jerusalem with no means or hope for reconstructing what had been lost and destroyed. Is it any wonder she proclaims that God could not be found?

Several decades ago Paul Hanson proposed the theory that the "my servant"–"but you" language found in Isa 65–66 (and other parts of Second and Third Isaiah as well) reflects the struggle between two communities that he named the Hierocrats and the Visionaries. The first of these represented the elite group that had been taken into exile and was now returning to rebuild Jerusalem and its cult; the second represented the group that had been left behind.[37] His purposes for delineating these two groups revolved around the rise of biblical apocalypticism and its literature. Although Hanson's conclusions were critiqued as too simplistic and agenda driven, his insight into the voices found in Second and Third Isaiah and specifically Isa 65–66 has proven helpful. In essence he was reading these texts dialogically. He suggested the Visionaries represented the group from which the apocalyptic literature came and that in the fifty-year period between the destruction of Jerusalem and the edict from Cyrus the two communities, separated by time and space, developed very differently and consequently had very different visions for a rebuilt Jerusalem and temple cult. I am not so interested in deciphering what those differences may have been, only that differences would have naturally existed. This leads me to a concluding question: Is the voice of the community that laments in 63:7–64:11 (Eng. 12), the community that Daughter Zion represents, the voice of a faithless remnant? Or does she represent a faith-filled community that understood God in new and different ways, with the result that she was ostracized by an elitist, dominant group?

37. Paul Hanson, *The Dawn of Apocalyptic: The Historical and Sociological Roots of Jewish Apocalyptic Eschatology* (rev. ed.; Philadelphia: Fortress, 1979), 134–208.

THE DAUGHTER'S JOY

Mark J. Boda

Carleen Mandolfo's recent work on Daughter Zion[1] has highlighted the painful condition and expression of this key literary figure throughout the Hebrew Bible and the tension between her voice in the laments and God's voice in the prophets.[2] The work was largely focused on the more negative forms of expression, that is, on Daughter Zion's embittered cry of disorientation. Largely absent from her treatment, however, are those texts that suggest a more positive stance for Daughter Zion and especially those addresses to Daughter Zion in the Book of the Twelve.[3] Thus in this present chapter I take as my point of departure three texts that appeal to Daughter Zion at the close of the Book of the Twelve and that call her to a different response than the bitter lament championed by Mandolfo. I will suggest their place within a typology of speech forms associated with Daughter Zion, highlight the striking absence of some of these forms in relation to Zion, and finally reflect on the appropriation of the voice of Daughter Zion in texts responding to the fall of Jerusalem.

---

1. See the vigorous debate over the translation of the phrase בת־ציון between Michael H. Floyd, "Welcome Back, Daughter of Zion!" *CBQ* 70 (2008): 484–504; and J. Andrew Dearman, "Daughter Zion and Her Place in God's Household," *HBT* 31 (2009): 144–59. See Floyd's essay in the present volume, "The Daughter of Zion Goes Fishing in Heaven." For the sake of dialogue with Mandolfo and others, I will use the phrase "Daughter Zion," although I find Floyd's arguments compelling.

2. Carleen Mandolfo, *Daughter Zion Talks Back to the Prophets: A Dialogic Theology of the Book of Lamentations* (SemeiaSt 58; Atlanta: Society of Biblical Literature, 2007).

3. Mandolfo does deal with Isa 54 in detail in her monograph, but does not focus on the invitation to joy; see ibid., 115–18.

THE SUMMONS TO JOY IN THE HEBREW BIBLE

DAUGHTER ZION AND THE SUMMONS TO JOY IN THE BOOK OF THE TWELVE

Daughter Zion does not play a significant role in the Book of the Twelve as a collection, an observation that may explain why this prophetic collection was not treated in detail in Mandolfo's volume. Some have suggested that (Daughter) Zion is the understood subject of the feminine singular imperative in Joel 1:8, a call to "wail like a virgin girded with sackcloth for the bridegroom of her youth,"[4] but there is no evidence in the immediate context to confirm this. Daughter Zion is explicitly mentioned in Mic 4:6–13, referred to in the phrase "hill of the Daughter Zion" in 4:8, and then by name in 4:10, 13. These references are a mixture of both judgment and salvation. On the one side they promise to the "hill of Daughter Zion" that it will recover its former dominion and kingdom (4:8), and, in an interesting metaphorical twist, to "Daughter Jerusalem" that she will even become a powerful ox that threshes the nations to gather in their wealth (4:13). On the other side they call Daughter Zion to experience her judgment, writhing as a woman in the agony of childbirth (4:10). Beyond these verses in one pericope in Micah, there are no other explicit references to Zion, until the final section of the collection, where three texts address Daughter Zion directly, in each case calling her to an exclusively positive response.

Zephaniah 3:14–15

רני בת־ציון הריעו ישראל שמחי ועלזי בכל־לב בת ירושלם:
הסיר יהוה משפטיך פנה איבך מלך ישראל יהוה בקרבך לא־תיראי
רע עוד:

Shout joyfully, O Daughter Zion, shout triumphantly, O Israel. Be glad and exult wholeheartedly, O Daughter Jerusalem. Yahweh has removed the judgments against you. He has removed your

---

4. E.g., Ronald Simkins, *Yahweh's Activity in History and Nature in the Book of Joel* (ANETS 10; Lewiston, N.Y.: Mellen, 1991), 131; Raymond B. Dillard, "Joel," in *Hosea, Joel, and Amos* (vol. 1 of *The Minor Prophets: An Exegetical and Expositional Commentary*; ed. Thomas Edward McComiskey; Grand Rapids: Baker, 1992), 230–313, here 261; with thanks to Joel Barker.

enemies. The King of Israel, Yahweh, is in your midst. Do not fear disaster again.

Zephaniah 3:14–15 is addressed to Daughter Zion/Daughter Jerusalem, employing the feminine singular imperatives of the roots רנן (shout joyfully), רוע hiphil (shout triumphantly), שמח (be glad), and עלז (exult). Verse 15 provides the motivation or reason for this expected rejoicing, identifying it as Yahweh's removal of judgment against the addressee, as well as the removal of her enemies. In addition, the presence of King Yahweh in her midst prompts such shouts of joy. The following verses identify this Yahweh in their midst as "a victorious warrior" who will reciprocate with his own shouts of joy: rejoicing (שיש) with gladness (שמחה) and rejoicing (גיל) with a joyful shout (רנה; v. 17).

Zechariah 2:14 (Eng. 10)

רני ושמחי בת־ציון כי הנני־בא ושכנתי בתוכך נאם־יהוה

Shout joyfully and be glad, Daughter Zion, because, take note, I am about to come and I will dwell in your midst, declaration of Yahweh.

In this prophetic piece in Zech 2:14 (Eng. 10), the addressee is once again Daughter Zion, and feminine singular imperatives from the roots רנן (shout joyfully) and שמח (be glad) are employed. Again the motivation for the rejoicing follows the exhortation, but this time the reason clause is introduced by the particle כי followed by the attention particle הנה, and the reason is identified as the impending appearance of Yahweh and his promise to dwell in the midst of the community. The preceding section (2:10–13 [Eng. 6–9]) describes Yahweh's violent retribution against the nations that plundered and abused his people.

Zechariah 9:9–10

גילי מאד בת־ציון הריעי בת ירושלם הנה מלכך יבוא לך צדיק ונושע
הוא עני ורכב על־חמור ועל־עיר בן־אתנות: והכרתי־רכב מאפרים
וסוס מירושלם ונכרתה קשת מלחמה ודבר שלום לגוים ומשלו מים
עד־ים ומנהר עד־אפסי־ארץ:

Rejoice greatly, O Daughter Zion, shout triumphantly, O Daughter Jerusalem. Take note, your king is coming to you, righteous and saved is he, humble and riding on a donkey, on a colt, the foal of a donkey. I will cut off the chariot from Ephraim, and the horse from Jerusalem, and the war bow will be cut off, and he will speak peace to the nations and his rule will be from sea to sea, and from the River to the ends of the earth.

The addressee in Zech 9:9–10 is the same Daughter Zion/Daughter Jerusalem encountered in Zeph 3, and the feminine singular imperatives are drawn from the roots גיל (rejoice) and רוע hiphil (shout triumphantly). As in Zeph 3:14–15, the particle כי does not introduce the reason clause, but as in Zech 2:14 (Eng. 10) the particle הנה does appear. The motivation for the joyous response of Daughter Zion is the return of Jerusalem's king and Yahweh's enforcement of a universal peace among the nations of the world. Underlying these motivations appears to be the march of Yahweh as Divine Warrior down the Levant that ends with Yahweh encamped around his temple in Jerusalem (9:1–8). Jerusalem's king emerges as one "saved," evidently by Yahweh's maneuvers in the previous verses. War is also a key theme in the verses following Zech 9:9–10 that depict Judah, Ephraim, and Zion in a war in which Yahweh will act on their behalf (vv. 13–15).

Conclusion

These three passages appear to reflect a rhetorical trend in the final phase of the Book of the Twelve, that is, the section comprising Haggai–Malachi.[5] With the conclusion of Zephaniah there is a shift in the rhetoric of the Book of the Twelve, from the dominating tone of judgment to the dominating tone of salvation.[6] For those responsible for this collection, Daughter Zion emerges as the key figure commissioned to announce this new era of salvation.[7]

---

5. For the shape, cohesion, and history of this subcollection within the Book of the Twelve, see Mark J. Boda, "Messengers of Hope in Haggai–Malachi," *JSOT* 32 (2007): 113–31.

6. See Paul R. House, *The Unity of the Twelve* (BLS 27; Sheffield: Almond, 1990), although it is important to note that in this final phase the dominance of salvation shifts after Zech 9 back to judgment.

7. Strikingly similar to her expected role in Isa 40–55; see Isa 40:9–11; cf.

These three passages highlight a particular form that is not unique to the Book of the Twelve but can be discerned in other sections of the Hebrew Bible. The form was identified long ago by Frank Crüsemann as the *Aufruf zur Freude* (summons to joy), which, he argued, consisted of three basic elements: (a) imperative address to an audience (city, land) personified as a woman; (b) vocabulary drawn from the semantic range of celebratory shouts (רוע‎, רנן‎, גיל‎); and (c) a clause that delineates the reason for rejoicing (following the style of the prophetic oracle of salvation rather than a psalm).[8] According to Crüsemann the original setting of this *Aufruf zur Freude* was in the sexual/fertility cult;[9] hence he agrees with

---

Annemarieke van der Woude, "Can Zion Do without the Servant in Isaiah 40–55?" *CTJ* 39 (2004): 109–16. See further discussion on Isa 54:1 below.

8. Frank Crüsemann, *Studien zur Formgeschichte von Hymnus und Danklied in Israel* (WMANT 32; Neukirchen-Vluyn: Neukirchener Verlag, 1969), 55–65. Some have suggested that Qoh 11:8–10 is in this form tradition; cf. Robert Gordis, *Koheleth: The Man and His World* (3rd ed.; New York: Schocken, 1968), 334–35; Norbert Lohfink, *Kohelet* (NEchtB 1; Würzburg: Echter, 1980), 81; J. A. Loader, *Ecclesiastes* (Text and Interpretation; Grand Rapids: Eerdmans, 1986), 130; James L. Crenshaw, *Ecclesiastes: A Commentary* (OTL; Philadelphia: Westminster, 1987), 183; R. Norman Whybray, *Ecclesiastes* (NCB; Grand Rapids: Eerdmans, 1989), 161; Ludger Schwienhorst-Schönberger, *"Nicht im Menschen gründet das Glück" (Koh 2,24): Kohelet im Spannungsfeld jüdischer Weisheit und hellenistischer Philosophie* (2nd ed.; HBS 2; Freiburg: Herder, 1996), 224–26; Alexander A. Fischer, *Skepsis oder Furcht Gottes? Studien zur Komposition und Theologie des Buches Kohelet* (BZAW 247; Berlin: de Gruyter, 1997), 156–57; cf. Werner Andre Lategan, "The Theological Dialect of Creation and Death in Hebrew Bible Wisdom Traditions" (Ph.D. diss., Rijksuniversiteit Groningen, 2009). Since the larger complex of 11:7–12:7 is concerned with youth and old age, life and death, it may be that there is a contrast motif here between the joy of life and the mourning of death that plays on the *Aufruf zur Freude* form (see further below). However, the motif of joy appears throughout Qohelet (e.g., 3:12–13, 22; 5:17–19; 8:15; 9:7–10); cf. R. Norman Whybray, "Qoheleth, Preacher of Joy," *JSOT* 23 (1982): 87–98; Shannon Burkes, *Death in Qoheleth and Egyptian Biographies of the Late Period* (SBLDS 170; Atlanta: Society of Biblical Literature, 1999), 72–74; and in the other cases does not reflect the *Aufruf zur Freude* tradition.

9. Crüsemann, *Hymnus und Danklied*, 63–65, in conversation especially with the research of Paul Humbert, "'Laetari et exultare' dans le vocabulaire religieux de l'Ancien Testament," *RHPR* 22 (1942): 185–214; repr. in Humbert, *Opuscules d'un Hébraïsant* (Neuchâtel: Secrétariat de l'Université, 1958), 119–45. See Gary A. Anderson, *A Time to Mourn, a Time to Dance: The Expression of Grief and Joy in Israelite Religion* (University Park: Pennsylvania State University Press, 1991), 38, for a critique of Humbert.

Westermann that it related to the oracle of salvation responding to the "uralte Klage der kinderlosen Frau,"[10] a situation exemplified in a passage like Gen 25:21 (Rebekah). It was only later that it developed into the forms found in the prophetic books, although reminiscences of the connections to the sexual/fertility cult can be discerned even there.

Other texts, however, bear striking similarities to the *Aufruf zur Freude*. At several points in the psalmic and prophetic literature, one finds invitations to the elements of creation to rejoice using the same range of terms associated with the *Aufruf zur Freude*. So, for instance, in Isa 49:13 the heavens are called to shout for joy (רנן, masc. pl.), the earth to rejoice (גיל, fem. sg.), and the mountains to break forth (פצח, masc. pl.) with joyful shouting (רנה).[11] Standing out from this list of elements of creation in Isa 49:13 is the "earth" (ארץ), a term similar to the "land" (אדמה), which, according to Crüsemann, is one of two key referents for the personifications in the *Aufruf zur Freude*. Other texts akin to Isa 49:13 include 1 Chr 16:31; Pss 65:9, 14 (Eng. 8, 13); 89:13 (Eng. 12); 96:11; 97:1; 98:6; Isa 35:1; 44:23; 49:13; and Jer 51:48. It appears that the joyous response of the land is related to a larger phenomenon in the Hebrew Bible in which elements in creation are called to rejoice.[12] Furthermore, at times one finds the use of this vocabulary (usually indicative, e.g., Isa 14:7; 24:14; 35:6; 65:14; but also imperative forms, e.g., 42:10–13) in relation to a broader audience. Can one, though, see any trends within the examples of *Aufruf zur Freude*

---

10. Claus Westermann, *Das Buch Jesaja, Kapitel 40–66* (ATD 19; Göttingen: Vandenhoeck & Ruprecht, 1966), 219.

11. Interesting is that this comes just prior to Zion's lament in 49:14 to which the later *Aufruf zur Freude* of 54:1 is related.

12. That the call to creation may be related to the setting I will suggest below (that of response to battle); see how Isa 49:13 does speak of the rejoicing that follows mourning because of the reference to "comfort." For the role of comfort as key to the shift from mourning to joy see Anderson, *Time to Mourn*, 84–86; cf. Xuan Huong Thi Pham, *Mourning in the Ancient Near East and the Hebrew Bible* (JSOTSup 302; Sheffield: Sheffield Academic Press, 1999); Saul M. Olyan, *Biblical Mourning: Ritual and Social Dimensions* (Oxford: Oxford University Press, 2004), 46–49. For the relationship between creation and mourning rites, see Katherine M. Hayes, *The Earth Mourns: Prophetic Metaphor and Oral Aesthetic* (SBLABib 8; Atlanta: Society of Biblical Literature, 2002); idem, "When None Repents, Earth Laments: The Chorus of Lament in Jeremiah and Joel," in *The Origin of Penitential Prayer in Second Temple Judaism* (vol. 1 of *Seeking the Favor of God*; ed. Mark J. Boda, Daniel K. Falk, and Rodney A. Werline; SBLEJL 21; Atlanta: Society of Biblical Literature, 2006), 119–43.

related to female characters like Daughter Zion? A closer look at these texts reveals striking similarities.

THE SUMMONS TO JOY

Isaiah 12:6

צהלי ורני יושבת ציון כי־גדול בקרבך קדוש ישראל

Cry out and shout joyfully, O female inhabitant of Zion, for great in your midst is the Holy One of Israel.

This *Aufruf zur Freude* begins with two feminine singular imperatives based on the roots צהל and רנן, followed by a feminine singular vocative based on ישב in construct with ציון. This "inhabitant" must refer to a female figure who lives within Zion, since Zion is a geographical location. The second clause, introduced by כי, identifies the reason for this joy as the presence of the Holy One of Israel (קדוש ישראל) in her midst (בקרבך).

This call to praise is the last of a series of future scenarios in Isa 12 that expect a response of thanksgiving/praise due to actions performed by Yahweh. The first two (vv. 1–2, 3–5) use a formula that begins with a similar description of the future response of the people, the first describing the response of an individual (ואמרת ביום ההוא, v. 1a; see first common singular verbs that follow in vv. 1b–2), and the second, the response of the community as a whole ("You will draw water joyfully from the springs of salvation, and you will say in that day [ואמרתם ביום ההוא]," vv. 3–4a).[13] The declarations proper in both scenarios (vv. 1b–2, 4b–5) begin with a hiphil form of the root ידה. The declaration in the first scenario is in the indicative mood, declaring thanksgiving to Yahweh directly ("I will give

<hr />

13. While Otto Kaiser (*Isaiah 1–12: A Commentary* [trans. John Bowden; 2nd ed.; OTL; Philadelphia: Westminster, 1983], 270), Hans Wildberger (*Isaiah 1–12* [trans. Thomas H. Trapp; CC; Minneapolis: Fortress, 1991], 501), and Walter Brueggemann (*Isaiah* [Westminster Bible Companion; Louisville: Westminster John Knox, 1998], 109) divide this section into vv. 1–3 and 4–6, the distinction between the first/second-person singular (vv. 1–2), first/second-person plural (vv. 3–5), and feminine singular (v. 6) divides the section into three portions; cf. Marvin A. Sweeney, *Isaiah 1–39, with an Introduction to Prophetic Literature* (FOTL 16; Grand Rapids: Eerdmans, 1996), 198; John Oswalt, *The Book of Isaiah, Chapters 1–39* (NICOT; Grand Rapids: Eerdmans, 1986), 294, although these last two do not separate v. 6 from vv. 3–5.

thanks to you, O Yahweh") with a reason clause ("for [כי] although you were angry with me, your anger is turned away, and you comfort me," v. 1b) followed by a testimony about God's salvation ("Take note, God is my salvation, I will trust and not be afraid; because my strength and my song is Yah, Yahweh, he has become my salvation," v. 2). The declaration in the second scenario begins with the masculine plural hiphil imperatival form of the root ידה, which introduces a series of masculine plural imperatival forms (call [קראו], make known [הדיעו], cause to remember [הזכירו], sing praise [זמרו]), followed by a reason clause ("for [כי] a glorious thing he has done that is known in all the earth"). Verse 6 clearly represents a third rhetorical unit, as the feminine singular subject of the verbs contrasts with the masculine singular referent in the first scenario and the masculine plural referents in the second scenario.

The first scenario (vv. 1–2) praises God for turning his anger away (v. 1), comforting (v. 1) and saving (v. 2) the worshiper, while the second scenario (vv. 3–5) praises God for a glorious deed that God has done (v. 5). The third unit (v. 6) is motivated by the greatness of the presence of God in the worshiper's midst.

These three units function as a literary conclusion to this section of Isaiah.[14] Chapter 13 opens up a new literary unit of the book, one that contains a series of oracles against the nations (chs. 13–23). These praise units in Isa 12 follow Isa 11, which predicts a great victory for Israel in the future over the nations that is accomplished by Yahweh and will result in the return of a remnant (see esp. 11:11–16). Isaiah 12:6 thus gives voice to the representative female inhabitant of Zion who is to rejoice in that future day when the victorious warrior has returned from battle.

Isaiah 54:1

רני עקרה לא ילדה פצחי רנה וצהלי לא־חלה כי־רבים בני־שוממה
מבני בעולה אמר יהוה

Shout joyfully, O barren one, you who has not given birth. Burst forth with a joyful shout and cry out, you who has not experi-

---

14. See R. E. Clements, *Isaiah 1–39* (NCB; Grand Rapids: Eerdmans, 1980), 128; Oswalt, *Isaiah 1–39*, 291; Brueggemann, *Isaiah*, 109; Peter D. Quinn-Miscall, *Isaiah* (2nd ed.; Readings: A New Biblical Commentary; Sheffield: Sheffield Phoenix, 2006), 59.

enced labor, because greater are the sons of the desolate one than the sons of the married one, says Yahweh.

Once again a female figure is commanded to shout joyfully, using feminine singular imperatives (רנן, פצח + רנה, צהל). This female is identified only as "the barren one who did not give birth" (עקרה לא ילדה) and as "the one who has not experienced labor" (לא־חלה). The reason clause is introduced by the particle כי and founds the joyful response of the barren woman on the fact that she has more sons than the married woman. The string of imperatives continues into verse 2 as the female addressee is told also to prepare for an influx of children by expanding the size of her dwellings, and also into verse 4 as she is told not to feel fear or humiliation.

Beyond the more generic terms in verse 1, this female figure is never identified in this passage, but the broader context of Isa 40–55 suggests it is the city Zion.[15] In particular, Isa 54 brings to a close the prophetic message responding to the cry of Zion in 49:14.[16] The immediate response in 49:15–26 speaks to the issue of lack of children, describing the situation as that of a woman whose children have died (49:20, 21). Although also envisioning a woman without children, Isa 54 moves in a slightly different direction, describing the woman as one who has never borne children. The prophet goes on to speak of this in terms of shame and humiliation in verse 4, a condition that can be traced back to her youth, which is identified as "the reproach of your widowhood." The term used here for widowhood, אלמנות, appears elsewhere in the Hebrew Bible only in reference to the state of Tamar in Gen 38:14, 19, and that of the ten concubines of David who David refused to touch after Absalom's revolt (2 Sam 20:3).

---

15. See further R. Norman Whybray, *Isaiah 40–66* (NCB; repr., Grand Rapids: Eerdmans, 1981), 184; Katheryn Pfisterer Darr, *Isaiah's Vision and the Family of God* (Literary Currents in Biblical Interpretation; Louisville: Westminster John Knox, 1994), 177; Patricia Tull Willey, *Remember the Former Things: The Recollection of Previous Texts in Second Isaiah* (SBLDS 161; Atlanta: Scholars Press, 1997), 231–32. This does not deny the allusion here to the early matriarchs of Israel, Sarah, Rebekah, and Rachel (Gen 21:1–7; 25:21; 29:31); cf. John L. McKenzie, *Second Isaiah* (AB 20; Garden City, N.Y.: Doubleday, 1968), 139; John Oswalt, *The Book of Isaiah, Chapters 40–66* (NICOT; Grand Rapids: Eerdmans, 1997), 415; Brueggemann, *Isaiah*, 151; Joseph Blenkinsopp, *Isaiah 40–55: A New Translation with Introduction and Commentary* (AB 19A; New York: Doubleday, 2002), 371.

16. See Whybray, *Isaiah 40–66*, 184; and Oswalt, *Isaiah 40–66*, 414, for connections between Isa 54 and Isa 49.

Both of these scenarios involve young women with a male partner who are unable because of the male partner to bear children. Isaiah 54:5 goes on to identify her husband as Yahweh and then to compare her in verse 6 to "a wife forsaken and grieved in spirit" and "a youthful wife" who has been rejected. Yahweh admits to forsaking her due to an outburst of anger in verses 7–8. The image formed here is of a young woman who married and yet prior to bearing children was abandoned by her husband. Joy here is founded on the expectation of a return of the husband along with many children.

The broader context does suggest the setting of a victory after war, especially in light of Isa 52:7–10, where the same verbs as here (פצח, רנן) are directed toward the ruins (חרבה) of Jerusalem (see below), after the revelation to Zion by the messengers that Yahweh has been victorious in battle.

Isaiah 10:30

צהלי קולך בת־גלים הקשיבי לישה עניה ענתות

Cry aloud with your voice, O daughter of Gallim.
Pay attention, Laishah and poor Anathoth.

Isaiah 10:30 employs two feminine singular imperatives, one from the root צהל and the second from the root קשב (hiphil). Interestingly the verb usually associated with the *Aufruf zur Freude* (צהל) is the one accompanied by the feminine singular vocative: daughter of Gallim. The reason clause is not explicitly marked by the particle כי, but most likely comprises 10:32, where a warrior figure stops his march at Nob and makes some gesture with his hand related to the mountain of Daughter Zion, the hill of Jerusalem. Most have argued that the pericope in which this *Aufruf zur Freude* is embedded (10:28–32) depicts the Assyrian attack against Israel. Thus the verb צהל here refers to cries of terror rather than of joy.[17] However, not only would this be the only time this word would have this negative connotation in the Hebrew Bible,[18] the context of Isa 10 suggests a more positive theme, since it speaks of Yahweh's salvation of Israel in the face of the Assyrian threat (e.g., 10:24, 33–34). A better approach is

---

17. E.g., Kaiser, *Isaiah 1–12*, 250.
18. See *HALOT* 3:1007.

put forward by John D. W. Watts, who treats this as a review of Yahweh's theophanic Divine Warrior march, which results in victory over Assyria.[19] Therefore, Isa 10:30 is a call for the daughter of Gallim to rejoice at the approach of her Divine Warrior.

Isaiah 23:12

ויאמר לא־תוסיפי עוד לעלוז המעשקה בתולת בת־צידון כתיים קומי
עברי גם־שם לא־ינוח לך

And he said, "You shall no longer exult, O violated virgin daughter of Sidon. Rise up, pass over to Kittim, even there it will not be peaceful for you."

Isaiah 23, an oracle against the Phoenicians, is punctuated by a series of imperatives, first calling the ships of Tarshish to wail over the destruction of Tyre (v. 1), then the inhabitants of the coastlands and merchants of Sidon to mourn[20] (v. 2), Sidon herself to be ashamed (v. 4), the inhabitants of the coastland to pass over to Tarshish (v. 6), the daughter of Tarshish to overflow (or till)[21] her land (v. 10), the ships of Tarshish again to wail (v. 14), and a forgotten harlot of Tyre to take up a harp and sing (v. 16).

It is in the midst of this series of imperatival addresses that one finds the prohibition of an *Aufruf zur Freude* in verse 12. Here a negative imperative expression prohibits a feminine subject from exulting (עלז). The subject is identified as a virgin daughter who has been violated (המעשקה בתולת בת), here linked to the city of Sidon. No reason clause is provided in this instance. While prohibited from rejoicing over victory, this female figure is encouraged to escape to Kittim, even though there she will find no rest, possibly referring to the fact that there will be no safety there

---

19. John D. W. Watts, *Isaiah 1–33* (rev. ed.; WBC 24; Waco, Tex: Word, 2005), 199–201. Thus the hand gesture in 10:32 indicates "God's claim to the city" and "is not threatening—on the contrary, the one who has it in his power to utterly destroy indicates his will for the city to prosper."

20. *HALOT* 1:226, II דמם; cf. Oswalt, *Isaiah 1–39*, 430, who notes that silence in grief is possible: Lam 2:10; Job 2:13. On the possible role of silence as a mourning rite see Pham, *Mourning*, 29–31.

21. See Clements, *Isaiah 1–39*, 194, who suggests עבד (work, i.e., till) for עבר (pass over) based on LXX and 1QIs[a].

from those who pursue her (cf. Lam 5:5). This passage as a whole envisions the military defeat of the Phoenicians, a context that would result in the rape of the virgin daughters of the city.[22] In such a context the usual joyful exultation of victory is not just inappropriate but impossible for those who had been violated.

Lamentations 4:21

שׂישׂי ושׂמחי בת־אדום יושׁבתי בארץ עוץ גם־עליך תעבר־כוס תשׁכרי ותתערי

Rejoice and be glad, O daughter of Edom, female inhabitant in the land of Uz. A cup will pass by you as well, and you will become drunk and expose yourself.

The addressee in Lam 4:21 is a feminine figure, the daughter of Edom, who is identified as a female inhabitant of the land of Uz, an area associated with Edom (see Gen 36:28; cf. Job 1:1; Jer 25:20).[23] Feminine singular imperative forms of the roots שׂישׂ and שׂמח are employed, but no reason clause is provided as is typical of the *Aufruf zur Freude*. Instead, this condensed form is used ironically to set up a statement of impending judgment. The idea is thus that the daughter of Edom should enjoy her present victory now since it will be short-lived; according to the following verse Yahweh's punishment of Edom is at hand and will parallel the reversal of fortunes for Daughter Zion (4:22). The context of this *Aufruf zur Freude* is that of military victory.

Isaiah 52:9–10

פצחו רננו יחדו חרבות ירושלם כי־נחם יהוה עמו גאל ירושלם חשׂף יהוה את־זרוע קדשׁו לעיני כל־הגוים וראו כל־אפסי־ארץ את ישׁועת אלהינו

---

22. See Oswalt, *Isaiah 1–39*, 434: the "young girl, fresh and untouched, laughing and dancing, is now beaten down and crushed," noting Isa 47:1, where Babylon is addressed this way; and, in contrast, Isa 37:22, where Virgin Daughter Jerusalem will not be so crushed by the Assyrians.

23. Claus Westermann, *Lamentations: Issues and Interpretation* (trans. Charles Muenchow; Minneapolis: Fortress, 1994), 197.

Break forth, shout joyfully together, O waste places of Jerusalem, because Yahweh has comforted his people. He has redeemed Jerusalem. Yahweh has bared his holy arm in the sight of all the nations and all the ends of the earth will see the salvation of our God.

While the addressees in Isa 52:9–10 are the masculine plural waste places, it is interesting that these waste places are those of Jerusalem. The reason clause is introduced by the particle כי and focuses on Yahweh's comfort of his people and redemption of Jerusalem in the sight of all the nations. Walter Brueggemann likens God's baring of his holy arm to a "warrior rolling up his sleeve so that all nations can see the powerful military muscle that assures Israel and intimidates the nations."[24] This same "holy arm" is associated with God's "right hand" in the victory paean of Ps 98:1. This invitation follows the reception of the news of Yahweh's military victory in Isa 52:7–8. Interestingly, in 52:8 the sentinels on the wall are described as shouting joyfully (רנן), a verb often employed in the *Aufruf zur Freude*.

Hosea 9:1

אל־תשמח ישראל אל־גיל כעמים כי זנית מעל אלהיך אהבת אתנן
על כל־גרנות דגן

Do not rejoice, O Israel, by rejoicing like the nations, because you have committed adultery against your God, you have loved a harlot's earnings on every threshing floor.

Similar to Isa 23:12, Hos 9:1 represents the opposite of an *Aufruf zur Freude*, here employing the negative imperative construction of the verb שׂמח accompanied by the noun גיל. Unlike other passages with their feminine singular subjects, this one employs the masculine singular because the addressee is the masculine Israel, even though the description that follows pictures this male Israel as an unfaithful wife and female prostitute. The reason clause is introduced with the particle כי. While the immediately preceding verse in Hos 8 speaks of Yahweh's judgment on Judah by burning down the royal dwellings in the various fortified cities, most

---

24. Brueggemann, *Isaiah*, 139, noting Isa 40:10.

likely a reference to a devastating siege on the nation, most interpreters set this prophetic indictment in the context of cultic celebration over harvest, rather than that of response following battle. Typical is Francis Landy: "this is an anti-festival, when joy is turned to mourning, libations are not poured out, sacrifices are not sweet, and the harvest is not brought into the house of YHWH."[25] The dominant motif is clearly that of harvest, but one should not miss the military motifs that spell the end of the festivities as "the bounty of the harvest will become the booty of the invading enemy" and the people are sent into exile.[26]

Joel 2:21–23

אל־תיראי אדמה גילי ושמחי כי־הגדיל יהוה לעשות אל־תיראו
בהמות שדי כי דשאו נאות מדבר כי־עץ נשא פריו תאנה וגפן נתנו
חילם ובני ציון גילו ושמחו ביהוה אלהיכם כי־נתן לכם את־המורה
לצדקה ויורד לכם גשם מורה ומלקוש בראשון

Do not fear, O land, rejoice and be glad, because Yahweh has done great things. Do not fear, O animals of the field, because the grazing places of the wilderness have sprouted, because the tree has borne its fruit, the fig tree and the vine have yielded their strength. Sons of Zion rejoice and be glad in Yahweh your God, because he has given you the early rain as salvation, he has poured down showers, early and latter rain as formerly.

Joel 2:21–23 contains a series of imperatival addresses to various addressees.[27] It begins in verse 21 with an address to the land (אדמה),

---

25. Francis Landy, *Hosea* (Readings: A New Biblical Commentary; Sheffield: Sheffield Academic Press, 1995), 111; see also Francis I. Andersen and David Noel Freedman, *Hosea: A New Translation with Introduction and Commentary* (AB 24; Garden City, N.Y.: Doubleday, 1980), e.g., 522; Philip J. King, *Amos, Hosea, Micah: An Archaeological Commentary* (Philadelphia: Westminster, 1988), 112; Graham I. Davies, *Hosea* (NCB; Grand Rapids: Eerdmans, 1992), 213; Bruce C. Birch, *Hosea, Joel, and Amos* (Westminster Bible Companion; Louisville: Westminster John Knox, 1997), 84.

26. James Limburg, *Hosea–Micah* (IBC; Atlanta: John Knox, 1988), 32. Notice also the "watchman" terminology of Hos 9:8, another military nuance.

27. David A. Hubbard (*Hosea: An Introduction and Commentary* [TOTC 24; Downers Grove, Ill.: InterVarsity Press, 2009], 68) notes that the entities addressed here are those who would have suffered extensively from the plague.

employing the feminine singular prohibition formula "do not fear" followed by two feminine singular imperatives based on the roots גיל and שמח. The reason clause that follows is introduced by כי and points vaguely to Yahweh's great actions (הגדיל יהוה לעשות). The animals of the field are addressed in verse 22 and told not to fear, because (כי) of renewed vegetation. Finally, verse 23 addresses the sons of Zion, employing masculine plural imperatives of the same roots used in verse 21 in the address to the land (שמח, גיל). The reason clause once again is introduced by כי and focuses on Yahweh's gift of rain and the resultant harvest (v. 23; cf. v. 24).

This series of addresses is located in an important point in the book of Joel. Beginning in 2:18–19a, the book describes Yahweh's response to the cry of the people (2:17) prompted by the prophetic message in 1:1–2:16. Yahweh's initial promise in 2:19b–20 speaks of God sending plenteous harvest to his people, promising never to make them a reproach among the nations, and removing "the northerner" from them by driving it away. This call for the land to rejoice is thus related to a reversal of an agricultural crisis brought on by the combined conditions of drought and a locust infestation. It is interesting, however, that the locust infestation is described in terminology related to an invading army in 2:5–11 and 2:25.

Conclusion

Broadening our analysis from the three examples of *Aufruf zur Freude* in the final phase of the Book of the Twelve, we have seen how the summons to joy form is a regular component within the prophetic corpus. Two more examples of the form were discerned in texts showcasing a female figure associated with Zion/Jerusalem (Isa 12:6; 54:1), two examples in texts portraying a female figure associated with other geopolitical units (Sidon, Isa 23:12; Edom, Lam 4:21), one example related to Israel portrayed as an adulterous woman (Hos 9:1), and one other related to the land personified (Joel 2:21). These texts provide a broader context for us to understand the summons to joy directed toward the female figure associated with Zion in Isaiah (12:6; 54:1) and the Book of the Twelve (Zeph 3:14–15; Zech 2:14 [Eng. 10]; 9:9–10). It is instructive that those examples that were associated with a female city figure revealed clear connections to the summons to joy related to a military victory (Isa 12:6; 23:12; 54:1; Zeph 3:14–15; Zech 2:14 [Eng. 10]; 9:9–10; Lam 4:21), while those not associated with the female city figure (Hos 9:1; Joel 2:21–23) are dominated by harvest motifs, with some subtle connections to the military context. The connections to the context of military victory thus suggest that texts related to Daughter Zion and joy should be read against the backdrop of this social context, rather than that espoused by Crüsemann and Westermann.[28] In order to do this we need to take a look at the larger complex of forms highlighted by Mandolfo and others in relation to the crisis experienced by Daughter Zion at the fall of Jerusalem and preserved in the book of Lamentations.

FEMININE FORMS OF JOY AND GRIEF IN OLD TESTAMENT SPEECH

The origins of the form of speech in which the cries of Zion/Daughter Zion have been cast in the book of Lamentations has been a matter of considerable debate over the past century. It was Hedwig Jahnow and Hermann Gunkel in the early era of form criticism, and later Nancy Lee,[29] who connected these poems with the longer funeral dirges scattered throughout the Hebrew Bible (e.g., 2 Sam 1:19–27; 3:33–34; Jer 9:16–21 [Eng. 17–22]; 38:22), the abridged forms found in prophetic sayings (e.g., Isa 1:21–23; Jer 9:9 [Eng. 10]; Ezek 26:17–18; Amos 5:2), and popular statements (e.g., Isa 14:4–21; 23:1–14; Ezek 19:1–9, 10–14; 27:2–36; 28:11–19; 32:12–16).[30]

That this form has influenced the early poems in Lamentations (chs. 1 and 2) is suggested by the appearance of the feminine voice of the city throughout these chapters. It is true that two funeral dirges in the Hebrew

---

28. See also Pss 48:12 (Eng. 11) and 97:8, where (Mount) Zion and the daughters of Judah are glad (שׂמח) and rejoice (גיל) over Yahweh's judgments. The judgments in view in both cases are Yahweh's military victories over his adversaries (48:4–7; 97:3). Isaiah 65:17 and 66:10 call others to join in Jerusalem's joy: 65:17: "be glad and rejoice forever in what I create, for behold I create Jerusalem for rejoicing and her people for gladness"; 66:10: "be joyful [שׂמח] with Jerusalem and rejoice [גיל] for her, all you who love her; be exceedingly glad [שׂישׂ משׂושׂ] with her, all you who mourn over her." Also note 30:19, where the people of Zion, living in Jerusalem, are told that they will weep (בכה) no longer.

29. Hedwig Jahnow, *Das hebräische Leichenlied im Rahmen der Völkerdichtung* (BZAW 36; Giessen: Töpelmann, 1923); Hermann Gunkel and Joachim Begrich, *Introduction to Psalms: The Genres of the Religious Lyric of Israel* (trans. James D. Nogalski; Macon, Ga.: Mercer University Press, 1998), e.g., 95; Nancy C. Lee, *The Singers of Lamentations: Communities under Siege, from Ur to Jerusalem to Sarajevo* (BIS 60; Leiden: Brill, 2002).

30. See Westermann, *Lamentations*, 6.

Bible are found on the lips of men (2 Sam 1:19–27; 3:33–34),[31] but several texts in the Hebrew Bible describe women voicing such dirges, even as a vocation (2 Sam 1:24; 2 Chr 35:25; Jer 9:16–17, 19 [Eng. 17–18, 20]; Ezek 32:16; Nah 2:8 [Eng. 7]).[32] The reason for women's role within this arena is because it was women who were most affected by the death of their male protectors, whether husbands or sons. The funeral dirges in 2 Sam 1:19–27 and 3:33–34 suggest that this form arose in relation to the defeat of an army in battle, an activity in which ancient women were not involved. [33]

---

31. It is most likely that Jer 9:18 (Eng. 19) is a lament of the community as a whole, which is then to be taken up by the women mentioned in 9:16–17, 19 (Eng. 9:17–18, 20); cf. Terence E. Fretheim, *Jeremiah* (SHBC; Macon, Ga.: Smyth & Helwys, 2002), 162. But there is a possibility that the lament in 9:18 (Eng. 19) is the lament called for in 9:16–17 (Eng. 17–18), with 9:19 (Eng. 20) a further instruction to teach the daughters the lament; cf. J. A. Thompson, *The Book of Jeremiah* (NICOT; Grand Rapids: Eerdmans, 1980), 316. For the possibility that this is a mockery of illicit lament over the dying Baal, see William Lee Holladay, *Jeremiah 1: A Commentary on the Book of the Prophet Jeremiah, Chapters 1–25* (Hermeneia; Philadelphia: Fortress, 1986), 313.

32. Cf. Daniel I. Block, *The Book of Ezekiel: Chapters 25–48* (NICOT; Grand Rapids: Eerdmans, 1998), 210; Olyan, *Biblical Mourning*, 49–51. Men could also play a role in such mourning rites according to 2 Chr 35:25 and Amos 5:16.

33. It must be noted that in recent years many scholars have linked these poems in Lamentations to Mesopotamian laments over destroyed cities and sanctuaries. These laments were often used as part of ceremonies related to the refounding and restoration of sanctuaries after defeat by an enemy due to a decision in the divine council and abandonment of the sanctuary by the chief god. In these compositions, a feminine character in the divine council, the city's patron goddess, voices concern over the destruction by lamenting the predicament and crying for the council to reconsider the fate of the city and sanctuary. However, most authors have been careful to note that this Mesopotamian form has undergone significant adaptation. These distinctions between the Mesopotamian and Hebrew works suggest that the features shared by the two are more likely linked to the universal practice of female mourning rites in these Semitic cultures, rather than to actual borrowing of oral or literary compositions. See Hans-Joachim Kraus, *Klagelieder (Threni)* (3rd ed.; BKAT 20; Neukirchen-Vluyn: Neukirchener, 1968); Norman K. Gottwald, *Studies in the Book of Lamentations* (SBT 1/14; London: SCM, 1962); William C. Gwaltney Jr., "The Biblical Book of Lamentations in the Context of Near Eastern Lament Literature," in *More Essays on the Comparative Method* (ed. William W. Hallo, James C. Moyer, and Leo G. Perdue; Scripture in Context 2; Winona Lake, Ind.: Eisenbrauns, 1983), 191–211; Delbert R. Hillers, *Lamentations: A New Translation with Introduction and Commentary* (2nd ed.; AB 7A; New York: Doubleday, 1992); Paul Wayne Ferris, *The Genre of Communal Lament in the Bible and the Ancient Near East* (SBLDS 127; Atlanta: Scholars Press, 1992); Westermann, *Lamentations*; Frederick W. Dobbs-Allsopp, *Weep, O Daughter*

In ancient Israel, females were thus cast in the position of awaiting news from a battle, evidence for which can be found in Judg 5:28–30. In the wake of a defeat at the hands of a more powerful enemy, women would have received the news of death and mourned their devastating loss. One can discern two speech forms throughout the Hebrew Bible related to the setting of the community in the wake of defeat, the first being the invitation to lament (see esp. Jer 9:16–21 [Eng. 17–22]; Joel 1:8; cf. Isa 13:6; 14:31; 22:12; 23:1, 6, 14; Jer 4:8; 25:34, 36; 48:20; 49:3; 51:8; Ezek 21:17 [Eng. 12]; 30:2; 32:18; Zeph 1:11),[34] and the other the lament itself with its accompanying physical rituals (see esp. Lam 1–2 and other texts noted above). Among the survivors of events such as those associated with the fall of Jerusalem, its monarch, and state, those experiencing the greatest loss would have been the widows and fatherless daughters who were dependent on their patriarchal and filial protectors for sustenance, protection, and honor. And it is their voice that would have dominated the social context of Jerusalem and Judah in the period following the fall of Jerusalem. It is not then surprising that such forms typified the speech of the communities throughout Western Asia in antiquity and in Judah in this period in particular.

Other passages, however, reveal the flip side to the receipt of news of defeat and its corresponding funeral dirge.[35] Those women who were on the winning side would have received news of victory and responded with songs of joy and its accompanying rituals. Representative songs are probably evident in the literary compositions now found in Exod 15:21 and 1 Sam 18:7, focusing on the military feats of the male victors (Yahweh, Saul, David). The rituals included dancing and the use of musical instruments, especially tambourines (Exod 15:20–21; Judg 11:34; 1 Sam 18:6). It is in this context that the *Aufruf zur Freude* was most likely employed. In the ancient social context, just as the invitation to lament permitted the articu-

---

of Zion: A Study of the City-Lament in the Hebrew Bible (Rome: Pontifical Biblical Institute, 1993); idem, *Lamentations* (IBC; Louisville: Westminster John Knox, 2002); Walter C. Bouzard, *We Have Heard with Our Ears, O God: Sources of the Communal Laments in the Psalms* (SBLDS 159; Atlanta: Scholars Press, 1997).

34. The summons to mourn is noted by Westermann, *Lamentations*, 7, in his review of Jahnow.

35. Notice the contrast between the expected response of the women of the victors and the women of the defeated in 2 Sam 1:20, 24, and also the contrast between the cry of triumph (קול ענות גבורה) and the cry of defeat (קול ענות חלושה) in Exod 32:18.

lation of pain upon receipt of news of defeat, so the summons to joy repre-sented a speech form with the rhetorical intent to transition the addressees from the receipt of news of victory to a response of joy. This would explain the consistent reference to war in contexts where the *Aufruf zur Freude* is found with feminine (and esp. Daughter Zion) vocatives in the prophets, and the importance of the presence of the king, that is, the warrior who has returned from victorious battle in these texts.

CONCLUSION AND REFLECTIONS

If this typology of forms related to the impact of a battle's outcome on a community can be sustained,[36] there are two forms related to military defeat (invitation to lament, mourning) and two forms related to mili-tary victory (summons to joy, joyful expression).[37] Of course, this neat typology assumes a more static view of form than that which Mandolfo rightly espouses.[38] But observing the basic contours of these forms and the typology of their interrelationship is helpful for looking at their rhetorical interplay within the biblical corpus. Instructive is that only two of these forms are actually employed in relation to Daughter Zion in the Hebrew Bible. Daughter Zion expresses her mourning to Yahweh, and she is called

---

36. See the contribution of Floyd, "Welcome Back," 484–504, which I consulted at the end of writing this piece. He makes similar comments on the role of women in ancient mourning and rejoicing (esp. pp. 500–502).

37. In this analysis I am well aware that there is a broader tradition of rejoic-ing and mourning evidenced in the biblical corpus. What is key in this analysis is the observation of how the feminine traditions of rejoicing and mourning related to Daughter Zion are so closely associated with those related to the military context. For connectivity between rejoicing and mourning, especially seen in the accompanying actions in the broader tradition, see Anderson, *Time to Mourn*, 49. For the broader tradition of texts, forms, and settings related to rejoicing and mourning, besides Anderson, see esp. Jahnow, *Leichenleid*; Humbert, "Laetari et exultare," 185–214 = Humbert, *Opuscules d'un Hébraïsant*, 119–45; Flemming F. Hvidberg, *Weeping and Laughter in the Old Testament* (Leiden: Brill, 1962); Pham, *Mourning*; Olyan, *Biblical Mourning*.

38. Mandolfo, *Daughter Zion*, 55–58.

to express joy. Strikingly missing is any invitation to Daughter Zion to lament[39] or any record of her expressing joy.[40]

The latter is showcased in the contrast between the figures of the Servant and Zion in Isa 40–55. This section of Isaiah is structured according to the laments expressed by these two figures.[41] After the introductory sections in 40:1–11 (a second prophetic commissioning) and 40:12–26 (a disputation series that challenges the nations and their idols, key themes in chs. 40–55), the lament of Jacob/Israel (the Servant figure) introduces 40:27–49:13 and the lament of Zion/Jerusalem introduces 49:14–54:17. Chapter 55 concludes chapters 40–55 with an invitation to renew the covenant. Striking, however, is that while the Servant figure's voice appears at the conclusion of 40:27–49:13, Zion's voice is absent at the conclusion to 49:14–54:17.[42]

This observation lends further support to Mandolfo's concern over the lack of sensitivity to this Zion figure and the absence of resolution to Zion's pain in the Hebrew Bible. Zion must voice her pain uninvited, and ultimately she is unresponsive to any call to rejoice over the changed circumstances.

These observations, however, invite some closing reflections on the role that (Daughter) Zion plays within the biblical corpus. One fault in

---

39. Some have suggested the invitation in Joel 1:8 is directed toward Daughter Zion, but this cannot be proved (see above). The invitation to lament is never directed explicitly toward Daughter Zion/Jerusalem. The only possible example is Jer 6:26, where an invitation is given to the "daughter of my people," who may be related to the Daughter Zion of Jer 6:23. If this identification can be sustained, then this is the only example in the Hebrew Bible.

40. In her analysis of Isa 40–55, Mandolfo notes the "nearly absolute silence" of Daughter Zion and the fact that "she maintains her silence" (*Daughter Zion*, 115, 117); cf. Willey, *Remember the Former Things*, 228; Kathleen M. O'Connor, *Lamentations and the Tears of the World* (Maryknoll, N.Y.: Orbis, 2002), 146.

41. See Mark J. Boda, "'Uttering Precious Rather than Worthless Words': Divine Patience and Impatience with Lament in Isaiah and Jeremiah," in *Lament: Israel's Cry to God* (ed. Mark J. Boda, Carol Dempsey, and LeAnn Snow Flesher; LHBOTS 552; London: Continuum, forthcoming).

42. Mandolfo (*Daughter Zion*, 108) contrasts the Servant's speech in 49:1–6 with that of Zion in 49:14. This observation does not take into account the presence of the Servant's lament in 40:27. The contrast is between the presence of the Servant's speech in 49:1–6 and the absence of a speech by Zion at the end of ch. 54. On the open-ended character of Second Isaiah in relation to Zion's expected role in 40:10–11, see van der Woude, "Zion," 115.

all of this discussion is the focus on the target rather than the source of the metaphor of Daughter Zion. Considered sociologically, Zion theology traces its roots to the elite. It is based on the preservation of the privileges of those in power, in particular in royal power, a power that was often sustained at the expense of the populace in general and especially females in particular.

By leveraging the vulnerable image of daughter in this ancient context, those responsible have captured the imagination and pathos of ancient and modern readers alike. But notwithstanding protests against this,[43] it is ironic that those seeking to redress the imbalance between male and female in the imagistic world of the ancient text end up affirming an elite male community that leveraged the female image to mourn the loss of their own privilege and hegemony over the vulnerable within the society. Certainly we can note the creativity of the image makers and highlight the power of metaphor on readers, but in the end should it not be a concern that male elites have so manipulated a modern audience?[44]

To rephrase this: on the one hand, the metaphor is drawn from a social location within the patriarchal matrix of ancient Israel. The employment of this metaphor within a text assumes this broader patriarchal matrix with all of its dysfunctions. The depiction of Daughter Zion within the prophetic corpus is dominated by a negative portrayal of this feminine image, suggestive of the dominant treatment of women within this patriarchal setting. The privileging of the voice of Daughter Zion within the book of Lamentations is rather surprising given its context and stands out as an important corrective. On the other hand, the metaphor is being drawn from this social location by patriarchal writers, not only for the negative portrayal within the prophetic corpus, but also for the more sympathetic portrayal within the book of Lamentations. That is, those responsible for depicting Daughter Zion's vehement response to the Deity are also males within the patriarchal social context. These males are thus exploiting this spousal abuse for their own purposes, leaving Daughter Zion ever the victim in this new context.[45]

---

43. See Mandolfo, *Daughter Zion*, 44, and works cited there.

44. See further Mark J. Boda, "The Priceless Gain of Penitence: From Communal Lament to Penitential Prayer in the 'Exilic' Liturgy of Israel," in *Lamentations in Ancient and Contemporary Contexts* (ed. Nancy C. Lee and Carleen Mandolfo; SBLSymS 43; Atlanta: Society of Biblical Literature, 2008), 81–101, esp. 99–100.

45. J. David Pleins observes this consistently in his review of the use of traditions

While one can understand why Mandolfo is concerned about the normative depiction of the abuse of wife Israel by her divine husband, it should be of equal concern to highlight the exploitation of this image by the males responsible for the book of Lamentations. Is it not interesting that it is the male voice of the poet who must come alongside and affirm and legitimize the voice of Daughter Zion? It is surprising to me that the prophetic witness that so often spoke on behalf of the poor and vulnerable is now castigated by those whose privilege has been lost in the wake of the fall of Jerusalem.

This to me is akin to the leveraging of apocalyptic themes and images by hegemonic powers fearful of losing their privilege after being attacked by insignificant forces, a phenomenon evident in the ancient as well as modern worlds. One can leverage the images and genres of the powerless for rhetorical purposes, but does this legitimize the claim of these hegemonic voices?

related to Daughter Zion, the poor, and servanthood; see *The Social Visions of the Hebrew Bible: A Theological Introduction* (Louisville: Westminster John Knox, 2001), 266–67, 314, 389, 441–42.

"Whose God Is This Anyway?": A Response to Carleen Mandolfo

Carol J. Dempsey

Throughout the centuries men and women of every generation have pondered the question, Who or what is God? Artists have sketched portraits and wall hangings; mystics have crafted poems and stories; contemplatives have rested and sighed; biblical scholars have mined historical documents;[1] theologians have written books and treatises;[2] and children have imagined and wondered. Perhaps one of the most influential groups to talk about God and who have had a profound effect on the religious consciousnesses, imaginations, and belief systems of ancient and present-day civilizations, and in particular Western civilization, has been Israel's ancient prophets whose proclamations and musings have been recorded in the Bible, the sacred text of Jews and Christians alike. The prophets' depiction of God, however, has not always been palpable for many listeners and readers of the biblical text who ask critically, Is this truly God, or is it the creation of an author, editor, or redactor who may have had a literary or theological agenda that came into play when the Bible was being shaped into its present canonical form?

In *Daughter Zion Talks Back to the Prophets: A Dialogic Theology of the Book of Lamentations*, Carleen Mandolfo explores the metaphorical

---

1. Among recent biblical scholarship on the topic of God, see the work of Mark S. Smith, *The Memoirs of God: History, Memory, and the Experience of the Divine in Ancient Israel* (Minneapolis: Fortress, 2004); see also idem, *The Early History of God: Yahweh and the Other Deities in Ancient Israel* (2nd ed.; Grand Rapids: Eerdmans, 2002).

2. Among contemporary theologians writing on the topic of God, see the work of Elizabeth A. Johnson, *Quest for the Living God: Mapping Frontiers in the Theology of God* (New York: Continuum, 2008); and John F. Haught, *God after Darwin: A Theology of Evolution* (Boulder, Colo.: Westview, 2000).

language of the Bible and dares to have Daughter Zion talk back to the prophets. One competing voice and character in the prophets besides those of the prophets and Daughter Zion is God, to whom Daughter Zion also talks back. For Mandolfo, the God of the biblical text is not only revelatory but also metaphorical and "entirely resistant to iconography of all sorts—discursive or imagistic."[3] With this understanding of God, Mandolfo holds up the God of the prophets for ongoing critical theological reflection and, in doing so, challenges not only the biblical view of God but also people's belief in this God. In this essay I explore, reflect upon, and respond to the topic of God as presented by Mandolfo in her study on Daughter Zion and the prophets. Among the biblical texts that I will treat in the discussion are Hos 1–3; Jer 2–3; 13:20–27; Ezek 16; 23; and Lam 1–2.

THE BIBLE AS THE "WORD OF GOD":
UNPACKING MANDOLFO'S HOPES IN DIALOGUE WITH
SANDRA M. SCHNEIDERS

By writing her book, Mandolfo hoped for two things: (1) "to contribute to the dethroning of biblical authority as it is now construed"; and (2) to have the Bible and biblical authority "resound as the 'words' of God, rather than the 'Word.'"[4] Both of these points are central to one's understanding of God as presented by the biblical text. Too long have readers of the text and believing communities alike assumed that the Bible is the "word" of God as if God were the one either dictating or writing the text. Such a notion is at the heart of a fundamentalist view of both God and the biblical text. Giving God these skills anthropomorphically presumes an anthropocentric view of God, one created in the image and likeness of humankind. Such a view does not take into account the layers of authorship, editing, and redacting that took place in the shaping of the biblical text, nor does this view understand the concept of metaphor, which is central to understanding God as a character in the Bible.

---

3. Carleen R. Mandolfo, *Daughter Zion Talks Back to the Prophets: A Dialogic Theology of the Book of Lamentations* (SemeiaSt 58; Atlanta: Society of Biblical Literature, 2007), 7.

4. Ibid., 5.

In her seminal work, *The Revelatory Text: Interpreting the New Testament as Sacred Scripture*,[5] Sandra Schneiders sheds light on "Word of God" as a metaphor. Her analysis establishes the groundwork for what Mandolfo hopes to accomplish in her text. Schneiders argues that "'Word of God' is first of all a linguistic expression"[6] and that "the expression 'word of God' does not, of course, refer to a single word uttered by God but to intelligible divine speech, to language or discourse attributed to God."[7] She also states: "Language … is a human phenomenon rooted in our corporeality as well as in our discursive mode of intelligence and as such cannot be literally predicated of pure spirit."[8] Schneiders makes a further point: "there is a second reason, perhaps less obvious but even more important, why we cannot literally attribute language to God, namely, the noncommenasurability of the essentially limited reality of language with the infinite God."[9] Schneiders is clear in outlining the limitations of language. She notes the "**polyvalent character of words**," and stresses that "**no language is fully translatable**," and that "**words change in meaning** over time."[10] Thus for Schneiders, "The expression 'word of God' is a metaphor, and metaphor is perhaps our most powerful use of language, our most effective access to the meaning of reality at its deepest levels."[11]

For Schneiders, the phrase "the word of God" as it pertains to the Bible is metaphorical. This understanding, however, does not detract from the authoritative nature of the Bible. Mandolfo entertains this point briefly in the introduction to her book; she hopes to "contribute to the dethroning of biblical authority as it is now construed."[12] For Schneiders, authority takes two forms: "unilateral absolute authority" and "dialogical relative authority."[13] In unilateral absolute authority, "the will of another or the evidence of the data imposes itself on the addressee. One must either respond appropriately or suffer the sanctions."[14] In dialogical relative

---

5. See Sandra M. Schneiders, *The Revelatory Text: Interpreting the New Testament as Sacred Scripture* (2nd ed.; Collegeville, Minn.: Liturgical Press, 1999).

6. Ibid., 27.

7. Ibid.

8. Ibid., 28.

9. Ibid.

10. Ibid.

11. Ibid., 29.

12. Mandolfo, *Daughter Zion*, 5.

13. Schneiders, *Revelatory Text*, 56.

14. Ibid.

authority, "something or someone is opened to us, and an invitation is issued to engage the reality so disclosed. To respond is to commit oneself, to be changed, to be initiated into a reality that one does not eventually dominate and control but in which one continues to participate at ever deeper levels."[15] In assessing both aspects of authority, Schneiders notes:

> Because of our natural human preference for certitude, we spontaneously tend to think that coercive, or at least evidential, authority is the primary analogue. Such is not the case. True personal authority is of the second type. This is the type of authority that God exercises toward humans.... The authority of scripture belongs, strictly speaking, to the second type of authority, that is, the dialogical.[16]

In her study, Mandolfo takes the theory and insights of Schneiders and develops them further. Mandolfo's work is, in fact, a dialogic theology, and one that does dethrone biblical authority as unilateral absolute authority in order to establish Scripture as dialogical relative authority. Furthermore, her attempt at understanding the Bible as the words of God instead of as the "Word of God" develops Schneiders's argument and truly does capture, respect, and give credence to the metaphorical fabric of Scripture that features God as one of the main characters who is portrayed in metaphorical terms, particularly as lover and husband to Daughter Zion—which portrayal is, in itself, also a metaphor.

Thus, because of the metaphorical nature of Scripture, Mandolfo is able to be critically playful with the text in an honest attempt to deepen the faith of believing communities while offering a way on how to read, understand, and make sense of the biblical text and story in a postmodern world. For those readers and believers who maintain a fundamentalist position for whom infallibility and inerrancy are essential to Scripture and who understand Scripture "to have originated miraculously (e.g., by divine dictation or verbal inspiration),"[17] Mandolfo's dialogic theology, along with her dynamic portrait of God, will be unequivocally challenging and downright disturbing. The search for Truth, however, is never meant to soothe us in our comfort zones. Rather, the search for Truth is to take us beyond that which we know for certain and to suspend us in the ineffable

---

15. Ibid.
16. Ibid., 57.
17. Ibid., 54.

mystery we call "God," whose felt presence and experiential existence are beyond whatever we can possibly imagine or even try to fathom, let alone express in written word.[18]

SETTING THE STAGE FOR MANDOLFO'S PORTRAIT OF GOD: HER APPROACH TO THE BIBLICAL TEXT AND "GOD"

Having unpacked Mandolfo's understanding of God's word(s) and biblical authority as they pertain to the biblical text and how the text portrays God, I consider Mandolfo's dialogic approach as the next major point relevant to the discussion. Mandolfo makes clear that "a dialogic approach that takes into account such disconfirming experiences requires that all texts be open to intense interrogation, and that even the character of God, as well as the way he has been interpreted by traditional biblical theologians, is susceptible to critique."[19] In viewing God as a character within the biblical text, Mandolfo is free to critique this God and to have the metaphorical Daughter Zion respond to this God whom Mandolfo treats as a construct of the text, which is how most literary critics view the God of the biblical text.

Furthermore, Mandolfo states that her approach "is not a systematic account of the divine—it is a reading of a character that I think has potentially profound ethical implications for human relationality beyond the text."[20] She admits that "to speak of the god of the Bible is to make no claims about 'God'; but at the same time such a focus does not preclude the fact that on the cultural level (both then and now) the two gods often overlap, nor does it preclude the possibility that the biblical characterization *points toward* some ontological truths."[21] Mandolfo's approach to the biblical text and to the character of God, then, offers listeners of the text a variety of ways for interpreting the text and for uncovering the polyvalent voice of a multidimensional God. Finally, Mandolfo brings out the point that "the beauty of the text that many prize as 'sacred' is that it allows dissenting voices into the conversation; it is, then, our responsibility to attend to them."[22] For Mandolfo, an ethical dimension exists with respect to how

---

18. See Mandolfo, *Daughter Zion*, 7 nn. 12 and 13.
19. Ibid., 7.
20. Ibid.
21. Ibid.
22. Ibid., 22.

one hears, interprets, and responds to the biblical text that extends to how one hears, interprets, and responds to God as portrayed by the text. This ethical dimension to which Mandolfo lays claim is a critical one because in some cases the depiction of God has called people to a deeper and fuller sense of compassion. In other instances, the portrait communicates a negative message and has had a profound effect on how people treat one another.[23] Mandolfo's study draws out this latter point, particularly with respect to the husband-wife metaphor found in Hos 1–3; Jer 2–3; 13:20–27; Ezek 16; 23; and similar imagery and metaphorical language heard in Lam 1–2. The God of the biblical text has shaped cultures and belief systems down through the ages. Biblical scholars have the responsibility to make the text intelligible and to hold it up for ongoing critical theological reflection, which includes the character of God and the language and metaphors associated with this character.[24]

DAUGHTER ZION AND GOD: A MARRIAGE MADE IN HEAVEN?

Having set the stage for her engagement with and assessment of the biblical text, Mandolfo meticulously explores the relationship between two prominent characters in the prophets: Daughter Zion and God. Her analysis of Hos 1–3 begins a lively depiction of a troubled marital relationship. What begins as a metaphorical situation, whereby Hosea is told by God to take back his unfaithful wife Gomer to symbolize how God will take back unfaithful Israel, quickly shifts into something else, as Mandolfo notes:

> The collapsing of the prophet's marriage into the relationship between YHWH and the people in chapter 2 is where the metaphor gains real force; it is no longer mediated by the image of Hosea and Gomer's marriage. The people are now forced to assume fully the mantle of adulterous woman and thus the punishment attendant upon such a construction:

---

23. See Mandolfo's comments on ways that the Bible can sanction violence. Here she engages with the thought of Kathleen M. O'Connor, who also comments on the biblical text in relation to the U.S. culture, which she sees as being "saturated in violence" (*Daughter Zion*, 125).

24. See chs. 2 and 3 of Mandolfo, *Daughter Zion*, 29–77. For a succinct discussion on the role of the biblical scholar-theologian with respect to evaluating the God-language of the biblical text see the classic work of Leslie J. Hoppe, O.F.M, "Biblical Theology," *The Collegeville Pastoral Dictionary of Biblical Theology* (ed. Carroll Stuhlmueller; Collegeville, Minn.: Liturgical Press, 1996), li–lv.

"I will strip her naked, and expose her as in the day she was born; and make her like a wilderness, and turn her into a parched land, and kill her with thirst" (Hos 2:5).[25]

Mandolfo then points out how metaphorically the "children" will be affected adversely and how the audience is drawn into feeling the "full force of YHWH's fury and disillusionment."[26] In the course of her analysis, Mandolfo shows us how brutal God can be; even when the covenant is reestablished in Hos 3, the deed is not done mutually. God is the one who initiates and controls the entire situation. No other voice is heard but God's voice; no other action is seen but God's deeds. Mandolfo rightly reminds us that we hear only the words that God put into the woman's mouth.

God's tirade continues in Jer 2–3 and 13:20–27. Here Mandolfo points out the hostility that God shows toward Jerusalem, and the Israelite people by extension, because of their infidelity. No room exists for dialogue between the two parties. Jerusalem/Israel has no credibility before God, and God's language toward Jerusalem/Israel is pejorative and abusive. Even when God establishes a new covenant in Jer 31:31–34, as God did in Hos 3, God's "wife" is not included in this new covenant, which omission leads Mandolfo to question what kind of people can be tolerated in God's new vision.

The atrocities associated with the marriage metaphor come into full view in Ezek 16 and 23. Here Mandolfo points out that "the metaphor takes on a visceral power it lacks in Hosea and Jeremiah."[27] The woman in Ezek 16 is portrayed as someone who is "genetically flawed and carries with her the constant threat of defilement."[28] Mandolfo highlights how God plays "Henry Higgins" to "Eliza Doolittle"; and in making this association, Mandolfo draws attention to the patriarchal and imperial power dynamics that exist on God's part. God is portrayed as the one who tames barbaric Jerusalem. The language of God in Ezek 16 is harsh, barbaric, derogatory, and abusive to the point that God promises physical torture to his wife (see 16:35–40). And once again, when covenant is reestablished in 16:59–63, God initiates it; Jerusalem has no response and no voice in the matter.

---

25. Mandolfo, *Daughter Zion*, 33.
26. Ibid.
27. Ibid., 46.
28. Ibid., 47.

Ezekiel 23 draws Mandolfo's analysis of several clustered texts to a close. Here Mandolfo points out just how lewd God can be with respect to the female genitalia. She also notes that unlike Ezek 16, Ezek 23 ends with unmitigated violence. In comparison to the texts of Hosea and Jeremiah, Ezekiel, according to Mandolfo, is the worst of all with respect to its use of the marriage metaphor: "All in all, Ezekiel surpasses both Hosea and Jeremiah in his usage of the marriage metaphor as a way to strip the woman of any trace of subjectivity. She is rendered as hopelessly perverse and deviant."[29] Although the biblical writers are responsible for creating this image of Jerusalem/Israel, in the context of the stories themselves, God is the one who paints the horrific picture of the metaphorical woman who is made to appear rotten to the core.

Lamentations 1–2 is different from the other texts analyzed thus far. In Lam 1–2 Zion silences the voice of God, which lament, according to Mandolfo, is a fitting response to all of the accusations leveled against her. Mandolfo concludes:

> In Lam 1–2 the people cannot accept the consequences of acquiescing to belief in God's justice without undermining their own integrity. In the case of Lam 1–2, the apparent dominance of Daughter Zion's voice seems to serve a crucial ethical purpose—to offer a counterstory and bolster a voice that is in danger of falling into the abyss, a voice that has been brutalized first by prophetic pronouncements and delivered a final blow by God's hand.[30]

Hence, in each one of these texts, Mandolfo has allowed us to see the deeply violent side to God that has come to the fore in the context of the marriage/familial metaphor. Is this any way for a husband to act toward his wife in the face of adversity in marriage? Righteous anger over infidelity is understandable, but deep-seated violence that wishes or promises physical harm is not acceptable because it violates one's personhood and well-being.

A Look at Why Dialogic Reading Matters

Mandolfo's study thus far has been a rich one, but the best chapter of the book is the final one, in which she draws out several important points.

---

29. Ibid., 53.
30. Ibid., 122–23.

First, she concludes that God has failed in his duty as a husband insofar as he was not a responsible listener, not to mention the violent outbursts and threats that God rendered. Second, although God does not seem to be exercising justice, this failure on God's part does not exclude the human person and community from exercising justice. Third, the marriage metaphor is one way that the Bible can sanction violence and, as Mandolfo suggests, "can be found in the advice priests, pastors, and even friends sometimes give to women suffering from spousal abuse."[31] Furthermore, if God can be cruel in a metaphorical way, what is to stop the human person from being cruel in a literal way, especially if one perceives him- or herself as acting like God acts? Fourth, Mandolfo rightly cautions that:

> we must beware of a God who abuses because such an image has the potential to sanction oppressive human structures. But the fact is that God in the Bible *sometimes* ... abuses. The issue is not to find some way around that fact, but what we do with it. We must bring voices forward to challenge God's abusing voice. We must not accept his hegemony as narrated uncritically. *The dialogic structure of the canon gives us sanction for resisting seemingly irresistible power in our own contexts.*[32]

Fifth, Mandolfo asserts that for many biblical theologians, divine wrath is fitting for human sin. Sixth, Mandolfo thinks that because people are "caught in a religious conflict of global proportions"[33] in addition to a growing rigidity, people tend to "play God" with respect to punishing evildoers, whether these evildoers are on a personal or professional level.

Finally, Mandolfo makes one last point that brings together all of the issues and questions she raised throughout her study. This last point gives purpose and meaning to her entire endeavor:

> If I am reading the god in these particular texts correctly, why continue to turn to this book [the Bible] for moral sustenance? ... The Bible's authority for me rests in its ability to mirror the diversity and complexity of human existence. It brings together in one book voices with, at the most extreme, diametrically opposed worldviews.... And rather than expunge, whitewash, or ignore the "dangerous" books as some are wont to do..., I agree with O'Connor wholeheartedly when she says:

---

31. Ibid., 125.
32. Ibid., 127.
33. Ibid.

To excise the difficult texts erases possibilities of the texts to mirror present horrors, saves us from having to grapple with our own abuse and violence, and erases the cultural realities out of which the Bible emerged.[34]

CONCLUDING REMARKS

Mandolfo's study is a challenge and a gift to scholars and believers alike who have read and will read the Bible, because for the first time we have a sustained analysis of the biblical God of the prophets whose behavior is anything but desirable, much less worthy of our respect and admiration. Mandolfo is undeniably accurate in arguing that the God of the biblical text is a character within the text whose being and actions need to be viewed through a metaphorical and literary lens. She calls for a dialogic reading of the prophetic texts and their metaphors on a theological, social, cultural, and literary level, one that does not privilege one voice over another, namely, the voice of God over all other voices.

Without a doubt, the God of the Bible is historically, socially, culturally, and theologically conditioned, and to take the image of God literally is to do a disservice to the text and to the Sacred Presence whom we have labeled "God." Mandolfo opens the door to dialogue about how the biblical text portrays God metaphorically. She dares to question and be critical of this biblical God because she recognizes that the God of the text, especially the God of the prophetic texts, is a metaphorical construction that can be challenged and deconstructed, not to undermine the authority of the text but to allow the community of readers and believers to search for a new understanding of God that goes beyond the biblical tradition.

The entire Bible is revelatory insofar as it has the potential and capacity of revealing to us, its readers, that which is of God and that which is still in need of being transformed into God. What God, however, are we talking about? The God of the biblical text or the God beyond the text whom we can only glimpse? I daresay the answer rests somewhere in the middle of these two questions. While Mandolfo's focus is on deconstruction, somewhere the process of retrieval also needs to come into play because in addition to its metaphorical nature, the Bible also has a

---

34. Ibid., 128, citing Kathleen M. O'Connor, *Lamentations and the Tears of the World* (Maryknoll, N.Y.: Orbis, 2002), 118.

mystical dimension to it. The God of the prophets is not only a literary construct crafted for specific religious, political, and social agendas and times but also an experience that is perhaps best captured by another prophet, Micah:

> Who is a God like you, pardoning iniquity
>   and passing over the transgression
>   of the remnant of your possession?
> He does not retain his anger forever,
>   because he delights in showing clemency.
> He will again have compassion upon us;
>   he will tread our iniquities underfoot.
> You will cast all our sins
>   into the depths of the sea.
> You will show faithfulness to Jacob
>   and unswerving loyalty to Abraham,
>   as you have sworn to our ancestors
>   from the days of old. (Mic 7:18–20)

Centuries later the great mystic Meister Eckhart wrote:

> You may call God love
> You may call God goodness
> But the best name for God is compassion.[35]

In sum, Mandolfo reminds us that our words, our images for God all pale in light of the *mysterium tremendum*. Both the Bible and ourselves have limitations with respect to our God-language, and once we recognize these limitations and dare to let go of our false images of God, then and only then will we be able to encounter the Source of All Being who existed long before a word was ever uttered or written on parchment. In the words of theologian Elizabeth A. Johnson, "The quest continues. It will do so as long as the unfathomable mystery of the living God calls human beings into the future, promised but unknown, which is to say, as long as people exist."[36]

---

35. Matthew Fox, *Meditations with Meister Eckhart* (Santa Fe: Bear, 1982), 111.
36. Johnson, *Quest for the Living God*, 227.

One final but significant point I wish to make: for much of the Bible, the starting point for portraying God is an anthropocentric one that results in many portraits of God that reflect the human person and the human condition, for example, God depicted as warrior, and in the case of Daughter Zion, God as a male—a lover, a husband, a father figure. We humans, because we need relational metaphors for God, often use anthropocentric ones, but the truth is this: the Sacred Presence we have labeled "God" is none of the anthropocentric metaphors we find in the Bible, nor is this Sacred Presence any of the new anthropocentric metaphors we will devise in the future. Perhaps the closest understanding we can come to "God" is a cosmological one: God as Spirit, as light, as love, and even these descriptions are metaphors. Our starting point for understanding God can no longer be an anthropocentric one. Our starting point must be a cosmological one that flows from the experience of being one with all that exists. Only then will we begin to understand anew the wonder, the mystery, the beauty of the Sacred Presence we call "God." By exposing and interacting with the metaphorical language associated with "God," by having Daughter Zion talk back to "God" in a way that informs, instructs, and often shocks, Mandolfo has respectfully debunked the Bible's God whom human beings have created and has not only opened the door for dialogue about the God of the Bible but also pointed us toward the Truth if only we have eyes to see, ears to hear, minds to perceive, and hearts to know.

Daughter Zion Talks Back to Her Interlocutors

Carleen Mandolfo

This "dialogic" volume represents a humbling moment for me. My book, *Daughter Zion Talks Back to the Prophets,* no more deserves a volume of essays dedicated to it than countless other monographs written by my colleagues. But I do not want to brush off the gesture, either; rather, I want to express my sincerest gratitude to the editors and to everyone who took their valuable time and energy to contribute to it. Although *Daughter Zion* is clearly the product of someone trained in the academy as a biblical scholar, it was conceived out of a deep personal commitment, so I am particularly gratified that this volume has found resonance with some of my colleagues. As I read through these essays in the quiet of my office or home, I found myself engaged in vigorous dialogue and/or debate with each of them, and while I would have preferred to dialogue in person with their authors, I have to settle for a written response.

The essays in this volume engage *Daughter Zion* (and Daughter Zion) with diverse methodologies and varied critical assessments, ranging from strong disagreement to constructive appropriation (as you might imagine, my most spirited private engagements were with the former!). When I was considering how one goes about responding to fifteen essays (I find responding to a panel of papers challenging enough), it occurred to me that to take them on one by one, especially those I would be rebutting, would result in my having, for all intents and purposes, the "final say." The thought struck me as singularly ironic—bordering on hypocritical—for a scholar who so avowedly espouses a dialogic hermeneutic to make such a move. So I have decided to offer rather informal and not particularly systematic reflections of a more metacritical sort. Along the way, I will engage a number of the essays, but not all.

Musing on this collection of essays led me to consider the issue of critical engagement itself. I found myself asking questions having to do with the ways in which we choose to engage with one another. What assumptions and critical backgrounds do we bring that make us "agree" or "disagree"? Why do we choose to bring one method and not another to the conversation? Some of these essays engage quite directly with my methods and conclusions; others clearly find little resonance in the issues that are so pressing for me and choose to take up very different approaches, sometimes not even related to the questions I am trying to pose. In those cases, I wondered at how different our questions can be, even around the same text or topic. Illustrative of the divergences, Cheryl Kirk-Duggan, rather than critiquing my work, chooses to appropriate it for thinking about ways we can provide agential tools to those victimized by domestic abuse; while Michael Floyd points out the flaws in my conceptual assumptions by trying to recover the tradition-historical *intention* of the metaphorical "target" and demonstrating how I have conflated the various female figurations scattered throughout the prophets and Lamentations. In between these two are essays, like Mark Boda's, that share some methodological ground (in this case form criticism) with *Daughter Zion*, but move the particular conversation forward through both appropriation and critique.

My reflections here will be organized as follows. First, I will try to make some observations about my own hermeneutic commitments stimulated by observations made in my colleagues' fine essays. Second, I will make an attempt to organize said essays according to the intellectual commitments they seem to espouse. I am fully aware that doing so is an act of translation. That is, it is an interpretive move rather than a "scientific" procedure, and it is possible and perhaps likely that the authors of these essays may disagree with my placement of their work. Such a state of affairs is, of course, part and parcel of a dialogic hermeneutic—every reading is an act of authoring, and both authors (who were first readers) and readers (who are also authors) should be enriched by the process, a process that has no actual telos beyond the process. So I beg the indulgence of my contributor colleagues as I try to "make sense" of their essays, with the recognition that they will never make the sense to me that they made to them! If it is any comfort, I too had several times to remind myself of this fact as I read through the essays. I lost track of how many times I said to myself, "But that is not what I meant." The truth is, however, more often than not, their "misreading" turned out to be full of "meaning" that enhanced my own understanding. This point is not to advocate frivolous misreadings, of course. The lines may be fine, but understanding requires work. And below I will say more about this, drawing on Paul Ricoeur's insights about the hermeneutic process. The last section of my reflections will include some observations about how our disparate approaches work together to fulfill Ricoeur's thoughtful (and I think well-balanced) reading agenda.

MY READING OF MY HERMENEUTIC

Many of the remarks in this section have been inspired by Yvonne Sherwood's and Stephen D. Moore's recent (*brand new* at this writing) book, *The Invention of the Biblical Scholar*.[1] I was put in a metacritical frame of mind by their uniquely insightful chronicle of this equally unique (or "irreducibly strange," to use their terminology) discipline of ours. One of their primary points is that even those hermeneutic dispositions that the majority of our colleagues find "radical" (i.e., "theory") are merely carrying on the Enlightenment project of sustaining biblical authority through an emphasis on its cultural (rather than theological, per se) influence. While the point is well taken, my references to their work have more to do with several particular observations they make along the way. For instance, while addressing the interesting fact that biblical criticism quickly became "historical" criticism, they note that

> the zones of potential inquiry were myriad but also severely circum-scribed, not least because the emerging discipline eventually set aside and repressed what we are calling "moral critique"—critique of the morality of certain biblical material and even of the biblical God—though such critique had featured prominently in the discipline's earlier stages.[2]

I think many of our colleagues would have to concede that to describe one's work as "moral" is tantamount to surrendering our SBL membership cards. Indeed, biblical scholars have become "methodolaters" precisely in order to "keep our discourse on the Bible from being subjective, personal, private, pietistic, pastoral, devotional, or homiletical."[3] Of course, the aversion to moral considerations in biblical scholarship is not shared by every-

---

1. Yvonne Sherwood and Stephen D. Moore, *The Invention of the Biblical Scholar: A Critical Manifesto* (Minneapolis: Fortress, 2011).

2. Ibid., x. See also p. 59: "After the eighteenth century, the investigation of biblical morality was quietly dropped from the job description of the biblical scholar."

3. Ibid., 40. Relatedly, a couple of the scholars in this volume appear distressed by my seemingly "casual" analysis. I am not rigorous and exacting enough. Not coincidentally, these are essays that emphasize historical concerns (see Floyd and Tiemeyer).

one. And others are more or less unaware that this area of inquiry has been resurrected: "This repressed terrain does not ordinarily appear in standard histories of the discipline, even though its relationship to contemporary politicized forms of biblical scholarship, such as feminist, ideological, and postcolonial, is profound."[4]

My hermeneutic commitment may be first and foremost a moral-critical one, in the sense that it approaches texts with a feminist and postcolonial sensibility (toward the goal of freeing shackled voices).[5] That commitment, for me, certainly trumps "accuracy" in the sense of a singular, correct reading, based solely on a rigorous examination of the historical backdrop. That does not mean that I do not employ grammatical and historical analysis as a way to provide guardrails to my conclusions, but only that my principle impulse moves beyond "commentary" to judgment. I consider the ability to judge to be a primary index of human intellection and creativity. On this also I take my cue from Sherwood and Moore: "In biblical studies, the model of the good reader is the commentator. This self-effacing reader does not write but, as his name implies, merely comments.... For hundreds of pages at a time, there's little or nothing in his own text to indicate that it was written by a living, breathing human being."[6] Admittedly, my text may breathe too much humanity. Since I want my work to *matter* to other living, breathing humans (even if only a few), however, that seems best achieved by not trying to hide the humanity of my commitments.

Beyond my theoretical commitments is manifested another commitment that falls under the rubric of "moral" criticism—my theological emphasis. I consider *Daughter Zion* to be a book of biblical theology, but I am not interested in biblical theology in the sense of a better understanding

---

Still others object that my reading is inaccurate because it is not the interpretation original audiences would have come up with (see Green and Kim).

4. Ibid., xi. Out of curiosity, I did a word search in my *Daughter Zion* manuscript for the word *moral* only to find that I use it so many times I gave up the search. I was surprised; I would have thought that in most instances I would have substituted "ethical" for "moral" because I find that I am one of those whose default position is to think that moral inquiry tends to denote lack of critical rigor.

5. "Indeed, it was only in the last quarter of the twentieth century that feminist biblical critics, followed by womanist, ideological, and postcolonial critics, began in earnest to reawaken the moral question from its centuries-long slumber" (Sherwood and Moore, *Invention*, 117).

6. Ibid., 113.

of the supreme deity so much as I am interested in a theological discussion as a trope for better understanding human relationality—in other words, for ethical rather than metaphysical purposes. The general questions about human agency, subjectivity, and power I address through a theological lens are nothing new, at least not for theologians and philosophers; but the texts I choose through which to address them, in combination with the particular methods I utilize, add a unique dimension to these age-old questions. My commitment to a dialogic version of biblical theology is well known to anyone who has read my work; and I think the moral/ethical dimensions of that reading strategy require no more comment.[7]

I would like to explore, however, another aspect of my version of biblical theology that I do not explicitly discuss in my book. My theological understanding is akin to Ricoeur's version of narrative theology.[8] The texts I discuss (Hosea, Jeremiah, Ezekiel, and Lam 1–2) are not narratives in the formal sense, but the dialogue I stage between them amounts to a "story" about a challenging moment in Yhwh's and Israel's relationship. Although Ricoeur explicitly eschews a "morally oriented theology," what he means by that is best understood in reference to his use of Ulrich Simon's description of the "Christian Pattern," which I understand to mean the postcanonical distillation of the biblical narrative that has "concealed and buried the 'multiplex nature' (Barr) of both the Old Testament and the New Testament tradition."[9] In other words, "moral" for him—in this case—amounts to a christological/doctrinal imposition (especially the notion of *Heilsgeschichte* developed by early German biblical critics/theologians) on the "pure" biblical narrative.

> [O]ne of the tasks of a narrative theology would be to liberate the biblical narratives from the constraints of the "Christian pattern" and ultimately the multi-plex network of biblical narratives from the univocally chronological schema of the history of salvation. Then memory and hope

---

7. For those unfamiliar with Bakhtin's potential for biblical hermeneutics, including biblical theology, see Barbara Green, *Mikhail Bakhtin and Biblical Scholarship: An Introduction* (SemeiaSt 38; Atlanta: Society of Biblical Literature, 2000); and Carol Newsom, "Bakhtin, the Bible, and Dialogic Truth," *JR* 76 (1996): 290–306.

8. A version that is critical of the neo-orthodox movement coming out of Yale that gave rise to "narrative theology" in the first place.

9. Paul Ricoeur, "Toward a Narrative Theology: Its Necessity, Its Resources, Its Difficulties," in *Figuring the Sacred: Religion, Narrative, and Imagination* (ed. Mark I. Wallace; trans. David Pellauer; Minneapolis: Fortress, 1995), 236–48, esp. 237.

would be delivered from the *visible* narrative that hides that which we may call, with Johann-Baptist Metz, the "dangerous memories" and the challenging expectations that together constitute the unresolved dialectic of memory and of hope.[10]

While there is probably more of my Christian, particularly Roman Catholic, background than I would like to admit manifested in my reading, its primary commitments lie explicitly elsewhere. I am much more interested in offering a reading *for* marginalized voices than *for* the church, or even *for* God. The second half of Ricoeur's statement also reflects an aspect of my hopes for my own work, especially as pertains to its dialogic elements. What Ricoeur calls the "unresolved dialectic" could be replaced with Bakhtin's notion of the dialogic, in which discourses interact endlessly without the resolution that is implied by dialectic synthesis. I also think the "dangerous memories," like those preserved in Lamentations, are crucial participants in the full sweep of biblical theological claims.[11]

Neither a moral-critical approach nor a theological approach should be understood as methodological, but methods can be used to answer the questions such approaches imply. My methods are something of a hodgepodge. My primary training was firmly situated in the methods of historical criticism, but complemented by a wide variety of other criticisms, such as literary, linguistic/discourse analysis, social-scientific, and cultural, among others, each of which has connected to it a variety of methods. With regard to historical-critical method, form criticism is foremost among my methodological tools, but this method is not your grandfather Gunkel's form criticism.[12] For my purposes, attention to the intertextual relationship of genres aids in elucidating the message of the voices I am interested

---

10. Ibid., 238.

11. In their introduction to biblical theology, Leo Perdue et al. make a similar point when they note that for Walter Brueggemann "pluralism is a major characteristic that disallows any systematic presentation, that the cultural contexts of interpreters play an important role in interpretation, that voices from the margin in both scripture and the contemporary world are important to hear, that they must have a role in the world of authentic faith, that a 'grammar of faith' construing God through various parts of speech takes precedence over ontology and acts of salvation, and that scripture is not to be demeaned by reading it only through the eyes of Christianity and the New Testament" (Leo Perdue, Robert Morgan, and Benjamin D. Sommer, *Biblical Theology: Introducing the Conversation* [Nashville: Abingdon, 2009], 234).

12. See Marvin Sweeney and Ehud ben Zvi, *The Changing Face of Form Criticism*

in highlighting. In other words, very little exists that is "historical," per se, in my use of form criticism. In contrast to traditional form criticism, I have little to no interest in discovering the *Sitze im Leben* of the genres with which I am dealing, except perhaps insofar as the ideological tensions I uncover probably reflect similar tensions in the society that initially created these texts. Whether or not intentional, these tensions are "readable" today, as are the voices that give expression to them. So my intertextual/dialogic approach combined with deconstructive feminist and postcolonial emphases gives my form-critical endeavor a decidedly postmodern cast that serves my theological and moral agenda.

My Reading of the Hermeneutics of My Interlocutors

As stated above, I am going to attempt to catalogue the essays included in this volume in order to offer some perspective about the differences in our interpretive approaches. The final paragraph of the previous section illustrates how complex methodological descriptions tend to be. Very rarely do even the most rigorous scholars go about their critical task by choosing a single method and then mechanically applying it their subject texts. We tend to read texts, get a sense of what they mean (Ricoeur calls this initial reading the "first naïveté"), and then pick and choose whatever tools seem most appropriate for helping us support, refine, and check our interpretive instincts. This way of reading and interpreting is often done subconsciously, especially by those committed to traditional historical-critical methods, because the assumption in those cases is often that historical-critical tools are the "natural"—and so only—tools for such a task. In any case, because our hermeneutic approaches are often chosen and applied organically rather than self-consciously, untangling their strands in order to describe them proves to be surprisingly difficult.

I have decided to divide the essays into those that are more author-oriented and those that are more reader-oriented. This distinction could also be understood as that between "meant" and "means." My choice of this ordering is related to a tension that became readily apparent to me as I was reading through them. The majority of those most critical of *Daughter Zion* were dissatisfied with my apparent lack of respect for the "intention"

---

for the Twenty-first Century (Grand Rapids: Eerdmans, 2003), for a useful assessment of the continuing evolution of form criticism.

of the text. Beyond (and perhaps because of) their "genetic" commitments, these essays are marked by particularly strong methodologies and rigorous analysis. Interestingly, the essays broke down fairly evenly between these two categories. Those that I read as having a greater orientation toward the author include: Mark Boda, Michael Floyd, Barbara Green, John Hobbins, Brittany Kim, Christl Maier, Kim Lan Nguyen, and Lena-Sofia Tiemeyer. Those in the reader camp include: Mary Conway, Stephen Cook, Carol Dempsey, Mignon Jacobs, Cheryl Kirk-Duggan, Jill Middlemas, and LeAnn Snow Flesher. Those that rely largely on form criticism to make their case (like Boda and Middlemas) are particularly tricky to categorize because form criticism is inherently both synchronic and diachronic depending on the emphasis of the one applying it. I place Boda in the author camp because of his attention to the *Sitz im Leben* of the *Aufruf zur Freude*; and Middlemas goes into the reader camp because she more firmly situates her observations on the forms themselves.

The only two in the reader camp who strongly disagree with me are Cook and Conway, and their disagreements seem to hinge on faith commitments. Neither is pleased with my claim that Daughter Zion's condition remains unresolved and furthermore that in her case the deity is resolutely abusive. In order to counteract my negative assessment, Cook questions my philosophic principles, namely my insistence on ethics and reciprocity as the standards by which to judge the deity; and instead proposes an aesthetic standard of salvation. For him, the deity as deity is not open to the same ethical standards that humans are. To my mind, his position is *primarily* rooted in faith, not biblical speech. This is the point where my commitment to a type of narrative theology, rather than a canonical or doctrinal one, is simply irreconcilable with Cook's position. I certainly cannot *argue* with him, however, for loving God more than Zion! Conway comes at the theological questions posed by these texts from a methodological viewpoint very similar to mine—dialogic discourse analysis—but she has to make recourse to a different conversation to salvage the divine name; namely she permits the *geber* of Lam 3 into the conversation and keeps the prophets out of the equation. She seems to want to offer an alternative interpretation of the book of Lamentations itself, rather than an interpretation of God and Daughter Zion's relationship.

Several of the author-oriented essays level strong critiques at my work (that is not to say that they do not also generously accede that I have made some contributions). I am thinking specifically of Floyd, Green, Hobbins, Kim, and Nguyen. Floyd takes exception to the cavalier way I conflate the different figurative women in the prophets and Lamentations. He does this by a focus on the tradition history of the various female figurations, exploring what each may have *meant* in their varied contexts. His precise "explanation" of the various metaphorical targets seems sound to me. In other words, Floyd's work suggests that I am staging an improper conversation. Point taken; no question that I am *staging* a conversation in order to consider the impact of these texts on readers, but I would have to think more about what proper and improper mean in this context. I might at this point refer to Dempsey's comment that I am being "critically playful with the text." Not that I would want to suggest that authorial intention is the standard of meaning, but I agree with her. Green is sympathetic to my ethical concerns but has methodological objections to my reading. I think it is safe to say that she thinks I have played too fast and loose with the metaphor: "Has the metaphor been pulled so relentlessly out of context that we miss something vital by focusing narrowly on one linguistic referent?" She then performs a painstakingly careful and brilliant cognitive linguistic operation on the metaphor to compensate for my overindulgence. I have indeed pulled it "out of context" (if not necessarily "relentlessly"). If my book were the definitive word on these texts we would most certainly be missing "something vital." Fortunately, we have Green's observations, as well as countless others, to hold up alongside mine.

Ah, Hobbins. I love this essay. He may be my fiercest critic, but I am in thrall to his bold, "authorial" voice.[13] I am grateful for his recognition that I am executing a "strong misreading" (*à la* Harold Bloom) of Daughter Zion. I am not sure if he is congratulating me or admonishing me, but I think it is an apt characterization. In any case, he nobly claims to rescue Zion's voice from me and give it back to her. Given my stated ethical commitments, I am forced to concur wholeheartedly with the goal; but how exactly to do what he proposes? Merely quote her, verbatim, I wondered? Given that Hobbins wrote the longest essay of the bunch, apparently Zion had more to say than I realized![14]

---

13. In accord with Sherwood and Moore's implicit admonition against "dull and dreary" scholarship (*Invention*, 40–41).

14. If our medium were email, this is the point at which I would include a smiley face; but two serious issues should be raised in regard to Hobbins's essay, one intellectual, one political: (1) Pretty much every hermeneutic since Gadamer has understood that there is no way to avoid inflecting the voices that we engage with as readers. *Every act of interpretation is an act of appropriation.* (2) I would not be comfortable ignor-

Kim rightly acknowledges that the questions we bring to the text will determine the kinds of answers we derive. It just so happens that her primary question is the polar opposite of mine: she wants to know how the "*original* audience might have understood these texts." In short, she notes that my theological conclusions are colored by my context. True.

Nguyen has methodological and theological issues with my book. Her intention to recover the "author's strategy" does not resonate for me, but her rigorous form- and rhetorical-critical analysis helps to refine my conclusions. Specifically, she contests my claim that Lam 1 downplays Daughter Zion's sin by pointing out that "compared to the psalm laments, Lamentations says more, not less, about sin"—an excellent form-critical observation that were I to write *Daughter Zion* again I would definitely include.

Concluding Reflections

All of these critics, to a greater or lesser extent, object to my *appropriation* of Daughter Zion's voice for purposes that may be in conflict with the original intent of the poet. What should be clear at this point is that, for me, what the text "means" is only partially connected to what it "meant." For one thing, as dialogic theory teaches us, the utterance never possessed singularity. Roland Barthes captures it well: "We know now that a text is not a line of words releasing a single 'theological' meaning (the 'message' of the Author-God), but of a multidimensional space in which a variety of writings, none of them original, blend and clash."[15] I would venture to say that most of my colleagues contributing to this volume know this.[16] Still, as Sherwood and Moore demonstrate, the concern for origins (which is tied

---

ing his implication that by not being in more explicit dialogue with "Jewish exegesis" I am contributing to a "history of oppression and teaching of contempt that has characterized non-Jewish exegesis from time immemorial." It hardly needs to be said, and yet apparently must be said, that such essentialist claims dismiss decades of thinking on the issues of identity and subjectivity. In other words, his point may or may not be true, but it requires far more nuance. That said, his engagement with Jewish texts, ancient and modern, is profoundly moving and models a kind of poetic and yet critical dialogic I hope to emulate one day.

15. Roland Barthes, "The Death of the Author," in *Image-Music-Text* (trans. Stephen Heath; New York: Hill & Wang, 1987), 146.

16. After all, it has been noted countless times. For an early contemporary discussion see John Barton, *Reading the Old Testament: Method in Biblical Study* (Philadelphia: Westminster, 1984).

to the quest for "accuracy") has deep roots in our discipline, and as such still drives our hermeneutic endeavors. Biblical criticism's obsession with method is a symptom of this concern to find the original intent of the writing. In other words, since its inception, the field of biblical studies has been treated more like a science than a critical art—apply the correct methods in the right way, and achieve accurate results. "What other discipline in the humanities has striven more determinedly to perform the separation of the properly critical subject from the properly studied object?"[17]

None of this should be read as an anti-methodic manifesto, however, but rather as reflections meant to urge us to think more about what it means to be biblical *critics*, and to what degree "understanding" versus "explanation" should be our goal. The relationship between understanding and explanation (i.e., analysis) frames Ricoeur's observations about the hermeneutic circle.

> The interplay of explanation and understanding begins here: the initial impression can be tested, corrected, and deepened by recourse to the objective structure of the text. A sophisticated understanding must pass through the moment of explanation, and hermeneutics encompasses both procedures. Strictly speaking, Ricoeur says these are not two *methods* of approach, since only explanation is methodic: "Understanding is rather the nonmethodic moment which, in the sciences of interpretation, comes together with the methodic moment of explanation. Understanding precedes, accompanies, closes, and thus *envelops* explanation. In return, explanation *develops* understanding analytically."[18]

Traditional historical-critical analysis is most typically tied in our field to rigorously applied methodologies, which can be seen in the prototypical version of biblical criticism—the commentary. Commentaries are undeniably useful tools, but they usually stop short of "understanding" the texts on which they comment. Ricoeur suggests that interpretation is not complete until analysis gives way to understanding (and that understanding remains naïve unless tempered by analysis). This is not to say that the essays I characterize as author-oriented are empty analyses (they are not), but conversely to first suggest that my "understanding" might benefit from engagement with some of their "explanations." For

---

17. Sherwood and Moore, *Invention,* xii.

18. David E. Klemm, *The Hermeneutical Theory of Paul Ricoeur: A Constructive Analysis* (East Brunswick, N.J.: Associated University Presses, 1983), 91.

instance, as suggested above, Nguyen's essay is an excellent example of the way that rigorous analysis (i.e., explanation) can inform understanding. (Boda's essay, which does not really qualify as a "strong critique" of my work and so was not addressed in that section, is another example of rigorous form-critical analysis that would enhance, by balancing out, my reading of Daughter Zion's relationship with Yhwh.)[19] It is also to say, however, that too often biblical scholarship gets bogged down in analysis and thereby neglects to *say* much of anything, in the end.

This state of affairs seems risky to me, both for our profession and for the culture in which we are embedded. "Even as the general public has become less and less interested in what the professional biblical scholar has to say, the profession has become more and more interested in ensuring that the biblical scholar spend less and less time addressing himself or herself to the general public."[20] Biblical scholars are at absolute liberty, of course, to pursue purely intellectual commitments in regard to their work. Many, perhaps correctly, believe that political commitments of any kind only muddy the discipline and are transitory, in any case. I admit to a bias, since I choose to work at a seminary whose mission is explicitly both intellectual and political. Lest, however, the word *political* mislead anyone, let me clarify—"meaningful" does not need to connote explicitly "political" (though it often does). Once again, I fall back on Ricoeur to nuance the hermeneutical possibilities. The point of reading for Ricoeur is to "transfigure experience," and I take that to mean all types of human experience; but that can only happen in the engagement between reader and text. *Meaning* does not reside solely *in* the text. So all the digging in the world *into the text* will not uncover the meaning. It only becomes more meaning*less*, in fact. Analysis, yes. Interpretation, no.[21] Unless analysis is translated into meaning, analysis cannot transfigure experience. Biblical texts are first and foremost imaginative discourse, and only secondly historical facts to be verified, or grammatical particulates to be defined. Like the interpretation of all literature, biblical interpretation should point the reader to a "mode of being,"[22] whether defined socially/politically or personally. Now I am getting preachy. How one interprets the biblical text is

---

19. Boda concludes with some very interesting observations that I would include in the category of "understanding."

20. Sherwood and Moore, *Invention*, 78.

21. Ricoeur, "Toward a Narrative Theology," 240.

22. Klemm, *Hermeneutical Theory of Paul Ricoeur*, 91.

a personal/professional decision everyone has to make for herself or himself. I am simply aware that we are at a moment in our history when religious understandings, including the texts that undergird them, can offer significant insights into the global challenges we face. So I will conclude by admitting that I might choose to err on the side of *saying* too much.

Bibliography

Abma, Richtsje. *Bonds of Love: Methodic Studies of Prophetic Texts with Marriage Imagery (Isaiah 50:1-3 and 54:1-10, Hosea 1-3, Jeremiah 2-3)*. Studia semitica neerlandica 40. Assen: Van Gorcum, 1999.

Abu-Lughod, Lila. *Veiled Sentiments: Honor and Poetry in a Bedouin Society*. Berkeley: University of California Press, 1986.

Adams, J. *The Performative Nature and Function of Isaiah 40-55*. Library of Hebrew Bible/Old Testament Studies 448. London: T&T Clark, 2006.

Albertz, Rainer. *Israel in Exile: The History and Literature of the Sixth Century B.C.E.* Translated by David Green. Society of Biblical Literature Studies in Biblical Literature 3. Atlanta: Society of Biblical Literature, 2003.

Albrektson, Bertil. *Studies in the Text and Theology of the Book of Lamentations*. Studia theologica lundensia 21. Lund: Gleerup, 1963.

Alexiou, Margaret. *The Ritual Lament in Greek Tradition*. 2nd ed. Revised by Dimitrios Yatromanolakis and Panagiotis Roilos. Greek Studies: Interdisciplinary Approaches. Lanham, Md.: Rowman & Littlefield, 2002.

Alison, James. *Knowing Jesus*. Springfield, Ill.: Templegate, 1993.

Alonso Schökel, Luis. *A Manual of Hebrew Poetics*. Subsidia biblica 11. Rome: Pontifical Biblical Institute, 1988.

Alter, Robert. *The Art of Biblical Narrative*. New York: Basic Books, 1981.

———. *The Art of Biblical Poetry*. New York: Basic Books, 1985.

Amichai, Yehuda. *Poems of Jerusalem and Love Poems: A Bilingual Edition*. Riverdale-on-Hudson: Sheep Meadow Press, 1992.

Andersen, Francis I., and David Noel Freedman. *Hosea: A New Translation with Introduction and Commentary*. Anchor Bible 24. Garden City, N.Y.: Doubleday, 1980.

Anderson, Gary A. *A Time to Mourn, a Time to Dance: The Expression of Grief and Joy in Israelite Religion*. University Park: Pennsylvania State University Press, 1991.

Bach, Alice. "Reading Allowed: Feminist Biblical Criticism Approaching the Millennium." *Currents in Research: Biblical Studies* 1 (1993): 191–215.

Balentine, Samuel. "I Was Ready to Be Sought by Those Who Did Not Ask." Pages 1–20 in *Seeking the Favor of God*. Vol. 1: *The Origins of Penitential Prayer in Second Temple Judaism*. Edited by Mark J. Boda, Daniel K. Falk, and Rodney A. Werline. Society of Biblical Literature Early Judaism and Its Literature 21. Atlanta: Society of Biblical Literature, 2006.

Baltzer, Dieter. *Ezechiel und Deuterojesaja*. Beihefte zur Zeitschrift für die alttestamentliche Wissenschaft 121. Berlin: de Gruyter, 1971.

Baltzer, Klaus. *Deutero-Isaiah: A Commentary on Isaiah 40–55*. Translated by M. Kohl. Hermeneia. Minneapolis: Fortress, 2001

———. "Stadt-Tyche oder Zion-Jerusalem? Die Auseinandersetzung mit den Göttern der Zeit bei Deuterojesaja." Pages 114–19 in *Alttestamentlicher Glaube und Biblische Theologie: Festschrift für Horst Dietrich Preuss zum 65. Geburtstag*. Edited by Jutta Hausmann and Hans-Jürgen Zobel. Stuttgart: Kohlhammer, 1992.

Barstad, Hans M. *The Babylonian Captivity of the Book of Isaiah: "Exilic" Judah and the Provenance of Isaiah 40–55*. Oslo: Novus: Instituttet for Sammenlignende Kulturforskning, 1997.

———. *A Way in the Wilderness: The "Second Exodus" in the Message of Second Isaiah*. Journal of Semitic Studies Monograph 12. Manchester: University of Manchester Press, 1989.

Barthes, Roland. *Image-Music-Text*. Translated by Stephen Heath. New York: Hill & Wang, 1987.

Barton, John. *Reading the Old Testament: Method in Biblical Study*. Philadelphia: Westminster, 1984.

———. *Reading the Old Testament: Method in Biblical Study*. Rev. ed. Louisville: Westminster John Knox, 1996.

Bauer, Angela. *Gender in the Book of Jeremiah: A Feminist-Literary Reading*. New York: Peter Lang, 1999.

Baumann, Gerlinde. *Love and Violence: Marriage as Metaphor for the Relationship between Yhwh and Israel in the Prophetic Books*. Translated by Linda M. Maloney. Collegeville, Minn.: Liturgical Press, 2003.

Bautch, Richard J. *Developments in Genre between Post-exilic Penitential Prayers and the Psalms of Communal Lament*. Society of Biblical Literature Academia Biblica 7. Atlanta: Society of Biblical Literature, 2003.

————. "Lament Regained in Trito-Isaiah's Penitential Prayer." Pages 83–101 in *Seeking the Favor of God. Vol. 1: The Origins of Penitential Prayer in Second Temple Judaism*. Edited by Mark J. Boda, Daniel K. Falk, and Rodney A. Werline. Society of Biblical Literature Early Judaism and Its Literature 21. Atlanta: Society of Biblical Literature, 2006.

Bayer, Oswald. *Living by Faith: Justification and Sanctification*. Translated by Geoffrey Bromiley. Lutheran Quarterly Books. Grand Rapids: Eerdmans, 2003.

————. *Martin Luther's Theology: A Contemporary Interpretation*. Translated by Thomas H. Trapp. Grand Rapids: Eerdmans, 2008.

————. "Toward a Theology of Lament." Pages 211–20 in *Caritas et Reformatio: Essays on Church and Society in Honor of Carter Lindberg*. Edited by David M. Whitford. St. Louis: Concordia, 2004.

Begrich, Joachim. *Studien zu Deuterojesaja*. Theologische Bücherei 20. Munich: Chr. Kaiser, 1963.

Ben-Ze'ev, Aaron. "Envy and Jealousy." *Canadian Journal of Philosophy* 20 (1990): 487–516.

Berg, Werner. "Die Eifersucht Gottes: Ein problematischer Zug des alttestamentlichen Gottesbildes?" *Biblische Zeitschrift* 23 (1979): 197–211.

Berges, Ulrich. *Das Buch Jesaja: Komposition und Endgestalt*. Herders biblischen Studien 16. Freiburg: Herder, 1998.

————. "Personification and Prophetic Voices of Zion in Isaiah and Beyond." Pages 54–82 in *The Elusive Prophet: The Prophet as a Historical Person, Literary Character and Anonymous Artist*. Edited by Johannes C. de Moor. Oudtestamentische Studiën 45. Leiden: Brill, 2001.

Berkovits, Eliezer. *Faith after the Holocaust*. New York: Ktav, 1973.

Berlin, Adele. *Lamentations: A Commentary*. Old Testament Library. Louisville: Westminster John Knox, 2002.

Berquist, Jon L., and Claudia V. Camp, eds. *Constructions of Space I: Theory, Geography, and Narrative*. Library of Hebrew Bible/Old Testament Studies 481. New York: T&T Clark, 2007.

————. *Constructions of Space II: The Biblical City and Other Imagined Spaces*. Library of Hebrew Bible/Old Testament Studies 490. New York: T&T Clark, 2008.

Beuken, Willem A. M. "Isaiah Chapters LXV–LXVI: Trito-Isaiah and the Closure of the Book of Isaiah." Pages 204–21 in *Congress Volume: Leuven 1989*. Edited by John A. Emerton. Vetus Testamentum Supplements 43. Leiden: Brill, 1991.

———. *Jesaja deel IIA*. De Prediking van het Oude Testament 2A. Nijkerk: Callenbach, 1979.

———. "The Main Theme of Trito-Isaiah: The 'Servants of *Yhwh*.'" *Journal for the Study of the Old Testament* 47 (1990): 67–87.

Biddle, Mark. E. *Deuteronomy*. Smyth & Helwys Bible Commentary. Macon, Ga.: Smyth & Helwys, 2003.

———. "The Figure of Lady Jerusalem: Identification, Deification and Personification of Cities in the Ancient Near East." Pages 173–94 in *The Biblical Canon in Comparative Perspective*. Edited by K. Lawson Younger Jr., William W. Hallo, and Bernard F. Batto. Scripture in Context 4. Ancient Near Eastern Texts and Studies 11. Lewiston, N.Y.: Mellen, 1991.

———. "Lady Zion's Alter Egos: Isaiah 47.1–15 and 57.6–13 as Structural Counterparts." Pages 124–39 in *New Visions of Isaiah*. Edited by Roy F. Melugin and Marvin A. Sweeney. Journal for the Study of the Old Testament Supplement Series 214. Sheffield: Sheffield Academic Press, 1996.

Birch, Bruce C. *Hosea, Joel, and Amos*. Westminster Bible Companion. Louisville: Westminster John Knox, 1997.

Bird, Phyllis. "'To Play the Harlot': An Inquiry into an Old Testament Metaphor." Pages 219–236 in *Missing Persons and Mistaken Identities: Women and Gender in Ancient Israel*. Minneapolis: Fortress, 1997.

Black, Max. "Metaphor." Pages 63–82 in *Philosophical Perspectives on Metaphor*. Edited by Mark Johnson. Minneapolis: University of Minnesota Press, 1981.

———. *Models and Metaphors: Studies in Language and Philosophy*. Ithaca, N.Y.: Cornell University Press, 1962.

Blenkinsopp, Joseph. *Ezekiel*. Interpretation: A Bible Commentary for Teaching and Preaching. Louisville: John Knox, 1990.

———. *A History of Prophecy in Israel*. Philadelphia: Westminster, 1983.

———. *Isaiah 40–55: A New Translation with Introduction and Commentary*. Anchor Bible 19A. New York: Doubleday, 2002.

———. *Isaiah 56–66: A New Translation with Introduction and Commentary*. Anchor Bible 19B. New York: Doubleday, 2003.

Block, Daniel I. *The Book of Ezekiel: Chapters 1–24*. New International Commentary on the Old Testament. Grand Rapids: Eerdmans, 1997.

———. *The Book of Ezekiel: Chapters 25–48*. New International Commentary on the Old Testament. Grand Rapids: Eerdmans, 1998.

———. "Marriage and Family in Ancient Israel." Pages 33–102 in *Marriage and Family in the Biblical World*. Edited by Ken M. Campbell. Downers Grove, Ill.: InterVarsity Press, 2003.

Bloom, Harold. *The Anxiety of Influence: A Theory of Poetry*. New York: Oxford University Press, 1973.

Boase, Elizabeth. *The Fulfilment of Doom? The Dialogic Interaction between the Book of Lamentations and the Pre-Exilic/Early Exilic Prophetic Literature*. Library of Hebrew Bible/Old Testament Studies 437. New York: T&T Clark, 2006.

Boda, Mark J. "Messengers of Hope in Haggai–Malachi." *Journal for the Study of the Old Testament* 32 (2007): 113–31.

———. "The Priceless Gain of Penitence: From Communal Lament to Penitential Prayer in the 'Exilic' Liturgy of Israel." Pages 81–101 in *Lamentations in Ancient and Contemporary Contexts*. Edited by Nancy C. Lee and Carleen Mandolfo. Society of Biblical Literature Symposium Series 43. Atlanta: Society of Biblical Literature, 2008.

———. *A Severe Mercy: Sin and Its Remedy in the Old Testament*. Siphrut: Literature and Theology of the Hebrew Scriptures 1. Winona Lake, Ind.: Eisenbrauns, 2009.

———. "'Uttering Precious Rather Than Worthless Words': Divine Patience and Impatience with Lament in Isaiah and Jeremiah." In *Lament: Israel's Cry to God*. Edited by Boda, Carol Dempsey, and LeAnn Snow Flesher. Library of Hebrew Bible/Old Testament Studies 552. London: Continuum, forthcoming.

Botterweck, G. Johannes, Helmer Ringgren, and Heinz-Josef Fabry, eds. *Theological Dictionary of the Old Testament*. Translated by John T. Willis, Geoffrey W. Bromiley, David E. Green, and Douglas W. Stott. 15 vols. Grand Rapids: Eerdmans, 1974–2006.

Bourke, Angela. "More in Anger than in Sorrow: Irish Women's Lament Poetry." Pages 160–82 in *Feminist Messages: Coding in Women's Folk Culture*. Edited by Joan Newlon Radner. Urbana: Illinois University Press, 1993.

Bouzard, Walter C. *We Have Heard with Our Ears, O God: Sources of the Communal Laments in the Psalms*. Society of Biblical Literature Dissertation Series 159. Atlanta: Scholars Press, 1997.

Bradshaw, Paul F. "The Influence of Jerusalem on Christian Liturgy." Pages 251–59 in *Jerusalem: Its Sanctity and Centrality to Judaism, Christianity, and Islam*. Edited by Lee I. Levine. New York: Continuum, 1999.

Brenner, Athalya. "On Prophetic Propaganda and the Politics of 'Love.'" Pages 87–105 in *Reflections on Theology and Gender*. Edited by Fokkelien van Dijk-Hemmes and Athalya Brenner. Kampen: Kok Pharos, 1994.

Brettler, Marc Zvi. "Incompatible Metaphors for *Yhwh* in Isaiah 40–66." *Journal for the Study of the Old Testament* 78 (1998): 97–120.

Brichto, Herbert Chanan. "Case of the *Sōṭā* and a Reconsideration of Biblical 'Law.'" *Hebrew Union College Annual* 46 (1975): 55–70.

Briggs, Charles L. "Personal Sentiments and Polyphonic Voices in Warao Women's Ritual Wailing." *American Anthropologist* 95 (1993): 929–57.

———. "'Since I Am a Woman, I Will Chastise My Relatives': Gender, Reported Speech, and the (Re)Production of Social Relations in Warao Ritual Wailing." *American Ethnologist* 19 (1992): 337–61.

Bright, John. *Jeremiah*. Anchor Bible 21. Garden City, N.Y.: Doubleday, 1965.

Brown, Francis, Samuel Rolles Driver, and Charles Augustus Briggs. *Enhanced Brown-Driver-Briggs Hebrew and English Lexicon*. Electronic ed. Oak Harbor, Wash.: Logos Research Systems, 2000.

Brownlee, William H. *Ezekiel 1–19*. Word Biblical Commentary 28. Waco, Tex.: Word, 1986.

Broyles, Craig C. *The Conflict of Faith and Experience in the Psalms: A Form-Critical and Theological Study*. Journal for the Study of the Old Testament Supplement Series 52. Sheffield: JSOT Press, 1989.

Brueggemann, Walter. *A Commentary on Jeremiah: Exile and Homecoming*. Grand Rapids: Eerdmans, 1998.

———. "The Costly Loss of Lament." *Journal for the Study of the Old Testament* 36 (1986): 57–71.

———. *Isaiah*. Westminster Bible Companion. Louisville: Westminster John Knox, 1998.

———. *The Message of the Psalms: A Theological Commentary*. Minneapolis: Augsburg, 1984.

———. *Theology of the Old Testament: Testimony, Dispute, Advocacy*. Minneapolis: Fortress, 1997.

———. "Voice as Counter to Violence." *Calvin Theological Journal* 36 (2001): 22.

Brueggemann, Walter, and Hans Walter Wolff. *The Vitality of Old Testament Traditions*. 2nd ed. Atlanta: John Knox, 1982.

Brunson, Hal. "A Door of Hope." First Baptist Church of Parker Texas.

Preached 25 May 2005. Online: http://www.sermonaudio.com/ser-moninfo.asp?SID=52905145841.

Burkes, Shannon. *Death in Qoheleth and Egyptian Biographies of the Late Period*. Society of Biblical Literature Dissertation Series 170. Atlanta: Society of Biblical Literature, 1999.

Burnett, Anne Pippen. *Revenge in Attic and Later Tragedy*. Berkeley: University of California Press, 1998.

Buss, David M. *The Dangerous Passion: Why Jealousy Is as Necessary as Love and Sex*. New York: Free Press, 2000.

Callaway, Mary. *Sing, O Barren One: A Study in Comparative Midrash*. Society of Biblical Literature Dissertation Series 91. Atlanta: Scholars Press, 1986.

Carasik, Michael. *Theologies of the Mind in Biblical Israel*. Studies in Biblical Literature 85. New York: Peter Lang, 2005.

Caraveli [-Chaves], Anna. "The Bitter Wounding: The Lament as Social Protest in Rural Greece." Pages 169–94 in *Gender and Power in Rural Greece*. Edited by Jill Dubisch. Princeton: Princeton University Press, 1986.

———. "Bridge Between Worlds: The Greek Women's Lament as Communicative Event." *Journal of American Folklore* 368 (1980): 129–57.

Carr, David M. "Reading Isaiah from Beginning (Isaiah 1) to End (Isaiah 65–66): Multiple Modern Possibilities." Pages 188–218 in *New Visions of Isaiah*. Edited by Roy F. Melugin and Marvin A. Sweeney. Journal for the Study of the Old Testament Supplement Series 214. Sheffield: Sheffield Academic Press, 1996.

Carroll, Robert P. "Deportation and Diasporic Discourse in the Prophetic Literature." Pages 63–85 in *Exile: Old Testament, Jewish and Christian Conceptions*. Edited by James M. Scott. Journal for the Study of Judaism in the Persian, Hellenistic, and Roman Periods: Supplement Series 56. Leiden: Brill, 1997.

———. "Desire under the Terebinths: On Pornographic Representation in the Prophets—a Response." Pages 275–307 in *A Feminist Companion to the Latter Prophets*. Edited by Athalya Brenner. Feminist Companion to the Bible 8. Sheffield: Sheffield Academic Press, 1995.

———. "Exile! What Exile?" Pages 62–79 in *Leading Captivity Captive: "The Exile" as History and Ideology*. Edited by Lester L. Grabbe. Journal for the Study of the Old Testament Supplement Series 278. Sheffield: Sheffield Academic Press, 1998.

———. *Jeremiah: A Commentary.* Old Testament Library. Philadelphia: Westminster, 1986.

Carson, D. A. *Exegetical Fallacies.* Grand Rapids: Baker, 1984.

Ceccarelli, Leah. "Polysemy: Multiple Meanings in Rhetorical Criticism." *Quarterly Journal of Speech* 84 (1998): 395–415.

Chaney, Marvin. "Accusing Whom of What? Hosea's Rhetoric of Promiscuity." Pages 97–115 in *Distant Voices Drawing Near: Essays in Honor of Antoinette Clark Wire.* Edited by Holly E. Hearon. Collegeville, Minn.: Liturgical Press, 2004.

———. "Bitter Bounty: The Dynamics of Political Economy Critiqued by the Eighth-Century Prophets." Pages 15–30 in *Reformed Faith and Economics.* Edited by Robert L. Stivers. Lanham, Md.: University Press of America, 1989.

Childs, Brevard S. *The Book of Exodus.* Old Testament Library. Philadelphia: Westminster, 1974.

———. *Isaiah.* Old Testament Library. Louisville: Westminster John Knox, 2001.

Clements, Ronald E. *Ezekiel.* Westminster Bible Companion. Louisville: Westminster/John Knox, 1996.

———. *Isaiah 1–39.* New Century Bible. Grand Rapids: Eerdmans, 1980.

Collins, John J. "The Zeal of Phinehas: The Bible and the Legitimation of Violence." *Journal of Biblical Literature* 122 (2003): 3–21.

Conroy, Charles. "Reflections on Some Recent Studies of Second Isaiah." Pages 145–60 in *Palabra, Prodigio, Poesía: Im Memoriam P. Luis Alonso Schökel, S.J.* Edited by Vicente Collado Bertomeu. Analecta biblica 151. Rome: Pontifical Biblical Institute, 2003.

Cooey, Paula M. *Religious Imagination and the Body: A Feminist Analysis.* New York: Oxford University Press, 1994.

Cook, Stephen L. *Conversations with Scripture: 2 Isaiah.* Anglican Association of Biblical Scholars Study Series. Harrisburg: Morehouse, 2008.

———. "Cosmos, *Kabod,* and Cherub: Ontological and Epistemological Hierarchy in Ezekiel." Pages 179–97 in *Ezekiel's Hierarchical World: Wrestling with a Tiered Reality.* Edited by Stephen L. Cook and Corrine L. Patton. Society of Biblical Literature Symposium Series 31. Atlanta: Society of Biblical Literature, 2004.

Coulsen, Seana, and Todd Oakley. "Blending Basics." *Cognitive Linguistics* 11 (2000): 218–23.

Crenshaw, James L. *Ecclesiastes: A Commentary.* Old Testament Library. Philadelphia: Westminster, 1987.

Cross, Frank Moore. *From Epic to Canon: History and Literature in Ancient Israel.* Baltimore: Johns Hopkins University Press, 1998.

Crüsemann, Frank. *Studien zur Formgeschichte von Hymnus und Danklied in Israel.* Wissenschaftliche Monographien zum Alten und Neuen Testament 32. Neukirchen-Vluyn: Neukirchener, 1969.

Darr, Katheryn Pfisterer. "Ezekiel's Justifications of God: Teaching Troubling Texts." *Journal for the Study of the Old Testament* 55 (1992): 97–117.

———. *Isaiah's Vision and the Family of God.* Literary Currents in Biblical Interpretation. Louisville: Westminster John Knox, 1994.

Davies, Graham I. *Hosea.* New Century Bible. Grand Rapids: Eerdmans, 1992.

Day, Linda. "Rhetoric and Domestic Violence in Ezekiel 16." *Biblical Interpretation* 8 (2000): 205–30.

Day, Peggy L. "Adulterous Jerusalem's Imagined Demise: Death of a Metaphor in Ezekiel XVI." *Vetus Testamentum* 50 (2000): 285–309.

———. "The Bitch Had It Coming to Her: Rhetoric and Interpretation in Ezekiel 16." *Biblical Interpretation* 8 (2000): 231–53.

———. "The Personification of Cities as Female in the Hebrew Bible: The Thesis of Aloysius Fitzgerald, F.S.C." Pages 283–302 in *Social Location and Biblical Interpretation in Global Perspective.* Vol. 2 of *Reading from This Place.* Edited by Fernando F. Segovia and Mary Ann Tolbert. Minneapolis: Fortress, 1995.

De Martino, Ernesto. *Morte e pianto rituale: dal lamento funebre antico al pianto di Maria.* Torino: Boringhieri, 1975.

Dearman, J. Andrew. "Daughter Zion and Her Place in God's Household." *Horizons in Biblical Theology* 31 (2009): 144–59.

———. "The Family in the Old Testament." *Interpretation* 52 (1998): 117–29.

———. *Jeremiah/Lamentations.* NIV Application Commentary Series. Grand Rapids: Zondervan, 2002.

———. *Property Rights in the Eighth-Century Prophets: The Conflict and Its Background.* Society of Biblical Literature Dissertation Series 106. Atlanta: Scholars Press, 1988.

———. "Yhwh's House: Gender Roles and Metaphors for Israel in Hosea." *Journal of Northwest Semitic Languages* 25 (1999): 97–108.

Dempsey, Carol J. "The 'Whore' of Ezekiel 16: the Impact and Ramifications of Gender-Specific Metaphors in Light of Biblical Law and Divine Judgment." Pages 57–78 in *Gender and Law in the Hebrew Bible and the Ancient Near East.* Edited by Victor H. Matthews, Bernard M. Levinson, and Tikva Frymer-Kensky. Journal for the Study of the Old Testament Supplement Series 262. Sheffield: Sheffield Academic Press, 1998.

Diamond, A. R. Pete. "Playing God: 'Polytheizing' *YHWH-ALONE* in Jeremiah's Metaphorical Spaces." Pages 119–32 in *Metaphor in the Hebrew Bible.* Edited by Pierre van Hecke. Leuven: Leuven University Press, 2005.

Diamond, A. R. Pete, and Kathleen M. O'Connor. "Unfaithful Passions: Coding Women Coding Men in Jeremiah 2–3 (4:2)." *Biblical Interpretation* 4 (1996): 288–310. Repr. pages 123–45 in *Troubling Jeremiah.* Edited by Diamond, O'Connor, and Louis Stulman. Journal for the Study of the Old Testament Supplement Series 260. Sheffield: Sheffield Academic Press, 1999.

Dijk-Hemmes, Fokkelien van. "The Metaphorization of Woman in Prophetic Speech: An Analysis of Ezekiel 23." Pages167–76 in *On Gendering Texts: Female and Male Voices in the Hebrew Bible.* Edited by Athalya Brenner and Fokkelien van Dijk-Hemmes. Biblical Interpretation Series 1. 1993. Repr., Leiden: Brill, 1996. [A slight variation of an earlier publication: "The Metaphorization of Woman in Prophetic Speech: An Analysis of Ezekiel xxiii." *Vetus Testamentum* 43 (1993): 162–70.]

Dillard, Raymond B. "Joel." Pages 239–313 in *Hosea, Joel, and Amos.* Vol. 1 of *The Minor Prophets: An Exegetical and Expositional Commentary.* Edited by Thomas Edward McComiskey. Grand Rapids: Baker, 1992.

Dille, Sarah J. *Mixing Metaphors: God as Mother and Father in Deutero-Isaiah.* Journal for the Study of the Old Testament Supplement Series 398; Gender, Culture, Theory 13. New York: T&T Clark, 2004.

Dim, Emmanuel U. *The Eschatological Implications of Isaiah 65 and 66 as the Conclusion of the Book of Isaiah.* Bern: Peter Lang, 2005.

Dobbs-Allsopp, Frederick W. "Darwinism, Genre Theory, and City Laments." *Journal of the American Oriental Society* 120 (2000): 625–30.

———. "Daughter Zion." Pages 125–34 in *Thus Says the Lord: Essays on the Former and Latter Prophets in Honor of Robert R. Wilson.* Edited by John J. Ahn and Stephen L. Cook. Library of Hebrew Bible/Old Testament Studies 502. New York: T&T Clark, 2009.

———. *Lamentations.* Interpretation: A Bible Commentary for Teaching and Preaching. Louisville: Westminster John Knox, 2002.

———. "Linguistic Evidence for the Date of Lamentations." *Journal of the Ancient Near Eastern Society* 26 (1998): 1–36.

———. "Rethinking Historical Criticism," *Biblical Interpretation* 7 (1999): 235–71.

———. "The Syntagma of *bat* Followed by a Geographical Name in the Hebrew Bible: A Reconsideration of Its Meaning and Grammar." *Catholic Biblical Quarterly* 57 (1995): 451–70.

———. "Tragedy, Tradition, and Theology in the Book of Lamentations." *Journal for the Study of the Old Testament* 74 (1997) 29–60.

———. *Weep, O Daughter of Zion: A Study of the City-Lament Genre in the Hebrew Bible.* Biblica et orientalia 44. Rome: Pontifical Biblical Institute, 1993.

Dohmen, Christoph. "'Eifersüchtiger ist sein Name' (Exod 34:14): Ursprung und Bedeutung der alttestamentlichen Rede von Gottes Eifersucht." *Theologische Zeitschrift* 46 (1990): 289–304.

Dozeman, Thomas B. *Commentary on Exodus.* Eerdmans Critical Commentary. Grand Rapids: Eerdmans, 2009.

Duhm, Bernhard. *Das Buch Jesaia.* Handkommentar zum Alten Testament 3/1. Göttingen: Vandenhoeck & Ruprecht, 1892.

Duncan, Nancy. *Bodyspace: Destabilizing Geographies of Gender and Sexuality.* London: Routledge, 1996.

Durose, Matthew R., et al. *Family Violence Statistics: Including Statistics on Strangers and Acquaintances.* Bureau of Justice Statistics. Washington, D.C.: U.S. Dept. of Justice, 2005. Online: http://www.ojp.usdoj.gov/bjs/pub/pdf/fvs.pdf.

Eaton, J. H. *Festal Drama in Deutero-Isaiah.* London: SPCK, 1979.

Eichrodt, Walther. *Ezekiel: A Commentary.* Translated by Cosslett Quin. Old Testament Library. Philadelphia: Westminster, 1970.

Eslinger, Lyle. "Ezekiel 20 and the Metaphor of Historical Teleology: Concepts of Biblical History." *Journal for the Study of the Old Testament* 81 (1998): 93–125.

Evans, Redd, and John Jacob Loeb. "Rosie the Riveter." New York: Paramount Music Corporation, 1943.

Exum, J. Cheryl. "The Ethics of Biblical Violence against Women." Pages 248–71 in *The Bible in Ethics: The Second Sheffield Colloquium.* Edited by John William Rogerson, Margaret Davies, and M. Daniel Carroll R. Journal for the Study of the Old Testament Supplement Series 207. Sheffield: Sheffield Academic Press, 1995.

————. "Prophetic Pornography." In *Plotted, Shot, and Painted: Cultural Representations of Biblical Women*. Journal for the Study of the Old Testament Supplement Series 215. Gender, Culture, Theory 3. Sheffield: Sheffield Academic Press, 1996.

Facts about Violence. Online: http://www.feminist.com/antiviolence/facts.html.

Farrell, Daniel. "Jealousy." *The Philosophical Review* 89 (1980): 527–59.

Fauconnier, Gilles, and Mark Turner. *The Way We Think: Conceptual Blending and the Mind's Hidden Complexities*. New York: Basic Books, 2002.

Feldman, Emanuel. *Biblical and Post-Biblical Defilement and Mourning: Law as Theology*. New York: Ktav, 1977.

Ferris, Paul Wayne. *The Genre of Communal Lament in the Bible and the Ancient Near East*. Society of Biblical Literature Dissertation Series 127. Atlanta: Scholars Press, 1992.

Fischer, Alexander A. *Skepsis oder Furcht Gottes? Studien zur Komposition und Theologie des Buches Kohelet*. Beihefte zur Zeitschrift für die alttestamentliche Wissenschaft 247. Berlin: de Gruyter, 1997.

Fitzgerald, Aloysius. "*BTWLT* and *BT* as Titles for Capital Cities." *Catholic Biblical Quarterly* 37 (1975): 167–83.

————. "The Mythological Background for the Presentation of Jerusalem as a Queen and False Worship as Adultery in the Old Testament." *Catholic Biblical Quarterly* 34 (1972): 403–16.

Flesher, LeAnn Snow. "The Rhetorical Use of the Negative Petition in the Lament Psalms." Ph.D. diss., Drew University, 1999.

————. "The Use of Female Imagery and Lamentation in the Book of Judith: Penitential Prayer or Petition for Obligatory Action?" Pages 83–104 in *Seeking the Favor of God*. Vol. 2: *The Development of Penitential Prayer in Second Temple Judaism*. Edited by Mark J. Boda, Daniel K. Falk, and Rodney A. Werline. Society of Biblical Literature Early Judaism and Its Literature 22. Atlanta: Society of Biblical Literature, 2007.

Floyd, Michael H. "Welcome Back, Daughter of Zion!" *Catholic Biblical Quarterly* 70 (2008): 484–504.

Foley, Helene P. "The Ethics of Lamentation." Pages 145–71 in *Female Acts in Greek Tragedy*. Martin Classical Lectures. Princeton: Princeton University Press, 2001.

————. "The Politics of Tragic Lamentation." Pages 19–55 in *Female Acts in Greek Tragedy*. Martin Classical Lectures. Princeton: Princeton University Press, 2001.

Follis, Elaine R. "The Holy City as Daughter." Pages 173–84 in *Directions in Biblical Poetry*. Edited by Follis. Journal for the Study of the Old Testament Supplement Series 40. Sheffield: JSOT Press, 1987.

Fortune, Marie. *Sexual Violence: The Sin Revisited*. Cleveland: Pilgrim Press, 2005. Online: http://www.faithtrustinstitute.org/index.php?p=Q_%26_A&s=45.

Foucault, Michel. "Of Other Spaces." *Diacritics* 16 (1986): 22–77.

Fox, Matthew. *Meditations with Meister Eckhart*. Santa Fe: Bear, 1982.

Fretheim, Terence E. *God and World in the Old Testament: A Relational Theology of Creation*. Nashville: Abingdon, 2005.

———. "'I Was Only a Little Angry': Divine Violence in the Prophets." *Interpretation* 58 (2004): 365–75.

———. *Jeremiah*. Smyth & Helwys Bible Commentary. Macon, Ga.: Smyth & Helwys, 2002.

———. "Theological Reflections on the Wrath of God in the Old Testament." *Horizons in Biblical Theology* 24.2 (2002): 1–26.

Frymer-Kensky, Tikva. *In the Wake of the Goddesses: Women, Culture, and the Biblical Transformation of Pagan Myth*. New York: Free Press, 1992.

———. "Zion, the Beloved Woman." Pages 168–78 in *In the Wake of the Goddesses: Women, Culture, and the Biblical Transformation of Pagan Myth*. New York: Free Press, 1992.

Galambush, Julie. *Jerusalem in the Book of Ezekiel: The City as Yahweh's Wife*. Society of Biblical Literature Dissertation Series 130. Atlanta: Scholars Press, 1992.

Gane, Roy. *Cult and Character: Purification Offerings, Day of Atonement, and Theodicy*. Winona Lake, Ind.: Eisenbrauns, 2005.

Gärtner, Judith. *Jesaja 66 und Sacharja 14 als Summe der Prophetie: Eine traditions- und redaktionsgeschichtliche Untersuchung zum Abschluss des Jesaja- und des Zwölfprophetenbuches*. Wissenschaftliche Monographien zum Alten und Neuen Testament 114. Neukirchen-Vluyn: Neukirchener, 2006.

Gerstenberger, Erhard S. *Psalms, Part 2, and Lamentations*. Forms of the Old Testament Literature 15. Grand Rapids: Eerdmans, 2001.

Gibbs, Raymond, and Gerhard Steen, eds. *Metaphor in Cognitive Linguistics*. Amsterdam: John Benjamins, 1999.

Gile, Jason. "Ezekiel 16 and the Song of Moses: A Prophetic Transformation?" *Journal of Biblical Literature* 130 (2011): 87–108.

Gitay, Yehoshua. "The Poetics of National Disaster: The Rhetorical Presentation of Lamentations." Pages 1–11 in *Literary Responses to the*

Holocaust 1945–1995. Edited by Gitay. San Francisco: International Scholars, 1998.

Goldenstein, Johannes. *Das Gebet der Gottesknechte: Jes 63,7–64,11 im Jesajabuch.* Wissenschaftliche Monographien zum Alten und Neuen Testament 92. Neukirchen-Vluyn: Neukirchener, 2001.

Goldie, Peter. *The Emotions: A Philosophical Exploration.* Oxford: Clarendon, 2000.

Goldingay, John, and David Payne. *Isaiah 40–55.* 2 vols. International Critical Commentary. London: T&T Clark, 2006.

Gordis, Robert. "Conclusion of the Book of Lamentations (5:22)." *Journal of Biblical Literature* 93 (1974) 289–293.

———. *Koheleth, the Man and His World: A Study of Ecclesiastes.* 3rd ed. New York: Schocken, 1968.

Gordon, Pamela, and Harold C. Washington. "Rape as Military Metaphor in the Hebrew Bible." Pages 308–25 in *A Feminist Companion to the Latter Prophets.* Edited by Athalya Brenner. Feminist Companion to the Bible 8. Sheffield: Sheffield Academic Press, 1995.

Gottwald, Norman K. "Social Class and Ideology in Isaiah 40–55: An Eagletonian Reading." *Semeia* 59 (1992): 3–71.

———. *Studies in the Book of Lamentations.* Studies in Biblical Theology 1/14. London: SCM, 1962.

Goulder, Michael D. *Isaiah as Liturgy.* Society for Old Testament Study Monographs. Aldershot: Ashgate, 2004.

Graffy, Adrian. *A Prophet Confronts His People: The Disputation Speech in the Prophets.* Analecta biblica 104. Rome: Pontifical Biblical Institute, 1984.

Green, Barbara. *How Are the Mighty Fallen? A Dialogical Study of King Saul in 1 Samuel.* Journal for the Study of the Old Testament Supplement Series 365. Sheffield: Sheffield Academic Press, 2003.

———. *Mikhail Bakhtin and Biblical Scholarship: An Introduction.* Semeia Studies 38. Atlanta: Society of Biblical Literature, 2000.

Greenberg, Moshe. *Ezekiel 1–20: A New Translation with Introduction and Commentary.* Anchor Bible 22. Garden City, N.Y.: Doubleday, 1983.

———. *Ezekiel 21–37: A New Translation with Introduction and Commentary.* Anchor Bible 22A. New York: Doubleday, 1997.

Greenstein, Edward L. "The Wrath at God in the Book of Lamentations." Pages 29–42 in *The Problem of Evil and Its Symbols in Jewish and Christian Tradition.* Edited by Henning Graf Reventlow and Yair Hoffman.

Journal for the Study of the Old Testament Supplement Series 366. New York: T&T Clark, 2004.

Grosz, Elizabeth, and Elspeth Probyn, eds. *Sexy Bodies: The Strange Carnalities of Feminism*. London: Routledge, 1995.

Gunkel, Hermann, and Joachim Begrich. *Introduction to Psalms: The Genres of the Religious Lyric of Israel*. Translated by James D. Nogalski. Macon, Ga.: Mercer University Press, 1998.

Gunn, David M., and Paula M. McNutt, eds. *"Imagining" Biblical Worlds: Studies in Spatial, Social and Historical Constructs in Honor of James W. Flanagan*. Journal for the Study of the Old Testament Supplement Series 359. Sheffield: Sheffield Academic Press, 2002.

Gwaltney, William C. "The Biblical Book of Lamentations in the Context of Near Eastern Lament Literature." Pages 191–211 in *More Essays on the Comparative Method*. Edited by William W. Hallo, James C. Moyer, and Leo G. Perdue. Scripture in Context 2. Winona Lake, Ind.: Eisenbrauns, 1983.

Haag, Ernst. "Der Weg zum Baum des Lebens: Ein Paradiesmotiv im Buch Jesaja." Pages 35–52 in *Künder des Wortes: Beiträge zur Theologie der Propheten. Josef Schreiner zum 60. Geburtstag*. Edited by Lothar Ruppert, Peter Weimar, and Erich Zenger. Würzburg: Echter, 1982.

Hals, Ronald M. *Ezekiel*. Forms of the Old Testament Literature 19. Grand Rapids: Eerdmans, 1989.

Hanson, Paul D. *The Dawn of Apocalyptic: The Historical and Sociological Roots of Jewish Apocalyptic Eschatology*. Rev. ed. Philadelphia: Fortress, 1979.

———. *Isaiah 40–66*. Interpretation: A Bible Commentary for Teaching and Preaching. Louisville: John Knox, 1995.

Harris, R. Laird, Gleason L. Archer, and Bruce K. Waltke, eds. *Theological Wordbook of the Old Testament*. 2 vols. Chicago: Moody, 1980.

Harris, Wendell V. "Metaphor." Pages 222–31 in *Dictionary of Concepts in Literary Criticism and Theory*. New York: Greenwood, 1992.

Haught, John F. *God After Darwin: A Theology of Evolution*. Boulder: Westview, 2000.

Hayes, Katherine M. *The Earth Mourns: Prophetic Metaphor and Oral Aesthetic*. Society of Biblical Literature Academia Biblica 8. Leiden: Brill, 2002.

———. "When None Repents, Earth Laments: The Chorus of Lament in Jeremiah and Joel." Pages 119–43 in *Seeking the Favor of God*. Vol. 1: *The Origins of Penitential Prayer in Second Temple Judaism*. Edited by

Mark J. Boda, Daniel K. Falk, and Rodney A. Werline. Society of Biblical Literature Early Judaism and Its Literature 21. Atlanta: Society of Biblical Literature, 2006.

Hecke, Pierre J.-P. van. "Conceptual Blending: A Recent Approach to Metaphor, Illustrated with the Pastoral Metaphor in Hos 4,16." Pages 215–31 in *Metaphor in the Hebrew Bible*. Edited by van Hecke. Leuven: Leuven University Press, 2005.

Heim, Knut M. "The Personification of Jerusalem and the Drama of Her Bereavement in Lamentations." Pages 129–69 in *Zion, City of Our God*. Edited by Richard S. Hess and Gordon J. Wenham. Grand Rapids: Eerdmans, 1999.

Hermisson, H.-J. "Diskussionsworte bei Deuterojesaja. Zur theologischen Argumentation des Propheten." *Evangelische Theologie* 31 (1971): 665–80.

Heschel, Abraham J. *The Prophets*. New York: Harper & Row, 1962.

Hessler, Eva. *Das Heilsdrama: Der Weg zur Weltherrschaft Jahwes (Jes 40–66)*. Hildesheim: Olms, 1988.

Hillers, Delbert R. *Lamentations: A New Translation with Introduction and Commentary*. 2nd ed. Anchor Bible 7A. New York: Doubleday, 1992.

Hobbs, T. R. "Reflections on Honor, Shame, and Covenant Relations." *Journal of Biblical Literature* 116 (1997): 501–3.

Holladay, William Lee. *Jeremiah 1: A Commentary on the Book of the Prophet Jeremiah Chapters 1–25*. Hermeneia. Philadelphia: Fortress, 1986.

Holst-Warhaft, Gail. *Dangerous Voices: Women's Laments and Greek Literature*. London: Routledge, 1992.

Hopkins, Gerard Manley. *The Poems and Prose of Gerard Manley Hopkins*. Penguin Classics. Baltimore: Penguin Books, 1985.

Hoppe, Leslie J., O.F.M. "Biblical Theology." Pages li-lv in *The Collegeville Pastoral Dictionary of Biblical Theology*. Edited by Carroll Stuhlmueller. Collegeville, Minn.: Liturgical Press, 1996.

House, Paul R. "Lamentations." Pages 267–473 in Duane Garrett and House, *Song of Songs, Lamentations*. Word Biblical Commentary 23B. Nashville: Nelson, 2004.

———. *The Unity of the Twelve*. Bible and Literature Series 27. Sheffield: Almond, 1990.

Hubbard, David A. *Hosea: An Introduction and Commentary*. Tyndale Old Testament Commentaries 24. Downers Grove, Ill.: InterVarsity Press, 2009.

Hugenberger, Gordon. *Marriage as a Covenant: A Study of Biblical Law and Ethics Governing Marriage, Developed from the Perspective of Malachi.* Vetus Testamentum Supplements 52. Leiden: Brill, 1994.

Humbert, Paul. "'Laetari et exultare' dans le vocabulaire religieux de l'Ancien Testament." *Revue d'histoire et de philosophie religieuses* 22 (1942): 185–214.

———. *Opuscules d'un Hébraïsant.* Neuchâtel: Secrétariat de l'Université, 1958.

Hvidberg, Flemming F. *Weeping and Laughter in the Old Testament.* Leiden: Brill, 1962.

Jacobs, Mignon R. *Gender, Power, and Persuasion: The Genesis Narratives and Contemporary Portraits.* Grand Rapids: Baker Academic, 2007.

———. "YHWH's Call for Israel's 'Return': Command, Invitation, or Threat." *Horizons in Biblical Theology* 32 (2010): 17–32.

Jacobson, Diane. "Hosea 2: A Case Study on Biblical Authority." *Concordia Theological Monthly* 23 (1996): 165–72.

Jahnow, Hedwig. *Das hebräische Leichenlied im Rahmen der Völkerdichtung.* Beihefte zur Zeitschrift für die alttestamentliche Wissenschaft 36. Giessen: Töpelmann, 1923.

Jeppesen, Knud. "Mother Zion, Father Servant: A Reading of Isaiah 49–55." Pages 109–25 in *Of Prophets' Visions and the Wisdom of Sages: Essays in Honour of R. Norman Whybray on His Seventieth Birthday.* Edited by Heather A. McKay and David J. A. Clines. Journal for the Study of the Old Testament Supplement Series 162. Sheffield: JSOT Press, 1993.

Johnson, Benjamin. "Form and Message in Lamentations." *Zeitschrift für die alttestamentliche Wissenschaft* 97 (1985): 58–73.

Johnson, Elizabeth A. *Quest for the Living God: Mapping Frontiers in the Theology of God.* New York: Continuum, 2008.

Johnson, Elizabeth L. "Grieving for the Dead, Grieving for the Living: Funeral Laments of Hakka Women." Pages 135–63 in *Death Ritual in Late Imperial and Modern China.* Edited by James L. Watson and Evelyn S. Rawski. Berkeley: University of California Press, 1988.

Joüon, Paul, and T. Muraoka. *A Grammar of Biblical Hebrew.* Subsidia biblica 14/1–2. Rome: Editrice Pontifcio Istituto Biblico, 2000.

Joyce, Paul M. *Divine Initiative and Human Response in Ezekiel.* Journal for the Study of the Old Testament Supplement Series 51. Sheffield: Sheffield Academic Press, 1989.

———. *Ezekiel: A Commentary.* Library of Hebrew Bible/Old Testament Studies 482. New York: T&T Clark, 2007.

Kaiser, Barbara Bakke. "Poet as 'Female Impersonator': The Image of Daughter Zion as Speaker in Biblical Poems of Suffering." *Journal of Religion* 67 (1987): 164–82.

Kaiser, Otto. *Isaiah 1–12: A Commentary.* Translated by John Bowden. 2nd ed. Old Testament Library. Philadelphia: Westminster, 1983.

Kalluveettil, Paul. *Declaration and Covenant.* Analecta biblica 88. Rome: Pontifical Biblical Institute, 1982.

Kaminsky, Joel S. "Joshua 7: A Reassessment of Israelite Conceptions of Corporate Punishment." Pages 315–46 in *The Pitcher Is Broken: Memorial Essays for Gösta W Ahlström.* Edited by Steven W. Holloway and Lowell K. Handy. Journal for the Study of the Old Testament Supplement Series 190. Sheffield: Sheffield Academic Press, 1995.

———. "The Sins of the Fathers: A Theological Investigation of the Biblical Tension between the Corporate and Individualized Retribution." *Judaism* 46 (1997): 319–32.

Kamionkowski, S. Tamar. *Gender Reversal and Cosmic Chaos: A Study on the Book of Ezekiel.* Journal for the Study of the Old Testament Supplement Series 368. Sheffield: Sheffield Academic Press, 2003.

Kapelrud, Arvid S. *Et folk på hjemferd. "Trøsteprofeten"—den annen Jesaja—og hans budskap.* Oslo: Universitetsforlaget, 1964.

Kartveit, Magnar. "Daughter of Zion." *Theology and Life* 27 (2004): 25–41.

Keefe, Alice A. *Woman's Body and the Social Body in Hosea.* Journal for the Study of the Old Testament Supplement Series 338. Sheffield: Sheffield Academic Press, 2001.

Kelle, Brad E. *Hosea 2: Metaphor and Rhetoric in Historical Perspective.* Society of Biblical Literature Academia Biblica 20. Atlanta: Society of Biblical Literature, 2005.

Kiesow, Klaus. *Exodustexte im Jesajabuch: Literarkritische und motivgeschichtliche Analysen.* Orbis biblicus et orientalis 24. Fribourg: Éditions Universitaires, 1979.

Kim, Hyukki. "The Interpretation of בת ציון (Daughter Zion): An Approach of Cognitive Theories of Metaphor." M.A. thesis, McMaster Divinity College, 2006.

King, Philip J. *Amos, Hosea, Micah: An Archaeological Commentary.* Philadelphia: Westminster, 1988.

Kirk-Duggan, Cheryl. *Misbegotten Anguish: A Theology and Ethics of Violence.* St. Louis: Chalice Press, 2001.

———. "Slingshots, Ships, and Personal Psychosis: Murder, Sexual Intrigue, and Power in the Lives of David and Othello." Pages 37–30 in *Pregnant*

Passion: Gender, Sex, and Violence in the Bible. Edited by Kirk-Duggan. Semeia Studies 44. Atlanta: Society of Biblical Literature, 2003.

Klein, William W., Craig L. Blomberg, and Robert L. Hubbard Jr. *Introduction to Biblical Interpretation.* Dallas: Word, 1993.

Klemm, David E. *The Hermeneutical Theory of Paul Ricoeur: A Constructive Analysis.* Lewisburg, Pa.: Bucknell University Press, 1983.

Knohl, Israel. *The Divine Symphony: The Bible's Many Voices.* Philadelphia: Jewish Publication Society, 2003.

———. *The Sanctuary of Silence: The Priestly Torah and the Holiness School.* Minneapolis: Fortress, 1995.

Koehler, Ludwig, Walter Baumgartner, and Johann Jakob Stamm. *The Hebrew and Aramaic Lexicon of the Old Testament.* Translated and edited under the supervision of M. E. J. Richardson. 5 vols. Leiden: Brill, 1994–2000.

Koenen, Klaus. *Ethik und Eschatologie im Tritojesajabuch: Eine literarkritische und redaktionsgeschichtliche Studie .* Wissenschaftliche Monographien zum Alten und Neuen Testament 62. Neukirchen-Vluyn: Neukirchener, 1990.

Koole, Jan L. *Isaiah 40–48.* Vol. 1 of *Isaiah, Part 3.* Translated by Anthony P. Runia. Historical Commentary on the Old Testament. Kampen: Kok Pharos, 1997.

Kotzé, Zacharias. "Metaphors and Metonymies for Anger in the Old Testament: A Cognitive Linguistic Approach." *Scriptura* 88 (2005): 118–25.

Kövecses, Zoltán. *Metaphor: A Practical Introduction.* Oxford: Oxford University Press, 2002.

———. *Metaphor: A Practical Introduction.* 2nd ed. New York: Oxford University Press, 2010.

Krašovec, Joze. "The Source of Hope in the Book of Lamentations." *Vetus Testamentum* 42 (1992): 223–233.

Kratz, Reinhard Gregor. *Kyros im Deuterojesaja-buch.* Forschungen zum Alten Testament 1. Tübingen: Mohr Siebeck, 1991.

Kraus, Hans-Joachim. *Klagelieder (Threni).* 3rd ed. Biblischer Kommentar: Altes Testament 20. Neukirchen-Vluyn: Neukirchener, 1968.

Kristjánsson, Kristján. *Justifying Emotions: Pride and Jealousy.* Routledge Studies in Ethics and Moral Theory 3. London: Routledge, 2002.

Kugel, James L. *The Idea of Biblical Poetry: Parallelism and Its History.* New Haven: Yale University Press, 1981.

Kwok, Pui-Lan. *Postcolonial Imagination and Feminist Theology.* Louisville: Westminster John Knox, 2005.

Labahn, Antje. "Metaphor and Inter-textuality: 'Daughter of Zion' as a Test Case: Response to Kirsten Nielsen 'From Oracles to Canon'—and the Role of Metaphor." *Scandinavian Journal of the Old Testament* 17 (2003): 49–67.

Lakoff, George, and Mark Johnson. *Metaphors We Live By*. Chicago: University of Chicago Press, 1980.

Lakoff, George, and Mark Turner. *More Than Cool Reason: A Field Guide to Poetic Metaphor*. Chicago: University of Chicago Press, 1989.

Lanahan, William F. "The Speaking Voice in the Book of Lamentations." *Journal of Biblical Literature* 93 (1974): 41–49.

Landy, Francis. *Hosea*. Readings: A New Biblical Commentary. Sheffield: Sheffield Academic Press, 1995.

Lategan, Werner Andre. "The Theological Dialect of Creation and Death in Hebrew Bible Wisdom Traditions." Ph.D. diss., Rijksuniversiteit Groningen, 2009.

Lau, Wolfgang. *Schriftgelehrte Prophetie in Jes 56–66: Eine Untersuchung zu den literarischen Bezügen in den letzten elf Kapiteln des Jesajabuches*. Beihefte zur Zeitschrift für die alttestamentliche Wissenschaft 225. Berlin: de Gruyter, 1994.

Lee, David. *Cognitive Linguistics: An Introduction*. Oxford: Oxford University Press, 2001.

Lee, Nancy C. *The Singers of Lamentations: Cities under Siege, from Ur to Jerusalem to Sarajevo*. Biblical Interpretation Series 60. Leiden: Brill, 2002.

Lee, Nancy C., and Carleen Mandolfo, eds. *Lamentations in Ancient and Contemporary Cultural Contexts*. Society of Biblical Literature Symposium Series 43. Atlanta: Society of Biblical Literature, 2008.

Leene, Henk. *De Vroegere en de Nieuwe Dingen bij Deuterojesaja*. Amsterdam: Free University of Amsterdam Press, 1987.

Lefebvre, Henri. *The Production of Space*. Translated by Donald Nicholson-Smith. Malden: Blackwell, 1991.

Leveen, Adriane B. "Variations on a Theme: Differing Conceptions of Memory in the Book of Numbers." *Journal for the Study of the Old Testament* 27 (2002): 201–21.

Levine, Baruch. *Numbers 21–36: A New Translation with Introduction and Commentary*. Anchor Bible 4. New York: Doubleday, 2000.

Limburg, James. *Hosea–Micah*. Interpretation: A Bible Commentary for Teaching and Preaching. Atlanta: John Knox, 1988.

Linafelt, Tod. "The Refusal of a Conclusion in the Book of Lamentations." *Journal of Biblical Literature* 120 (2001): 340–43.

———. *Surviving Lamentations: Catastrophe, Lament, and Protest in the Afterlife of a Biblical Book*. Chicago: University of Chicago Press, 2000.

———. "Zion's Cause: The Presentation of Pain in the Book of Lamentations." Pages 267–79 in *Strange Fire: Reading the Bible after the Holocaust*. Edited by Linafelt. Biblical Seminar 71. Sheffield: Sheffield Academic Press, 2000.

Lipschits, Oded. *The Fall and Rise of Jerusalem: Judah under Babylonian Rule*. Winona Lake, Ind.: Eisenbrauns, 2005.

Loader, J. A. *Ecclesiastes*. Text and Interpretation. Grand Rapids: Eerdmans, 1986.

Lohfink, Norbert. *Kohelet*. Neue Echter Bibel 1. Würzburg: Echter, 1980.

Løland, Hanne. *Silent or Salient Gender? The Interpretation of Gendered God-Language in the Hebrew Bible, Exemplified in Isaiah 42, 46, and 49*. Forschungen zum Alten Testament 2/32. Tübingen: Mohr Siebeck, 2008.

Lund, Øystein. *Way Metaphors and Way Topics in Isaiah 40–55*. Forschungen zum Alten Testament 2/28. Tübingen: Mohr Siebeck, 2007.

Lundbom, Jack R. *Jeremiah 1–20: A New Translation with Introduction and Commentary*. Anchor Bible 21A. New York: Doubleday, 1999.

Macwilliam, Stuart. "Queering Jeremiah." *Biblical Interpretation* 10 (2002): 384–404.

Magrini, Tullia. "Women's 'Work of Pain' in Christian Mediterranean Europe." *Music and Anthropology* 3 (1998).

Maier, Christl M. *Daughter Zion, Mother Zion: Gender, Space, and the Sacred in Ancient Israel*. Minneapolis: Fortress, 2008.

———. "Psalm 87 as a Reappraisal of the Zion Tradition and its Reception in Gal 4:26." *Catholic Biblical Quarterly* 69 (2007): 473–86.

Malul, Meir. "Adoption of Foundlings in the Bible and Mesopotamian Documents: A Study of Some Legal Metaphors in Ezekiel 16.1–7." *Journal for the Study of the Old Testament* 46 (1990): 97–126.

Mandolfo, Carleen R. *Daughter Zion Talks Back to the Prophets: A Dialogic Theology of the Book of Lamentations*. Semeia Studies 58. Atlanta: Society of Biblical Literature, 2007.

———. *God in the Dock: Dialogic Tension in the Psalms of Lament*. Journal for the Study of the Old Testament Supplement Series 357. London: Sheffield Academic Press, 2002.

————. "Talking Back: The Perseverance of Justice in Lamentations." Pages 47–56 in *Lamentations in Ancient and Contemporary Cultural Contexts*. Edited by Nancy C. Lee and Carleen Mandolfo. Society of Biblical Literature Symposium Series 43. Atlanta: Society of Biblical Literature, 2008.

McDowell, Linda. *Gender, Identity, and Place: Understanding Feminist Geographies*. Minneapolis: University of Minnesota Press, 1999.

McEvenue, Sean. "Who Was Second Isaiah?" Pages 213–22 in *Studies in the Book of Isaiah: Festschrift Willem A. M. Beuken*. Edited by Jacques van Ruiten and Marc Vervenne. Bibliotheca ephemeridum theologicarum lovaniensium 132. Leuven: Leuven University Press, 1997.

McKane, William. *Jeremiah I–XXV*. Vol. 1 of *A Critical and Exegetical Commentary on Jeremiah*. International Critical Commentary. Edinburgh: T&T Clark, 1986.

McKenzie, John L. *Second Isaiah*. Anchor Bible 20. Garden City, N.Y.: Doubleday, 1968.

McKenzie, Steven L. *Covenant*. Understanding Biblical Themes. St. Louis: Chalice, 2000.

Meek, Theophile J. "The Book of Lamentations." Pages 3–38 in vol. 6 of *The Interpreter's Bible*. Edited by George Arthur Buttrick. Nashville: Abingdon, 1956.

Mein, Andrew. *Ezekiel and the Ethics of Exile*. Oxford Theological Monographs. Oxford: Oxford University Press, 2001.

Merendino, Rosario Pius. "Jes 49, 14–26: Jahwes Bekenntnis zu Sion und die neue Heilszeit." *Revue biblique* 89 (1982): 321–69.

Middlemas, Jill. "Did Second Isaiah Write Lamentations 3?" *Vetus Testamentum* 56 (2006): 505–25.

————. *The Troubles of Templeless Judah*. Oxford Theological Monographs. Oxford: Oxford University Press, 2005.

————. "The Violent Storm in Lamentations." *Journal for the Study of the Old Testament* 29 (2004): 81–97.

Milgrom, Jacob. "Case of the Suspected Adulteress, Numbers 5:11–31: Redaction and Meaning." Pages 475–82 in *Women in the Hebrew Bible: A Reader*. Edited by Alice Bach. New York: Routledge, 1991.

————. *Leviticus 1–16: A New Translation with Introduction and Commentary*. Anchor Bible 3. New York: Doubleday, 1991.

Miller, John W. "Prophetic Conflict in Second Isaiah: The Servant Songs in the Light of Their Context." Pages 77–85 in *Wort—Gebot—Glaube: Beiträge zur Theologie des Alten Testaments. Walther Eichrodt zum 80.*

Geburtstag. Edited by Hans Joachim Stoebe. Abhandlungen zur Theologie des Alten und Neuen Testamentum 59. Zurich: Zwingli, 1970.

Mills, Mary E. *Images of God in the Old Testament.* Collegeville, Minn.: Liturgical Press, 1998.

Mittleman, Alan. "The Job of Judaism and the Job of Kant." *Harvard Theological Review* 102 (2009): 25–50.

Moore, Michael S. "Human Suffering in Lamentations." *Revue biblique* 83 (1990): 539–43.

Morrow, William S. *Protest against God: The Eclipse of a Biblical Tradition.* Hebrew Bible Monographs 4. Sheffield: Sheffield Phoenix, 2006.

———. "The Revival of Lament in Medieval Piyyuṭīm." Pages 139–50 in *Lamentations in Ancient and Contemporary Cultural Contexts.* Edited by Nancy C. Lee and Carleen Mandolfo. Society of Biblical Literature Symposium Series 43. Atlanta: Society of Biblical Literature, 2008.

Morse, Benjamin. "The *Lamentations* Project: Biblical Mourning through Modern Montage." *Journal for the Study of the Old Testament* 28 (2003): 113–27.

Mossman, Judith. *Wild Justice: A Study of Euripides' Hecuba.* London: Bristol Classical Press and Duckworth, 1999.

Motyer, Alec J. *The Prophecy of Isaiah: An Introduction and Commentary.* Downers Grove, Ill.: InterVarsity Press, 1993.

Moughtin-Mumby, Sharon. *Sexual and Marital Metaphors in Hosea, Jeremiah, Isaiah, and Ezekiel.* Oxford Theological Monographs. Oxford: Oxford University Press, 2008.

Mowinckel, Sigmund. *The Psalms in Israel's Worship.* Translated by D. R. Ap-Thomas. 2 vols. Oxford: Blackwell, 1962.

Muilenburg, James. "The Book of Isaiah Chapters 40–66." Pages 381–773 in vol. 5 of *The Interpreter's Bible.* Edited by George Arthur Buttrick. Nashville: Abingdon, 1956.

———. "Form Criticsm and Beyond." *Journal of Biblical Literature* 88 (1969): 1–18.

Mukta, Parita. "The 'Civilizing Mission': The Regulation and Control of Mourning in Colonial India." *Feminist Review* 63 (1999): 25–47.

Mulvey, Laura. "Visual Pleasure and Narrative Cinema." Pages 28–40 in *Issues in Feminist Film Criticism.* Edited by Patricia Erens. 5th ed. Bloomington: Indiana University Press, 1991.

Nachama, Andreas. "Jerusalem und die jüdische Gebetskultur." Pages 76–79 in *Die Reise nach Jerusalem: Eine kulturhistorische Exkursion in die Stadt der Städte. 3000 Jahre Davidstadt.* Edited by Hendrik Budde and Andreas Nachama. Berlin: Argon, 1995.

Nel, Philip J. "'I Am a Worm.' Metaphor in Psalm 22." *Journal for Semitics* 14 (2005): 40–54.

———. "Yahweh Is a Shepherd." *Horizons in Biblical Theology* 27.2 (2005): 79–103.

Newsom, Carol A. "Bakhtin, the Bible, and Dialogic Truth." *Journal of Religion* 76 (1996): 290–306.

———. "Response to Norman K. Gottwald, 'Social Class and Ideology in Isaiah xl–lv." *Semeia* 59 (1992): 73–78.

Nouwen, Henri J. M. *Lifesigns: Intimacy, Fecundity, and Ecstasy in Christian Perspective.* Garden City, N.Y.: Doubleday, 1986.

O'Brien, Julia M. *Challenging Prophetic Metaphor: Theology and Ideology in the Prophets.* Louisville: Westminster John Knox, 2008.

O'Connor, Kathleen M. "Jeremiah." Pages 178–86 in *Women's Bible Commentary.* Edited by Carol A. Newsom and Sharon H. Ringe. Rev. ed. Louisville: Westminster John Knox, 1998.

———. *Lamentations and the Tears of the World.* Maryknoll, N.Y.: Orbis, 2002.

———. "'Speak Tenderly to Jerusalem': Second Isaiah's Reception and Use of Daughter Zion." *Princeton Seminary Bulletin* 20 (1999): 281–94.

Odell, Margaret S. *Ezekiel.* Smyth & Helwys Bible Commentary. Macon, Ga.: Smyth & Helwys, 2005.

Olyan, Saul M. *Biblical Mourning: Ritual and Social Dimensions.* Oxford: Oxford University Press, 2004.

———. "Honor, Shame, and Covenant Relations In Ancient Israel and Its Environment." *Journal of Biblical Literature* 115 (1996): 204–6.

Oorschot, Jürgen van. *Von Babel zum Zion: Eine literarkritische und redaktionsgeschichtliche Untersuchung.* Beihefte zur Zeitschrift für die alttestamentliche Wissenschaft 206. Berlin: de Gruyter, 1993.

Oswalt, John N. *The Book of Isaiah: Chapters 1–39.* New International Commentary on the Old Testament . Grand Rapids: Eerdmans, 1986.

———. *The Book of Isaiah: Chapters 40–66.* New International Commentary on the Old Testament . Grand Rapids: Eerdmans, 1998.

Otene, Matungulu, S.J. *Celibacy and the African Value of Fecundity.* Translated by L. C. Plamondon, S.J. Spearhead 65. Eldoret: Gaba, 1981.

Otto, Rudolf. *The Idea of the Holy: An Inquiry into the Non-Rational Factor in the Idea of the Divine and Its Relation to the Rational.* Translated by John W. Harvey. New York: Oxford University Press, 1958.

Paganini, Simone. *Der Weg zur Frau Zion, Ziel unserer Hoffnung: Aufbau, Kontext, Sprache, Kommunikationsstruktur und theologische Motive in Jes 55,1–13*. Stuttgarter biblische Beiträge 49. Stuttgart: Katholisches Bibelwerk, 2002.

———. "Who Speaks in Isaiah 55.1? Notes on the Communicative Structure in Isaiah 55." *Journal for the Study of the Old Testament* 30 (2005): 83–92.

Patton [Carvalho], Corrine L. "'Should Our Sister Be Treated Like a Whore?': A Response to Feminist Critiques of Ezekiel 23." Pages 221–38 in *The Book of Ezekiel: Theological and Anthropological Perspectives*. Edited by Margaret S. Odell and John T. Strong. Society of Biblical Literature Symposium Series 9. Atlanta: Society of Biblical Literature, 2000.

Perdue, Leo, Robert Morgan, and Benjamin D. Sommer. *Biblical Theology: Introducing the Conversation*. Nashville: Abingdon, 2009.

Perry, Tyler. *Diary of a Mad Black Woman*. DVD. ASIN: B00097DXFS, 2005.

Petersen, David L., and Kent Harold Richards. *Interpreting Hebrew Poetry*. Minneapolis: Fortress, 1992.

Pham, Xuan Huong Thi. *Mourning in the Ancient Near East and the Hebrew Bible*. Journal for the Study of the Old Testament Supplement Series 302. Sheffield: Sheffield Academic Press, 1999.

Pleins, J. David. *The Social Visions of the Hebrew Bible: A Theological Introduction*. Louisville: Westminster John Knox, 2001.

Premnath, D. N. *Eighth Century Prophets: A Social Analysis*. St. Louis: Chalice, 2003.

Pressley, Arthur. Unpublished Presentation on Domestic Violence. Society for the Study of Black Religion, Charleston, S.C., 2008.

Prine, John. "Fish and Whistle." Disc 1, Band 19 in *The John Prine Anthology: Great Days*. Los Angeles: Rhino Records Inc., 1993.

Provan, Iain W. *Lamentations*. New Century Bible. Grand Rapids: Eerdmans, 1991.

———. "Past, Present and Future in Lamentations III 52–66: The Case for a Precative Perfect Re-examined." *Vetus Testamentum* 41 (1991): 164–75.

Quinn-Miscall, Peter D. *Isaiah*. 2nd ed. Readings: A New Biblical Commentary. Sheffield: Sheffield Phoenix, 2006.

Ravikovitch, Dahlia. *Hovering at a Low Altitude: The Collected Poetry*. Translated by Chana Bloch and Chana Kronfeld. New York: Norton, 2009.

Reif, Stefan C. "Jerusalem in Jewish Liturgy." *Judaism* 46 (1997): 159–68.

Renaud, Bernard. *Je suis un Dieu jaloux: Evolution sémantique et significa-tion théologique de qineʾah*. Paris: Cerf, 1963.

Renkema, Johan. *Lamentations*. Translated by Brian Doyle. Historical Commentary on the Old Testament. Leuven: Peeters, 1998.

Richards, I. A. "The Philosophy of Rhetoric." Pages 48–62 in *Philosophical Perspectives on Metaphor*. Edited by Mark Johnson. Minneapolis: University of Minnesota Press, 1981.

Ricoeur, Paul. *The Rule of Metaphor: Multi-disciplinary Studies of the Creation of Meaning in Language*. London: Routledge, 1978.

———. "Toward a Narrative Theology: Its Necessity, Its Resources, Its Difficulties." Pages 236–48 in *Figuring the Sacred: Religion, Narrative, and Imagination*. Edited by Mark I. Wallace. Translated by David Pellauer. Minneapolis: Fortress, 1995.

Roberts, Robert C. *Emotions: An Essay in Aid of Moral Psychology*. Cambridge: Cambridge University Press, 2003.

Ryken, Leland, James C. Wilhoit, and Tremper Longman III, eds. *Dictionary of Biblical Imagery*. Downers Grove, Ill.: InterVarsity Press, 1998.

Sanders, James A. *The Psalms Scroll of Qumrân Cave 11 (11QPsa)*. Discoveries in the Judaean Desert IV. Oxford: Clarendon, 1965.

Sanderson, Judith E. "Nahum." Pages 232–36 in *Women's Bible Commentary*. Edited by Carol A. Newsom and Sharon H. Ringe. Rev. ed. Louisville: Westminster John Knox, 1998.

Sawyer, John F. A. "Daughter of Zion and Servant of the Lord in Isaiah: A Comparison." *Journal for the Study of the Old Testament* 4 (1989): 89–107.

Scarry, Elaine. *On Beauty and Being Just*. Princeton: Princeton University Press, 1999.

Scheuer, Blaženka. *The Return of YHWH: The Tension between Deliverance and Repentance in Isaiah 40–55*. Beihefte zur Zeitschrift für die alttestamentliche Wissenschaft 377. Berlin: de Gruyter, 2008.

Schmitt, John J. "The City as Woman in Isaiah 1–39." Pages 95–119 in vol. 1 of *Writing and Reading the Scroll of Isaiah: Studies of an Interpretive Tradition*. Edited by Craig C. Broyles and Craig A. Evans. 2 vols. Vetus Testamentum Supplements 70. Leiden: Brill, 1997.

———. "Motherhood of God and Zion as Mother." *Revue biblique* 92 (1985): 557–69.

———. "The Wife of God in Hosea 2." *Biblical Research* 34 (1989): 5–18.

Schneiders, Sandra M. *The Revelatory Text: Interpreting the New Testament as Sacred Scripture*. 2nd ed. Collegeville, Minn.: Liturgical Press, 1999.

Schroeder, Jonathan E. "Consuming Representation: A Visual Approach to Consumer Research." Pages 193–230 in *Representing Consumers: Voices, Views and Visions*. Edited by Barbara B. Stern. London: Routledge, 1998.

Schüngel-Straumann, Helen. "Mutter Zion im Alten Testament." Pages 19–30 in *Theologie zwischen Zeiten und Kontinenten: Für Elisabeth Gössmann*. Edited by Theodor Schneider and Helen Schüngel-Straumann. Freiburg: Herder, 1993.

Schwartz, Baruch J. "Ezekiel's Dim View of Israel's Restoration." Pages 43–67 in *The Book of Ezekiel: Theological and Anthropological Perspectives*. Edited by Margaret S. Odell and John T. Strong. Society of Biblical Literature Symposium Series 9. Atlanta: Society of Biblical Literature, 2000.

———. "Repentance and Determinism in Ezekiel." Pages 123–30 in *Proceedings of the Eleventh World Congress of Jewish Studies*. Division A: *The Bible in Its World*. Edited by David Assaf. Jerusalem: World Union of Jewish Studies, 1994.

Schwienhorst-Schönberger, Ludger. *"Nicht im Menschen gründet das Glück" (Koh 2,24): Kohelet im Spannungsfeld jüdischer Weisheit und hellenistischer Philosophie*. 2nd ed. Herders biblische Studien 2. Freiburg: Herder, 1996.

Segal, Charles. "The Ethics of Antiphony: The Social Construction of Pain, Gender, and Power in the Southern Peloponnese." *Ethos* 18 (1990): 481–511.

———. "The Gorgon and the Nightingale: The Voice of Female Lament and Twelfth Pythian Ode." Pages 17–34 in *Embodied Voices*. Edited by Leslie C. Dunn and Nancy A. Jones. Cambridge: Cambridge University Press, 1994.

Seitz, Christopher R. *Word without End: The Old Testament as Abiding Theological Witness*. Grand Rapids: Eerdmans, 1998.

———. *Zion's Final Destiny*. Minneapolis: Fortress, 1991.

Sekine, Seizo. *Die Tritojesajanische Sammlung (Jes 56–66) redaktionsgeschichtlich untersucht*. Beihefte zur Zeitschrift für die alttestamentliche Wissenschaft 175. Berlin: de Gruyter, 1989.

Seremetakis, C. Nadia. *The Last Word: Women, Death, and Divination in Inner Mani*. Chicago: University of Chicago Press, 1991.

Shea, William H. "The *qinah* Structure of the Book of Lamentations." *Biblica* 60 (1979): 103–7.

Sherwood, Yvonne. *The Prostitute and the Prophet: Hosea's Marriage in Literary-Theoretical Perspective.* Journal for the Study of the Old Testament Supplement Series 212; Gender, Culture, Theory 2. Sheffield: Sheffield Academic Press, 1996.

Sherwood, Yvonne and Stephen D. Moore. *The Invention of the Biblical Scholar: A Critical Manifesto.* Minneapolis: Fortress, 2011.

Shields, Mary E. "An Abusive God? Identity and Power/Gender and Violence in Ezekiel 23." Pages 129–51 in *Postmodern Interpretations of the Bible: A Reader.* Edited by A. K. M. Adam. St. Louis: Chalice, 2001.

———. "Circumcision of the Prostitute: Gender, Sexuality, and the Call to Repentance in Jeremiah 3:1–4:4." *Biblical Interpretation* 3 (1995): 61–74.

———. *Circumscribing the Prostitute: The Rhetorics of Intertextuality, Metaphor and Gender in Jeremiah 3.1–4.4.* Journal for the Study of the Old Testament Supplement Series 387. London: T&T Clark, 2004.

———. "Multiple Exposures: Body Rhetoric and Gender Characterization in Ezekiel 16." *Journal of Feminist Studies in Religion* 14 (1998): 5–18.

Simian-Yofre, Horacio. "Exodo en Deuteroisaías." *Biblica* 61 (1980): 530–53.

———. "La teodicea del Deuteroisaías." *Biblica* 62 (1981): 55–72.

Simkins, Ronald. *Yahweh's Activity in History and Nature in the Book of Joel.* Ancient Near Eastern Texts and Studies 10. Lewiston, N.Y.: Mellen, 1991.

Smith, Mark S. *The Early History of God: Yahweh and the Other Deities in Ancient Israel.* 2nd ed. Grand Rapids: Eerdmans, 2002.

———. *The Memoirs of God: History, Memory, and the Experience of the Divine in Ancient Israel.* Minneapolis: Fortress, 2004.

Smith, Paul A. *Rhetoric and Redaction in Trito-Isaiah: The Structure, Growth and Authorship of Isaiah 56–66.* Vetus Testamentum Supplements 62. Leiden: Brill, 1995.

Smith-Christopher, Daniel L. *A Biblical Theology of Exile.* Overtures to Biblical Theology. Minneapolis: Fortress, 2002.

Soderbergh, Steven. *Sex, Lies, and Videotape.* ASIN: 0767812158, 1989.

Sohn, Seock-Tae. "'I Will Be Your God and You Will Be My People': The Origin and Background of the Covenant Formula." Pages 355–72 in *Ki Baruch Hu: Ancient Near Eastern, Biblical, and Judaic Studies in Honor of Baruch A. Levine*. Edited by Robert Chazan, William W. Hallo, and Lawrence H. Schiffman. Winona Lake, Ind.: Eisenbrauns, 1999.

Soloveitchik, Joseph B. מסורת הרב קינות *Eicha, Kinot, Tefilot for Tisha b'Av: The Complete Tisha b'Av Service with commentary by Joseph B. Soloveitchik*. Bilingual Hebrew/English edition. Edited by Simon Poser. Translation of *Kinot* by Tzvi Hersh Weinreb and Binyamin Shalom. Translation of *Tefilot* by Jonathan Sacks. Jerusalem: Koren, 2010.

Sommer, Benjamin D. *A Prophet Reads Scripture: Allusion in Isaiah 40–66*. Contraversions. Stanford, Calif.: Stanford University Press, 1998.

Soskice, Janet Martin. *Metaphor and Religious Language*. Oxford: Oxford University Press, 1985.

Spykerboer, Hendrik Carel. "Isaiah 55:1–5: The Climax of Deutero-Isaiah. An Invitation to Come to the New Jerusalem." Pages 357–59 in *The Book of Isaiah*. Edited by Jacques Vermeylen. Bibliotheca ephemeridum theologicarum lovaniensium 81. Leuven: Leuven University Press, 1989.

Steck, Odil Hannes. *Bereitete Heimkehr: Jesaja 35 als redaktionelle Brücke zwischen dem Ersten und dem Zweiten Jesaja*. Stuttgarter Bibelstudien 121. Stuttgart: Katholisches Bibelwerk, 1985.

———. *Gottesknecht und Zion: Gesammelte Aufsatze zu Deuterojesaja*. Forschungen zum Alten Testament 4. Tübingen: Mohr Siebeck, 1992.

———. *Studien zu Tritojesaja*. Beihefte zur Zeitschrift für die alttestamentliche Wissenschaft 203. Berlin: de Gruyter, 1991.

Stinespring, William F. "No Daughter of Zion: A Study of the Appositional Genitive in Hebrew Grammar." *Encounter* 26 (1965): 133–41.

Sweeney, Marvin A. *Isaiah 1–39, with an Introduction to Prophetic Literature*. Forms of the Old Testament Literature 16. Grand Rapids: Eerdmans, 1996.

Sweeney, Marvin A., and Ehud Ben Zvi. *The Changing Face of Form Criticism for the Twenty-First Century*. Grand Rapids: Eerdmans, 2003.

Tadmor, Hayim. "The Babylonian Exile and the Restoration." Pages 159–82 in *History of the Jewish People*. Edited by H. H. Ben-Sasson. Cambridge: Harvard University Press, 1976.

Thoennes, K. Erik. "A Biblical Theology of Godly Human Jealousy." Ph.D. diss., Trinity Evangelical Divinity School, 2001.

Thompson, J. A. *The Book of Jeremiah*. New International Commentary on the Old Testament. Grand Rapids: Eerdmans, 1980.

Tiemeyer, Lena-Sofia. "Geography and Textual Allusions: Interpreting

Isaiah 40–55 and Lamentations as Judahite Texts." *Vetus Testamentum* 57 (2007): 67–85.

———. "Two Prophets, Two Laments, and Two Ways of Dealing with Earlier Texts." Pages 185–202 in *Die Textualisierung der Religion*. Edited by Joachim Schaper. Forschungen zum Alten Testament 62. Tübingen: Mohr Siebeck, 2009.

Tjaden, Patricia, and Nancy Thoennes. *Full Report of the Prevalence, Incidence, and Consequences of Violence against Women: Findings from the National Violence against Women Survey*. Washington, D.C.: U.S. Dept of Justice, 2000. Online: http://www.ojp.usdoj.gov/nij/pubs-sum/183781.htm; http://www.abanet.org/domviol/statistics.html#prevalence.

Trible, Phyllis. *Rhetorical Criticism: Context, Method, and the Book of Jonah*. Guides to Biblical Scholarship. Minneapolis: Fortress, 1994.

———. *Texts of Terror: Literary-Feminist Readings of Biblical Narratives*. Overtures to Biblical Theology 13. Philadelphia: Fortress, 1984.

Tuell, Steven. *Ezekiel*. New International Biblical Commentary. Peabody: Hendrickson, 2009.

Turner, Mary Donovan. "Daughter Zion: Giving Birth to Redemption." Pages 193–204 in *Pregnant Passion: Gender, Sex, and Violence in the Bible*. Edited by Cheryl A. Kirk-Duggan. Society of Biblical Literature Symposium Series 44. Atlanta: Society of Biblical Literature, 2003.

VanGemeren, Willem A., et al., eds. *New International Dictionary of Old Testament Theology and Exegesis*. 5 vols. Grand Rapids: Zondervan, 1997.

Vincent, Jean M. *Studien zur literarischen Eigenart und aur geistigen Heimat von Jesaja, Kap. 40–55*. Beiträge zur biblischen Exegese und Theologie 5. Frankfurt am Main: Lang, 1977.

Walker, Alice. *The Color Purple*. New York: Pocket Books, 1982.

Washington, Harold C. "Violence and the Construction of Gender in the Hebrew Bible: A New Historicist Approach." *Biblical Interpretation* 5 (1997): 324–63.

Watson, W. G. E. *Classical Hebrew Poetry: A Guide to its Techniques*. Journal for the Study of the Old Testament Supplement Series 26. Sheffield: JSOT Press, 1984.

Watts, John D. W. *Isaiah 1–33*. Rev. ed. Word Biblical Commentary 24. Waco, Tex.: Word, 2005.

———. *Isaiah 34–66*. Word Biblical Commentary 25. Waco, Tex.: Word, 1987.

Watts, Rikki E. "Consolation or Confrontation? Isaiah 40–55 and the Delay of the New Exodus." *Tyndale Bulletin* 41 (1990): 31–59.

Weems, Renita J. *Battered Love: Marriage, Sex, and Violence in the Hebrew Prophets.* Minneapolis: Fortress, 1995.

Weigel, Sigrid. *Topographien der Geschlechter: Kulturgeschichtliche Studien zur Literatur.* Reinbek: Rowohlt Taschenbuch, 1990.

Weil, Simone. *Waiting for God.* Translated by E. Craufurd. Harper Perennial Modern Classics. New York: HarperCollins, 2000.

Weinbaum, Batya. "Lament Ritual Transformed into Literature: Positing Women's Prayer as Cornerstone in Western Classical Literature." *Journal of American Folklore* 114 (2001): 20–39.

Westermann, Claus. *Das Buch Jesaja, Kapitel 40–66.* Das Alte Testament Deutsch 19. Göttingen: Vandenhoeck & Ruprecht, 1966.

———. *Isaiah 40–66.* Translated by David M. G. Stalker. Old Testament Library. Philadelphia: Westminster, 1969.

———. *Lamentations: Issues and Interpretation.* Translated by Charles Muenchow. Minneapolis: Fortress, 1994.

———. *Praise and Lament in the Psalms.* Translated by Keith R. Crim and Richard N. Soulen. Atlanta: John Knox, 1981.

Whybray, R. Norman. *Ecclesiastes.* New Century Bible. Grand Rapids: Eerdmans, 1989.

———. *Isaiah 40–66.* New Century Bible. Repr., Grand Rapids: Eerdmans, 1981.

———. "Qoheleth, Preacher of Joy." *Journal for the Study of the Old Testament* 23 (1982): 87–98.

Widengren, Geo. *The Accadian and Hebrew Psalms of Lamentation as Religious Documents.* Uppsala: Almqvist & Wiksells, 1936.

Wildberger, Hans. *Isaiah 1–12.* Translated by Thomas H. Trapp. Continental Commentaries. Minneapolis: Fortress, 1991.

Willey, Patricia K. Tull. *Remember the Former Things: The Recollection of Previous Texts in Second Isaiah.* Society of Biblical Literature Dissertation Series 161. Atlanta: Scholars Press, 1997.

———. "The Servant of YHWH and Daughter Zion: Alternating Visions of YHWH's Community." Pages 267–303 in *The Society of Biblical Literature 1995 Seminar Papers.* Society of Biblical Literature Seminar Papers 34. Atlanta: Scholars Press, 1995.

Williamson, Hugh G. M. *Ezra, Nehemiah.* Word Biblical Commentary 16. Nashville: Word, 1985.

———. *Isaiah 1–5*. International Critical Commentary. London: T&T Clark, 2006.

Wischnowsky, Marc. *Tochter Zion: Aufnahme und Überwindung der Stadtklage in den Prophetenschriften des Alten Testaments*. Wissenschaftliche Monographien zum Alten und Neuen Testament 89. Neukirchen-Vluyn: Neukirchener, 2001.

Woodruff, Paul. *Reverence: Renewing a Forgotten Virtue*. New York: Oxford University Press, 2001.

Woude, Annemarieke S. van der. "Can Zion Do without the Servant in Isaiah 40–55?" *Calvin Theological Journal* 39 (2004): 109–16.

———. "'Hearing Voices while Reading': Isaiah 40–55 as a Drama." Pages 149–73 in *One Text, a Thousand Methods: Studies in Memory of Sjef van Tilborg*. Edited by Patrick Chatelion Counet and Ulrich Berges. Biblical Interpretation Series 71. Leiden: Brill, 2005.

———. "What Is New in Isaiah 41:14–20? On the Drama Theories of Klaus Baltzer and Henk Leene." Pages 261–67 in *The New Things: Eschatology in Old Testament Prophecy. Festschrift for Henk Leene*. Edited by F. Postma, K. Spronk, and E. Talstra. Maastricht: Shaker, 2002.

Yee, Gale A. "Hosea." Pages 197–336 in vol. 7 of *The New Interpreter's Bible*. Edited by Leander E. Keck. Nashville: Abingdon, 1996.

———. "Hosea." Pages 207–15 in *Women's Bible Commentary*. Edited by Carol A. Newsom and Sharon H. Ringe. Expanded ed. Louisville: Westminster John Knox, 1998.

———. *Poor Banished Children of Eve: Woman as Evil in the Hebrew Bible*. Minneapolis: Fortress, 2003.

Zenger, Erich. *A God of Vengeance? Understanding the Psalms of Divine Wrath*. Translated by Linda M. Maloney. Louisville: Westminster John Knox, 1996.

———. "Der Gott des Exodus in der Botschaft der Propheten—am Beispiel des Jesajabuches." *Concilium* 23 (1987): 15–22.

Zimmerli, Walther. *Ezekiel: A Commentary on the Book of the Prophet Ezekiel*. Translated by Ronald E. Clements. 2 vols. Hermeneia. Philadelphia: Fortress, 1979–1983.

———. "Jahwes Wort bei Deuterojesaja." *Vetus Testamentum* 32 (1982): 104–24.

Zuckerman, Jocelyn Craugh. "Victims of Sexual Violence in Zimbabwe Say ... We Must Stop the Rape and Terror." *Parade Magazine* (22 March 2009).

Contributors

Mark J. Boda, Ph.D. (Cambridge), Professor of Old Testament, McMaster Divinity College; Professor in the Faculty of Theology, McMaster University, Hamilton, Ontario, Canada

Mary L. Conway, Ph.D. cand. (McMaster), McMaster Divinity College, Hamilton, Ontario, Canada

Stephen L. Cook, Ph.D. (Yale), Catherine N. McBurney Professor of Old Testament Language and Literature, Virginia Theological Seminary, Alexandria, Virginia, U.S.A.

Carol J. Dempsey, OP, Ph.D. (The Catholic University of America), Professor of Theology (Biblical Studies), University of Portland, Portland, Oregon, U.S.A.

LeAnn Snow Flesher, Ph.D. (Drew), Professor of Old Testament, Academic Dean, American Baptist Seminary of the West at Berkeley, Graduate Theological Union, Berkeley, California, U.S.A.

Michael H. Floyd, Ph.D. (Claremont), Advent-St. Nicholas Church, Quito, Ecuador

Barbara Green, O.P., Ph.D. (University of California Berkeley and Graduate Theological Union), Professor of Biblical Studies (Old Testament and Christian Spirituality), Dominican School of Philosophy and Theology at the Graduate Theological Union, Berkeley, California, U.S.A.

John F. Hobbins, L.Th. (Waldensian Theological Seminary, Rome), Adjunct Faculty, Department of Anthropology and Religious Studies, University of Wisconsin-Oshkosh, Oshkosh, Wisconsin, U.S.A.

Mignon R. Jacobs, Ph.D. (Claremont), Associate Professor of Hebrew Bible/Old Testament, Fuller Theological Seminary, Pasadena, California, U.S.A.

Brittany Kim, Ph.D. cand. (Wheaton), Wheaton College, Wheaton, Illinois, U.S.A.

Cheryl A. Kirk-Duggan, Ph.D. (Baylor), Professor of Religion, Director of Women's Studies, Shaw University Divinity School, Raleigh, North Carolina, U.S.A.

Christl M. Maier, Th.D. and Habilitation (Humboldt-University Berlin, Germany), Professor of Old Testament, Faculty of Protestant Theology, Philipps-University Marburg, Germany

Carleen Mandolfo, Ph.D. (Emory), Associate Professor of Hebrew Bible, Claremont School of Theology; Associate Professor of Religion, Claremont Graduate University, Claremont, California, U.S.A.

Jill Middlemas, D.Phil. (Oxford), Research Associate, Department of Old Testament, Theology Faculty, University of Zurich, Zurich, Switzerland

Kim Lan Nguyen, Ph.D. (University of Wisconsin-Madison), Assistant Professor of Old Testament, Bible Division, Cornerstone University, Grand Rapids, Michigan, U.S.A.

Lena-Sofia Tiemeyer, D.Phil. (Oxford), Senior Lecturer in Hebrew Bible, University of Aberdeen, Aberdeen, U.K.

Index of Ancient Sources

Index of Modern Authors

Lightning Source UK Ltd.
Milton Keynes UK
UKOW04f1422081117
312394UK00002B/497/P